D0871827

THE REAL DEAL ON PEOPLE

Straight Talk on How the CHRO Creates Business Value

Les Dakens

CARSWELL®

© 2013 Thomson Reuters Canada Limited

NOTICE AND DISCLAIMER: All rights reserved. No part of this publication may be reproduced, stored in a retrieval system, or transmitted, in any form or by any means, electronic, mechanical, photocopying, recording or otherwise, without the prior written consent of the publisher (Carswell).

Carswell and all persons involved in the preparation and sale of this publication disclaim any warranty as to accuracy or currency of the publication. This publication is provided on the understanding and basis that none of Carswell, the author/s or other persons involved in the creation of this publication shall be responsible for the accuracy or currency of the contents, or for the results of any action taken on the basis of the information contained in this publication, or for any errors or omissions contained herein.

No one involved in this publication is attempting herein to render legal, accounting or other professional advice. If legal advice or other expert assistance is required, the services of a competent professional should be sought. The analysis contained herein should in no way be construed as being either official or unofficial policy of any governmental body.

ISBN: 978-0-7798-6064-7

A cataloguing record for this publication is available from Library and Archives Canada.

Composition: Computer Composition of Canada

Printed in Canada by Thomson Reuters.

TELL US HOW WE'RE DOING
Scan the QR code to the right with your smartphone to send your comments regarding our products and services.
Free QR Code Readers are available from your mobile device app store.
You can also email us at carswell.feedback@thomsonreuters.com

THOMSON REUTERS

CARSWELL, A DIVISION OF THOMSON REUTERS CANADA LIMITED

One Corporate Plaza
2075 Kennedy Road
Toronto, Ontario
M1T 3V4
www.carswell.com
E-mail www.carswell.com/email

Customer Relations
Toronto 1-416-609-3800
Elsewhere in Canada/U.S. 1-800-387-5164
Fax 1-416-298-5082

Praise for *The Real Deal On People*

"Les has had an incredible career in multiple companies and roles. This book offers an exceptional synthesis of his experiences in ways that will edify the next generation of HR professionals. He shares specific experiences, but offers broad principles and practices that are grounded in reality, but will nurture future HR professionals. With his insights and lessons drawn from the best CHROs and CEOs, this book is a treasure trove of insights, tools, and actions that move the HR profession to a new standard."

Dave Ulrich, Professor, Ross School of Business, University of Michigan & Partner, The RBL Group

"This book has brought together many voices to describe how the CHRO can add great value in an organization. Les has been the quarterback in driving the HR strategy along with the cheerleader for his HR team in their execution. A great read for current and aspiring CHRO's and some great insights for CEO's."

Bill Conaty, former SVP, Corporate Human Resources at General Electric, and author of the book *The Talent Masters: Why Smart Business Leaders Put People Before Numbers*

"In *The Real Deal on People*, Les distills complex interpersonal and business challenges to craft a clear and concise guidebook for professionals at all levels, providing a better understanding of how a strong CRHO can significantly benefit a company. His entertaining anecdotes and real-world experiences provide countless helpful tips and direction for aspiring CHROs and seasoned executives alike."

John Brock, Chairman & CEO, Coca-Cola Enterprises

"Les has combined first class HR practice with years of experience to create a comprehensive must read for CEOs, Corporate Boards and their HR Committees, and all those involved with the HR function. From total rewards to talent management, Les looks at the most senior HR role from every angle to create sage advice that is business driven and people focused. A great contribution to the HR field."

Stephen Wetmore, President & CEO, Canadian Tire Corporation

"In any company there are many business drivers that determine success. Strategy in general and people strategy in particular also play a key role to how a company performs. People can be your number one competitive advantage, they can be the differentiator. The CHRO plays a vital role as a business partner to the CEO in helping to develop a people strategy and Les articulately describes throughout his book with real life examples how the CHRO is a major contributor to it. A must read for CEOs, CHROs and Boards."

John Sullivan, Chief Executive Officer, The Cadillac Fairview Corporation Limited

"This is an excellent book, not only because it provides an internal perspective of what an effective CHRO should look like, but it also gives real life examples of how a CHRO should behave, and is perceived by their colleagues, CEO and Board members. It is very inspirational and instructive! Congratulation Les!"

Renée Légaré, SVP, Human Resources, Vice Présidente Principale, RH The Ottawa Hospital, L'Hopital d'Ottawa

"*The Real Deal on People* is a thoughtful practitioner's guide to the extensive challenges and huge responsibilities held by today's CHRO. Written by an accomplished CHRO himself, who shares both solid advice and practical experiences. The book covers the vast expanse of CHRO duties and is a useful reference for anyone in business – whether you're a CHRO today, aspire to be one or frankly, for any executive in any function who wants to better understand how a top-flight CHRO can help his or her organization."

"Les Dakens' knowledge and insights abound in this book – worth a read and delivered in an easy to digest format. As a CHRO, from "sounding board" to the CEO to developer of talent to ambassador to the Board, this book has good lessons for all about the ever increasing critical role of the CHRO."

Doug Tough, Chairman and CEO, International Flavors and Fragrances

"Les has done a brilliant job of capturing the essence of a high-performing Chief Human Resources Officer, and it's all the more credible because of his personal track record. This is a must-read for HR professionals and business leaders alike."

Dean A. Connor, President and Chief Executive Officer, Sun Life Financial

"While big strides have been made in all areas of Human Resources Management, there is more to be done. CHROs and all practitioners must strategically integrate their initiatives, processes and advice, and truly lead at the top, with measurable value and impact, to business success. Through his stories and insights, Les Dakens provides a deep, "insiders' view" of how tomorrow's HR leaders can achieve that impact."

Rose Patten, Special Advisor to CEO, BMO Financial Group

"As the former CEO of a large company, Les' insights really resonated with me and my experience in leading a successful company with great employees. Les captures the essence of the CHRO as business strategist, not just people strategist, which is absolutely key as people are the business. The content is real, practical and no-nonsense and offers great insights into the use of HR technology, which Les notes is really about managing information and not about the technology itself. *The Real Deal on People* is a must-read for executives as well as HR committee directors."

Laura Formusa, former CEO, Hydro One & Board Director

"A true wealth of experience distilled into one book."

"I found myself nodding in agreement so many times. *The Real Deal on People* is the candid advice and observations of an HR pro. Early in your career it will inspire and guide. Later in your career it will remind you of what it takes.Through out it deals with the myriad of challenges and complexity of the top HR job in a breadth, depth and honesty I have not seen before."

Peter Edwards, VP Human Resources & Labour Relations, Canadian Pacific

"In a matter of fact, conversational way, Les delivers a powerful and practical guide in sharing his 30+ years of experience in the human resources field – as valuable to current CHROs as those aspiring to the position."

John Silverthorn, Senior Vice President, Human Resources, CIBC

"Les has assembled a very practical, comprehensive playbook for leaders who care deeply about talent and its impact on business. This book is filled with terrific insights and great advice on how to manage all facets of the employee life cycle from hire to retire. This is an invaluable toolkit."

Julie Murphy, CHRO, Direct Energy Business

"*The Real Deal on People* is exactly that. Les Dakens has pulled together insights and experiences from some of the most challenging business environments in North America, and turned them into lessons that would serve every aspiring CHRO. His practical insights are borne of experiential learning that jumps off every page. Put it on your bookshelf, because you will want to use it as a reference when facing your next tough human resources challenge."

Bill Morneau, Executive Chairman, Morneau Shepell

About the Author

Les Dakens became Senior Vice President and Chief Human Resources Officer for Maple Leaf Foods Inc. in January 2011 and retired in December 2013.

From 2008 to 2010, Les was the principal of Pineridge Consulting Inc., a human resources consulting firm through which he provided executive level coaching to Human Resources leaders and Human Resources Committees of Corporate Boards of many leading Canadian companies.

Previously he held the executive position of Senior Vice-President, People with CN Rail which he joined in 2001. Prior to that he spent most of his years in the food business, holding progressively senior roles in human resources with Cadbury Beverages before joining H.J. Heinz in 1990 as the North American Vice-President of Human Resources. He began his career with Nortel in 1975.

He has accumulated a wealth of knowledge and expertise over more than 30 years working with top tier companies and is widely recognized for his leadership in developing best practices as one of North America's top human resource professionals. Les is also the author of two successful business books: *Switchpoints, Culture Change on the Fast Track to Business Success* and *Employee Performance Scorecards*.

Mr. Dakens holds a Bachelor of Arts degree from York University, a Business Administration diploma in marketing from Sheridan College and is a graduate of the Institute of Corporate Directors' Directors Education Program. Additionally he is a faculty member at Rotman's HRC Program. Les is a Board Director with Equitable Life of Canada, Walden House, and the Alzheimer Society of Toronto.

All of the author's proceeds from the "Real Deal" book will be donated to the Alzheimer Society of Canada, to support their research efforts.

Dedication

This book is dedicated to the three most important women in my life.

My mother, Annie Dakens, the wife of a coal miner, was the leader of our family and its strength; she countered my father's introverted nature with energy and spirit and she raised four children within a strong moral framework that valued hard work and constancy. A product of the great depression, my mother developed a heightened sense of the importance of education and a steady job; and so even as she expressed great pride when I was the first in my family to graduate university, she also worried about me when I left one company to work for another.

Like a growing number of victims every year, my mother died too soon from Alzheimer's disease; and so, as a final tribute to her, I am active in the fight to find a cure. To that end I am also donating the proceeds of the sale of this book to the Canadian Alzheimer's Society. My mother was my biggest fan, and I miss her.

Marijane and I were married 31 years ago as of this writing – we met at the recruitment firm we both worked for. Her very successful career culminated in a partnership at a large Human Resources consulting firm where Marijane was considered the best in her field vetting candidates for senior corporate roles; and over the years, using me as her daily assessment victim, she only got better. Her capabilities as a business-savvy coach have been instrumental in the development of my own strengths and without her guidance in helping me to develop my career, I literally would not be where I am now. She is my life partner and I cannot imagine my life without her.

And last, but not least, this book is dedicated to Carolynn Walda who started me down this path in the first place – and I'm not even sure she knows the extent of the impact she had on my career.

Table of Contents

Preface

Along time ago, in a city far, far away (38 years ago in Brampton to be precise), my journey in the HR world began and ever since that time I have been accumulating enormous amounts of information and insights; and now, with the guidance and coaching of so many colleagues and advisors along the way, I have the privilege of being able to share my stories with you.

Many of these tales could not have been told in real time because of their sensitive nature; and looking back, there were some hair-raising situations that at the time could have completely changed the North American corporate landscape – and in some cases did. A few names have been changed to protect the innocent, and to keep the litigious at bay, but mostly everything recounted here is the real deal – the people, the places, the companies and the situations – all undisguised and exactly as they were.

So – what do I hope to achieve with this book – and what exactly does the title mean?

Although this is primarily a business book, my hope is that you will also find it a bit entertaining; at the risk of ticking some people off, I have made a point of adding personal details throughout the book that may not add to its value as a business text, but will definitely put the situations into a much more human and interesting perspective.

From a business viewpoint, my intent is to expand my role as coach and mentor within the HR community – especially to HR professionals who aspire to reach the C-suite, and not just as CHRO. Current CHROs – hopefully you will learn some new tricks, and aspiring CHROs – my goal is to provide you with something of a roadmap to help you achieve your objective sooner. This book is also for CEOs and Board Directors interested in better understanding the role of CHRO and how to better leverage their CHRO.

As for the title, it is a reference to this book as an exposé on the very special role the CHRO plays in corporate affairs, as well as the opportunity, and the responsibility, to be confidante to the CEO and purveyor of the unvarnished truth to the uppermost executive levels of the company. Importantly, it is also a reference to the very real requirement for today's CHRO to be every bit as business savvy as their C-suite colleagues.

Throughout my HR journey I have been blessed with great coaching and help from others willing to share their insight and knowledge – and ultimately that is what I hope this book becomes – a resource that offers guidance and insight that helps you in your career.

Acknowledgements

There are a lot of people who contributed to the writing of this book. I wish to thank them for their kind and thoughtful work. I will list them into separate groups to recognize their efforts.

I wish to thank my wife, Marijane, for her great insight and selective editing. Also, special thanks to the Carswell team: Sheila McLeish, Product Process & Development Manager, Joanne Gordon, Marketing Manager, Todd Humber, Managing Editor, Canadian H.R. Reporter, John Hobel, Publisher, Canadian H.R. Reporter, and Nance Fleming/Alexandra Hutchinson, Content Editors. I have included several articles that I co-wrote with Bonnie Flatt and Judy Johnson- thank you ladies! I would also like to thank Peter Edwards and Steve Jacobs for agreeing to include "the 17 out of 17" chapter from the *Switchpoints* book.

A special "well done" to the great human resources staff at Maple Leaf Foods who volunteered to help write much of the HR Products & Services sections – they include, Ian Henry, Cheryl Fullerton, Paul Clipson, Norm Sabapathy, Carmen Klein, Lynn Langrock, Mike Habel, Emma Horgan, and David Harman. Also, thanks to Ken Campbell, SVP Manufacturing, MLF for his assistance with the Health & Safety section and to Lynda Kuhn, SVP, Communications, MLF for her great help with the Employee Communications Overview.

My interviews with current and former CHRO's were very exciting and awe-inspiring. These people encouraged me to write my book and they brought real life stories. Special thanks to Bill Conaty (formerly with General Electric), Katy Barclay (Kroger), Yvonne Jackson (formerly of Pfizer), John Lynch (General Electric), Jim Grossett (Agrium), Ferio Pugliese (WestJet), and Peter Goerke (Prudential). Rose Patten at BMO was very supportive of my work. Finally, David Ulrich from the University of Michigan provided wonderful input to the book and has been a thought leader to many of us in the HR world.

I had the great pleasure of interviewing five great CEO's including Claude Mongeau (Canadian National), Joe Jimenez (Novartis), Mike Wilson (Agrium), Hunter Harrison (Canadian Pacific), and Michael McCain (Maple Leaf Foods). They were very giving of their time and most importantly, they were extremely insightful towards the CHRO role. Also, they provided some very helpful perspectives on the future CEO roles.

The Board Directors who I spoke to were incredibly seasoned and wise in their description of the CHRO role and the relationship to the Human Resources Committee of the Board. These distinguished leaders included David Emerson, Ed

Lumley, Purdy Crawford, Yvonne Jackson, Sarah Raiss, Gordon Ritchie, Claude Lamoureux, James Olson, and Geoffrey Beattie. In addition, Stan Magidson (The Institute of Corporate Directors), Peter Gleason (National Association of Corporate Directors), and Chris Bart (The Directors College) provided their very valuable perspectives.

The following media organizations have either supported my previous articles or wrote articles about my HR team's work and I would like to thank them for their support – they include the HR Reporter, HR Professional, Progressive Railroading, Financial Post, ICD Journal, and the Globe & Mail.

I would like to thank Chris McCain for her dedication to the Alzheimer's cause.

I would also like to thank all of the HR staff that worked with me during my career – you made me a better HR leader with your contributions.

In particular, there are three people who were my "go-to" staff: Julie Murphy (Heinz), Peter Edwards (CN), and Cheryl Fullerton (Maple Leaf Foods).

I have had the great fortune of working with some very special consultants during my career. They provided their own perspectives about working with the CHRO in the book. Thanks to Marty Parker, (Waterstone), Judith Humphrey (The Humphrey Group), Helen Handfield-Jones (Handfield Jones), Cliff Grevler (Boston Consulting Group), Sandro Iannicca (SICG), Luis Navas (Global Governance Advisors), Steve Jacobs (CLG), Art Horn (Horn), Ralph Shedletsky (Knightsbridge), Israel Chafetz (TJC Law), Bernard Morency (La Caisse), Al Schnur (PCI Human Resource Consulting), and Mark Dahlman (Dahlman Human Capital Corp.).

In addition to working with the right consultants in gathering content for this book, it was important to me that I work with the right consultant in *writing and producing* this book. My initial thought was to work with a well-known non-fiction writer who I know socially, but after discussing the project with him he said "I'd love to work with you, but I'm not the right kind of writer for the job – you need someone with solid business experience and business-writing experience."

And so my friend introduced me to Ken Webster – a communications veteran with more than 30 years' experience and a solid track record of writing and producing for some of North America's top business leaders. Ken has the kind of practical business experience and academic understanding that made us a great match to work together, and his story-telling ability made the project, and the end product, more fun than it might have been otherwise. Ken did the bulk of the heavy lifting and provided great ideas on context, relevance, chapter layout and process; I hope we will be able to work together again.

1

Les Dakens: My Journey as CHRO

> "21st century – the CHRO title should be changed to
> Chief Strategy Execution Officer."
>
> Dr. Chris Bart, Principal and Lead Professor, The Directors College

INTRODUCTION

The simple fact is I had no intention of ever working in Human Resources. Perhaps, more accurately, I should say that I barely knew the role or the department even existed – it wasn't even on the consideration list – and as far as my future was concerned, the HR department was nothing more than a hurdle to be jumped – the gatekeeper to my exciting new career in some other department, any other department. But all that changed not too long after I met Carolynn Walda.

After high school I didn't have the money for college, so I worked on the assembly line at Nortel – the jewel of Canada's burgeoning high-tech sector and one of the world's leading telecommunications companies – and I took my college courses at night. My goal was to earn enough to be able to quit Nortel and go to school full time in my final year.

Coincidentally, one of my instructors at night school was an HR executive with Nortel, Carolynn Walda. Young, smart, well-educated, and totally ambitious, she was among the first cohort of post-war university grads who were destined to redefine North American corporate culture in the latter part of the 20th century. To me, she was absolutely someone to pay attention to and so when she suggested that after I finished college I should apply for a full time job at Nortel, it was an easy decision to make and that's exactly what I did.

Naturally, as a graduate with a Marketing degree, I thought I would be interviewing for a position in Nortel's Marketing Department; and although a marketing position was indeed discussed, it was Carolynn's advice that instead I should consider a position in the "Personnel" department. By that time, Carolynn had become the first female HR director at a very male-dominated Nortel. She was a successful 28-year-old business executive with an eye to the future and so I took her advice and the rest, as they say, is history.

My first HR position at Nortel was called a "Personnel Specialist", an analyst position working on employee attendance and related projects. What struck me immediately about Nortel's HR department was that very few were professionally trained in HR and not only that, it soon became apparent that some had even failed at their previous position and were one step away from being out the door. It was not an auspicious beginning, and many times I found myself asking, "What the hell am I doing here?"

Occasionally, I had the opportunity to pose that question to Carolynn and that's when she would tell me about her vision of the future of the HR world; a world where HR executives were valued senior members of the core business management group and where human resources departments were staffed with ambitious professionals dedicated to the company's most dynamic resource and its most valuable asset. She was committed to transforming the HR department at Nortel into such a place and she was indeed the catalyst for making that transformation a reality.

Carolynn saw something in me that convinced her I would be successful in the HR world and so I took that position in Nortel's HR department. That was 1975 and I am glad all these years later that I trusted her instincts; Carolynn's 70s-era vision of creating a new breed of Human Resources professional has not only become a reality, it has been a significant focus of my career.

In many ways, my career and the way I approached the HR roles I've held over the years might be considered by many to be "unconventional," and so in keeping with that tradition, let's begin the rest of my story… at the end.

CHAPTER 1:   JOURNEY'S END

> "Without doubt, the head of HR should be the second most
> important person in any organization", I said. "From the point of view
> of the CEO, the director of HR should be at least equal to the CFO."
>
> J. Welch and S. Welch, *Winning*
> (New York: Harper Business, 2005), p. 99

"F@*k your consulting practice and come f@*king work for me."

It was November 2010 and he was loud and he was smiling ... and "he" was an icon of the Canadian food industry... he also happened to be the president of Maple Leaf Foods, one of North America's leading food processors, and he was Michael McCain. To say the least, I was shocked. Oh not by the colourful language – my father was a coal miner, and, like Michael, I'm from the Maritimes, so it takes more than the casual dropping of the "f-bomb" to shock me. What did surprise me, though, was the spontaneous job offer.

I first met Michael McCain through Wayne Hanley, Canadian president of the United Food & Commercial Workers Union, who knew that I was working on a book about the best management/union relationships in North America. Despite a very confrontational beginning that included serious strikes, layoffs, plant closures and wage roll-backs, Maple Leaf Foods and the UFCW eventually developed a very strong and positive working relationship and Wayne thought I should meet Michael as part of the research for the book.

Barely 30 minutes into the interview, McCain made the profanity-laced job offer and it took me by total surprise. He had been looking for a CHRO for over 12 months and, in fact, had found one – only to have that candidate withdraw his acceptance due to family reasons. Ironically, I had turned down the same job offer some months earlier when I was approached by MLF's external search firm. I was happily retired, busy with my consulting business and working on my book. I didn't need or want another corporate job, even if it was to work with one of Canada's food industry giants.

So, although I was flattered, I also had an interview to finish and I didn't want to p@#s McCain off by simply saying "no". I promised I would think about it over the coming weekend, even though I had no real intention of doing any such thing. But something gnawed at me over the weekend. I became intrigued by the challenge that McCain had laid out – a massive transformation at Maple Leaf Foods, the most significant strategic change in the company's history; it was hard not to be really interested and I was definitely conflicted.

It was Marijane who orchestrated the analysis that followed. Basically a 3-year stint at MLF represented a small percentage of what (I hoped) would be the remaining years of a long life, and the challenge and the role was really drawing me in; I could be around for 30 more years to regret not taking the challenge.

And so I became CHRO at Maple Leaf Foods in January 2011 – my first position with that title.

When I first became CHRO at MLF, the title and the role itself was still relatively new compared to most other C-suite positions – a decade at most – and there are still many companies that do not have direct human resources representation at that level. But as corporate human relations functions have evolved over the last 20 years in response to fundamental changes in the workforce and in labour relations and in the size and nature of the talent pool, and as complex global networks of employees are formed in response to changes in the marketplace, the strategic requirement for the CHRO role has also expanded and is still expanding. It is also still evolving. At some point in the not so distant future, the role of CHRO will be as ubiquitous as CFO or any of the other more traditional C-suite roles.

"The CHRO is one of the two key jobs in the organization reporting into me. I can buy lots of lawyers and CFO's in the marketplace, but, I can't easily find a great HR Chief with people assessment skills."

Hunter Harrison, CEO, Canadian Pacific

CHAPTER 2:   "YOU ARE A NECESSARY EVIL!"

> "There are two types of HR people – those who like
> other people or those who like to screw people."
>
> John Lynch, SVP, Corporate Human Resources, General Electric

When I was given the North American HR job at Heinz, in Pittsburgh, my new boss was the head of the North American unit, Bill Springer. When I first introduced myself to Bill, his first words to me were "I'm not convinced that we need this role but let's move on. As a former finance guy, I view HR as a necessary evil." Not an auspicious beginning. I told him that I was there to prove him wrong and, if I didn't, then my tenure would be short. He smiled and said "you're on!" Later, I learned that he respected guys with balls that stood up to him. That made me smile.

Bill's opinion was not to be taken lightly. He was the head of Heinz's North American business, the largest and most profitable division in the company and we sold the famous Heinz ketchup brand which dominated the condiment market. Bill was the former CFO of this unit and had been promoted several years before my meeting with him. He reported to Tony O'Reilly, the charismatic Chairman and CEO for the HJ Heinz Company and it was Tony who gave Bill his telling nickname – the "Prince of cost control."

Bill's opinion about HR was not unique. In many ways it represented the norm amongst those executives who did not have a background in HR and sometimes even within the HR world itself – and in some quarters that is still true today. I had a lot to prove and I had set myself up for a really tough challenge, to prove to Bill and others like him that they were wrong about HR.

Bill's job was to protect our brands, squeeze out costs and grow our business with a conservative mindset. Despite Bill's concerns about the nature of my role, I felt it was my job to support not only his objectives, but also his strategies and his business philosophy. I was able to do that, but it didn't happen by chance. I had to create a strategy of my own and execute it.

The secret to working successfully with Bill was to show a financial return for every HR initiative I proposed – not always an easy thing to do, as you may know – but not only did the pure discipline of calculating a cost/benefit return make me a better business person, it also gave Bill the confidence and the ammunition he needed to fully support my initiatives and give them the backing they needed to be adopted and to be successful.

My tenure with Bill lasted 5 years before he promoted his successor and took on a new role at Heinz, and since that first meeting in 1992, and throughout all that we went through together at Heinz, we have remained good friends and still occasionally golf together. I guess I wasn't so evil after all. There's more about my tenure at Heinz later in the book.

CHAPTER 3:   BUY OR SELL?

> "A successful CHRO knows when to stroke or choke."
>
> Mike Wilson, CEO, Agrium

The Board of Directors was in a heated discussion about potential internal successors for the CEO role – they were divided. One faction was solidly behind the two mainstream candidates: the CFO and the EVP, Sales and Marketing. The other, more aggressive group argued that the dark horse in the race was John, another C-suite executive. They all liked working with John and felt he knew the business well and had great political connections within the federal government. After letting the debate go on for some time, the veteran chair of the Human Resources committee turned to me and asked "Les, as the CHRO what is your opinion of John as a viable CEO successor?"

I was surprised he asked me but I didn't think long about my answer and said in an unintentionally loud voice: "I would sell my stock."

Clearly this was not an answer they were expecting – the room went silent and John's backers looked shocked. Naturally they wanted a more detailed answer, so I told them: "John is very bright and technically sound, however, he is a poor leader and his peers do not trust him. If he became CEO, I would sell my stock."

Putting both the question and the answer in a context that the Board of Directors understood intimately was the key to ending the argument. Apparently the Board agreed with my assessment because John was no longer considered a viable candidate from that point on.

The moral of the story is that the role of the CHRO is to advocate the right talent for every critical role in the company, especially the C-suite. Asking the question, "Would you buy stock in the company if this person was put into the CEO role or any C-suite role?" puts the issue squarely into a value creation perspective.

CHAPTER 4:   ONE MILLION DOLLARS!

> "Future CEOs need to create a vision, lead the organization, and drive value for all stakeholders."
>
> Claude Mongeau, CEO, Canadian National

There are dozens of apt euphemisms for what is relevant in this chapter. "Putting your money where your mouth is", "walking the talk", "skin in the game", etc., etc. – but they all refer to one simple concept which shareholders of companies expect – that company executives will substantially win or lose in the same way as them – and that is through owning stock.

Prior to 1995, most companies did not have stock ownership requirements for C-suite executives, with the possible exception of some CEOs and maybe Board Directors. But shareholders began to demand more executive accountability for companies' share performance and requiring executives to own stock is the obvious way to achieve this.

When I arrived at CN in 2001, we introduced a broader stock ownership policy that expanded the requirement to the top 200 executives in the firm. The CEO was expected to own 5x his salary and the direct reports had to own 3x their salary – that was the new standard. At lower levels, we introduced a 1x salary expectation. A lot of executives didn't like the program at all and complained bitterly about it.

That's when the rubber first hit the road for me, when I was required to purchase $1 million of CN Rail stock; that was an interesting day – my wife just about fainted when I told her what we had to do and, I have to admit, I felt a bit light-headed myself. This was truly a transformative mind shift for me and my fellow executives. A significant slice of our personal wealth was now going to be tied to the company's share performance, the result of which meant that we thought differently about how we approached our day-to-day functions, the kind of actions and risks and the long-term implications of our decisions. Gittin'er done was different now.

For us at CN, accountability for company results became something of a common rallying cry. It also served to bring the executive team closer; we became more connected. We were all in the same boat. We had invested heavily in our own company and now we had to deliver, not only for shareholders, but for ourselves as well – we truly had skin in the game. Of course, it didn't hurt to know that the company's biggest single shareholder at the time was Bill Gates of Microsoft fame – we liked to think he knew what he was doing. Given CN's outstanding share value performance since then, none of us are complaining about that policy now.

When I joined Maple Leaf Foods, the CEO and I went to the Board and convinced them to increase the share ownership guidelines to a larger group of executives. The nasty e-mails began in earnest (it was déjà vu all over again), but a short 2 years later, the dust has settled and executives are buying MLF shares with confidence. For my part, I sold a small part of my stake in CN and bought MLF shares and frankly it was easy to do and didn't cost a penny in new money. I find there is something very positive psychologically about being connected to my employer and company shareholders this way, not to mention I have a lot of confidence it will turn out to be an excellent investment and I have every intention of owning MLF shares after I retire and leave the company.

Stock ownership is a real motivator for executives to focus on delivering long-term success for the business and taking business risks becomes a different animal when senior executives all have skin in the game.

"As an investor, the toughest thing is to find out about the company's culture."

Claude Lamoureux, Board Director

CHAPTER 5: PERSONAL DEFINITION OF SUCCESS

> "The CHRO needs to balance the needs of the business and be an advocate of employees. We sometimes forget why we are at the table."
>
> Bill Conaty, former SVP, Corporate Human Resources, General Electric

As I mentioned at the beginning of the book, I was not a traditional candidate for the CHRO role; I graduated with a marketing major – a focus that has stayed with me during my 38 years in HR. My personal sense of success is driven by a need to show quantifiable results in my work – again, not a typical HR metric, but one that I believe has enhanced my abilities as an HR professional. And although I personally do feel more comfortable focusing on quantifiable results (as opposed to more emotional or relationship outcomes), I certainly do appreciate the value of the wonderful experience of working with others to achieve collective success.

The Human Resources function by design has both strategic and tactical elements and my first definition of success in that role is the creation of a successful People Strategy that supports the company's long-term business strategy. A significant part of that People Strategy is to ensure that the C-suite team is made up of individuals who know how to make money, who know how to lead people, and who can work together to achieve the company's objectives. Another related and equally important definition of success is the creation of a vibrant succession plan for the critical C-suite roles. Ultimately, the CHRO will be judged on how well they have influenced the company's culture in a way that maximizes its performance; the bottom line is the Bottom Line and so the CHRO must strategically support the CEO and the team to deliver maximum shareholder value.

From a tactical point of view, the company's employees and managers are our clients and expect great customer service. Our HR products and services need to be relevant and delivered in a timely way, and we need to make them more accessible so our clients can access them at their convenience. Managers need to have the HR tools at their fingertips and we need to educate managers and employees about how to be better consumers of our HR products and services.

And finally, for me at this point in my career (Maslow might call it "self-actualization"), I feel another definition of success is being in a position to start giving back to my profession – to be able to define personal legacy more by helping others than by stroking the ego. Writing this book falls into that category (it certainly isn't for the financial rewards!) and so, for me, success also includes an element of "giving back".

2

My Philosophy about the CHRO Role

> "The CHRO must be a strong leader willing to take on
> tough discussions with the CEO and others."
>
> Geoff Beattie, Board Director

CHAPTER 6: BUSINESS PERSON FIRST – HR PROFESSIONAL SECOND

> "The CHRO can't be afraid of numbers –
> they must have business acumen."
>
> Ferio Pugliese, EVP & President, WestJet Encore (former CHRO)

There is a lot written about the need for all C-suite roles to be business partners at the table. The CHRO is one of those roles that require a business mindset simply because most of the other members of the C-suite believe they, themselves, are people experts and therefore feel comfortable challenging the CHRO on people issues. The CHRO needs to be able to respond accordingly.

This perception is not true, however, for most of the other C-suite roles. Take the CFO, for example. There are very few C-suite executives who will go "toe to toe" with the CFO on technical financial matters. Similarly, manufacturing/ supply chain executives could have plenty of autonomy and authority because of the complexity of their area of expertise. And depending on the nature of the industry, the sales/marketing executives might also be relatively immune to challenges from their peers.

The point is that, unlike the other C-suite roles, the CHRO will only command respect among their peers when they demonstrate a very good understanding of the business in general, and more specifically the areas of responsibility of the other C-suite executives. In my opinion, the best CHROs out there have the level of leadership skills and business acumen to step into other C-suite roles and be effective on day one. Being a business person first begins with simply knowing "how do we make money in this business and how do all of the functions work together to deliver exceptional performance." Later on we will go deeper into how the CHRO develops these skills and knowledge.

CHAPTER 7:   START WITH THE BUSINESS STRATEGY

> "The CHRO should eat, sleep, breathe, and talk about strategy execution. They need to be passionate about it."
>
> Dr. Chris Bart, Principal and Lead Professor, The Directors College

"You can't fix stupid." Unlike wilful ignorance, when it comes to the raw brain power we are all individually born with, this truism is unfortunately quite true – and as it might apply to your mother-in-law or the guy down the street, it is also mostly irrelevant. But, as it might apply to an HR professional and their ability to contribute to their company's business success, not only is it relevant, it could also be a sign of a career going nowhere. If we as HR professionals are "stupid" about our companies' fundamentals, we limit our ability to add value and we downgrade our influence with our colleagues. Fortunately, in this context, we can, in fact, fix "stupid". I know we can because I did it – more than once.

With every new HR role I took on, the first thing I did was to get a copy of the business plan and associated strategies. What I was looking for was the deep-down insight into how the company makes money – both short and long term – what is the environment, what are the challenges?

For example, at Cadbury I needed to understand the business relationship between the soft drink bottler and the franchise owner. And, perhaps more importantly, I needed to know how they got the Caramilk into the Caramilk bar – I made a special trip to the plant to find that out. If we ever meet, feel free to ask me how – you won't be disappointed.

At Heinz, I needed to know how we could sustain our ketchup's incredible market share against the onslaught of private label products into the category. The ketchup business was also under attack from salsa-related products and easily challenged with the many "me-too" private label entries. How could Heinz thrive in such an environment?

When I first joined CN, the only thing I knew about that industry and that company is that it moved Heinz and Cadbury products around the continent. The rail industry is incredibly complicated and I had a lot to learn – so that's what I did. I learned how the railroad business could provide consistent service and maintain profitability in the face of incredible cost challenges.

And finally, at Maple Leaf Foods, I needed to understand how branded and private label products could co-exist within the company. How do you maintain a distinctive brand, the company's profitability and the platform for a successful future when you also package your customer's competitive products?

At every company I worked for, either as the head of HR or as a consultant, I spent time meeting the critical leaders in sales, marketing and operations to really understand their respective strategies and tactics. There were plenty of times I asked really "stupid" questions because I simply did not understand the business. But it was worth it. For the sake of a few awkward moments I gained a much deeper understanding of each company's business model, department by department, and in preparing myself that way I was able to provide much greater support to my colleagues, and much greater value to the company as it faced the inevitable business challenges.

Too often I see senior HR professionals who really don't understand their business and as a result advocate HR solutions that don't precisely fit the company's business needs. As a CHRO, I understand that my primary responsibilities are talent, capabilities and corporate culture, but as an influential and respected CHRO I know that by understanding the fundamentals of my company's business, I have a much greater chance of not only creating the most appropriate people strategy, but also confidently articulating it and gaining greater acceptance of it with my C-suite colleagues.

To read more about how we created a people strategy at Maple Leaf Foods, please see Appendix 11.

> "The CEO is a very lonely job. They don't need staff who are time wasters (chin waggers). Be focused in your discussion with the CEO."
>
> John Lynch, SVP, Corporate Human Resources, General Electric

CHAPTER 8:   BUILDING YOUR BUSINESS ACUMEN – AKA, HOW WE MAKE MONEY

> "CEO has to bring the CHRO into every decision and strategy. There is a healthy dose of mutual respect for each other."
>
> Katy Barclay, SVP, Human Resources, The Kroger Company

In my opinion, the CHRO cannot underestimate the importance of becoming intimately knowledgeable about how the company makes money. I discussed earlier the importance of "fixing stupid" and its impact on our ability as HR professionals to influence company strategy and tactics way beyond the archetypal 'personnel' function. One of the best ways I know to do this is to job shadow executives and front-line personnel, especially those who are responsible for creating the product and those who sell it. My normal practice when joining a company is to spend a day with a sales representative, a day with a production supervisor, and a day with the marketing manager. When I combined these job shadow days with intensive discussions with my C-suite counterparts and one-on-ones with the CFO, my understanding of how the company works grew to the point where I was not only able to align HR solutions more closely to the business reality, I was able to add value in a proactive way beyond my HR responsibilities. Keep your eyes on those who make and sell your product and it will be good for the company and good also for career growth.

One of the more difficult examples of building business acumen this way was when I joined CN Rail. Not only did I know nothing about their business model, I am probably the last guy you would think of as "railroad material". I am mechanically challenged (I took wood shop in high school and it's a miracle I still have all ten digits), I flunked auto mechanics (you have to be really inept to do this) and I can get lost on a small island – true story, just ask Marijane about a certain excursion to a Hawaiian golf course.

As a candidate for leading the HR function at a major continental transportation company, at face value, I did not exactly fit the bill. Thinking about it now, it sort of makes sense that someone who gets lost easily might well work for a company that transports goods and people by rails permanently fixed to the ground – but I digress.

So, here I was joining CN and I didn't know a thing about their business. How was I going to "fix stupid" this time? The learning curve was incredibly steep and

I needed help. It was at this point I began to get to know one of the great executive leaders of our time, and a name synonymous with "railroad" – Hunter Harrison, CN Rail's iconic CEO.

Hunter facilitated an amazing array of opportunities for me to learn the intimate details of our company and our industry from the direct line employees who ran the railroad every day. I went on day-long trips with locomotive engineers and conductors and I asked them a thousand questions about how we operated our trains and why. I asked them about customer service and what it took to keep customers happy and loyal. I asked them about the pitfalls and the things that we screwed up – and what that did to the business. I asked them what were the opportunities to do better and what did the senior executives not know about the business that they ought to know. I sat on trains for 10 to 12 hours straight and took it all in.

Just as important as what happens on the trains, is the big picture management of the whole system – which in CN's case was comprised of a network that spanned the continent – and so I spent a day in the control room with the folks who had their finger on the pulse of every route, every train, every railcar and every customer requirement throughout both Canada and the United States. It was an incredible experience, not only because of the staff expertise and dedication I witnessed there, but also what I began to understand about the railroad business; how incredibly complex the processes were and how precise and accurate and consistent everything must be within that framework. I began to understand just how difficult it was to make money and just how fragile profitability was.

As much as I enjoyed my time on the trains and in the control room, my favourite way to learn about CN's business first hand was to spend time with Hunter Harrison and pick his brains, especially in this case, when spending time with a CEO was such a positive experience.

One of the hallmarks of a good CEO in my opinion is the ability to succinctly and precisely articulate the top three to five success factors for their business – I've heard them called "business drivers". Hunter Harrison called them his five guiding principles. Similarly, a really good CFO should be able to succinctly and precisely articulate the financial implications of each of these business drivers. And so, starting with the CEO's list and filling in with the CFO's assessment, a new CHRO should be able to quickly capture the essence of the business at its most fundamental core and use it to create a detailed blueprint of how the company is intended to generate revenue and profit. At CN, this blueprint also gave me a good basis to assess the information provided by other execs and company personnel as I continued through the process of learning the intimate details of how CN made money.

> "The CHRO role is dynamic and changing – they need to be looking out into the future (5-10 year horizon) for talent decisions versus a look back approach."
>
> Geoff Beattie, Board Director

CHAPTER 9:   FUNCTIONAL VISION AND VALUES GUIDELINES

> "CEO should set incredible HR expectations and the CHRO will need to step up."
>
> Bill Conaty, former SVP, Corporate Human Resources, General Electric

Every CHRO needs to have a vision for the HR team; a statement intended to be the rallying cry for the HR team members. When I arrived at MLF, for example, I created not only a functional vision detailing the operations of the team, but also a behaviours vision that I would use as a leadership guide.

When I arrived at MLF, the HR function was split into a number of autonomous HR teams for different business units as well as a small corporate HR group. Not surprisingly, there was no teamwork between the corporate team and the business units or between the business units themselves.

I was determined to change this and so the MLF Functional Vision that I created was "Operate as One HR Team". Not only was this new functional vision in stark contrast to the past, most people on the HR team were looking for more consistency in our HR practices and were in fact looking forward to having strong leadership from the CHRO and acceptance of the new functional vision was widespread and immediate.

The second part of the HR vision I put in place at MLF was the behaviours vision outlining what I believed were the desired and positive behaviours I wanted our HR personnel to exhibit – individually and as a team. I communicated these guidelines by sharing my own behaviours detailing the way I wanted to be part of the team and the objectives I set for myself and the HR team at MLF. They were:

- Strive to be a Q4 leader.
- Set high performance standards.
- Love developing people.
- Enjoy creating and being a part of one strong HR team.
- Overcome my natural introversion and try to have a good time.
- Hire smart, motivated, and results-oriented people.
- Be a force for good that helps everyone succeed.
- Help the business make money.
- We are the "people experts".
- We are "One HR Team".

The operational and values vision was my first leadership directive at MLF and once they were accepted by the whole team, which was very quickly, we moved on to developing a People Strategy consistent with these guidelines; and the People Strategy became the focal point for our entire team for the next 3-5 years.

CHAPTER 10:   THE CHIEF HUMAN RESOURCES OFFICER AS THE VOICE OF THE SYSTEM

> "A great CHRO can simultaneously educate the HRC and management on the key questions that need to be answered. Both parties will be thankful."
>
> Sarah Raiss, Board Director

At the time I write this, the global economy is recovering, though still uncertain and turbulent. C-suite executives are challenged to make crisp business decisions or to encourage innovation and creativity. Some management teams will succumb to the inertia and take a wait and see stance and risk being left behind as a result.

There is much to suggest, however, that businesses can survive and even flourish in this environment by actually taking advantage of the uncertainty, and they can do so by facilitating diverse conversations throughout the organization; getting to the core of the challenges and exploring new possibilities to overcome them.

The CHRO is in a unique position then to listen to all the stakeholders – employees, customers and suppliers – and organize and redistribute the results of these conversations.

A strategic-minded, business-aligned CHRO acting as the information conduit can create a corporate culture better equipped to deal with uncertainty and to drive higher performance at the Board and C-suite levels.

Sound's great, right? Well, let's just say it's easier said than done – let's take a closer look.

(a)   Historical Context – Relating to the Board

In the past, the Board's relationship with the company was primarily via the CEO who controlled all links between the Board and the management team. Today, two other senior executives also directly interact with the Board: the CFO, by way of the Board's audit committee, and the CHRO by way of the Board's compensation/ human resources committee. This interaction will vary, of course, from company to company, but in organizations that favour strong corporate governance, the Board's level of interaction with the CFO and the CHRO can often be significant.

The CHRO is typically unique in that they are not looking to become the next CEO or CFO, and so may be better positioned to collect and share input from all constituents. Additionally, forward-thinking companies are beginning to appoint more CHROs to their boards because of their technical knowledge and their skills in building teams.

Exact numbers are hard to come by of course, but indications are that as more companies recognize the strategic importance of HR, and increase the senior HR executive's strategic role, the result is bottom line improvements. If this trend is accurate, and I think it is, HR's strategic influence within organizations will continue to grow.

(b)   The Role the CHRO can Play in the Organization

Just as the CHRO is uniquely positioned to interact with the Board, they are also ideally positioned to be "the voice of the system" to the rest of the organization; collecting, synthesizing, reporting and facilitating dialogue between senior management, the Board, outside suppliers, customers, employees, third parties and even competitors. It means connecting with all the disparate groups to build common understanding and common purpose. The more that HR can help build alliances at all levels within and outside of the organization, the more a company can realize sustainable business results.

In addition to attaining good business results, good governance is also about a positive reputation; and so the more the CHRO can collect and share diverse information the more aware the Board and senior management will be of issues that could affect the organization's optics. In all these examples the success of the CHRO as "the voice of the system" will depend on the CEO's willingness to allow these communications, as well as the CHRO's ability to play in this arena and their willingness to take the inherent risks.

Here are some examples of how the CHRO can facilitate and drive organizational performance:

1. *Organizational culture:* defining the purpose and values of the company, and supporting their linkage to the business strategy. Creating this culture and communicating it internally and externally will capture the hearts and minds of employees, thus creating the "stickiness" for employees to stay and the productivity that generates sustainable business results.

2. *Management's relationship with the Board:* helping build stronger relationships by:

    - facilitating dialogue around strategy development and risk identification;
    - creating a culture of openness, transparency, and sharing between management and Board members:
    - facilitating conflict resolution between Board members and the CEO.

3. *Talent management at the Board level:* the CHRO has a unique opportunity to play a role in building a stronger Board by assisting with the following activities:

    - recruiting and selecting new Board members;
    - developing and running orientation programs for new Board members;
    - developing and supporting a Board-effectiveness assessment process;
    - researching, sharing and implementing best practices in Board governance and operation.

4. *Talent management within the organization:* identifying emerging talent issues and creating a plan to manage them by:

    - creating a process for Board members to be more aware of talent within the company;

- developing a performance-management process that maximizes individual, team and organizational performance;

- developing social media and employer branding strategies and creating a risk management scenario with respect to corporate governance and reputation as it pertains to recruiting, collaboration and innovation;

- identifying global human capital trends and forecasts and developing strategies to attract, retain and motivate staff;

- working with the Board to develop a company value proposition that appeals to both current and future employees; and

- assisting in the evaluation of the CEO by the Board.

5. *Aligning relationships at the executive level:* becoming a trusted advisor to all executives, facilitating a culture that values all voices and where minority opinions are respected and disagreements do not have negative repercussions – a culture that encourages the exploration of different ideas and options and new ways of looking at problems and situations.

6. *Building stronger relationships between the company and its customers, suppliers and third-party entities:* creating an inclusive environment that encourages new ways of working together by asking and answering these questions:

- how can we work together to realize results for each other?

- what is working, what's not working, and what can we do better?

- do we have a common purpose, and if so, what is it?

As the CHRO I went on a sales call with the company's sales group and met with his HR counterpart in the customer organization. The result was a much stronger understanding of the customer's business and its needs which created a more sound partnership and a competitive advantage.

Other examples could include building similar HR-to-HR relationships with government and regulatory agencies and with suppliers and other third-party entities.

7. *Being a coach to the organization*: strategically savvy CHROs will have the intimate understanding of the business needed to create personal development plans for highly-placed executives and targeted candidates for top executive positions and either do the coaching themselves or engage the appropriate outside coaching resources.

Most people want to feel like they are adding value and making a difference to their employer. As the voice of the system, the CHRO is uniquely positioned to give a voice to all the organization's stakeholders – giving each a greater opportunity to contribute safely and confidently to the achievement of the company's objectives and contributing to superior, sustainable business results.

> "I expect my CHRO to be the eyes and ears of the organization. He/she needs to understand the undercurrents of engagement levels and mood of the organization, and help me manage that."
>
> Joe Jimenez, CEO, Novartis

CHAPTER 11: PEOPLE EXPERT ON THE TEAM

> "Along with being an excellent assessor of talent, the CHRO has to have a huge capacity for complex problem solving."
>
> Bill Conaty, former SVP, Corporate Human Resources, General Electric

There was a time when most companies did not have a Human Resources department. So why did that begin to change and why do most companies have them now? In hindsight, the answer seems obvious: changing circumstances around the recruitment, hiring and retention of employees and an increasingly complex regulatory environment made it necessary to create a department specializing in employee relations. But as correct as that answer is… it's not the bottom line answer. The reason most companies have HR departments now is that it has become a competitive necessity. Over time, companies with HR departments have performed better than those without. Nonetheless, this connection between HR and enhanced competitiveness is still regularly not recognized and HR professionals everywhere are underutilized.

In my view, the best reason to have a Human Resources department is to have people experts on the payroll responsible for educating managers on how to hire, develop and lead people to achieve great results. Many companies have outsourced a lot of traditional people administration services. This is fair game because these outside service suppliers are potentially better able to deliver superior service and technology to your employees.

Let's talk about the real "people experts" – the skilled practitioners who have been trained and have experience in all aspects of people leadership. They know how to:

1. expertly assess and recruit talent,
2. develop total rewards programs,
3. provide leadership training and development,
4. coach leaders with great feedback,
5. ensure strong employee relations and communications,
6. manage culture change,
7. advise senior leadership.

Sure, you can hire this expertise temporarily from consultants, but you don't get the right leverage. In my experience, with the right "people experts" on the team, companies can significantly increase company performance through engaged employees.

The CHRO that runs the HR department must be the ultimate "people expert" on the senior executive team. Yes, there could be several C-suite executives who have many of the skills to manage people. Ultimately, as the CHRO, my goal was to have a senior leadership team that was capable of leading people successfully. Is it possible that the CHRO can eliminate their role by making every leader self-sufficient? Stay tuned for the answer to that question later in the book.

> "Great CHROs are plugged into the 'authentic truth' in people and organizational awareness. They know what is going on with people and are lead advisors to the CEO."
>
> Michael McCain, CEO, Maple Leaf Foods

CHAPTER 12: SIMPLIFIER VS. COMPLICATOR

"Above all, the head of HR must be and be seen to be a straight shooter. I require absolute honesty in the relationship between the HRC chair and the head of HR. Our contacts should be frequent, candid and confidential. The head should not wait to be asked but should provide the chair with advance warning on all significant matters, including a careful reading of the internal atmosphere and concerns of and about key individuals. The head should earn and keep the trust of the chair but also be trusted by other members of the organization from the CEO to the plant workforce."

Gordon Ritchie, Board Director

During the interview process with CN Rail, I had the pleasure and the challenge of having several long conversations with the CEO, Paul Tellier. A gifted executive, Paul had transformed CN from a bloated government run, money-losing entity through the privatization process; but by the time I met Paul, he had been CEO for close to 10 years.

Paul's most challenging question during the interview process was "Les, are you a simplifier or are you a complicator?" Before I could answer I had to admit to him that I wasn't sure what he meant, so I asked, and here's what he told me: "A simplifier gets to the issue quickly and provides practical solutions and a complicator does the opposite."

Well my momma didn't raise no dummies and I knew the right answer so I promptly responded "I am a simplifier!" – forgetting for the moment that, in fact, I truly was.

What I found out later is that it was the simplifiers on Paul's team who were the key players in the transition that took CN from bloated bureaucracy to capitalist enterprise. In government, the complicators would prevail, and this made Paul crazy, but in the new CN it was the simplifiers who drove massive improvements in productivity. I was very pleased when he asked me to join him and the other simplifiers at CN.

About 18 months into my stay at CN, Paul walked into my office and told me about his interest in taking over the CEO position at Bombardier; he was on their Board and knew the company well. At first I was shocked – at the time he was 63 – and so I had to ask: "Why in the world would you want to start a new CEO job at your age?" He seemed somewhat bemused by the suggestion he was too old to start something new and stated quite simply: "CN is in great shape, I have plenty of time to do other things and I want a new challenge."

He took the job and although I was happy for him, I was sad for me. I had learned a lot from Paul and I was looking forward to more years working together. Of course when Paul left that's when things really got interesting at CN.

CHAPTER 13: CHRO: "TWO TO HIRE, ONE TO FIRE"

> "The hiring of the CHRO is ultimately the responsibility of the CEO but the chair of the HRC and eventually the committee itself should be closely consulted. It would be most unwise for the CEO to insist on proceeding with an appointment that was not fully supported by the chair of the HRC – this has never happened in my experience."
>
> Gordon Ritchie, Board Director

"Two to hire, one to fire." Although I didn't coin this concise phrase, I wish I had. It perfectly describes a complex set of relationships inherent to how "Matrix" leaders are hired and managed. I first heard it at Maple Leaf Foods and I think it also directly applies to the working relationships of today's CHRO.

Today it takes "two to hire" a CHRO – the CEO and the HRC Chair – both will have to agree on a new CHRO whether it's an internal promotion or an external hire, and so effectively the CHRO will have two bosses to manage. This is quite like the CFO and their relationship with the CEO and the Audit Committee Chair.

I can tell you from personal experience that it's not easy to work for two different bosses; keeping both happy requires a real juggling act and sometimes you do end up p*#sing one of them off. If this persists, the unhappy individual can pull the trigger and you are gone – that's the pithy "one to fire" part of the phrase.

I can also tell you from personal experience that losing your job to just one of your two bosses really sucks. In my case, the HRC Chair retired and was replaced with a new person – someone I did not see eye-to-eye with – and the result was that I left and he didn't. You may have heard the expression "you don't get to pick your family", well that's mostly true. Replace "family" with "boss", however, and it is absolutely true; and so for me it was adapt or get lost, and at that time I was too stubborn to adapt.

The lesson I learned, of course, is that the CHRO needs to be adaptable in the face of the "two to hire, one to fire" scenario and if you're like me, and you were not born with the requisite patience and political skills, you should seriously consider getting the appropriate training and/or coaching.

> "The CHRO has a delicate relationship with the CEO and HRC chair. CHRO is first and foremost aligned with management. However, there is a reporting line into the HRC chair which could be in conflict with their first loyalty. The HRC is increasingly reliant on external third parties to address this conflict."
>
> Michael McCain, CEO, Maple Leaf Foods

CHAPTER 14: DOING THE RIGHT THING VERSUS FOLLOWING THE CROWD

> "I always look at HR through a business lens. Do the right things with no compromise. Be true to yourself and be ready to take the consequences if needed."
>
> Peter Goerke, Group Human Resources Director, Prudential PLC

If I was sitting across the table from you over a coffee and asked, "As HR professionals should we always do the right thing?" You would be hard pressed to say anything but yes. You might say "it depends", but you wouldn't flat out say "no".

Of course, the tough part of the choice presented in the heading is how to be sure what is right, or who is right (you or the crowd), and, even more complicated, determining if those who are "wrong" in your view are willing to "fall on their sword" in support of their stance on an issue and in so doing present you with dire consequences for insisting on being right. To even further complicate the choice, when it comes to doing the right thing on a people issue, everyone involved may genuinely believe they are not doing or advocating anything wrong.

As a CHRO, I faced exactly this kind of choice and I had to decide whether or not to follow my instinct on what was "right" or follow the crowd. Beginning in the early 1990s many companies started to drop Defined Benefit pension plans for their salaried employees in favour of the new Defined Contribution pension plans. There were a lot of good bottom-line reasons for making this move and it became something of a groundswell. Although I wasn't convinced it was the right thing to do, I was one of those CHROs who followed the crowd.

Now today, as a natural evolution of that kind of change, there is a growing trend for companies to get out of the employee pension business altogether. The rationale is that it is the "right" thing to do for employees who today are more transient and want more control over their pension and who would rather have higher salaries in lieu of pension contributions. The assumption, and the basis for thinking this is "right", is the notion that employees will use their incremental salary to fund their own pensions. In terms of cost control and cost certainty, this move is, of course, right for the companies. Salaries and salaried personnel are much more easily controlled than the cost of pension benefits or even pension contributions.

But in my view, the basic premise is flawed because it relies on an assumption that, in fact, is statistically untrue. Employees for the most part will use salary increases to fulfill their short term financial requirements or even to fund a different lifestyle before they will invest it in a pension. For most of us, it is in our nature to think in the immediate before we think about the long term. Not surprisingly then, a very large percentage of employees do not have enough invested for their retirement and that number is growing, coincidentally, just as the number of companies getting out of employee pensions is growing.

If this trend continues, and if more companies get out of the employee-pension business, I believe we will have a national disaster on our hands. If there is no "captive" way to effectively force people to save for their retirement, we will see more and more retired and elderly who will need to rely on government assistance programs because they do not have the pension funds available. Think of the Boomer, Gen X and Echo Boomer cohorts and the kind of life expectancies anticipated for these generations and this effect could be both immediate and sustained; and everyone will suffer the consequences including those companies who saved the costs in the short term.

And so, for me, this is where the rubber hits the road in terms of doing what's "right" versus following the crowd. Some will argue that you can't force people to do the right thing like save for retirement, and that people should be allowed to make their own mistakes and learn from them. The problem in this case is that at the point the lesson is learned it's too late to do anything about it.

In my view, the right thing is to protect employees from their own potential weakness or lack of planning, and in so doing protect not only their future, but also the future of the following generations and even the country. I for one will not be following the crowd on this new trend and will continue to advocate strongly for a defined benefits or defined contribution company pension plan.

CHAPTER 15:   CHRO – CONSCIENCE OF THE ORGANIZATION?

> "CHRO's need to stand tall behind line managers. Every line manager is accountable for talent – put people first. They must walk the talk."
>
> Claude Mongeau, CEO, Canadian National

When I first started in HR so many years ago, my personal mantra was that "the HR department is the conscience of the organization", and indeed back then it seemed no one else in the corporate world was at all interested in taking responsibility for the moral and ethical stature of the company and its employees. In the past, some companies were run by cowboys who had no moral conscience and typically it fell to the CHRO to address any undesirable treatment of employees.

But as much as that HR mandate made sense back then, in the intervening years it has become outdated, and today it might even be a little dangerous.

Today, not only do the majority of leaders know right from wrong, they also behave accordingly because the consequences of not doing so are immediate, long-lasting, and usually harsh. Business codes of conduct are the norm in virtually every company and the most senior executives are held accountable for the company's adherence to them. And waiting in the wings to pounce on any misstep is the "social media", or, more precisely, whistle-blowers and "wronged" employees who use social media to tell their story with pictures and video to millions of people everywhere – including the press and the Board of Directors. The court of public opinion, rightly or wrongly, is, in fact, the new conscience of the organization. Accordingly, the CHRO should no longer be the "cop" tasked with policing the organization for bad leaders; it should happen by design by way of standardized whistle-blower programs and 360 surveys. Bad leaders today cannot hide nearly as well as they have in the past.

As the CHRO, I sit on the Ethics Committee at MLF which is chaired by the CEO, who in turn will ask the committee to rule on any issue involving the CEO's own behaviour. There are more checks and balances in most corporate systems today than at any point in history and so it seems that my old mantra is now not needed and redundant – ready for retirement. This is not to say, of course, that the CHRO no longer needs to be the employee advocate in the C-suite, but more on that elsewhere in the book.

> "The stronger the CEO, the greater the need for the CHRO to communicate and deal with Board Directors."
>
> Edward Lumley, Vice Chair, BMO Nesbitt Burns

CHAPTER 16: EVERY PEER IS AN HR EXPERT

> "The CHRO can't get upset if the CEO asks others for their opinions on people issues."
>
> John Lynch, SVP, Corporate Human Resources, General Electric

When it comes to the financial matters of a company, the CFO and the accounting group tend to work without much oversight or input from employees at large. Their area of expertise is such that generally no one outside the department would think to meddle with what they do or how they do it. The same is true for most departments – IT, operations, facilities, and even sales and marketing to some degree.

The one area in the company where it seems that everyone is an expert is human resources. When it comes to things like pay, benefits, training, coaching, promotions, culture, etc., every executive in the company thinks they know what's best and are usually not shy about sharing their ideas; and every executive in the company has a vision that is usually different from everyone else's.

Accordingly, one of the most difficult challenges I have faced as CHRO, is getting the other executives to sing from the same songbook regarding people issues. Getting consensus is like herding cats and a great deal of time can be spent negotiating between many different solutions.

On the one hand, it's good when other senior execs are engaged in the subject, but on the other hand, it's difficult to arrive at a unanimous decision when individuals become entrenched in their own solution, usually citing past success as the reason for their intransigence. The notion that HR matters should be left to the purview of the HR experts hasn't quite got there yet.

The most common people issue that every executive seems to have their own solution for is employee turnover; and the most prevalent non-HR solutions out there include some form or another of increased compensation – i.e., more money. But if salaries and benefits are competitive with the rest of the industry, money is almost never the reason for higher-than-usual levels of turnover, and therefore money will not be the solution. I talk elsewhere in the book about using money to motivate people and frankly the conclusion is that it is a poor motivator.

The other common people issue that my peers have had instant answers to is low employee morale; and usually the first solution to leap to the front is to "pay them more", or "increase the bonus". So again, the notion that money is at the root of all happiness/unhappiness becomes the facile underpinning to the most popular non-HR HR solutions.

Too often, however, the "other HR experts" in the company either ignore, or do not know how to recognize, the non-financial reasons why employees might leave the company in higher than usual numbers: bad management, no development, workload issues, few promotional opportunities, and many more. In fact some of these executives might even be one source of the problem.

If salaries and benefits are truly below par with the industry, then, of course, high turnover could very well result. I'm not saying here that money is never the problem; and, indeed, sometimes when pay and benefits are at the low end of the industry scale it can exacerbate other problems and even mask them. But even then, more money is rarely the sole solution.

Applying solid and consistent processes to understand high turnover is the key to finding the right solution. As the CHRO, I believe that as the true people expert on the team I need to be fact-based in developing my own preferred solution, using the HR tools and team to delve to the bottom of each resignation – and here I use a consistent and positive exit interview strategy as one means to gather relevant information.

As the CHRO I also feel it is important to be assertive in taking control of the solution-development process and sometimes I felt the need to take the discussion outside of the group dynamic. In some cases, I've felt it necessary to take the conversation out of the group setting and go one-on-one with my peers to discuss their take on the issue; it gives them a sense that I truly care about their opinion and am open to it, and it gives me an opportunity to bring them around to my point of view without having to talk over half a dozen other voices. Although this process could be more time consuming, it can pay dividends in terms of the executive group coming to a consensus on a people issue.

CHAPTER 17: INTERNAL FILL RATE

"Rewarding past performance with promotion is relevant but understanding skills needed for the future is the key to success."

Geoff Beattie, Board Director

How would you feel if you joined a new company only to discover that they rarely promoted from within? Well, if you're like me and I suspect the vast majority of people are, you wouldn't feel very good about your impending employment and you would almost immediately begin planning your exit. Surprisingly, a lot of companies do not regularly promote from within and seem oblivious to the effects on its employees.

One of the most important accountabilities for the CHRO is to create a culture/work environment where internal talent is valued and developed for future promotional opportunities. At CN, we had a goal to promote internal staff for at least 85% of all management openings. So, as an example, if we were looking to fill a supervisory job, we would look at our unionized workforce to find suitable candidates.

Obviously, this created a positive work environment for those interested in their career development, but to be fair one of the reasons for this high internal objective was the lack of qualified candidates in the external market. There are only six major railroads in North America and they are geographically isolated from each other. Additionally, stealing employees from your competitors creates a revolving-door type bidding war and employees that come with bad habits and sometimes other baggage. And so for all these reasons, it was imperative that CN develop its own leadership talent from within the organization.

In the consumer-packaged goods industry, it is very common to find a much lower internal fill rate than CN. This is in part due to the wide availability of qualified candidates and the industry's high turnover culture. In addition, the CPG industry is more broad and generic than the railroad industry and talent is therefore more transferable. Of course, this is not to say that you should not, or could not, have a high internal fill rate in the CPG world. In fact, at MLF, we set a goal to reach a 70% fill rate and at Hormel Foods, they currently fill 85-90% of all openings internally.

I believe an obvious outcome of a high internal fill rate is a lower turnover rate, as well as an attractive company attribute when you do have to recruit outside. On the other hand, there is no compelling reason to want a lower internal fill rate. The one I hear most to justify going outside is that it is faster to hire outside than to develop an internal employee – a short-sighted and lazy excuse in my opinion. I believe one of the core competencies of great leaders is the development of talent, but too often senior managers will succumb to the siren call of expediency and will default to hiring outside. And, of course, this kind of short-term management strategy for hiring becomes self-perpetuating as potential internal candidates leave the company to advance their career.

Obviously, building an internal pipeline of talent takes time and patience, and, of course, the corporate determination to put the appropriate processes in place; but once the pipeline is up and pumping, the company will continuously reap the rewards of lower recruitment costs and, most importantly, a higher success rate for internal promotions versus external hires.

"We always told our business leaders, 'You own the businesses. You're renting the people.' Bill Conaty and I felt we had personal responsibility for the top 750 managers. We looked after their development, their rewards, and their advancement. We ran the people factory to build great leaders."

J. Welch and J. Byrne, *JACK: Straight From The Gut* (New York: Business Plus, 2003), p. 388

CHAPTER 18:   HR PERFORMANCE METRICS

> "Today, and certainly for the future, CHROs and their teams
> need to have strategic alignment and relevant metrics."
>
> Katy Barclay, SVP, Human Resources, The Kroger Company

To say that every company will have different people issues may fall into the "duh!" category, but across the board I believe there are a number of HR "success predictors" that virtually all companies will have in common; predictors that need to be managed and importantly, need to be measured.

Here are my top 10 common HR success predictors:

1. *Top talent retention:* the CHRO should have an eye on how effectively the company is retaining the high flyers in the company. This group should be limited to 20% of the salaried workforce.

2. *Employee stock ownership:* there are two groups of people to measure here. Your executive team should be adhering to the company's mandatory stock ownership requirement, so that should be an easy group to measure. Obviously, a high level of ownership in this group isn't as meaningful as it may be for the second group – the balance of the employees who voluntarily buy company shares, sometimes with a financial incentive, but often not. Measuring share ownership amongst this group can give you a grass roots' indication of how many employees are "believers" in the company.

3. *Internal management fill rate:* how many management openings are being filled with existing employees? In my view, the higher the internal fill rate, the greater the company's opportunities for success because internal talent has the greatest potential to be successful. In addition to the fill rate, I also recommend that CHROs keep track of the diversity of promotions to ensure that their communities are represented in management.

4. *Productivity per employee:* measured by the number of products produced, divided by the number of employees and the sales revenue, divided by the number of employees. The metric to look for here is continuous improvement in products produced and sold.

5. *Spans and levels:* the CHRO needs to be the organizational architect constantly measuring the span of control for managers and the number of

management levels in the company. My goal was to ensure large spans of control for managers and few levels of management.

6. *Employee engagement levels:* the CHRO must be aware of how well the employee population is being led by management. The metric here isn't exactly "happiness", but rather whether or not employees feel motivated to do a good job, and if they feel connected to their supervisors and the company. Regular focus groups and surveys can assist in taking this measurement, perhaps every 12 to 18 months.

7. *Supervisory development:* in my opinion, the prospects for the long-term success of a company is greatly enhanced by having very well-trained front-line supervisors and managers, and my goal as CHRO is to measure the amount of hours of training the company provides with a view to increasing that number every year.

8. *Total rewards cost:* in most companies where employee costs are a large component of the cost base, the CHRO is responsible to ensure the total rewards program is competitive for employees yet provides for very efficient delivery. The metric here is the total cost of compensation and benefits averaged per employee.

9. *Q4 leadership level:* Q4 leaders get the right results by using positive consequences and by creating high levels of commitment; they foster an environment of high performance and dedicated employees; and they tend to develop self-maintaining systems. Obviously, the objective is to maximize the number of Q4 leaders in the company and I usually set my goal at 80%. The metric here is by way of the PMP and 360 Degree survey process.

10. *Employee performance scorecards:* in my opinion every employee, including all unionized employees, deserves to receive feedback on their performance in the form of annual written reviews from their managers. These scorecards would be designed to reflect the individual's contribution and the minimum acceptable measure here is 100% completion.

I've had a lot of time and many opportunities to develop these 10 HR performance metrics and they work for me. Other CHROs have their own metrics and philosophies and I will share some of them with you throughout the book.

CHAPTER 19: WHO IS THE CONFIDANTE TO THE CHRO?

> "The CHRO is like the utility in-fielder in baseball – they need to know so much about so many things in the company."
>
> Peter Gleason, Managing Director & CFO, National Association of Corporate Directors (NACD)

Top HR executives occupy a unique spot on the senior management team and often become confidantes to their peers and even the CEO, and in so doing they often become something of an informal coach, which makes them the easy and obvious go-to person when a sounding board, trusted advisor or mentor is needed.

On the other hand, it can be difficult for peers to give frank feedback to the top HR executive. After all, who wants to risk upsetting the person who has input on succession or promotion and holds the key to confidential personnel files? Similarly, depending on how open their relationships are, a CHRO may feel constrained in seeking confidential input from the CEO and other senior managers.

Who, then, can play the role of confidante for an HR executive?

A CEO can provide direct feedback on performance, but as the CEO is also usually HR's boss, there are some constraints on what an HR executive may feel comfortable disclosing. The chair of the Board of Director's Human Resources Committee (HRC) is a likely mentor if they have the skills and interest but the chair of the HRC is also a member of the Board with influence in top-level executive hiring and promotion and so, again, the HR executive may feel uncomfortable discussing difficult subjects with them.

In some cases, a strong and credible peer on the executive team can serve as an internal coach and provide another source of feedback, but for some very important practical and professional reasons there are risks associated with being too open with a fellow executive. So where is an HR executive to go to have a free-ranging dialogue without the baggage of internal politics?

An external coach might be the best solution to provide an objective voice and a source of straight-talking feedback and they can be a safe and trusted sounding board with no axe to grind and no agenda that might not mesh with yours. An external coach can listen to your frustrations or disappointments and they can offer a different perspective and advice on the most difficult issues, all in the context of objectivity and privacy.

"When talking with my coach, I felt as though I was talking with a wise Yoda", says Doug Cable, senior HR director at Cangene Corporation, a Winnipeg-based biopharmaceutical firm. "That is to say, as a coach, he was part oracle, part father confessor, and always had practical, put-in-action advice."

Naturally an external coach does not replace the feedback or advice from the CEO or the HRC chair or even your peers. Instead they are a different resource who can provide personal support as you deal with the more difficult aspects of your role. So, for example, if there are messages on performance that need to be delivered, that will naturally fall to you as CHRO, but your coach can be there to help you deal with the subsequent feedback and help you decide the best way to respond.

Bottom line: in addition to helping HR executives get a handle on the feedback as they deal with the Board and the other C-suite executives, a coach is an important developmental resource for HR executives who want to continue to grow in their roles.

There are a number of situations where an HR executive will find a specialized coach useful.

Personal development: There are coaches who specialize in a range of services directly targeted at HR executives who want to continuously improve their professional performance; it's important to know precisely what your needs and goals are and look for the coach best suited to helping you achieve them.

On the subject of personal development coaches, this is how Diane Nyisztor, former senior vice-president of global HR at SNC-Lavalin put it: "As a senior vice-president of HR, engaging a coach was the most relevant personal development initiative I have taken. Learning from someone who has 'been there' is one of the best ways to develop yourself professionally."

Succession planning: Many CEOs believe promoting from within for the top HR position has the greatest chance of success. An external coach, with senior HR experience, can work with the designated internal successor to prepare for the senior HR role. Chances of a smooth transition are improved when a coach works with an incumbent vice-president of HR and the CEO to "tag team" the execution of the new vice-president's development plan, which helps co-ordinate the hand-off of responsibility.

Performance issues: Not everyone is open to feedback and an HR executive may be no exception. If there is reason to believe the individual has value to offer, but some personal or leadership behaviour is getting in the way, an external coach can be a practical answer.

A coach can deliver very specific performance feedback to an HR executive and work with them to make changes in behaviour. A very useful exercise can have the coach undertaking a 360-degree feedback process that helps to highlight areas of strength and obvious problems to be explored in the coaching relationship.

"It's very easy for an HR executive to develop a functional blindness to their own defects. It's not that they can't resolve them, it's that they can't see them. A great coach, in my experience, has the insight and proven HR track record to help any HR executive resolve these blind spots", says James Grossett, Senior Vice-President of Human Resources at Agrium, a Calgary based fertilizer producer.

Maximizing HR leadership: Some senior HR executives have a deep understanding of the HR field, but may have some barriers in communicating their knowledge and connecting with staff or the senior team. When major business challenges are confronting an organization, and deep change will be needed, it can be helpful for the CHRO to work with a coach on how to communicate ideas, set a pace that gives staff a fair chance to execute plans and develop a process to measure effectiveness. Other leadership aspects, such as evaluating staff objectively, setting a realistic strategy, learning how to support rather than staying hands-on, and enhancing strategic leadership skills can also be addressed through coaching.

Like so many other forms of developmental assistance, coaching will likely show its results over time and not immediately. Nonetheless, for a forward-thinking HR executive who plans on continuously moving to the next level in their professional performance, an objective decision about engaging a specialized coach will, in fact, show both short- and long-term benefits.

"The CHRO role can be a very lonely place. You need to develop a strong external network of CHROs that can be a confidential sounding board and help you stay externally focused and current."

Katy Barclay, SVP, Human Resources, The Kroger Company

CHAPTER 20: CULTURE CHANGE – DOES IT REALLY MATTER?

> "Cultures change one funeral at a time."
>
> Ascribed to Margaret Mead

It has been my experience that not only is it hard to change a company's culture, it can actually be hard to measure or define it in the first place, especially when there are no preferred cultural values or desired behaviours established, or when they are different between management levels and business units. But just how significant is it, that we may not be able to measure a company's culture?

For example, at CN there were two very different cultural eras – pre-1995, when the company was basically a government bureaucracy, and post-1995, when it became a publically-traded company focused on meeting shareholder expectations. Post-1995, the company had no articulated cultural values, but instead it was driven by five guiding business principles – Service, Safety, Cost Control, Asset Utilization, and People.

These five principles drove everything CN did from a leadership perspective; we used them to evaluate leadership and employees' performance and we even evaluated departmental performance using the same metrics.

So what's my point? Well, CN was, and still is, a very successful company despite not having a defined and measurable company culture. During my tenure, I resisted doing annual employee satisfaction surveys because they were not effective in measuring our leadership effectiveness as measuring against the five guiding principles. The moral of this story is that you don't have to have a laundry list of company values to be successful; but, nonetheless, you do need leadership that is focused on what matters to be successful in your industry.

On the other hand, at Maple Leaf Foods, the CEO was instrumental in creating a very clear set of behavioural values that made a difference in how the company was managed – and in this instance it was absolutely needed. Today's MLF was created by the acquisition of over 30 different companies of various sizes – each with their own management and employee values, each with their own corporate culture – and so in order to bring all these disparate entities together into a single, homogenous, smooth-running company, the CEO Michael McCain established and imposed some very specific cultural norms. By giving all the employees the cultural direction they needed, right from the top, he made it possible for a very diverse management team to become unified in its operations and in its vision of business success.

So, of course, culture matters. But what matters more is making sure the company's leadership knows how to make money in an ethical and inspiring manner. Everything else is window dressing. Consultants make a lot of money in selling culture change services, but if you have a leadership team that is very good on the people development, a lot of the bad culture stuff never rears its ugly head. Making money and treating people well can go very nicely together if that is your focus.

For more on the culture change at CN Rail, see Appendix 3, Working with Human Nature to Change CN.

> "The CHRO is the keeper and co-definer of the culture-values and behaviours expected of people."
>
> Sarah Raiss, Board Director

CHAPTER 21:   USING MONEY AND BENEFITS TO MOTIVATE PEOPLE

> "The CHRO should know the social costs of running the business (hire to retire costs). Do we really manage these costs effectively?"
>
> Geoff Beattie, Board Director

When I talk to people about what motivates employees, the usual first thing on their list is money and benefits, and then a long silence as they try to figure out what else there might be. In fact, you probably read the headline and said to yourself, "Well, duh … what else is there?"

Due to the fact that "how much we make" is almost always the number one metric used to determine how well we are doing in our job, I guess it makes sense that most people also assume it is our prime motivator as we go about doing our job; yes, money does talk, but the truth is only for a short time.

So now that I've said that, you might not be surprised to learn that I don't believe pay and benefits alone, even good ones, are sustainable daily motivators for the majority of employees. Naturally, if your pay is totally commission-based or piece work, making enough money to survive is clearly a short-term motivator, but not necessarily a positive one, especially if the question of making enough is in doubt. Fortunately, most of us do not have to be selling every minute to put bread on the table for our families.

To put this idea into a more memorable and more concise statement, I like to use a phrase that has always resonated with me as CHRO – "you can't buy a good team with just money, but you can lose a good team by underpaying them." A competitive money and benefits program for your employees is simply the entry-level cost of doing business. It's what gets you in the game, but it isn't what keeps you in the game. After a very short while, the bi-weekly paycheque becomes almost invisible; the money goes into the account and, for most employees, quickly disappears. Pay is what you get for showing up, pay is what you get for the 8 hours you put in, and pay is what you get no matter what company you work for. The truth is, pay simply doesn't motivate on a daily basis.

What's missing from this equation are the intangibles that on a daily basis truly motivate employees to do a great job, to look out for the company's best interests, and to eagerly come back the next day to do it again – intangibles that stem from top notch leadership practices – intangibles that don't necessarily add cost.

If you consider how much time most of us spend at our jobs – almost literally a third of our life and often more during our working years – it should come as no surprise that our work and our workplace are huge factors in our emotional, intellectual and even physical well-being. Successfully addressing these factors is what will truly create a fully motivated and committed workforce; the idea isn't to necessarily create a group of "happy" employees, but that often is a related, if unintended, consequence.

So now the question is: what kind of top notch leadership practices address these intangible factors that so greatly impact our employees? I can't speak directly to the practices themselves – that will vary from company to company and even from one leader to another – but what I can do is offer the objectives: things like interesting work, inspiring leaders, people development, great feedback, promotional opportunities, family-friendly policies, high performance standards and a positive learning environment. You can likely think of your own workplace right now and add a couple yourself. And as you think about these objectives, think about delivering on them in terms of leadership practices that feature honesty, consistency, respect, recognition, reason, and access/high-visibility.

You can probably think of leaders in your own situation that have these characteristics and some that don't, but don't mistake this for a list of personality traits. What I'm talking about are corporate policies and systems and processes, as well as the leadership training that may be necessary to ensure that these policies, systems and processes are successfully put into action.

There are few movie lines as memorable as "Show me the money!" – but in the end it's Jerry Maguire's new-found honesty and his focus on the intangibles in Rod Tidwell's life (Cuba Gooding Jr.) that keep him in the game and put him in a position to succeed both personally and professionally – a rare instance where the movie plot actually rings true.

> "In another case, the CEO had made a very dramatic argument for increasing compensation for his senior staff who, he feared, would otherwise be looking aggressively at outside opportunities. It fell to me as chair of the HRC to advise him that the committee had reached its own, very different conclusions and the compensation increase would not be forthcoming."
>
> Gordon Ritchie, Board Director

CHAPTER 22:　COACHING YOUNG TALENT

> "The CHRO has to have a real opinion on the assessment of the talent in the organization to reduce the subjectivity of the CEO and others."
>
> Geoff Beattie, Board Director

One of the more important and rewarding roles of the CHRO is recognizing young talent throughout the company and becoming a positive influence in the development of their personal skills and their careers, in some cases even taking on the role of mentor and coach.

One recent example I'd like to share with you is from my time with Maple Leaf Foods. Maple Leaf has a very successful university recruitment program called Leadership Track; in operation for over 10 years, several of the company's senior executives were hired through this program.

During the 3-year LT program, the graduate is rotated through three different positions in various departments and when they're finished they take on a job that best suits their university training and work experience. Graduates go into sales, operations, supply chain, finance, marketing, food safety, and recently, for the first time, we had a graduate come into the program destined for HR. Her name is Stephanie Hauck and she has a Masters in Labour Relations from the University of Toronto.

Stephanie was assigned a mentor from HR and I developed a 3-year plan which started in mid-2012 and will see her rotate through three positions – a production supervisor, a sales representative, and an HR specialist. At the end of her LT program, Stephanie will become an HR manager in a plant location.

At first I was a bit reluctant to get personally involved in her development, but because she was the first HR graduate to enter the LT program I decided I should take more ownership for her coaching. What really convinced me to coach her directly, however, were the circumstances of her becoming a front-line supervisor at a plant that was scheduled to close in 2 years.

Although Stephanie was very keen to take on this role she was also quite nervous about it because she had never managed people before and she had no experience in a food plant. It was my idea for her to get this kind of experience, so I felt an added obligation to become her coach and help her through it. Fortunately, for both Stephanie and for me, she worked for a very talented production manager who also took an active role in her development.

My coaching plan was to spend time every 2 weeks to discuss Stephanie's progress and for her to send me a weekly summary of her day-to-day activities with a special emphasis on what she has learned about the supervisory role and herself as a person. These weekly notes to me were so good I decided to send them to all the HR staff, and to every VP in the company, as well as the C-suite team including the President and CEO. Here is a great example of one of her weekly notes which she called, "Shop Floor Weekly":

#31 – Shop Floor Weekly

Monday, February 25th 2013 – Friday, March 1st 2013

This week I had both an impactful and inspiring conversation that ignited the topic of plant closure and the reality many members of my team will face over the next two years. Kirk is a long-standing dynamite employee who has dedicated 30 years of his life to Maple Leaf Foods. Kirk is the type of team member that will do anything and everything for the sake of the department and team. My supervisor team and I are greeted every single morning by Kirk, usually with a long list of things that need immediate attention. Although, hearing these unfortunate items can be frustrating, especially first thing in the morning, his passion and enthusiasm for doing what's right is infectious making it impossible to turn away.

On numerous occasions Kirk and I have spoken regarding various topics. In a recent discussion we spoke about education, which eventually lead to a discussion about the plant closing and his feelings towards this upcoming change. "I have been working here for 30 years and when you work somewhere for that long it becomes a part of you, a part of your life – actually it becomes your life", Kirk explained. During the conversation, Kirk expressed that when the company first announced the closure he felt as though it was years away and he did not have anything to worry about just yet. However, now as it gets closer to the end he is starting to worry about how he will market himself moving forward and most importantly how he is going to provide for his family down the road. "I didn't go through school, (laughs) I didn't even need too. Back when I was your age, your fathers age, being a hard-worker was usually what got you the job and you worked hard and that was that – things have changed." Overall the conversation was very moving and will likely reside with me throughout my career.

For nearly all of us, change is an inevitable part of our careers and lives. For some of us it is planned, others sudden but in either case we are often forced to adapt and move on. As a supervisor, I realized over the course of my journey working in an environment undergoing change how important it is to be cognitive of the plant closure and what it means for my team, collectively and individually.

I remember when I first started and had my 'pedal to the floor' with change, the resistance I experienced, the comments and the fear. My colleagues and I can recall several members of the team turning their heads to process improvements because they honestly viewed these important improvements as a waste of time, "Who cares, this place is closing" some of them would say. Of course, as a young, enthusiastic LT this type of resistance was very challenging but looking back also very powerful because it helped me conceptualize the reality of my environment, adjust my style and push forward.

It was at this stage and even more so after my conversation with Kirk that I developed an increased level of empathy and understanding. This is not to say that I have stopped pushing for both process and behavioural change but I have thought about my approach a lot more critically while also being conscious of the emotions and feelings some of my long-standing employees may have to these abrupt changes. In essence getting to know your employees on both a professional and personal level enhances your ability to truly understand the complex balance between productivity, people management and human interaction.

On numerous occasions I have been inspired by the spirit of this company, but I am most inspired by the dedication and spirit of those who continue to come to work and work hard in a time of such uncertainty.

I look forward to your feedback and thank-you for your continued support.

Have a wonderful week!

Stephanie

The response from those who received Stephanie's note was wonderful. Vice Presidents wrote to her to encourage and compliment her efforts on the front line, as did several executives. Operations leaders became more educated about the daily life of a production supervisor, and the HR folks learned more about the daily challenges of a supervisor. Everyone is benefitting from watching and being part of the professional and personal growth of a very talented young person.

Most importantly, of course, this process is helping Stephanie build confidence and develop leadership skills that will benefit her throughout her career. At the time of writing this book, Stephanie is in her second year of the LT program as a sales representative. My prediction is Stephanie will someday be a CHRO and it gives me great satisfaction to have been there at the very beginning of her career and to have been a positive influence in her professional life.

CHAPTER 23: SEVEN YEARS IS ENOUGH

> "Future CHRO's need to manage: globalization, the social costs on the bottom line and transforming the HR department."
>
> John Lynch, SVP, Corporate Human Resources, General Electric

There's a common theory in many industries and with many types of jobs that there is a time limit, or a "best before" date that starts counting down the day you first start the new job. A common number we often hear is 5 years, especially in the high-tech industries. The reasons for this belief are varied and generally non-scientific, but they can best be summed up by the aphorism: "familiarity breeds complacency", or as Mark Twain put it, "familiarity breeds contempt – and children".

The notion of job fatigue is the subject of a lot of popular writing today, and there doesn't seem to be much debate about whether or not it actually exists – it does. And not only do those of us in HR need to be aware of it with respect to our talent, we need to be aware of its possible effects on us. Based on my own experience, I believe that with respect to the CHRO position, 7 years is enough. Generally speaking, I begin to get restless after 5 years in the same job and bored and unproductive after seven.

Things that can make this number shorter or longer are such influences as the CEO and other C-suite members. How often do the other executive positions turn over? Are you always working with someone new, or does the team stay intact over a long period of time? New colleagues in the C-suite can serve to reinvigorate how you feel about your job and the company, and so maybe 7 years is too short – assuming they want to keep you. Sometimes, however, you won't mesh with the new CEO and the idea of moving on quickly becomes an attractive one.

On the other hand, perhaps the entire team has stayed in place for 7 years or more, and perhaps everyone should be looking for something fresh. CEO's tend to move on after 5 years in the same role and CFO's the same or sooner. Most C-suite executives have CEO aspirations and generally they want to gain experience quickly and be seen as upwardly mobile as evidenced by regularly acquiring new, more responsible, better paying positions.

I also believe the age of the new CHRO can influence when they might start experiencing job fatigue or feel the need to move on. On day one a new CHRO appointed in their early 40s likely knows they will not retire with that company and may even have a career plan with three or four more promotional moves mapped out and penciled in. On the other hand, a CHRO appointed in their early 50s is likely to at least include retirement in their plans and may at this stage of their career value stability over promotional opportunity. At 50, this CHRO may be less effective as a change agent than they might have been at 40.

Based on my experience, the reality is that most experienced CHROs, and other traditional C-suite executives, get bored after 6 or 7 years in the same position and it requires almost super-human self-motivation to re-invent oneself within the same company. I also believe the same is true for CEOs but of course they are usually asked to leave before they ever start feeling the onset of career fatigue.

CHAPTER 24: THE POWER BEHIND THE CEO

> "The CEO sets the tone at the top. The most critical part of the
> CEO & CHRO relationship is the CEO listens to the
> CHRO and agrees to take action."
>
> Purdy Crawford, Board Director

For me to say that the CHRO is the "power" behind the CEO is, yes, a bit presumptuous – okay, a lot presumptuous, but it needs to be said that because of their close relationship with the CEO, and because of the nature of their role and the information they have access to, the CHRO does wield a lot of power, both actual and perceived, and they need to be careful how they use it.

Naturally the CHRO is seen by most in the company as the career-maker or career-breaker and that critical power, operating at such a personal level, can impact the way other employees behave regardless of the CHRO's actual intention. Instead of focusing solely on doing a good job, some employees can also become concerned about their personal relationship with the CHRO and behave in ways intended to put them on the CHRO's "good side".

For example, I was told that the CHRO at PepsiCo was so powerful that even senior management was very careful to keep in his good books. They apparently managed their behaviour to ensure the CHRO felt positively about them, sometimes at the risk of other relationships or even their job performance. I heard this story time and time again, told to me by so many ex-Pepsi people during hiring interviews that I concluded it was true.

In my own career, I have dealt with people who honestly believed my role was one of king/queen maker (as opposed to hiring talent for the best interest of the company) and I became very sensitive to this perception. I felt that I was more effective in my role if I was seen as a company advocate with no personal feelings about any individual's career except in that context. Despite my efforts, the perception persisted and I had to go to lengths to make sure that I did not use this power, and was not seen to be using it – that is, in most situations.

There are times, however, for the good of the company, when it is necessary to use this power to change behaviour. One example comes to mind. I was the head of HR in a company during a CEO succession and one of the senior contenders for the position used the possibility that he might become my boss to try and change my position on a matter. I did not give him what he wanted because I didn't feel it was in the best interest of the company, but his response was more personal, along the lines of, "Well, I will remember this Les when I become CEO."

I guess in the moment he forgot that he wasn't yet CEO and that I might actually have some influence in who eventually would get the job because 30 minutes after I told him, "If you continue to behave this way, I can assure you the CEO job will not go to you," he was in my office, tail between his legs trying to make amends. Although I must admit it felt good at the time to put this jerk in his place, the fact is that it can become too easy to use this power to simply get your way; and the perception in the company could become "if you want to get ahead, do whatever it takes to get on the good side of the CHRO." As much as we, as HR professionals, would not like to see that scenario play-out with any manager or supervisor, we also have to make sure that in reality, and in perception, it does not happen with us as CHRO.

The CHRO has the serious responsibility of advocating strong internal talent for promotions within the company and they need to exercise a certain level of diplomacy in dealing with leaders who naturally want to protect their talent pool. The CHRO has enterprise-wide accountability for talent and therefore should not have to negotiate with a senior manager in order to move critical employees between business units. If necessary, this is another example of when the CHRO might need to use their "perceived" power.

Another scenario when it is appropriate to use the CHRO's power is when it supports a message from the CEO to the senior team. Occasionally, the CEO will want to emphasize that message with one individual and to make the point, will ask the CHRO to meet with them and reinforce the message. By involving the CHRO, the CEO makes his point without the need for personal intervention, and the receiver of the message is led to understand that it is important, and that there may be HR implications if they don't get it.

Based on my long-standing experience in HR, I believe the vast majority of HR professionals, and CHROs specifically, are realistic and will use integrity in deciding if and when to project the power of the CHRO office. Using the power of the CHRO office wisely will engender increased trust with the senior team and, in my opinion, is the hallmark of a successful CHRO.

> "In working with the CEO, you need to build a high level of trust including asking tough questions. Sometimes, it got me into trouble. It can be a funny little dance."
>
> Yvonne Jackson, Board Director & former CHRO

3

Leadership Characteristics
of a Good CHRO

> "The CHRO should be the trusted confidante to the CEO,
> Board Chair and HRC Chair. They can head off potential
> conflicts and pave the way to consensus."
>
> Edward Lumley, Vice Chair, BMO Nesbitt Burns

CHAPTER 25: INTRODUCTION – WHAT MAKES A SUCCESSFUL CHRO

> "The CHRO often has a difficult balancing act to perform. If he simply
> serves as the tool of the CEO he will be doing a disservice to the
> organization. He must be prepared to "speak truth to power" in the
> form of his direct superior, the CEO, and his indirect superior, the
> chair on behalf of the HRC. He must be prepared to speak on behalf
> of the other people in the organization, senior and junior. Above
> all, he must be guided by a keen sense of the interests of all the
> stakeholders in the organization and particularly those employees
> who are giving their time and energy to the company."
>
> Gordon Ritchie, Board Director

The question about what makes a good CHRO is much like asking, "How long is a piece of string?" There is no direct answer and it could vary significantly depending on the industry, the company, and even the other personalities that make up the rest of the C-suite. So let me start by acknowledging that there is no right or wrong answer to this question and if you are a CHRO or aspiring to be one and you do not fit the description that follows, I am not saying you aren't, or would not be, a good CHRO. Having said that, one of the benefits of being around for as long as I have is that I have a significant body of experience to draw from, so I also feel confident in saying that if you do fit this description – or aspire to – my money is on you for being a good CHRO.

To start with, unlike the "personnel" managers of days gone by, the successful CHRO should possess the same range of solid technical and leadership competencies required of the other C-suite executives. There will be a lot more on this subject in other areas of the book.

More specific to the CHRO role, the number one competency required to be successful is the ability to accurately assess talent. In my view there is nothing more fundamental or more important to the role. To me it's like the requirement to have an engineering degree to become a good engineer. So think in terms of having a Masters or even PhD in "talent assessment" as being a requirement for a good CHRO.

The ability to accurately assess talent can be learned through academic study as well as behavioural training and observation; I could write a whole book about this one subject, but I won't, because the book has already been written. Bill Conaty, in his book, Talent Masters, asserts that the best CHROs are the ones who are the really great assessors of talent – and I couldn't agree more.

The second most important competency required to be a successful CHRO is, in my opinion, the ability to "courageously challenge the status quo", although I think you could argue that this is more of a skill or a mindset or a business practice or even a personal attribute. Whatever you decide to call it, it's important.

Traditionally, the Personnel or HR role has included the reduction of conflict – the creation of a smooth-running organization – the development of people who are comfortable fitting in and going with the flow. But that isn't what's needed in a high-performing executive team and, in this regard, the CHRO can be a unique catalyst and a uniquely valuable member of the C-suite.

As with most teams, the members of an executive team tend to gravitate towards protecting each other and maintaining the status quo. Conflict is uncomfortable, change is unwelcome, and going with the flow and working to fit in becomes the norm. This can be especially true if the CEO is a dominating figure on that team. But in the C-suite, a conflict-free and "smooth-running" team becomes a source of inertia and is less capable of making the difficult "game-changing" decisions; and in extreme cases the C-suite can become little more than an extension of the CEO's personality and business philosophy.

With no vested interest in any one area of the company over another, and with responsibilities to the whole organization, the CHRO is in a unique position to challenge other C-suite executives, including and especially the CEO, and to push for change when it's needed but not likely to happen because of the inertia of the status quo.

Starting at the top, the CHRO needs to have ongoing open and honest dialogue with the CEO on critical issues regarding, for example, the company's strategy, senior talent and rewards – being undiplomatic, challenging and confronting when necessary. The same opportunity/need exists with all other members of the C-suite and lower-level executives.

This will not be an easy or comfortable thing to do (hence the inclusion of the word "courageously" in describing this trait), but if you approach the task with honesty and sincerity and with the organization's best interests clearly the basis for everything you advocate, your efforts will be appreciated by everyone with the same basic interests. In my case, I knew I was on the right track in adopting this approach because of the positive feedback I received from many of my peers; most of them were mature enough and confident enough about themselves to accept my "brutal honesty" and "direct feedback" for what it was – a sincere attempt to make the company better.

Now that's not to say that over the years some of my colleagues didn't mistake my advocacy for a better company as an attack on them, and several individuals have even attempted to undermine my credibility with the CEO. Letting the facts speak for themselves is usually enough to block any such attempt.

There are a host of other characteristics that make a successful CHRO. They include the following:

1. Business acumen
2. Independence
3. Technical knowledge
4. Negotiator/influencer
5. Power broker
6. Communicator
7. Strategic & Results delivery
8. People leader
9. Team player
10. Street smarts

Throughout the remainder of the book, I will describe these competencies in more detail.

> "CHRO's are the chief talent scouts in companies."
>
> Hunter Harrison, CEO, Canadian Pacific

CHAPTER 26: "CHRO MOJO" – PERSONAL LEADERSHIP APPROACH

> "The CHRO is the 'Brave' person to give feedback to the CEO and team as well as being the independent voice to the Board's HRC."
>
> Sarah Raiss, Board Director (former CHRO)

As business leaders we all face the same dilemma, how do we fight fires and meet day-to-day business demands and still keep an eye on what's coming over the horizon that might impact the company's future success?

Working closely with top corporate leaders over the years I have compiled a list of the most effective strategies that are proven to work for successful leadership; what's more is that these strategies can be adopted by any leader in any company of any size in any industry.

1. *Manage your culture.* The behaviour of every employee, from the front line to the executive suite, is what makes a company successful – or not. At every level in the company employee behaviour is directly influenced by their manager, and so by definition the managers set standards, communicate, measure, and create consequences for the people they are responsible for. The managers' collective behaviour is what determines the workplace culture and performance; an organization's spirit, feel, and attitude stems mostly from its leaders' behaviours.

2. *Measure what you want your employees to achieve.* Do your employees know exactly what your company's goals are? Most employees will do their jobs well and with pride when they know what their company values are. Too

many priorities will cause confusion, as will conflicting priorities, or those that are not clear. Clearly define no more than five or six company objectives and then measure employees' performance against each one.

3.   *Be open to challenge and disagreement. But then make the decision with confidence.* Listen to everyone's ideas and let others have their say – this stimulates debate, fosters ideas, leads to better decisions, and generates greater buy-in for the eventual decision.

4.   *Focus on what you directly observe.* If an employee is not performing, consider only what you actually see and hear in the workplace. It's tempting to ponder the employee's personal life or listen to hearsay, but more often than not this is misleading and may actually impede remediation.

5.   *"Would you do it if your life depended on it?"* Ask this about an underperforming employee to determine if the problem is poor motivation. If the answer is "yes" then, indeed, poor motivation is the problem. Motivation is driven by consequences. What happens as a result of certain behaviour? To encourage an employee to improve, manage the consequences to support their performance.

6.   *Turn good performers into great performers.* The difference between a good team and a great team is the leader's ability to motivate – to apply positive consequences. The best ways are through engagement, commitment, and the resulting pride of team members.

7.   *Deal quickly with poor performers.* Some supervisors try to avoid conflict and won't deal with poor performers, leading to an eventual crisis and a lose-lose situation for everyone. By acting early, you can guide most people back on track through coaching and feedback.

8.   *Get face-to-face.* Talking one-on-one, face-to-face, is the most effective way to influence others. Receiving positive feedback from a supervisor in person is highly motivating; the best way for leaders to thank employees for their hard work is not money – it's a simple handshake and a smile. The same is true when confronting poor performance. When you are face-to-face, the employee can't avoid the issue.

9.   *Balance your consequences.* Consequences for behaviour can be positive, constructive, or missing altogether. Each consequence has its own effect on people. To build a positive relationship over time, provide a balance of consequences; a good rule of thumb is to provide four positive consequences (like praise) for each constructive consequence. Providing no consequences can make your leadership ineffective, and the employee will rely on other

consequences in the environment to encourage or discourage behaviour; this takes you out of the equation and leaves performance to chance.

10. *Manage the learning curve to lead better.* Intelligent, aggressive employees can seem farther along than they really are, and so, despite appearances, a green employee can still make fatal mistakes – literally. Be objective and realistic in assessing competency and don't place people in roles they're not ready for; help them stretch, but make sure they don't break. An employee assessed as skilled and confident can be coached for even higher performance.

These strategies will give you and your leaders the tools to keep an eye on the future of the business while fighting the day-to-day fires and creating an environment where employees feel engaged and valued . . . a win-win for all!

CHAPTER 27: LOOKING FOR WAYS TO SAY YES

> "The CHRO must have a wide bandwidth – from efficient operator and executor to deliver low cost, service based HR support functions, to organizational strategist, to leadership psychologist and to hard-nosed compensation negotiator."
>
> Michael McCain, CEO, Maple Leaf Foods

"I like to do things differently." Although I like to think that I, in fact, do things differently, here I am actually quoting one of the most successful plant managers in the Cadbury Schweppes system. This was in the mid-1980s, early on in my career, and his success meant he was someone I wanted to learn more about. Some might have considered him to be "old school" because he had been trained in the "command and control" leadership style. When I asked him what he meant by "differently", I expected some variation on the "it's my way or the highway" management style.

So imagine my surprise when he actually said this: "When I am out on the shop floor, I look for opportunities to say yes to my employees." This was something you never heard back then and it has stuck with me ever since, and right from the first time I heard it, I believed he was on to something big, and yes, at the time, really different.

As I enter the next chapter in my life, I still try to use this simple mantra of, "looking for ways to say yes", because it still helps me approach every leadership situation with a positive attitude about the outcome of that situation and about the ongoing relationships with the people I work with. To be sure, this approach can be difficult to apply in tough situations – plant closures, for example – and, of course, there will always be some who will try to take advantage of you, knowing you, but, even then, it is important to look for ways to say yes to help people.

I hope all of you will try this simple approach. It definitely makes work more fun and challenging.

CHAPTER 28:   PERSONAL TOUCH – CASSIE UPDATES

"That's why the best HR people are a kind of hybrid: one part pastor, who hears all sins and complaints without recrimination, and one part parent, who loves and nurtures, but gives it to you fast and straight when you're off track."

J. Welch and S. Welch, *Winning*
(New York: Harper Business, 2005), p. 102

For a number of good reasons, the CHRO is often considered the most approach-able person on the senior leadership team – after all, "people" is topmost in the job description – but, even with that consideration, it is important for the CHRO to do whatever they can to increase their visibility and the perception of availability and contact. Maximum engagement is the objective because that is what creates a positive communications environment.

For a lot of people this is not so easy to do – me, for example. As an introvert, I need to work harder to make myself seem more approachable because by nature I am relatively quiet and shy. It wouldn't be so bad if employees assumed my introverted behaviour was just me being me, but a lot of times, especially with people in senior executive positions, there is an automatic assumption that this kind of behaviour is aloofness and even arrogance, not a good thing when we are trying to create positive contact and engagement.

One of the tools I created to increase my personal visibility and contact with employees is a weekly email which I send to my staff and senior executives; I call it, "Les On Line" – or LOL. In showing my personal side, I offer details of my life outside of work; I talk about my wonderful wife and our marriage; I talk about the things I do for recreation – our cottage and tennis, for example – but perhaps the one topic that seems to resonate the most with a lot of employees is our dog, Cassie. Make a list of the best ice-breakers out there and dogs are either number 1 or 1A, right after children – and, in my case, Cassie is both.

So in many of my weekly emails I include a "Cassie Update". I talk about her personality, things she does, sometimes health issues, etc., and I know they resonate with employees because of the response I get. It's not unusual for a staff member to stop me or even drop by my office to comment about my Cassie story, and to share their own stories with me. It makes for a great personal connection, a lot of laughs, and a wonderful enrichment of a working relationship.

One day a colleague dropped by to tell me that his dog had unexpectedly died and I could tell he was really suffering for it. As all pet owners would, I felt a lot of sadness for him and comforted him as best I could; I knew that he had something of a healing process ahead – a process that included sharing his grief with me and with others. As sad as the occasion was, however, I was actually grateful that my colleague felt comfortable enough to share his grief with me because it meant we had a personal connection – a connection that I have no doubt started with me sharing stories about Cassie.

As much as enriching personal relationships this way is its own reward, there are, of course, the improved business outcomes we started this section with, and so my conclusion is that CHROs earn great personal consideration and professional credibility if they are prepared to share some of their personal life with the staff and peers they want to connect with – think of it as putting the "human" in HR professional.

Here is an example of a Cassie Update also featuring my wife Marijane (MJ):

Cassie up-date

Due to Cassie's medical problems (ear infection and eye cyst), Cassie has been under medical attention for the last 4 weeks. I am confident her Vet has already bought his new Florida condo using the money we have paid him. The good news is Cassie is back in fine form.

As a treat for her (and MJ), I took her to the cottage alone for the weekend. She frolicked in the snow and was dive bombing her head into the snow banks. At night, she would join me on the couch in my "Man Cave" where I have a large TV/ loud stereo. We watched music videos together (she slept through Lady Antebellum) but wanted her belly rubbed with her four legs in the air when I had Bon Jovi roaring through the speakers. The other reason for going to the cottage with Cassie (without MJ) is I get to listen and watch great music videos at supersonic volume levels. When MJ is at the cottage, I am forbidden from turning up the volume (much to my displeasure). With Cassie and I alone, I crank it up to ear splitting levels (which might explain my partial deafness). We returned home on Sunday with big smiles on our faces. Although MJ probably knows already, I am turning Cassie into a Rock & Roller!!

CHAPTER 29:   READY, FIRE, AIM – ACTION JACKSON

> "It is not your "God given right as CHRO"- you must earn respect from the CEO and other executives."
>
> John Lynch, SVP, Corporate Human Resources, General Electric

Not too long after we got married, Marijane told me she thought I was "very expedient". For a fraction of a second I was hopeful she meant it as a compliment, but the tone of her voice and the look on her face made it clear this was not a good thing. Being married to a psychologist has its special rewards and special challenges and this was looking like an example of the latter; fortunately for me, however, she wasn't talking about that "unfortunate" expediency a new husband might immediately think of. Phew!

There's something about the way I look and the way I talk that makes people think that I am naturally a thoughtful planner; someone who weighs the pros and the cons, considers all the factors, thinks about alternatives and only then makes a decision and acts on it. Well, as much as I most often fooled everyone else, it didn't take Marijane too long to figure out that I wasn't by nature anything close to a thoughtful planner. My natural process, if you can call it that, is all about getting things done as fast as possible.

When I joined Maple Leaf Foods as CHRO, I'm fairly certain that my outward persona initially convinced my C-suite colleagues that, in me, they were getting a thoughtful planner and they were probably looking forward to the calming, rational influence on the leadership of the company. But it wasn't too long before Michael McCain starting describing my methods as "ready, fire, aim" and calling me "Action Jackson".

The truth is that I am fully aware of my natural tendencies and over the years I have made a point of learning how to be the thoughtful planner I appear to be – and yes, these are processes that can be learned and applied in lieu of what comes naturally. There are forces, however, that can work against this; for example, the confidence that comes from long and wide experience and a record of success. The notion that if you are a good shot then you don't need to aim before firing is just a rationalization of resorting to unplanned expediency.

That's what happened with me at MLF and that's how I came be known as Action Jackson with a tendency to fire before aiming and a budding reputation for implementing solutions before consulting with others. Michael liked the "action" part, but wasn't crazy about some of the other "ready, fire, aim" baggage that came with it – the key was to find the balance – and so that's what I did at MLF.

Because of my natural tendencies, I make a point of applying the thoughtful planner processes I've learned over the years to ensure that a certain amount of "aiming" takes place before I fire my action pistol (and yes, in light of the first paragraph I realize in hindsight that this is probably an inappropriate metaphor) – so the balance is this: on the larger issues, I take a thoughtful, planned approach, and when the issues are small, or whenever the company is dragging its feet on a good idea, I sometimes choose a more expedient route to the conclusion – and they call me Action Jackson.

CHAPTER 30: TAKING THE "HIGH ROAD"

> "Total objectivity is required from the CHRO in CEO succession planning – free of internal bias and historical baggage."
>
> David Emerson, Board Director

By definition, when it comes to critical people issues in the organization, the buck stops with the CHRO even though there will likely be many others involved in arriving at a solution – many who feel they have the most vested interest in the outcome and therefore a primary role in the solution. In managing the development of the solution it is therefore important for the CHRO to take the "high road" with all parties involved; clearly more easily said than done, especially for someone like me who simply wants to get the job done expeditiously.

For me, taking the high road means always appearing to be above the fray (assuming there is conflict involved) by always being objective and neutral and avoiding petty or confrontational arguments. The CHRO should be a fair and impartial arbiter – the one with a non-personal, corporate view – and should favour the best long-term solution – ignoring the perhaps easier and more immediately-satisfying short-term solution.

If the CHRO is directly involved in the issue, and is the senior person in the debate, it is their responsibility to ensure the other party gets a fair and impartial hearing – avoiding even the appearance that their seniority and the power of their office is being used to push a personal agenda.

Another way to think of this approach is to consider how an "elder statesman" might view the situation, perhaps adopting the role of a wise grandfather sagely guiding his grandchild in the process of maturing into a good person. This kind of approach is characterized by the wisdom and the emotional control to see the issue in an objective manner; helping the other party to see the wisdom of the solution and in fact embrace it themselves versus the CHRO arbitrarily imposing it.

I am the first to admit that it is almost always easier to simply tell someone, "Stop arguing and just do it." And while that might solve the issue in the short-term, the long-term implications are usually negative and persistent.

Taking the "high road" requires great patience and persistence to be sure, but the long-term results of using this approach are better for the individuals involved and the company, and it has the added benefit of enhancing the company's image in the mind of anyone observing how the issue is being dealt with.

CHAPTER 31:   ACTING THE PART – ALWAYS ON THE STAGE OF LEADERSHIP

> "The CHRO needs to be the role model for leadership behaviours such as ethics."
>
> Sarah Raiss, Board Director

Just like the CEO and other members of the C-suite, the CHRO must be aware that they are always on the corporate stage and must act accordingly – no pun intended.

Even in non-corporate situations, the CEO, the CHRO and other senior executives will be monitored for their disposition. Do they look happy or satisfied? Or do they look sad, disappointed, angry, or dismayed? Whatever their appearance, others will try to derive some meaning from it about the state of the business.

And there's not too many ways to win here, either. If you look unhappy (even if it's just the fish taco you had for lunch), your face could be telling the troops there's a problem with the company, or with them. On the other hand, if you're constantly smiling no matter what, you could be seen as phony or insincere.

The best approach for the CHRO is to always be on the stage of leadership – and, yes, I know this is somewhat vague. Your objective should be for your outward appearance and your stature to convey genuine confidence and a genuine concern for the people of the company. Your actions should always convey a sincere desire to help people, to provide support and inspiration, to demonstrate thoughtfulness. At all times you should convey a sense of optimism for the company's future even in hard times. People want to see a confident leader who is passionate and caring.

Of course, it's easiest to appear to be all these things if, in fact, you are – and that's something else to consider: if you don't naturally feel this way about your company or your situation, then perhaps that's a signal to re-evaluate your course or tackle issues that may be outstanding. On the other hand, perhaps you genuinely feel confident and positive, but your outside simply doesn't accurately reflect what's on the inside. That too, you can work on.

As an introvert, being on the stage at all times, I have to be constantly aware of my surroundings. Earlier in my career, when I was a new HR Manager at Cadbury Schweppes, I had a tendency to keep my head down (literally and figuratively) and concentrate on getting my job done as quickly as possible. They didn't call me Action Jackson yet, but that's who I was back then. Anyway, one of the long-time employees I worked with was a lady who never smiled at me. This went on for a while until one day as we passed in the hall she muttered, "For a guy in HR, you're not very friendly." In one split second I got it! I had never smiled at her either. From that point on, it was clear to me that I had to take personal responsibility for the reactions I prompted in others. The impression the rest of the world had of me was mine to make and I wasn't ever going to leave it to chance (or my nature) again.

There is no escaping the reality that senior executives today, including and perhaps especially the CHRO, are constantly in the spotlight and under the microscope, and no matter what the real situation is, employees, the Board of Directors, the shareholders and even colleagues in the C-suite need to see a confident, caring, relaxed and competent leader. To whatever degree your public persona reflects these attributes – or others that may be important to you – the outcome should not be left to chance or the whims of others but instead should be yours to measure and manage.

"The CEO must have their game face –
people look up to you at all times."

Claude Mongeau, CEO, Canadian National

CHAPTER 32: THE MAYANS DISCOVERED IT ... NOW THIS OUTRAGEOUS CONCEPT CAN CHANGE YOUR LIFE FOREVER!*

"The CHRO needs to help me influence our people to work
their a**es off and have fun doing it."

Hunter Harrison, CEO, Canadian Pacific

One of the hallmarks of effective communications is the headline. You see them in newspapers, magazines, online, on billboards, on buses and subway cars. Basically anywhere people might be available to read them. The tabloid newspapers are particularly good at headlines – just try and not read them as you're standing in the check-out line at the drug store. How else would we ever know about the dog-boy – even if it's just that he exists?

If you watch TV at all you probably know about CNN Headline News, where the entire product is basically one headline after the other, either coming out of the mouth of the announcer, or presented in the graphics panel, or scrolling along the bottom of the screen. More often than not the headline is outrageous, or contentious, or enigmatic, and usually only remotely related to the subject. And sometimes the headline is repeated dozens of times before they actually get around to telling the story. In truth, its only job is to capture your attention, and the fact that you are now wondering, "where the hell is the rest of the story" means it did its job.

The reason headlines exist in the first place is because all day long we are bombarded with messages – visual and verbal – and over time we have all developed immunity to communications that don't first capture our attention and our imagination. Present most people with the proverbial wall of text and chances are they won't even start reading it. If they wanted to read a book they would crack open the Kobo and download one; and we've all heard of death by PowerPoint – same cause, same effect.

The ability to frame the essence of a communication in a super-precise and engaging manner is what effective headlines are all about – simple one-liners that capture the eye and the imagination and literally force the reader to continue. To say that the ability to effectively present your message this way is a useful communication skill is to seriously understate its importance. For any HR professional, but especially the CHRO, effective communication is everything. You could be the most talented, most concerned, most respected HR pro on the planet and it wouldn't mean much if you didn't know how to capture your audience's attention in order to communicate to them.

If you are a successful HR professional, chances are you are already a decent communicator – it goes with the territory – but there are always improvements that can be made and crafting the headline is probably one of them. It is a skill that typically does not come naturally, but can be honed with practice and with a process to follow.

As the CHRO, you need to capture the people issues in simple headlines in order to capture the hearts and minds of your staff and peers. The key to being able to develop effective CNN headlines is to distil the issue down to a simple action or concept that says enough to capture the audience's attention, but not so much that they feel there is no need to read the rest of the content. Spending an inordinate amount of effort finessing the headline is probably a good use of your time if it means the difference between effectively delivering your message or not.

---

* The Mayans had many effective means of getting people's attention and delivering their message – throwing virgins down the stairs of a pyramid was one, and cutting off people's heads and putting them on display was another; if these methods are not available to you, crafting beguiling headlines might just be the alternative you're looking for.

CHAPTER 33: LES' TOP CHRO LEADERS

> "Over time, you will find that there are some people in your organization who have a special gift for picking out stars and phonies. Rely on them. Bill Conaty, my HR head, was a master at this. Whether it was with a handshake, a smile, or a way of talking about their family, job candidates were transparent to him."
>
> J. Welch and S. Welch, *Winning*
> (New York: Harper Business, 2005), p. 94

This chapter of the book is dedicated to what I think are the best attributes of a good CHRO, and so I thought it would also be a good idea to offer you a list of those CHROs who I think best personify these characteristics. Although I have not worked for any of them, I am familiar with their work and their successes and their philosophies on being a CHRO, and I was fortunate enough to have spoken to all of them for the purpose of including their expertise throughout the book.

Based on my prior knowledge of high-profile CHROs, and further research for the book, there were many excellent CHROs to choose from – which made this a fun exercise – but in the end I chose eight individuals who have reached the pinnacle of the HR profession and continue to add value to it with their continuing work. To those great HR professionals who I did not include on the list please accept my apology for any unintentional slight.

My goal here is to summarize and share some of their experiences, wisdom and suggestions. I interviewed each one individually, but used a standard set of questions. I hope you enjoy reading this information as much as I did in collecting it. In my opinion, the CHROs profiled here are real HR heroes and have been instrumental in transforming our profession around the world.

Bill Conaty is the former CHRO at General Electric and currently an Advisory Partner at Clayton, Dubilier & Rice. Bill is a legend in the HR world having worked with the other GE legend, Jack Welch, and together they transformed not only the HR function at GE, but the entire company which boasts some incredible credentials – being one of the world's biggest, most admired, best led, and most innovative companies. Bill's book, Talent Masters, is the new bible for HR leaders who want to step up their executive assessment skills. He has been a great inspiration to me during my career and so I was thrilled when he agreed to offer his thoughts and encouragement for this book.

Peter Goerke is the Group Human Resources director at Prudential PLC. A real business maverick who has taken the HR function to the highest business level, Peter's focus on value- added contribution has made him the "go to person" on the management team. His insights are great thought provokers for senior HR leaders in all industries.

Katy Barclay is SVP, Human Resources at The Kroger Company, the world's fourth largest retailer, and before that she was the top HR executive at General Motors Corporation where her leadership contributions helped guide GM through some of its most turbulent years. Katy's input into this book offers excellent lessons for any HR pro.

Ferio Pugliese is the President of WestJet Encore and before that was EVP, People, Culture and Inflight Services. Ferio has been instrumental in creating a truly unique culture at WestJet and his move from the CHRO role to the presidency of a regional airline serves as an excellent case study in executive succession planning. **John Lynch** is the SVP, Corporate Human Resources, at General Electric and Bill Conaty's successor. Bringing his own financially-focused transformation to the HR function at GE, John has created his own legacy. John's sense of humour and candour has brought new views to the HR scene and his sharp wit is evident in his contributions to this book.

Yvonne Jackson is the former CHRO at Pfizer, one of the world's leading pharmaceutical companies, and is now providing HR and management consulting services through her own firm, Beecher Jackson. Yvonne has made the transition from successful CHRO to Board Director and her insights into the two roles are captured in this book. Yvonne remains a role model for aspiring HR professionals.

Sarah Raiss is the former EVP, Corporate Services, at TransCanada Corporation and like Yvonne Jackson, Sarah is also a successful Board Director. She is an engineer and MBA graduate, and is regularly named to Women Executive Network's annual list of Canada's top 100 powerful women and, in fact, was named to the inaugural list in 2003.

Dave Ulrich is technically not a CHRO and never was, but when great HR leaders seek advice and counsel, Dave is at the top of the list. He is a professor at the Ross School of Business, University of Michigan, and a partner at The RBL Group, and his HR thought leadership is represented in over 200 articles and 23 books. I got to know Dave when he was on a 3-year sabbatical in Montreal, and I am very pleased he agreed to contribute to this book.

To capture this esteemed group's collective HR intelligence, I asked them all a series of the same questions and you will find their answers scattered throughout the book in various formats.

For example, the first question that I asked them is: "What are the most important skills future CHROs will require?" In no particular order, here are their initial thoughts on the subject:

Bill Conaty

- Trust and confidence in the senior leadership team.
- Good fit with the CEO and CFO.
- Excellent assessor of talent.
- Huge capacity for complex problem solving.
- Decisive with courage to make tough calls.

Yvonne Jackson

- Business acumen.
- Compensation DNA knowledge.

Ferio Pugliese

- Strategic thought leadership.
- Influencing CEO and peers without authority.

Peter Goerke

- Strategic focus on scarce resources.

John Lynch

- Business bottom line mastery vs. social work.
- Use of technology.
- Strong communications skills.

Katy Barclay

- Great change management skills.
- Linking People initiatives to Business Strategy.

Sarah Raiss

- Solid business acumen and industry knowledge.
- Don't need to be an HR expert, but you need a strong HR team.

Dave Ulrich

- Strategic thinker with change management expertise and passion.
- High integrity person who is an HR innovator.
- A technologically savvy person who can build HR capabilities.

Looking at the excellent input from these great HR leaders throughout the book, their combined experience and thought leadership will serve as a strong HR foundation for any executive. For more details about their biographical information go to Appendix 9.

"Peter Goerke believes in the role of HR as a source of competitive advantage. He sees it as a core element of business success, especially in the context of a global financial institution, so he makes sure that leaders throughout the business talk about business and HR as one and not as independent entities. Since HR is part of the business, the HR organization needs to match the business structure and have clear priorities."

D. Ulrich, J. Younger, W. Brookbank, and M. Ulrich, *HR from the Outside In: Six Competencies for the Future of Human Resources* (New York: McGraw-Hill, 2012), p. 228

CHAPTER 34:   DO IT FASTER THAN YOU THINK

"CHRO needs to be an advocate for the CEO – his disciple
– an extension of the CEO."

Hunter Harrison, CEO, Canadian Pacific

If there's one thing I've learned about corporate life over my 35-year career in HR, it's this: change is difficult – and determining how fast to institute change, is just as difficult. When change is required, by nature I'm inclined to start and finish the process as quickly as possible – and, in fact, I do believe that there are circumstances where that approach is the best. But there are other types of change that could benefit from taking things a bit slower and being more methodical. Over the years, I've developed a formula to help me decide at what pace to institute various changes at a number of different companies; and here it is.

If the change will be perceived as a very negative one by the affected employees and managers, it's often natural to want to delay the announcement, but that's not the right way to do it, in my opinion. In instances where the change will be perceived as negative – closing a factory, for example – the affected employees will appreciate being told as soon as the decision is made.

They will, of course, be angry and distressed, so it may not be immediately apparent that they appreciate the timing of the announcement. In addition to the timing, it's important to consider the message too; no matter how quickly you want to get started, it is critical that the communication be complete and as transparent as possible, and totally free of condescension, especially with respect to the "why" of what's happening. By the end of the process, the affected employees will appreciate being treated as adults with a right to know, and they will appreciate having the maximum notice period to make the plans necessary to adjust to their new reality.

Unfortunately, I had the need to put this change-process into practice at Maple Leaf Foods, and in a series of plant closings we gave the affected employees 2 years advance notice of our plans. Intuitively, you might think that morale would drop and that productivity would suffer and there might even be other manifestations of anger, but the reality is that all these plants closed with the highest productivity levels we ever recorded there.

What we learned is that the employees returned the respect we paid them in the way we communicated the need for change and our plans to make it happen. Indeed, they appreciated having the maximum time to adapt. The process we followed – created and rolled out in an environment of respect – allowed employees to maintain their personal pride and their pride in their work and it showed in high productivity. For me, the ultimate expression of appreciation we received were the many statements from employees like this one: "If I owned MLF, I would have closed the plants too – and I would have done it the same way you did."

Sometimes the change itself needs to be completed as quickly as possible – and not just the announcement of change as in the example of plant closings. This is the case, for example, when a company like MLF acquires another company and there is a need to integrate the newly-acquired employees into an existing set of systems and processes. In this scenario, for the case of existing employees and the new ones, the integration needs to take place as quickly as possible and should not be dragged out for any length of time. It's important for the acquiring company to get back to normal as quickly as possible, and it's important for the "new" employees to adapt to their new normal as quickly as possible. In this case, a deadline works to motivate everyone concerned and adds the right kind of pressure that most employees will respond to with the appropriate sense of urgency.

Other types of change can benefit from a more methodical approach, often with other changes required in advance; for example, the introduction of new equipment or new processes. Although these kinds of changes can be stressful to the affected employees, with the right kind of planning for communications, training, roll-out and positive consequences, the normal uncertainty and resistance to change can be minimized.

Despite our natural tendencies to avoid change or be wary of it, what I have learned is that with the right kind of communication and the right kind of approach, most employees will adapt readily to even the most extreme change. The key is to treat employees like adults and to be thorough and honest in answering the questions "why" and "what's in it for me?" And, if you do that, the majority of employees will adapt readily and willingly to the change and be a positive force in making the transition successful.

"Future CEOs need to take more calculated risks, act bold on beliefs (long-term decisions) and stand up to short-term activists."

Mike Wilson, CEO, Agrium

CHAPTER 35: WHEN SHOULD YOU FIRE THE CHRO?

> "It is very apparent when you have a weak CHRO – they are more focussed on managing administration activities versus organizational talent and cost management."
>
> Geoff Beattie, Board Director

If you have already read the chapter on job fatigue (Chapter 23) you also need to know the corollary: any CHRO in the same position for 7 years should be fired. No, I am not advocating mass firings without cause and yes, I am being just a little facetious, but the fact is that job fatigue is not just a risk for the incumbent, it is also a risk for the company.

Companies do better with new blood regularly infused into the senior executive roles, including the CHRO. In the past, it was easier for the CHRO to avoid the implications of poor performance because the metrics were simply not there to support letting them go. Prior to 2000, the only performance issue that ever threatened my employment was whether or not I was able to successfully negotiate a collective agreement and avoid a labour strike. I did, and so I wasn't fired. It was that simple.

Today, however, the CHRO has many accountabilities that are easily and regularly measured, and their feet are constantly to the fire on critical issues; issues raised by the results for the HR team. To my mind, there are some easily determined reasons for terminating a CHRO for a performance shortfall.

The CHRO should be asked to leave when ...

1. The People Strategy has failed to deliver the expected results or there is no People Strategy.
2. The chemistry between the CHRO and the CEO/HRC Chair has become toxic.
3. The trust with the C-suite peers has been violated.
4. The HR team does not respect the CHRO.
5. The Labour Unions refuse to deal with the CHRO.
6. The CHRO is bored and simply going through the motions, a.k.a. the 7-year itch.

There are many repercussions to the firing of a CHRO that are unique to that role. Many employees will believe, naively, that they are losing their advocate in the C-suite and so that loss can sometimes send shock waves throughout the company, not unlike the firing of a CEO. It's advisable then to carefully manage the change process; the messaging must be clear, consistent, and specific about what changes are likely to follow. And, of course, it will be less traumatic if the CHRO can be convinced to jump before they are pushed.

CHAPTER 36: "LES ON LINE" – TALKING WITH THE TROOPS

> "The CHRO keeps me grounded and provides a heads up on culture, organization and people issues."
>
> Mike Wilson, CEO, Agrium

As a way to have regular communications with my HR team and the senior leadership team at Maple Leaf Foods, I wrote a weekly e-mail called LOL ("Les on Line"). I have included a number of these emails in Appendix 13, but here is a sample of one of these LOLs:

Les on Line - 2012 Week #2: January 9th – 14th

This week's focus continued to be execution of the People Strategy. We met with several senior executives to discuss their role in championing the People Strategy initiatives in 2012, and beyond. I feel we are really getting the traction needed to execute with excellence – which is what it's all about!

People Strategy Tracking and Management

People Strategy Champions

This week we met with the following executives who expressed keen interest and engagement in supporting various People Strategy initiatives:

- Michael McCain – who will champion CEO Workouts, Q4 People Leadership Model, the Academy, Talent / Succession Management processes, Engagement Surveys and the PAD.

- Stephen Graham – who will champion our Employment Branding initiative, as well as the alignment of our recruitment processes with the Brand, once it's clearly defined.

- Scott McCain – who will champion the MLCF Transformation project and our HR Team Development initiatives.

- Mike Vels – who will champion the review of our TakeStock program, and join Richard Lan in championing our Compensation initiative.

Business Unit Discussion

Ian MacPherson and I met with the Fresh Bakery Management Committee and presented the People Strategy. There was a lot of interest and a number of great questions from the team. I really enjoyed the hour we had with them, and appreciate their support of our Strategy.

Strategy Focus Area #1: Strengthen Our Culture of Accountability CEO Leadership Workout Sessions

Bob Hedley and I are fine-tuning the agenda with Michael – and I spent time with Michael discussing the February session. There is a great deal of interest in the program. Participants are very keen to attend and spend two days with our CEO.

My Own Accountability

One of the projects that I have been personally managing got derailed this week from a financial perspective. There is a cost overrun which is unacceptable – and I own this mistake. I am not happy with my performance and am going do whatever I can to mitigate the financial impact.

Strategy Focus Area #2: Develop People Leaders Who Deliver Sustainable Results ABC Training Rollout

Unfortunately, our main contact at CLG (the firm that is training our in-house ABC trainers) has left CLG to join another firm, BCG. Bob Hedley and I spent several hours with her, and her replacement at CLG, to discuss the planned transition.

In addition, I spoke with Ian MacPherson and Walter Miller about the launch of ABC training at Trillium beginning in late February. I am excited about this Trillium opportunity.

Best Practice Benchmarking

Bob and I spoke with the head of leadership development at RBC – we plan to meet with the RBC team in the future to exchange best practices.

Strategy Focus Area #3: Implement Robust Talent and Succession Management Executive Coaching

I spent several hours with one of the executives that I currently coach. Our focus was on debriefing the 360 Survey along with the assessment report with Dr. Minden.

Following this session, I had dinner with the executive and his spouse. We have agreed on the next steps which will include a meeting with his boss to finalize the personal development plan.

In addition, I ramped up work on the new coaching assignment I started last week with one of our senior executives.

I met with a second potential external coach to determine if they could be a future coach for one of our executives. I also met with an executive who is seeking an external coach for support in developing a technical area. There are a variety of external coaches in the marketplace: most are leadership coaches but there are some specialized technical coaches who help executives in areas such as Marketing, Sales, Strategy Development, Finance and Supply Chain.

PAD Process

This will be my first time directly involved with the PAD process at MLF. Cheryl is coaching me on the mechanics of the system and I am preparing my feedback for my direct reports. The career and performance discussions and resulting development plans are a very important element of our Talent Management process. And recording the information from these discussions / plans in MMP helps simplify the follow up processes greatly – since we can pull and summarize information quickly, for purposes such as Functional Talent Reviews, avoiding or minimizing additional effort.

In addition, I am working with the BU Presidents to provide them with feedback on the HR Leaders. To confirm – the process for BU Function Leader PADs is as follows:

- The Business Unit Head is responsible for managing the PAD process in partnership (shared accountability) with the Function Head.

- The Business Unit Head conducts the PAD. (Best practice would be to conduct the PAD jointly with the applicable Function Head.)

- The Function Head will provide input into all components of the PAD but with particular focus on Development and Career Plans.

- Support and consultation will be provided by Business Unit HR as needed.

Internal Fill Rates

As I've mentioned before, the internal fill rate for leadership positions is one way to measure the strength of our talent pool and the effectiveness of our talent management/succession processes. Although we have a way to go to get from good to great on this across MLF – Malcolm Jones shared some interesting statistics that show we are having great success in some areas of the company:

- Of 10 MLCF Operations HR Manager vacancies in the last 12 months, 9 were filled with internal candidates – an internal fill rate of 90%.

- Of 11 MLCF Plant/Production Manager vacancies in the last 12 months, 8 were filled with internal candidates – an internal fill rate of 72%.

Strategy Focus Area #4: Fully Engage Our People with a New Focus on Hourly Employees Supervisory Foundations Program Update

This past week Lynn Langrock provided the Fresh Bakery Atlantic Operations Leadership team an overview of the new Supervisory Foundations program. They were very interested in learning more about the content of the specific modules, and potentially piloting a couple of modules as they wait for the full roll out.

In addition Lynn and Mike Habel met with the Six Sigma resources who will be peer coaching the pilot of the Continuous Improvement module in Courtland Avenue plant.

Support from a Board Member

Ken Campbell and I spent two hours with MLF Board Member Jim Olson to discuss our new People Strategy. Since Jim's background is in Operations/Supply Chain, we discussed specifically the new Supervisory Development program, hourly employee engagement and the ABC concept. He was very interested in our plans, and is very interested in supporting us.

Strategy Focus Area #5: Maximize HR Value and Service Hourly Employee Pension / Benefits Employee Service Centre

Leslee Wills, who is our Project Leader on this initiative, met with Cheryl last week for an initial discussion on the overall objective and scope. There are a number of complex factors involved with getting to solution on this one – including the fact that although all our hourly employees will be on SAP shortly, information about their pension/benefits won't be. This information sits in a number of systems – including with third party vendors. Dave Aird, Nancy Forrester and Patti Hamilton have provided some initial input – and the next step will be for Leslee to arrange for a full blown scoping session with all the key players.

SAP UFAR Hourly Update (UK, Fresh Prepared, Agri-Farms, Rothsay). The UFAR project team is working on the specific configuration requirements and setup in SAP for the Business Units involved in this phase. In parallel the BU subject matter experts are busy collecting and cleansing the employee data required for conversion.

This coming week the first of three scheduled conversion tests will take place. Each test allows us to learn a little bit more about where we can improve the quality and completeness of the employee records. Then when we finally convert to the production environment before going live we can be confident the data is accurate.

Pension Plan Administration Committee Meeting (PPAC). We had a PPAC meeting this past week to discuss and approve some administrative plan amendments. There are a number of new players on the Committee – and Patti Hamilton did a great job of providing historic context for the discussions.

HR Moves

I am very pleased to share that Sheona Koroman has accepted the position of Human Resource/Health and Safety Manager at the Consumer Foods facility in Guelph. Sheona started with MLF in May 2011 as Human Resource Advisor in the MLCF Hamilton plant – and has very strong past experience in unionized environments. I enjoyed getting to know Sheona at the HR Manager Coaching session in the summer, and have every confidence that she will excel in her new role.

HR Case Studies and HR Manager Challenges Last Week's Case Study: Implementing the People Strategy at Your Plant

Situation: As the HR Manager in a manufacturing plant at MLF, you are excited to begin the execution of the new MLF People Strategy at your facility. The plant management team has asked you to describe what the People Strategy is all about and the implications for the plant. The Plant Manager has heard a little bit from his VP but is not really clear on what he should be doing to support this People Strategy. He is a bit concerned that this is more work for him and his team but does not know what the benefits to his plant will be and when.

Question for you: As the HR Manager, how do you plan to communicate the People Strategy and the specific initiatives that will be relevant to your plant in 2012?

My response: First have a deep dive discussion with the Plant Manager regarding the overall People Strategy (full three year picture) and the specific 2012 initiatives that will affect the plant (i.e. Supervisory Development, Compensation Structure, RFE changes, potentially ABCs etc.). Then, along with the Plant Manager, present the People Strategy to the rest of the plant leadership team. Solicit their feedback and questions. Indicate the timing of the various initiatives and ask for some champions to help you execute the Strategy. Most Managers are interested in the components of the People Strategy – let them know how they can help ensure its success. Good luck and have fun with the execution plan.

Special thanks to...

Leanne for her hospitality at the Olivieri plant ... Bob Hedley for his work on the CEO sessions ... Norm for a great update meeting ... Our senior leaders for their support of the People Strategy ... Michael for his strong belief in the People Strategy ... and special thanks to the ThinkFood group for their kind gesture.

I look forward to your LOL feedback. Thanks for your continued support.

Les

4

Developing Successors
for the CHRO Role

> "I'm surprised that companies don't understand the importance of an experienced CHRO. Too many companies look to the CHRO role as a good development role for young high potential executives. Unfortunately, they don't know how to manage and support the executive team – blatantly missed skill."
>
> Mike Wilson, CEO, Agrium

CHAPTER 37: HEAD OF NORTH AMERICAN HR AT 30 – TOO YOUNG?

> "As Lafley (CEO, Procter & Gamble) reminds us, talent development is not only about developing and growing leaders but also testing the best with complex and challenging stretch assignments that will reveal which ones have CEO potential. "Running a tough country like Korea, Indonesia, Russia or Nigeria, or a tough business that we're not winning in, or a newly acquire business we don't understand, or a chronically underperforming business – all of these are stretch assignments." He says, "But we have to be careful not to blow up very good people with very strong potential by moving them a 'bridge too far', and subjecting them to more challenge, complexity and difficulty than they were ready for.""
>
> B. Conaty and R. Charan,
> *The Talent Masters, Why Smart Leaders Put People Before Numbers*
> (New York: Crown Publishing Group, 2010), p. 124

In 1982, not long after Marijane and I got married, I joined Cadbury Schweppes as the Training Manager in the Canadian corporate office. I was really looking forward to the challenge and I could see myself growing with this company.

The new-job high didn't last long, however, because just 3 months later my boss Don Phaneuf told me that the company had decided to eliminate the Canadian corporate HR function. What he didn't tell me though is that my job was targeted as the first to go; what he told me instead was that my job was safe for the moment and that he was going to be the first to leave. This was a rare and amazing gesture, and I think of Don fondly for it.

So I eventually left the corporate office and found myself in one of the business units and was quickly immersed in a field HR job in a factory setting. As luck would have it, the new head of the global beverage business, Jim Schadt, wanted to create a Beverage North American Business Unit based in Stamford CT and so when the Canadian Business Unit leader, Norm Fawcett, was promoted to the U.S. operation, he put in a good word for me, and the next thing I knew, I was hired to become the HR Director, North American Beverages. Marijane and I relocated to Stamford and lived there for 3 years.

In hindsight, I can tell you that I was not qualified for the role: my background was more of a training and recruitment specialist (versus an HR generalist), I had never managed a large HR team before, and last, but not least, I had no U.S. experience.

What's more, this job nearly cost me my marriage. Marijane had to quit her job in Canada and could not work in the U.S., and I travelled a lot, which meant leaving her home alone. And when I was at home, I wasn't very good company as the stress of doing a job I wasn't qualified for was making me miserable.

We managed to stick it out in Stamford for 3 years until Jim Schadt offered me the position of Canadian Corporate HR Director with responsibility for both beverage and chocolate business units. For the sake of my sanity and my marriage, we jumped at the chance to get back to Canada. It almost didn't matter that the job was a good one.

When I reflect back on my first big North American HR role, I am surprised that I lasted as long as I did. I'm sure there was a bullet with my name on it pushed into the chamber on a regular basis, but not only did Jim give me one of the best learning experiences of my entire career, he also made sure that the mistakes I made while learning did not cost me my job.

When I left Cadbury Schweppes to take on the VP, HR role at Heinz Canada, I wrote to Jim to tell him how much his support meant to me both personally and professionally. I told him how much I admired his leadership and that he was a powerful force in making me a better HR executive.

So, the question is do you take a 30-year-old and put them in a position that forces them to stretch beyond their qualifications? As you might imagine, I believe the answer is a qualified yes – as long as the intention is to let them learn and grow into the position without the usual ramifications of the mistakes that will be made. I certainly benefitted from my experience and I think the company did too. The irony, of course, is that one of the reasons I was able to carry on and persevere is that I had no idea just how unqualified I was. Confidence certainly trumped competence in this situation.

CHAPTER 38:   DISAPPOINTMENT AT HEINZ

> "In fact, almost half (44 percent) of the CHROs did not achieve the position from an internal succession process. They were directly hired from outside the firm (31 percent), hired from outside with the promise of being promoted into the CHRO role (3 percent), or promoted from outside HR within the firm (10 percent). In fact, only 36 percent reported that they had been promoted from within the HR function."
>
> P. Wright, J. Boudreau, D. Pace, E. Sartain, P. McKinnon, and R. Antoine, *The Chief HR Officer: Defining the New Role of HR Leaders* (San Francisco: Wiley, John & Sons, Inc. 2011), p. 293

In 1990, when I joined the Canadian subsidiary of HJ Heinz Company as VP Human Resources, I was 35 years old and this was the second time I was the top HR person in Canada working for an international food company.

It was something of a crazy time because the Canadian food industry was still learning how to compete under the new Free Trade Agreement with the United States as the competitive landscape was turned upside down and the "rules" were completely different. Ironically one of the principal architects of the Free Trade Agreement was Gordon Ritchie who I would get to work for at Maple Leaf Foods some 20 years later.

In response to these new competitive pressures, Heinz created a new organizational structure for North America and I became the new North American VP, Human Resources for Heinz North America. I relocated to Pittsburgh to work for Bill Springer, President, Heinz North America.Our primary responsibility was to consolidate North American manufacturing facilities and develop a new Sales structure.

Another Heinz big business unit that had operations in the U.S. and around the world was the Heinz Pet Foods and Star-Kist company headquartered in Cincinnati and run by Bill Johnson who was supported by his long-time HR person, Bill Goode. Bill Goode and I were peers and we worked together on many projects. We both had a dotted line reporting into the CHRO at the time, George Greer, and George reported to Tony O'Reilly, the Chairman and CEO.

When Tony O'Reilly retired, Bill Johnson was promoted to Chairman and CEO of the HJ Heinz Company and he promptly brought Bill Goode on board to fill the CHRO position left vacant when George Greer retired shortly before. Although I was disappointed I didn't get the job, it made sense that Bill Goode was rewarded for his loyalty to Bill Johnson, plus he was 10 years older than me, with that much more experience.

So there I was, 43 years old, 5 years into my current job and the CHRO position I aspired to had been filled by my former peer; I was definitely at a crossroads in my career. Stay or go? It was time to make a decision; maybe it was time to take a gamble.

So I did the math. I figured that, at 55 some odd years old, Bill Goode the new CHRO would stay in that position for 3 to 5 years and would probably retire at 58 to 60 years old – paving the way, hopefully, for me to step in; and so that's the bet I made.

Fast forward 3 years and it was clear that not only had my relationship with Bill soured a bit over disagreements about how to integrate his old business unit, Pet Food and Tuna, it became increasingly clear that he had no intention of retiring any time soon.

So my bet went bust and 3 years after deciding to stay, I concluded that it was time now to leave. So, in 2001, I was hired by CN Rail to become their new CHRO.

But the disappointment I reference in this chapter title isn't the fact that I did not become CHRO of Heinz; rather it's that during my time at Heinz I had failed to help develop my successor. Heinz eventually hired from outside to fill the job I left, but if I had been smarter, less selfish and more patient, I could have developed my successor internally. There were at least two people who could have been considered for my role. Unfortunately, I was so pre-occupied with my own career aspirations that I failed to do the right thing and help prepare and groom one of them for my own succession.

The failure to identify and prepare my successor at Heinz was something I regretted at the time and something that I learned from. When I joined CN Rail I made a commitment to myself that I would never repeat that mistake again.

CHAPTER 39: CHRO SUCCESSION AT CN

> "The CHRO has a special role in reflecting on the CEO's agenda."
>
> Claude Mongeau, CEO, Canadian National

The year was 2001... the month was June... I was 46 years old and I couldn't imagine being in a better place in life. On the career track I had just landed the HR role of a lifetime – CHRO at CN Rail, led by the iconic Paul Tellier. His resume reads like a piece of fiction: law degree from Oxford, recipient of the Order of Canada, former Clerk of the Privy Council, the driving force behind the privatization of CN, and the architect of CN's purchase of Illinois Central, which turned an unprofitable east-west carrier into a North American rail giant. Yeah – I was the new CHRO of that CN and I was going to work for that Paul Tellier.

Once the euphoria of winning the position wore off, however, the reality of just how daunting the job was began to sink in. In addition to the HR team I also had direct responsibility for the Information Services function – a large 650-employee shop – and the HR department I inherited was fragmented and in conflict, and the corporate HR functions, like compensation and benefits, were not aligned with the HR field operations. Today the younger execs would call it a "hot mess."

Nonetheless, I was determined to create the efficient team that I wanted to run the show, and so the remedies were harsh – I had to terminate about 60% of the senior HR leadership team to clear the decks for the team I wanted to put in place. Another priority of mine was succession planning, including identifying and developing my own replacement. I wasn't going to make the same mistake I made at Heinz.

Throughout this clearing-out process, however, some individuals actually began to stand out from their colleagues and show themselves to be exceptional, and that's how I came to know Peter Edwards and Kim Madigan. When I started at CN, Peter was head of HR for the Eastern business unit and Kim was running the U.S. HR team in Chicago, but it wasn't long before I had them both in Montreal filling two critical roles.

I brought Peter into the corporate team to become VP, HR & Leadership Development, and Kim was brought in to become VP, Labour Relations. More than just filling these critical positions, I also pegged both as potential successors for my job, and having them with me in Montreal gave me the opportunity to work with them on their development – and what a process it was.

For Kim, we developed an internal Railroad MBA program; a 9 to 12-month cross-functional learning program that taught the railroad business from the inside out, focused on how we made money. She became a certified conductor and actually ran trains, and she became well versed on track and engine repair functions, to name just a few of her accomplishments. By the time she returned to the corporate office, she had become a true railroader. As an added bonus, her travels also gave her the opportunity to get to know all the key leaders in the company, and perhaps more importantly, they got to know her.

In Peter's case, we gave him a variety of new assignments including running all of the field HR departments in the company. In addition, he successfully led many cultural programs (Q4 leadership and ABC processes mentioned in the Switchpoints book) that truly transformed the company and he was the architect of several groundbreaking initiatives including the two company books written by Hunter Harrison, the CEO after Paul Tellier.

Fast forward 7 years and by early 2008 I had hit the wall professionally on several fronts – I was bored and, even worse, my relationship with the new HRC Chair was strained. After talking it over with Marijane and my boss, Hunter Harrison, I decided to take early retirement at the ripe old age of 53. What made the decision to take early retirement easier for me was the knowledge that there were at least two great internal candidates capable of taking on the CHRO job.

When I left CN in May 2008, Kim and Peter began a formal 12-month competition for the job, at which point Kim Madigan was promoted into the top HR job.

Peter Edwards decided to become a free agent and subsequently took on the top HR job at CP Rail, CN's major Canadian competitor; and interestingly enough, as I write this book, Hunter Harrison and other executives have left CN and joined Peter at CP.

The most rewarding part of this CHRO succession story is I got to train two people who eventually became CHROs. It does not get better than that!!

> "The Diversity movement has pushed functional experts on to Boards. Boards are pursuing HR experts for people specific companies such as retail."
>
> Sarah Raiss, Board Director

CHAPTER 40: CHRO SUCCESSION AT MLF

> "The CHRO and the CEO have complete trust, transparency and respect for each other's skills."
>
> Michael McCain, CEO, Maple Leaf Foods

If you started reading this book at the beginning, you know that I was kidnapped and forced against my will to join Maple Leaf Foods as the CHRO. Well not exactly, but being pulled out of a comfortable retirement and thrust back into the working world on some days did feel like an abduction.

By the time they hired me, MLF had been looking for a CHRO for quite a while – had found one, only to lose them due to a family matter – and so the search for another outsider continued until I entered the picture and became entangled in McCain's web. At the same time, interestingly, the one question on many people's minds, including mine and Michael McCain's, was how long would I stay?

The significance of MLF's search for a CHRO is that it was focused solely on outside candidates. Obviously, there were no viable candidates at MLF at that time, so the question was, where would my successor come from when it was time for me to leave?

There were two good reasons for me to take responsibility for finding my own successor; first, because it was a point of personal pride for me stemming from my time at Heinz, and second, because McCain wasn't going to let me "re-retire" until we had someone to take my place. And so, beginning literally on my first day at MLF, I began the process of identifying possible candidates to take my job.

The first step was to look at the entire HR team from an organizational perspective. As a result of that process, we eliminated about 40% of the HR leadership team due to poor spans and excessive layers. During that process we were also able take the measure of the HR leaders who had survived the cuts, and what came next was very surprising.

What surprised me almost immediately was not only was there a qualified candidate at MLF, there were several who I believed could be ready to take my job within 3 years; and so the CHRO succession plans at MLF began to coalesce.

Within a short time after I started we identified four potential candidates to take my job. The fourth candidate however did not have the necessary labour relations experience, which was considered a must-have prerequisite, and so we were left with three well-qualified HR leaders, each potentially capable of stepping into my role when I left.

The question now was, how would we go about preparing the successor and eventually choosing who it was to be? And so with the blessing of the CEO, I created a multi-year development plan that would serve as a training and development tool, as well as a means to assess each candidate's progress.

The plan included the following elements:

1. Management assessments from an external psychologist.
2. A Q4 360 survey.
3. Access to an external executive leadership coach.
4. Participation in the HRC meetings.
5. Attending a formal HRC training workshop.
6. Rotating "Chairs" for the HR Council.
7. Job rotations and task forces.
8. Quarterly People Strategy presentations to the CEO.
9. C-suite interviews and functional talent reviews.
10. Communications and media training.
11. Leading the annual MLF HR Conferences.
12. External presentations at industry HR functions.

As I am writing this book, I am 2 ½ years into my stay at MLF, and 6 months away from retiring – again – at the age of 59, and, importantly, a seamless and internal CHRO succession is about to take place.

If I may say so myself we had an excellent succession process in place at MLF. The result is three candidates from distinctly different backgrounds, each capable of stepping into the role of CHRO. One candidate has an LR background, another is an HR generalist, and the third has a leadership talent orientation.

The C-suite players are actively engaged in the dialogue about who is best suited to replace me and it speaks well of the process, and the candidates, that no one is the favourite – they are all very strong. Do I have a favourite? Actually, yes I do, but I'm not telling who it is because choosing my successor is not my decision to make. My job was to provide the CEO and the Board with several viable successors, and in this case I feel really good about the results and I feel I have definitely lived up to my part of the bargain.

In late July 2013, Michael announced Ian Henry as my successor and during my last few months I will be acting as an advisor to Michael and Ian both, and on January 1, 2014 I begin to write the next chapter in the story of my career in HR. In early 2014, Ian is attending the University of Michigan's 2-week Advanced HR program with Dave Ulrich. I know he will enjoy it immensely.

Here is the announcement of Ian Henry's appointment made by Michael McCain:

July 30, 2013

ANNOUNCEMENT

I am very pleased to announce that Ian Henry, Vice President Labor Relations and Home Office HR will be assuming the role of Chief Human Resources Officer (CHRO) effective August 1st, reporting to me. Ian will also be joining the Executive Council and the Transformation Steering Team. Les Dakens is retiring from his position as CHRO, but remaining with Maple Leaf Foods until year end to support the transition of his responsibilities and complete work on other projects.

As CHRO, Ian will assume overall responsibility for the direction and execution of Human Resources programs and strategies across the company. He will continue to maintain overall responsibility for Labor relations, working closely with our Business Unit HR leaders, and for Home Office HR, with strong support from Emma Horgan. Paul Clipson, Cheryl Fullerton, Lynn Langrock and Emma Horgan will report to Ian, as will the senior Business Unit HR leaders on a dotted line basis.

Ian's career in Human Resources began in 1986 at Westfair Foods, where he worked for seven years before joining Pacific Press, where he advanced to the role of VP Human Resources. He was Director of Labor Relations for CBC Canada from

2000-2002 before joining Maple Leaf Foods as VP Labor Relations. In 2011 Ian assumed additional responsibility as VP Human Resources for Home Office salaried staff and Facilities Management.

Les joined Maple Leaf as CHRO two and a half years ago with the understanding that he would return to retirement once the HR structure was enhanced and the People Strategy well established. I want to thank Les for his deep dedication to Maple Leaf and his many contributions during his tenure, most especially building a very strong and high impact HR organization.

Ian has made an extraordinary impact on Maple Leaf through his experience, judgment and ability to drive business results through strong HR strategies and execution. I know that he will bring all these skills to his new role, and further embed the importance of people development and engagement in all our business initiatives. Please join me in congratulating Ian on this well-deserved appointment.

Leadership Edge, Michael McCain

As a further testament to this CHRO development process, another of my succession candidates, Norm Sabapathy, has gone on to a CHRO role at Cadillac Fairview, a leading commercial real estate company with an international portfolio valued at more than $21 billion and growing. He is reporting to John Sullivan, President & CEO, who is a strong supporter of the CHRO role, and who also gladly endorsed this book.

CHAPTER 41:   GENERALIST VS. SPECIALIST TRACK

> "Thus, it seems that working outside HR does not hurt one's career and potential to become a CHRO, but neither is it a requirement for effectively executing the role."
>
> P. Wright, J. Boudreau, D. Pace, E. Sartain, P. McKinnon, and R. Antoine, *The Chief HR Officer: Defining the New Role of HR Leaders* (San Francisco: Wiley, John & Sons, Inc., 2011), p. 295

The key question about what path should an HR professional take to reach the CHRO position is a tough one to answer. In my case, I had a short specialist career path before I was picked to take on the large generalist role. In most cases today, the CHROs are people who have been around the track and have worked in multiple specialist roles before taking on the bigger business unit HR leader roles.

If it was possible to take an HR professional and expose them to the ideal set of jobs and experience, here's what I would choose for them in the first 10 years of their career in HR:

1. Start the HR graduate in a production supervisor and sales representative role for 2 years. They will learn the business.

2. Move them into a recruiting specialist role for 2 years. They will learn to assess talent and learn about the different roles in the company.

3. Move them into a field HR manager role for 2 years. They will learn all aspects of the generalist role.

4. Move them into one speciality function like compensation or labour relations or leadership development for 2 years. They will learn about another technical area.

5. Move them into a multiple site HR role. They will learn to manage staff and bigger customers.

I believe that to best develop the rising HR star, they need to be selectively exposed to a variety of specialist and generalist assignments. Today, graduates with a Masters of Human Resources degree come pre-wired with the technical aspects of the HR profession, so what they need is the opportunity to put their great education to good use, starting with a ground-level exposure to the business. Working in a sales or production supervisory role will give them unique insights they might not otherwise get and a wonderful business foundation.

There's nothing like real-world experience to round out a good education – and the best employees will relish the opportunity.

CHAPTER 42:   MUST CHRO SUCCESSORS COME FROM HR?

> "Seasoned CHRO's know the difference
> between right versus dead right."
>
> Mike Wilson, CEO, Agrium

Whenever I have been asked this question my instinct is to answer "Why are you even asking this question?" After all, would you put a non-Finance person in the CFO role, or appoint someone with no legal background as the Chief Legal Officer?

And then there's the flip side question: "Why would you even consider a non-HR person for the CHRO job?" The answer is, because some senior executives don't see the CHRO as a technical position in the same way that CFO, COO, or CLO positions are, and the selection of CHRO is sometimes driven by factors other than background or relevant experience.

For example, sometimes a company will fill the CHRO position with a high-potential executive for developmental purposes, or sometimes a company will have a valued executive in transition and need a place to park them. These kinds of scenarios, however, represent risk to the company.

The risk is inherent to the perception that the non-HR executive is only a short-term caretaker and is therefore likely to be more disruptive than helpful in the execution of the People Strategy. The other scenario that happens when you put a non-HR person in the CHRO role is they over stay their welcome due to a lack of movement for them, or they tend to treat the assignment as a way to leverage their relationship with the CEO at the expense of other C-suite executives.

The CHRO role has developed into a very skilled position in the C-suite; it is a role that requires an individual to be HR technically savvy along with being the best people expert on the team. It is no longer a great rotation for wannabes.

Would you put a non-financial person into the CFO role? No way. It's the same answer for the CHRO role. Today there is no substantive difference.

Must CHRO successors come from HR? The answer is unequivocally, "Yes!"

CHAPTER 43: TURNING THE TABLES – COACHING THE CHRO

> "Never forget why you are at the table.
> The first HR person who cares about human beings."
>
> Bill Conaty, former SVP,
> Corporate Human Resources, General Electric

In many respects I wasn't ready for retirement when I retired from CN at age 53. I was still vitally interested in my work; I was healthy and energetic and I felt that, as much as I had achieved virtually all of the professional goals I had set for myself, there were still opportunities out there to add value and make a difference. I didn't want a job, but I didn't want to leave my profession either. The route I chose to go was to offer coaching services dedicated to helping HR people grow in their profession – and so Pineridge Consulting was born.

In all the time I worked as a CHRO, I never had the opportunity to work with an outside coach that actually knew the CHRO role intimately. I would have liked to, especially earlier in my career, for example when I joined CN.

Today, more than ever, talented HR professionals with an ambition to grow and move up can benefit greatly from coaching by someone who has been successful as a CHRO. And it seems that many of my fellow HR professionals agree, as my coaching practice was very busy and I worked with some great HR people. Having said that, the work of a CHRO coach is not easy. There's the constant temptation to simply tell the client what to do (I've been there, done that, got the T-shirt), rather than create a learning path and guiding them along it.

Nevertheless, the CHRO can call on the coach to bounce ideas off and role play certain situations. The most fun I had as a CHRO coach was to help my clients develop their People Strategy and to develop and recruit their HR teams.

When I retire from MLF at the end of 2013, I will return to Pineridge Consulting; I still feel I have a lot to offer and I hope to continue to give back to my wonderful profession. Nothing would please me more than for this book to become an inspiration or a resource for the next generation of HR leaders.

5

Working with the HR Team

> "The first statement the Board chair made to the CEO was,
> "Everything starts with people – I want to know about your HR
> department."
>
> Claude Lamoureux, Board Director

CHAPTER 44: TAKING A SEAT AT THE TABLE

"There is an expression that I have heard multiple times throughout my career – 'HR deserves a seat at the table.' Every time I hear that I cringe. In fact, when interviewing HR candidates, if they use that phrase I automatically will not hire them. Why? Because no one gives you anything. You have to take it. That's like saying 'HR deserves to be respected.' Of course they do. But the only way HR will be respected is if they earn it. And, as I've always said, 'They earn it in the trenches every single day.' HR gets the respect it deserves. No different than how individuals earn the respect of their peers."

The quote above is the opinion of James Grossett, the Senior Vice President, Human Resources for Agrium, one of the world's largest agricultural chemical companies. Jim has overall responsibility for Agrium's global HR function, covering over 10,000 employees, and he has over 25 years of Human Resource management experience.

This short chapter is intended to be an introduction to Jim and to refer you to Appendix 2 where you will read his much more detailed and complete discourse on the subject of HR earning respect in the C-suite.

> "The big difference between the staff role of
> CHRO versus an operating role is the day to day
> sense of urgency that comes with operations."
>
> Ferio Pugliese, EVP & President, WestJet Encore (former CHRO)

CHAPTER 45: CORPORATE VS. BUSINESS UNIT HR
DEPARTMENTS

"Creating an efficient, linked-up global HR function in a multi-national company is a major undertaking. The ingredients for success are a simple set of global HR priorities linked to the company's business strategy and plans; a global infrastructure of HR standards, tools, systems, definitions, and competences; a single HR organizational model with similar roles in businesses and functions; and a cadre of well-trained, motivated HR professionals. At Shell we have been working toward that goal for a decade. And we are starting to achieve it."

P. Wright, J. Boudreau, D. Pace, E. Sartain, P. McKinnon, and R. Antoine, *The Chief HR Officer: Defining the New Role of HR Leaders* (San Francisco: Wiley, John & Sons, Inc., 2011), pp. 235-236

In most medium to large organizations there is usually a corporate HR group and field or business unit HR groups. Depending on how centralized or decentralized the organization is, the relationship between the corporate and field HR groups will vary.

In companies that are centralized, the corporate HR group will be more dominant in the HR policy setting/design process and very active in the execution of HR products and services. With companies that are decentralized, the corporate HR function will be relatively small and only focused on a few critical HR policies; the business units will independently carry out these policies and will likely develop a broad range of their own HR products and services.

I have worked in both centralized and decentralized HR structures and I have come to the conclusion that to make either of them work, some members of the corporate HR group must have worked in a business unit role in order to be successful in their corporate roles.

The biggest contributing factor to the failure of a corporate HR team, small or large, is that the corporate HR people have no clue what actually happens out in an operating business unit. And this factor tends to be self-perpetuating, as corporate HR people are more likely to hire in their own image – preferring candidates with just corporate HR experience. The result is a corporate team that has never gotten their hands dirty in a true operating business. This not only hurts their credibility, but also impedes their practical day-to-day interaction with the business unit teams.

For example: A manufacturing company hires a CHRO without any plant HR or labour relations experience who is then expected to lead the HR function which is predominately comprised of plant employees – they are like a duck out of water.

Then there is the problem of corporate HR teams not knowing what they don't know, and assuming that corporate experience trumps business unit experience. When I was the business unit leader at Heinz I had to deal with that kind of situation.

I remember one particular instance when a corporate HR team member was visiting all the business units presenting the next new "innovation" in field operations HR. Part way through the presentation, when it became apparent to me that he didn't know what he was talking about and the idea would never fly, I asked him pointedly if he had ever actually tried his idea in a manufacturing environment.

His answer epitomizes for me the arrogance that is sometimes resident in corporate HR team members who have no field experience: "No, but I am confident it will work." I couldn't resist, I had to respond. So I told him right there in front of his boss, "You're part of the corporate team – you're supposed to be smarter than me and more experienced than me and you're supposed to know this business from the ground up, but based on your presentation today, it's clear that you are none of those things. I can tell you right now that this idea can't work here." And then I went on to explain why it wouldn't work. I guess he wasn't the only cocky one in the room.

Later, I felt bad for embarrassing him. To his credit, when he calmed down he was willing to work with us to make it right. The result was that never again did corporate HR float an idea that wasn't first pre-screened by the field teams. Of course, the whole episode could have been avoided in the first place, if someone on the corporate team had spent some time in the field.

The bottom line concept is pretty simple: the more complete corporate HR team member is the one who also has field experience – they will better support a centralized HR function, and they will have a greater sensitivity and a broader experience base to bring to bear on any HR issue that involves the field.

For a lot of reasons I prefer a more centralized HR function. I really like the concept of "One HR Team." I don't mean the business units should not have their own HR teams, but rather that the HR processes are the same throughout the company; the corporate team and all the field teams – together One HR Team unified in their vision, values, processes and their outcomes.

My rationale is the employee or manager that moves from one business unit to another should still see the same HR practices. In other words, the employee should not feel that they are going from one company to a new company from an HR perspective.

Some companies do this very well; for example, Procter & Gamble employees can move to a different country and still experience the same fundamental HR processes wherever they go. Other companies do not insist on this common HR approach and in my opinion they suffer for it.

At each company that I joined as CHRO, I made sure that my corporate team had field HR experience as a minimum requirement. Even some of our compensation and benefits experts were sent out to work in a field role so they could earn their" field cred." This may not be possible for every specialist role on the corporate team, but it is doable in some form or another for most team members.

At both CN and MLF, several of my direct reports on the corporate team had burned their bridges with the field HR groups, creating toxic relationships in some cases. The bottom line is they had to leave the company because they could not live up to the requirements of "One HR Team". Similarly, some of the business unit HR leaders had a preference for running their shops independently, without working with me or the corporate team, and so those that couldn't or wouldn't change, also had to leave.

There are good arguments for both approaches – centralized and decentralized – but having worked in both environments I firmly believe that in the long run a centralized HR function will add greater value.

CHAPTER 46: HR STRUCTURE AND REPORTING RELATIONSHIPS

"Make your company flatter. Managers should have ten direct reports at the minimum and 30 to 50 percent more if they are experienced."

J. Welch and S. Welch, *Winning*
(New York: Harper Business, 2005), p. 116

In a centralized HR function, business unit HR leaders can report directly to the CHRO, or they might have a dotted line relationship with both CHRO and the business unit president. As CHRO, it doesn't bother me to have members of my HR team reporting to me on a dotted line basis. In fact, there's a lot of good to it.

For example, when I was a business unit HR leader I liked having the dual reporting relationship. If the CHRO was a good leader I could learn a lot from them, and they might be a positive factor in my career development; and I liked having a closer relationship with the business unit president because it brought me closer to their business and their team. And again, another high-level contact never hurt.

Having been a business unit HR leader, I know how important it is that they be accountable to their customers and have a certain amount of latitude in living up to that responsibility. The only condition that I believe is 100% immutable is that they must work within the "One HR Team" organization and its processes. If they don't, or won't, in my opinion, they must be shut down. If you have rogue HR leaders in the field you will eventually pay a price.

In one extreme example, the European business unit of a well-known Canadian company fell into difficulty when the president and HR leader did their own thing and the corporate people allowed them to run rogue. I'll jump straight to the outcome: the business unit president is in jail for bribery, the HR person was fired for not blowing the whistle, and the CHRO paid a very high price for turning a blind eye to the situation.

Regarding the structure of the HR function, I believe a very flat organization is the best. I personally didn't want to go through too many levels in the HR function to get things executed. The other reason for having very few levels in HR is you do not want to be too removed from the employees and supervisors who comprise most of the company's workforce. For me, a large company with an HR function should have four levels as shown below:

1.   CHRO
2.   Business Unit /Corporate HR leaders
3.   HR Managers
4.   HR Specialists

More levels than the above-mentioned structure will lead to bureaucracy and a lack of urgency within the HR function. I believe in a great span of control for managers and so with 8 to 10 people reporting directly to the CHRO, including dotted line business unit HR leaders, there will never be too many levels.

CHAPTER 47:   WHO OWNS THE MONEY – LINE VS. STAFF

"Tell us about your business."

"That's how we like to start when we sit down to work with senior HR professionals. We find that it is a good litmus test for assessing the current state of HR in a company."

"Most replies start with discussing the latest challenges or innovations in HR practices (hiring people, training leaders, building incentive compensation, doing HR analytics, and so forth), relating to business leaders (having a voice at the table, getting buy-in), or managing the increased personal demands of the HR job (allocating time, staying upbeat in the face of over-whelming demands). That is, HR professionals almost invariably define business as "HR business" and are inclined to talk about their current initiatives in leadership training, recruiting, engagement, or rewards – the areas where they focus their attention on the job."

"These efforts are important, but they are not the business. They are in support of the business."

D. Ulrich, J. Younger, W. Brookbank, M. Ulrich, *HR from the Outside In: Six Competencies for the Future of Human Resources* (New York: McGraw-Hill, 2012)

Within most companies there is an ongoing debate about who should "own" people-related expenses. Everyone agrees that managers' budgets should carry staff salaries, travel, equipment and benefit costs, but when it comes to the costs of things like recruiting, training, bonus, relocation, coaching, tuition aid, employee engagement & recognition initiatives, there seems to be two distinct opinions on how to account for them.

On the one hand, some CFOs will argue that line managers should take on all people-related costs, while other CFOs prefer to have them put into central budgets so they can be better managed and to see the full magnitude of the costs to the company.

As the CHRO, the most important issue to me, regardless of what accounting method is used, is to make sure there is sufficient money to spend on all the important people priorities like training and development, and so if the budget isn't centralized for these kinds of core programs it will be much more difficult to leverage resources across the company. Another benefit of centralized budgets is their usefulness in diagnosing company-wide issues like high turnover, represented in a central budget by high recruiting costs which are more readily visible to senior management.

On the other hand, the downside of centralized budgets for people-related activities is, in fact, their visibility to senior management; they can become easy targets for CFOs looking for budgets to cut when times are tough.

My answer to the question is to centralize certain people-related costs into a corporate budget and then allocate the charges proportionally to the business units. This approach will ensure that critical people initiatives are funded in a consistent manner. This does not suggest the business units do not have training budgets, but they should be more technical training in nature. The key is to balance the need for leverage with the need for specific business unit needs.

CHAPTER 48:   THE HR COUNCIL APPROACH

> "Roles and structures will continue to evolve. In our data,
> an increasing proportion of respondents over time are
> individual contributors. HR departments, like other functions,
> are delayering. There are fewer true managerial roles and more
> working managers with smaller staffs; efforts are being made
> to consolidate where possible. The impact of outsourcing and
> technology has been a reduction in staffing; we have seen some
> leading global organizations essentially cutting their full-time HR
> staffing levels in half. Project contractors and consultants play an
> increasingly large role in the full-time equivalent staffing of HR. And
> we are seeing a new mix of functions. Over the period of the HRCS,
> we have seen an evolution of emphasis toward compensation,
> strategy, organization development, recruiting, and training, and
> away from benefits, Labor relations, and HR generalist work."
>
> D. Ulrich, J. Younger, W. Brookbank, and M. Ulrich, *HR from the
> Outside In: Six Competencies for the Future of Human Resources*
> (New York: McGraw-Hill, 2012), at pp. 259-260

Whether you have a centralized HR structure or a decentralized approach, the CHRO needs to create a formal means to bring HR leadership together to support the One HR Team concept, and to participate in the development of the common strategies and processes they will all be asked to support and to put into action within their own areas of responsibility.

My solution to this need was to create the HR Council, consisting of senior staff from the corporate and business unit HR groups, and typically including the corporate heads of leadership development and total rewards, along with the business unit HR leaders.

This HR Council should meet in person or by phone each month to discuss the business results, People Strategy initiatives, new or revised HR policies, HR staff development and movement, and identify HR issues that need resolution. The format would be half day sessions with pre-arranged agenda and pre-meeting hand-outs.

The CHRO chairs the meeting, but there may be times that one of the HR Council members will chair the meeting to get some development. In my last year at MLF, I asked my three potential successors to rotate the chairperson role so they could get real live experience in leading their peers.

There will be times when a Council member does not agree with the final HR Council decision, but consistent with the One HR Team approach, they will be expected to fully support the decisions of the Council. In fact, I expect the Council to be the strongest advocates of the One HR Team approach.

Even though the objective is to create a stronger HR team, the CHRO can derail that goal by dominating the Council meetings – easy enough to do especially if the CHRO feels the need to be right all the time. The trick to avoiding this is to provide your direction but to allow debate on your thinking. If you dissuade Council members from offering their input, you will disempower the team and become out of touch.

The flip side of that coin is the CHRO that lets the team drive the bus which could erode their authority as the ultimate leader of HR. So walk the fine line between both extremes and you will find that great minds working together as one team produce great results. That is your mission with the HR council.

CHAPTER 49:   HR COACHING WITH LES

> "Every CHRO is the coach for a number of people – certainly your boss, the CEO, but also members of the senior leadership team. And do not forget the responsibility to coach and develop the top HR people within your organization."
>
> P. Wright, J. Boudreau, D. Pace, E. Sartain, P. McKinnon, and R. Antoine, *The Chief HR Officer: Defining the New Role of HR Leaders* (San Francisco: Wiley, John & sons, Inc., 2011), at p. 37

If you believe, as I do, that the People Strategy of a company is one of the key factors vital to its success, then you must also believe that the HR management team that executes the People Strategy every day it every bit as important. Put another way, the People Strategy of a company will only be as effective as the front line HR team that interacts with managers and employees. Naturally, the effectiveness of the HR team is dependent on the quality of the HR managers on the team and, like most teams, it will be only as effective as its weakest member.

All of this preamble is to set up the statement that I did not tolerate anything less than high-performing HR managers on my team. If we had weak players in these jobs, it did not matter how good the rest of us were in HR.

At this point you might be expecting me to present another list of people I fired, but that's not where this is going. Instead, I took a personal interest in the HR managers who worked on my teams and that included ways and means to improve individual performance and team spirit. At Cadbury, Heinz, CN and Maple Leaf Foods, we would bring in HR managers for development sessions. In particular, I enjoyed running my 2-day "HR Coaching with Les" seminars.

These sessions were designed for current and up-coming HR managers and my staff would participate in certain sections of the agenda. Attendance was usually limited to just 12-15 people and before each session, I would meet every one in person or by phone so I would get to know them better and understand their backgrounds and career objectives.

With that information in hand, it made it easier to create an agenda that addressed as many of the concerns as possible; a typical agenda looked like this:

1. Role of CHRO
2. Business Plan/Strategy
3. People Strategy
4. HR role & responsibilities
5. Coaching leaders
6. Business acumen/company financial information
7. Dealing with difficult HR situations
8. ABCs – leadership behavioural science

The key success criteria for the participants was to learn more about the People Strategy and to connect with their CHRO. For me, I wanted each person to feel connected to me as the CHRO and me as a person. As an introvert, I had to be totally transparent about my belief system, leadership approach and my feelings about the HR team. At the end of the 2-day program, I would hand out a small business card inviting them to call me if they needed my assistance.

This card is good for one

CHRO Helping Hand

Keep in your back pocket and use if you
need me to help you out in a situation

Les Dakens-416-926-2012

The participants usually laughed when they read the card. However, the room would get very serious when I would say, "I want you all to know I have your back covered at all times." At that point, someone in the room would break the silence and say, "Can I have a few more of these cards, I'm going to need them."

It was a real treat for me to spend 2 full days with each group of HR managers. It was a great bonding experience which made for excellent team dynamics. What's more, it gave me the insight I needed to better help these key team members down the road, and it also gave me the chance to keep my assessment of the HR talent on my team up-to-date.

There are few CHRO roles as important and as rewarding as developing people and I always took it as a personal responsibility and a revered accountability, because I know it involves not only the success of the company, but also the future career development of so many people.

CHAPTER 50:   FIRING AN HR PROFESSIONAL

> "The new HR competencies challenge HR professionals to contribute both more and differently. HR must continue to flawlessly deliver transaction and administrative services in most organizations, whether directly or by attending to the quality of outsourced work, and its practices must both adapt to and lead organizational capability.
>
> The new wave is a change in context as well as competence. HR professionals must have the skills to interpret environmental events and trends, co-create a strategic agenda that informs the human capital implications of business strategies and priorities, and play a leading role in ensuring the leadership, culture, and talent required for future success."
>
> D. Ulrich, J. Younger, W. Brookbank, and M. Ulrich, *HR from the Outside In: Six Competencies for the Future of Human Resources* (New York: McGraw Hill, 2012), p. 203

There are few things in the HR world more distasteful or unwelcome than firing an employee, and in some respects it is doubly so when firing someone from your own HR team. And yet, statistically speaking, it will happen on a regular basis because HR employees are not immune from the same circumstances that sometimes make firing any other employee a necessity.

In my career, I have had to fire quite a number of HR people and although many terminations were the result of company consolidations or re-structuring situations that were no fault of the individuals, many were not.

It is these "performance" cases that are the subject of this chapter. Here then, are examples of situations where I had to terminate an HR professional because they were not skilled enough in their roles, or because they did not "fit" with their customers, or because they did not "fit" with me or the company.

(a) Big Lack of Discipline

My first example is actually someone I originally hired – yes sometimes the root cause of a firing stems from mistakes made in the original hire. In this case, the person was large and loud; and although overweight, he stated during the interview that his plan was to lose weight and get into shape. He also said he felt he was an underdog for the position because of his weight and just needed an opportunity to demonstrate his abilities. I have to admit that I let this notion get in the way of better judgement.

Unfortunately, this employee's lack of discipline with his health also became evident in his work habits; he was late for meetings, took a casual ad hoc approach to giving HR advice, and on occasion even fell asleep during meetings and other work situations. It wasn't long before he became a real embarrassment for the HR team and the company, and despite numerous warnings and promises to change, his behaviour did not change.

After his termination, I reflected on what I could have done differently to change him. My conclusion was his lack of discipline was core to everything he did and I did not have the energy, patience or expertise to fundamentally change him; he was destined to fail the day I hired him.

(b) Cultural Mismatch

This VP of HR was technically very sound and had been promoted into a broader role which required her to demonstrate strong interpersonal skills. Her previous roles were more "consultant-like" and required her to give expert advice and then execute the technical solutions. Unfortunately, her new role was more suited to someone who could deal in the "gray" area and then work with others in a collaborative manner. This was not really her DNA.

So, by the time I arrived on the scene, she had already pi@*ed off not only her critical internal clients, but also many of her HR peers. We tried to turn the situation around, but the damage had been done. I asked her if the performance feedback was a surprise and she admitted it wasn't. She had received similar feedback in the past. In this case, we were able to part ways in a very professional way and she has since gone on to another company and a role better suited to her cultural style.

(c)   The Peter Principle

This person had a very strong labour relations background and wanted to become an HR manager at a plant site – a generalist role. The new role required someone capable of handling the full range of the HR manager role from recruiting, training, coaching, and handling grievances. We had some reservations in promoting this individual into this role since he did seem to be very narrow in his expertise and he had a strong "do it my way" personality. He had been successful in the LR specialist role because he knew his stuff so well and managers appreciated his "black and white advice" in most cases. However, he totally bombed in the new role because he was too prescriptive in his advice as an HR manager; he didn't listen first to better understand situations, plus he was taking far too long to resolve issues. As the CHRO, I watched this scenario unfold and was truly saddened by the outcome. In working with his manager, we came to the conclusion that this individual would not be successful. We were at fault for putting him into the role and we needed to rescue him from the situation. He left the company because we did not have a better alternative – something I felt responsible for.

(d)   Control Freak

This person was successful in managing a part of the HR function and was eventually promoted to replace his boss who ran the HR function for one of the business units. Although the role required his prior experience, the more important criteria were the ability to hire and develop HR managers in his business unit.

Unfortunately, this manager had such a need to control everything that his existing staff started to leave or ask for transfers to other business units. In their exit interviews, they described a very controlling manager and an untenable situation for them. We initially chalked this up to the insecurity of a new leader and some sour grapes from the staff, so we treated the situation with coaching and 360-degree survey data to help point out the path to being a better leader.

New people were hired to replace those that had left, but unfortunately his controlling leadership behaviour continued. It was at this point that I joined the company and the issue was brought to my attention. I spoke directly to his staff and they were all upset and ready to leave and eventually one of them went to the business unit president to broach the subject. Unfortunately, it is a common situation where a control freak becomes the leader and ends up disempowering his staff. In this case the only remedy was dismissal.

Most of the descriptions above focus on the individual and the part of their make-up that creates an untenable situation, but as much as these personal traits might make the individual unsuited for the job, those of us responsible for giving them the job in the first place have to share a big part of the responsibility.

Frankly today there are no excuses that justify the kind of terminations I mention above because we are the people experts with the assessment tools capable of screening for these mismatch situations. They should be viewed as much a failure of the HR selection processes as the individual – and ultimately that buck stops at the CHROs desk.

6

HR Products and Services

"It is the combination of knowing clearly what one believes and the courage to stand up for those beliefs that leads every successful CHRO to be willing to have that "put your badge on the table" moment. Only through knowing yourself internally can you define yourself externally."

P. Wright, J. Boudreau, D. Pace, E. Sartain, P. McKinnon, and R. Antoine, *The Chief HR Officer: Defining the New Role of HR Leaders* (San Francisco: Wiley, John & Sons, Inc., 2011), p. 302

This section, and part of Section 9, Leading and Interacting with Employees, includes a series of articles contributed by the HR staff at Maple Leaf Foods. As any leader can tell you, it makes your life a good deal easier when you have great people working with you.

The start, of course, is technical expertise. People who know their subjects in depth can not only be concise and thorough in their particular subject area, but can offer ideas across a variety of topics. As most HR issues are at least to some degree interrelated, it can be rewarding to watch the team offer insights from their individual perspectives. The final product is richer and stands up better to the reality testing that is needed to implement new processes or programs.

I thank all my colleagues who contributed to these two sections:

- Supervisory Development: Lyn Langrock, Mike Habel
- Talent Acquisition Centre: Emma Horgan
- Leadership Development and Training: Carmen Klein
- Change Management: Carmen Klein, Paul Clipson
- Succession Planning: Carmen Klein
- Total Rewards Program: Cheryl Fullerton
- Diversity and Inclusion: Paul Clipson
- University Graduate Development: Carmen Klein

- Performance Management: Am I doing a good job?: Paul Clipson
- EmployeeTerminations and Facility Closures: Norm Sabapathy
- Plant Level Management: Norm Sabapathy
- HR Technology Solutions: Cheryl Fullerton
- Employee Engagement: Cheryl Fullerton
- Positive Leadership: Cheryl Fullerton, Norm Sabapathy
- High Performance People Systems: Dave Harman, Steve Jacobs (CLG)
- Labour Relations: Ian Henry

CHAPTER 51: MARKETING THE HR FUNCTION

> "As a new CHRO, take the time to assess the talent on the HR team and build credibility for the entire HR team."
>
> Ferio Pugliese, EVP & President, WestJet Encore (and former CHRO)

As you may remember from my Introduction, I went to college and graduated with a 3-year Business diploma with a major in Marketing (today, it would have been a degree level). I was rated as the number two student in Marketing in my class. Therefore, I had a basic understanding and affinity to marketing products and services. This academic expertise was used throughout my career in HR. I treated the HR function like a service business. We had products and services to sell to our customers.

Some of the HR products were highly valued by our clients and others were ideas that required some selling to convince line managers they really could use these services to make their jobs easier. As an introvert, I was not always the best person to sell the ideas so I relied on people within the HR functions who were more outgoing to help influence the customers.

The cornerstone for marketing the HR function is to identify the different populations that you are trying to service. The HR products and services for the management staff in your company are very different than the products and services consumed by front-line employees. In other words, you must differentiate your customers and develop products that meet their needs.

The best vehicle for marketing an HR function is a well-designed People Strategy. However, the People Strategy document cannot sit on a desk or bookshelf collecting dust. It is a marketing brochure that needs to be put into the hands of every customer (managers and employees). Each of the strategic initiatives is like a product extension in your product portfolio. Sometimes these products need to be killed or re-promoted; and because the People Strategy has a limited shelf life, occasionally it will need to be completely revamped.

Here is a good example of how the People Strategy can outlast its usefulness. In one company, one of their strategic priorities in the early 2000 period was to "top grade" their staff through external hiring. Unfortunately, this top grading mentality carried on beyond the initial 3-year time frame and resulted in significant turnover because staff that were hired 3-5 years earlier were consequently not being considered for internal positions. It became a vicious circle. Your HR products need to be revamped constantly to ensure you are on your People Strategy.

So, as the CHRO, I always felt I had two critical roles: support the executive team and run a successful HR service business. My marketing training helped me in both roles.

CHAPTER 52: SUPERVISORY DEVELOPMENT

> "I believe leadership can be taught. I do believe some people are natural leaders, but I question whether they're as great as they could be. There's always room for refinement, for gaining new insights, for changing with the times, for being more aware of what's important now versus what was important five years ago."
>
> **Rose Patten, Special Advisor to CEO (former CHRO),**
> **BMO Financial Group**

What is "front line" leadership? Sometimes we forget the origin of the "front line" analogy and its implications for business because its use has become so common it is now part of our everyday business lexicon, independent of its origins.

During World War I, the "front line" was one place you did not want to be. This was where you literally stood toe-to-toe with your enemy and could look them in the eye across a very narrow ribbon of dirt known as no-man's land. This was trench warfare at its most horrendous, yet out of the futility of this kind of battle came a number of very apt business analogies still in use today – including "front line leadership".

Just like their WWI military counterparts, today's front line business leaders are relied upon by both senior management and employees to get the business of business done. They need to be agile on their feet, quick thinking but with good judgement, prepared to handle any exigency with grace and flexibility – and they need to be good leaders.

Front line leadership is not easy, and it's not something that individuals are born into (although some might dispute this), but instead good front line leaders are created either by experience and trial and error, or by training – and ideally by both.

Because of the nature of the role of front line leader, however, there are a number of challenges in developing and managing a relevant front line leadership training and development program.

For example:

- Often this employee group works different shifts in a variety of locations. They often lack a large group of peers that serve to provide a "community of practice" that would allow them to learn from others performing the same work.

- These employees have a very full roster of duties that are often required to be accomplished in a set routine/time frame (quality checks, shift changes, crew meetings).

- The nature of their work often requires them to change and adapt on a moment's notice to meet urgent unplanned business requirements.

- Often employees in this group are technical experts who have come to these leadership roles with very little preparation or development of their leadership capabilities, and will default to leading others as they may have been led in the past, rather than what would be considered as best practice leadership.

All of these elements serve to create an environment that is not necessarily conducive to traditional classroom or even to Web-based facilitated learning. The organizational challenges to respond to these factors are:

- to understand the non-negotiable skill set that is required of this group of employees. Getting multiple viewpoints and alignment on this is critical. A way to approach this is to survey the current environment and assess what the high performers are currently saying and doing that is contributing to their success;

- to understand what the future skill set is that will allow the organization to maintain or increase market competitiveness. This is best achieved by engaging a broader group or analysis to understand strategic business direction as well as the labour market trends and forecasts;

- to understand the current skill gaps existing within the organization. This evaluation can be done based on manager perception, but is much more robust if done in conjunction with the employee group. Engagement of the employee group allows the organization to validate assumptions as well as to identify the early adopters and enlist their support for championing the programming that is developed; and

- to develop a program that is flexible enough to accommodate the needs of the employees and the business as the environment continues to change, often at a rapid pace.

As the program is developed the following elements need to be addressed:

- *Flexibility of design.* Adults learn at different speeds and in a variety of different styles. A blended learning approach incorporating a variety of learning methods will allow a program to meet the needs of the greatest number of employees. The creation of self-directed learning modules allows a learner to leverage exercises or approaches for learning the material which addresses both their style and their pace.

- *Flexibility of delivery.* In order for all employees to have equal access to the materials as well as an equal opportunity to use them, a Web-based portal for hosting the materials and which is open to the employees, is ideal. This approach allows employees to access the information as often as required on their own schedule.

- *Resources to support.* Peer mentors or functional coaches should be made available to the adult learner to reinforce the learning or to create a safe place to ask questions and get clarity of concepts. Ideally the coach is an expert who has practiced the skill and who can easily relate to the adult learner and his or her situation.

- *Measurement.* An organization wants to be able to measure its return on investment for any training dollars spent. In order to manage this, a learning outcome has to be established up front and linked to a benefit to the business.

A learning contract is a good vehicle for this where it is agreed upon by the employee and the manager and documented for future measurement.

- *Adaptability.* The program should be developed in small modules that focus on one skill or concept. This bite-sized approach allows for quick learning and the opportunity for the employee to practice one focused development area at a time. Should all employees become proficient or the skill become redundant, this module can be pulled and replaced with something new and more relevant – without a full scale redesign of a larger program.

- *Sustainability.* Internal resources dedicated to monitoring and tracking the program will aid in the ongoing success of the program.

As with so many concepts in development training, excellent implementation is key, including making sure the target learner understands the purpose of the program, and is able to access the program with relative ease. The goal is to encourage maximum participation and maximum buy-in.

Establishing why the program exists and what value the program brings to the learner is important to the adult learner's motivation. When working with operational learners, who are constantly bombarded with information, it is best to err on the side of over-communicating versus under-communicating.

A necessary and effective method for communicating the purpose of the program would include a well-scripted top down approach where the operational leaders relate the importance of the learner's participation in the program to the success of the organization and to the leader. Involving the chain of command in the messaging drives ownership into the leaders as well as buy-in from the learner group. Other methods to be considered could include an internal marketing campaign (engage your marketing department), regular e-mail updates to the learners, and information sessions on the program.

It is a good idea to ensure the learner's one-up manager understands how to manoeuver the training program very early on so that he or she can demonstrate their interest in the learner's development. When the one-up is unable to demonstrate competence in the program, there is a risk they will shy away from it. Whatever the process for accessing the learning program, it should be designed in a way that people who do not access the program regularly are able to easily navigate the process. There is no sense in creating a great training program if the process to access the training requires hours of training; learners will be turned off.

The end result training process should include the following steps:

- *Assessment.* By completing an annual assessment of the learner's current skills compared to the needs of the organization, the learner and manager can gain clarity on where skill gaps exist. Including the learner in the assessment process is important to ensure the learner connects with the value of the learning later on. Skill gaps should be prioritized to ensure the learner is focusing on the right objectives.

- *Commitment to learning.* Once the learner and manager have established the priority skill gaps, they review the materials available and decide on the appropriate training material for the learner to work through. A "learning agreement" is a great way to clarify learning objectives as well as the roles of the learner and the manager in the learning process. Where possible, learning objectives should be linked to appropriate business results, this will help the learner connect with the value and importance of the learning.

- *Gather resources.* When the learner is ready to begin the training, they should be able to easily access the resources needed. This could include accessing content via a SharePoint site, accessing an online learning link and/or being introduced to a mentor or peer coach. Regardless of the material the learner needs to access, the process of accessing the material should be easy and relatively quick to do.

- *Learn and practice.* All learning should involve a practical application on the job. By applying the learning on the job the learner gains confidence in their ability to demonstrate the new skills and begins to add the new skills to their regular rhythms. Where appropriate, the learner should have access to a mentor or coach who can answer questions and provide clarity.

- *Achieve the objectives.* When the training is complete, the learner and manager should review the original objectives as well as the target business results to see if the desired objectives were met.

To say that measuring the effectiveness of training is crucial to any training and development program is like saying, "Three on a match will get you shot in the head". In other words, "duh"!

Feedback should be gathered immediately after training to gain information on content and process, even if the overall effectiveness of the training may not yet be apparent. It may be necessary to check in on the effectiveness of the training at regular intervals (i.e., every 2 months for 6 months) to see whether the training is having the desired results. For a large organization it is advisable to have a standardized survey for these check ins so there is consistency; over a period of time it should become clear whether or not the learning objective was met.

The overall effectiveness of the program should show up in business results as well as in the annual assessments completed on the learners. By analyzing the assessment data over time and looking for changes, skill gaps, trends, and progress you can see how the training and development program has improved the learner population's skill set.

CHAPTER 53:   TALENT ACQUISITION CENTER

"Finding great people happens in all kinds of ways, and I've always believed "Everyone you meet is another interview"."

J. Welch, J. Byrne, *JACK: Straight From The Gut*
(New York: Business Plus, 2003), p. 156

Behind the dire headlines about skyrocketing unemployment during this most recent recession, was the rarely newsworthy fact that in North America, even at the worst depths of the recession, there were hundreds of thousands of jobs that remained unfilled because the employer could not find the right candidate. If you are an HR professional or senior executive this is not news to you, because you or someone you know is experiencing this phenomenon right now.

The implications of this fact are far-reaching; if we can't find the right candidate when times are tough, how do we fare when the economy is booming and the competition for talent becomes even fiercer? The answer is, we become industry leaders in recruitment.

When I joined Maple Leaf Foods as CHRO I discovered I had inherited a centralized recruitment department called the Talent Acquisition Center (TAC). That was the good news, the not-so-good news was that it wasn't fully implemented, it did not cover all geographies or all positions, and the kicker was that it wasn't mandatory for anyone to use it. I guess the last part was understandable given that the incomplete implementation presented too many challenges for too many potential users.

This kind of centralized recruitment model was new to me and frankly, I wasn't sure if it could work; especially as it related to the internal candidate experience. One of the things I brought with me to MLF was my personal emphasis on hiring from within – which I translated at MLF as a renewed focus on identifying and grooming internal candidates for job openings and succession.

The concept behind the TAC seemed limited for internal recruitment because the recruiters' typical skill set seemed more in line with recruiting from outside the company – such as might be the case with an external recruitment agency.

With our renewed focus on hiring from within, however, I wanted HR managers in the field to be properly connecting with both successful and unsuccessful internal applicants, ensuring they were getting the proper career coaching and feedback. Early on, we decided that all internal recruitment would be the purview of our HR managers, with the TAC taking the lead on external recruitment.

The main area of my concern with this model was the business case. It seemed like a big team of people and, from what I understood, the result was an incremental headcount above HR resources already in the field.

Normally I would expect to see a reduction in field HR as the recruitment portion of their roles became centralized, but this did not seem to have happened. After digging into it, I discovered the business case was built almost exclusively on agency fee savings. The group was measuring its success on the basis that every single role they filled was an agency fee saved.

I struggled with this because it relied on the notion that 100% of hires would be through an agency if all recruitment was still with field HR and were it not for TAC. It was difficult to compile the appropriate data, but as it turns out the number was more like 25%, and so recalculating the business case on that basis presented a completely different picture: at best it was break even. That's when we started to get into benchmarking – was there still room for improvement in the Return on Investment? And if cost neutral is the best we can expect, what model (centralized or decentralized) makes the most sense for MLF?

One thing that jumped out from the benchmarking was that those organizations that had moved to a centralized recruitment model weren't going back! Another thing that was clear from the benchmarking was the importance of technology as an enabler. The organizations we spoke to all had an Applicant Tracking System (ATS) which acts as a centralized database for open and closed roles, as well as for potential candidates. In some organizations, it was also fully integrated with their other HR systems. At the time we were benchmarking, Maple Leaf's TAC was only just in the process of implementing an ATS, and although it is in now, arguably it would have been beneficial for Maple Leaf to have had it sooner.

Another insight from the benchmarking was that although the other organizations may not have gone so far as to use the word "mandatory," it was nevertheless understood by hiring managers and HR generalists in the field that using their TACs was not optional. This enabled the maximum efficiencies to be gained, and enabled the organizations to fully understand their hiring volumes and costs of recruitment. In turn, they had better enterprise-wide metrics, for example, true "cost per hire", which enables management to ensure recruitment, is done as cost effectively as possible.

Aside from reduced spending on agency fees and efficiencies gleaned from a shared candidate pool, I came to appreciate the benefits associated with the skill set and mindset of the recruiters versus our HR generalists when it came to finding talent. With competition for top talent in the market being just as tough as ever, the generalist's "post and pray" approach to recruitment just doesn't cut it; especially with the growth of social networking as a recruitment medium and the increased popularity of specialty career sites like LinkedIn. Knowing how to navigate and fully leverage LinkedIn to find talent is a must today.

At some point I came to fully appreciate the advantages of a TAC for an organization like Maple Leaf; and over time it evolved from the partially implemented state to fully implemented, at least for salaried roles, with the added benefit of facilitating full management of all recruitment-related costs.

An element that requires some serious consideration is the potential relationship strain put on those organizations that the internal recruiters may target to find talent. While the outcome could be the same as an external recruiter targeting and calling potential candidates directly, having the third party in-between can help dilute some of the natural tension of the situation. The risk of not managing this well is that your organization in turn becomes a target. To help mitigate this, and in response to issues that have arisen from this, Maple Leaf has entered into informal agreements with certain organizations that they will not "poach" from each other.

As a result, there is a list of do not call organizations that the recruitment team has to work around; although even this can present a challenge, for example, when people from those organizations apply directly to a posting. The key is to understand internally who "owns" the particular relationship in question, and ensure there is transparency through the process. This has on occasion meant we have had to ask candidates to be transparent with their current employers about the fact they are interviewing with us, before they know whether they are going to be offered the position or not. Understandably some opt not to do this, and instead withdraw their candidacy.

So at the end of the day you can count me as "in favour" of centralized recruitment departments because of the potential for significant benefits that extend beyond simply hard savings. That being said, I will offer the caveat that the ROI is still critical. Clear baseline data must be set from which to work the business case. This can be challenging to collect in decentralized models, but it is worth the effort. Given that the benefits do extend beyond the hard savings, if reviewing the merits of implementing a centralized recruitment model, make sure you are clear on all the objectives your organization wants to achieve from it.

If your organization is moving towards this kind of centralized model, it is important to have a full implementation plan. This should include getting to the point that all recruitment goes through the team for in-scope hires, versus managers being able to opt for their own route. It should also include getting to the point that all recruitment-related costs and vendor relationships for in-scope hiring goes through the centralized team, so economies can be maximized, and the true cost of recruitment to your business can be measured and benchmarked.

Finally, if an organization is committing to the centralized model, ensuring the implementation of supporting technology as part of the early plan is a must if your business is not already using an ATS. Arguably Maple Leaf would have benefited from getting theirs in earlier than they did.

CHAPTER 54: LEADERSHIP DEVELOPMENT AND TRAINING

"Seven Principles of the Talent Masters

1. An enlightened leadership team, starting with the CEO.

2. Meritocracy through differentiation.

3. Working values.

4. A culture of trust and candor.

5. Rigorous talent assessment.

6. A business partnership with human resources.

7. Continuous learning and improvement."

B. Conaty and R. Charan, *The Talent Masters,*
Why Smart Leaders Put People Before Numbers
(New York: Crown Publishing Group, 2010), pp. 18-20

Strong leaders drive performance. Organizations wanting to survive and thrive recognize the need to continuously develop the quality and caliber of leadership skills in their talent. This means ensuring they have the right talent in the right place at the right time for all critical leadership positions. This is the essence of leadership development and is essential for driving the business today and in the future.

Best practice leadership development frameworks are aligned with business strategy and organizational direction; they are carefully laid out programs and processes to flow potential leaders through the talent pipeline so that the right leaders are in place when needed without disrupting business results. These programs include:

- Tailored leadership competencies that are important to the business, denoting behaviours at each stage of leadership. This becomes the foundation for all talent-related processes including recruitment, performance management and succession planning.

- Performance assessments that measure the performance, competencies and future potential of the leadership population. This also includes assessment tools such as 360s and other leadership assessments, and leads to individual development action plans to help employees achieve the desired level of performance or take their careers to the next level.

- Development programs that focus on building leadership skills. There are numerous tools for leadership development, including training, mentoring, special assignments and project teams. While many best practice organizations have focused primarily on formal leadership type academy and workshops, this is rapidly changing to include more informal methods. A best practice is to incorporate many of these methods into a program.

- Focused programs and processes to identify and develop high potential talent (the 10% of leaders who have what it takes to eventually fill critical roles in the business) and succession planning – and execution of that plan – for critical roles in the organization.

- Career paths that outline the experiences leaders need to accumulate as they move up through the organization – both horizontal and vertical. Leaders learn best through the work they do, and defining these, as well as managing the flow of talent through them, is critical for ensuring the succession plans have talent who are ready to move up.

Wrapped around these components are conversations on talent at all levels of the organization – identifying future leaders, measuring their performance and potential, and proactively monitoring their development and roles to keep talent moving through the pipeline.

The headline on leadership development is that it is evolving. Over the last decade there have been some major developments that are transforming how organizations nurture and develop their leaders. The first of these is the accessibility and functionality of technology. While this does include traditional e-learning (essentially the online equivalent of courses), the real innovation space is in the realm of social media. Over the last 5 years a number of vehicles have burst on the digital social scene (e.g., Google, YouTube, Wikipedia, SlideShare and Yammer) and employees have more resources at their fingertips (literally!) than ever before through knowledge portals, video sites, online communities, discussion boards, blogs, Webinars, and so on.

A second development is the changing definition of organizational leadership. Ten years ago, hierarchical one-way leadership styles were the common model. Today, the heroic leader who has all the answers and saves the day has given way to 21st century leaders who engage and collaborate in a network-centric, participatory way.

Leadership is evolving and the development methods are also evolving; status quo programs and approaches won't resonate with today's emerging leaders. They know that to stay ahead they need to learn continuously, and while formal training plays a role, traditional methods and programs only provide a fraction of what they need to know. Much like their leadership style, they are self-directed, collaborative and social in their approach to learning.

As such, leadership development today is a time of experimentation. Organizations are reviewing in light of these changes and experimenting with methods and approaches that will enable them to achieve their talent and business end goals. Some themes coming through include:

- *Go beyond the classroom.* Organizations are challenging the classroom training/workshop format to develop leadership skills: either blending it with other methods or replacing it altogether. The reason? The busy work environment is resistant to workers stepping away from work for days at a time. Also, more powerfully, leaders want learning options that are available right now, in the moment of need. While workshops and training have received the lion's share of organizations' budgets, the shift is to methods that are more immediate and informal in nature, including coaching, special projects, special assignments, and communities of practice. Course-type programs will still factor in, but not as the default solution.

- *Individual driven development.* Organizations are loosening the reins on leadership development and letting employees take the driver's seat in determining what they need to learn in the context of their work. Many employees are, in effect, already doing this, for example, Google and YouTube are among the most popular online learning vehicles, and networking through online communities such as LinkedIn is a common practice. Leadership development departments (and leaders themselves) are evolving from providing the answers to enabling and equipping employees to find the answers by surrounding them with performance support resources (content, experts – both internal and external), removing the blocks on key social sites such as YouTube and Facebook, helping them filter through the information out there, and connecting them to the right resource in the moment of need.

- *Increased team and group collaboration.* 21st century leaders are social learners. They like to learn with and from others and not just in formal learning contexts. Organizations are leveraging techniques where learners learn collaboratively with others beyond their immediate teams, across functions, and with other organizations. They learn from the resources, ideas and experiences that are shared. Communities of practice, peer coaching, and share groups, both in person and online, are leveraged to facilitate this.

- *Build collective leadership.* The focus is broadening from that of high performer. Organizations are developing supervisory and mid-level leaders as much as they develop executives, senior leaders and high potentials. The rationale is that leadership is a key skill required by jobs at all levels. A secondary reason is because these roles are the gateway to a significant percentage of the frontline workforce: key engagers of the workforce whose behaviours drive the top and bottom lines.

> "Future CEOs need to have better leading capability
> since they will have more direct reports."
>
> Joe Jimenez, CEO, Novartis

CHAPTER 55: CHANGE MANAGEMENT

> "When implementing changes, give all employees a seat at the table.
> They will step up when they feel their input is valued and
> appreciated."
>
> J. Izzo, *Stepping Up: Why Taking Responsibility Changes Everything*
> (San Francisco: Berrett-Koehler Publishers, Inc., 2012), p. 156

The Greek philosopher Heraclitus said, "Nothing is permanent, except change." Heraclitus, who died in 475 BC, reminded us that change is certainly nothing new. Today in business, change such as an acquisition, new software, or a new organizational structure, is essential for organizations to stay relevant and profitable.

Historically, organizations executed change by giving employees a heads up, throwing the switch and hoping for the best. The staffing implications of this approach are well documented and dire: productivity plummets, absenteeism doubles, and "A" players leave – all of which erode profits. Why? We can look to evolution, which tells us that only those who have learned to adapt to change will survive. In any organization, about 10 to 20% of employees adapt instinctively, but the rest struggle and/or actively resist and won't make the transition on their own.

Change management, the practice of helping the other 80% of employees make the transition to the change end state, is fairly recent. The concept emerged through consulting firms in the 1980s that recognized this area was an untapped opportunity and fairly lucrative. Over the last decade, companies began to bring this practice in-house to support transformation work. Because change management is about people, this expertise often finds its home in HR. It is a skill all HR practitioners are increasingly called upon to master.

Googling "change management" yields a plethora of thought leaders, bloggers, authors, researchers and consultants, all with their own take on how to help people through change, creating a tangled, ambiguous body of knowledge. At its simplest, a change management approach can be summed up in three phases, which need to be addressed for critical stakeholders affected by the change:

- *Awareness (Head).* "What is the change? What is the business rationale? What does it mean to me and my team?" Build awareness of the change, including the business case. Ensure employees' questions are answered. Build strategies to sway the resistors.

- *Feelings (Heart).* "How do I feel about the change? Why? How can I view the change as an opportunity instead of a threat?" Build employee support for the change, using messaging and counselling to alleviate and/or reframe fears and anxieties.

- *Behaviour (Hands).* "What do I need to do differently? Can I do it? Do I want to do it?" Define what employees need to start doing in the end state and encourage these new behaviours.

However, this is all easier said than done; traditional change management will tackle some of this through tactics such as executive alignment, structure communication and technical training. While this helps mitigate some talent risk, it can fall short of realizing the full benefit of the change.

The two things that often get underemphasized during change are detailed end state and success metrics. The end state is the future vision once the change is complete and sustained (long after "go live"). Robust change efforts take the time to define this with sufficient detail and analyze it so that the stakeholder change impact becomes clear. This is accompanied by a set of leading and lagging metrics (business and people) with clear ties to the original business case. This information is used to:

- Keep the business metrics within the line of sight for the change management team so that the team can monitor implementation and sustainment.

- Scope and diagnose the change effort as it pertains to talent (who is impacted? how?). This focuses change effort on the critical employees who are most impacted and who carry the biggest risk.

- Help answer critical "me" questions that accompany change. Answers help provide clarity to employees who may be struggling to support the change.

Pinpointed critical end state behaviours, or what people say and do, are where the rubber hits the road to realize full benefits. Much of organizational performance is rooted in people doing the right things to deliver results. Traditional change management approaches address some of this through training, but the training is never sufficient to sustain the desired behaviours in the end state. So what to look for with respect to a behaviours change plan?

- The critical new behaviours for driving performance are identified, object-ively described and measured for each stakeholder group in scope. There are clear ties between the behaviours and the business case metrics.

- There are actions identified to trigger and sustain these behaviours through the sustainment phase.

- Leaders are providing feedback – and lots of it – to their team to reinforce these behaviours.

Note, however, that aligning the "head" and "heart" is an important prerequisite for changing behaviours. Typically, impacted employees need to understand and support the change to move forward with new behaviours.

Front line leadership engagement: One of the most influential assets in helping employees transition to the change end state is their one-up manager. Managers reinforce change messages, counsel employees, help employees navigate their feelings, and provide a lot of support and positive feedback as their teams adopt a new mindset and new behaviours.

Periods of change are also very challenging times for managers. Managers are often sandwiched between executives who are pushing the messages down and a stressed, anxious, uncertain team. And managers are also most likely equally stressed, uncertain and anxious – which is a very natural reaction to have. To effect-ively leverage this resource in providing support to the front line, leaders must:

- Take care of these stakeholders first. They won't be effective if they do not align and support the change. In fact, they will be detrimental to it as teams look to them for cues on how to interpret events. Help them come to terms with their own feelings and reframe it into something more positive.

- Equip them with the knowledge and skills to help their teams do the same. Don't assume they have the experience to provide the right support needed during times of change. This is a good time to invest in developing these skills.

- Ensure their efforts are visible to and supported by their own leaders in the form of face time and encouragement.

As per Heraclitus, change is indeed constant and comes in all shapes and sizes – from the continuous change in our day-to-day work (such as a new policy or template) to major transformational events (facility network transformations or a new ERP system). Organizations that can build the adaptability of their employees will be faster, more flexible, more nimble and more effective than their peers. Investing in change management capabilities is a great way for HR to add value directly to the top and bottom line.

CHAPTER 56: SUCCESSION PLANNING

> "The CEO and senior vice president of HR know the top
> six hundred people in the company intimately – their families,
> their hobbies, their likes and dislikes, their skills, strengths,
> psychological tendencies, and development needs.
> These six hundred executives have become almost family."
>
> B. Conaty, R. Charan, *The Talent Masters,*
> *Why Smart Leaders Put People Before Numbers*
> (New York: Crown Publishing Group, 2010), p. 29

Succession planning is the organizational effort directed to identifying and developing potential future leaders so they can fill critical business positions when they become available. It is about having the right quantity and quality of leaders to meet business needs and deliver desired business results.

Planning processes are executive sponsored and supported. Ideally, they are also simple, straight forward, and well integrated with other talent management processes, including performance reviews, development action planning, and talent reviews. The process itself typically includes:

- Identify and assess the most critical positions in the organization – for both today and the future.

- Identify and assess potential talent who could eventually fill these roles.

- Create individualized development action plans that accelerate talent development, typically with a focus on new roles or special assignments.

- Ongoing monitoring and review of progress.

Organizations will devote a number of tools and vehicles to this process including leadership competency models, performance and potential assessments, and leadership development programs.

Best practice succession planning processes ensure that the plans are not a once a year event. They place considerable effort and focus on managing the plan; that is, ensuring the development plans and other activities are completed and tracking talent progression and retention. Follow through is more important than the plan itself.

There are a number of challenges to succession planning. Currently there is a mass exodus of the senior leader workforce as boomers retire – the demand for talent outstrips supply. Gen Xs and Ys are generally less devoted to organizations and may not stick around for the next role. In addition, work/life balance and flexibility are increasingly important so high potential talent may not even want roles with increasing responsibility – climbing the ladder and increased salaries are not worth the sacrifice of time and increased stress that often accompanies these roles.

There are several significant trends occurring in succession management including:

- *Creating talent pools.* Organizations are creating succession pools versus 1:1 or 2:1 match. Organizations may have up to four candidates as replacements for a senior role. This helps offset the risk potential of turnover or sudden changes in leadership needs due to alterations in business direction.

- *Increasing transparency of the plan.* In many organizations, succession planning is a secretive process where even the potential successors don't know they are on the "list." Successor retention risk is greater if staff believes there is no career plan for them – they will create their own via leaving for other organizations. Other high potentials may not even aspire to that role or may not want to make the investment required to get there. The risk of these types of surprises can be mitigated. Transparency of the plan, clarity around the career paths to get there and candid two-way conversations with potential successors about desires and aspirations help to mitigate these risk areas and make the plan more realistic.

- *Going deeper.* Originally succession management was limited to executive roles (CEO, CFO) – these are, after all, often the most critical roles in the organization. As organizations mature in their succession planning, they are going broader and deeper within the organization, planning for critical roles that are outside the executive realm.

- *Expanding talent pools to the external market.* Of course the preference is to promote from within. The success rate of leaders who come from within the organization far outstrips those recruited externally. However, it may not be possible to fill every succession need and companies may want to expand their pool to the external. This is not reactive recruitment; rather, it is proactive planning. Where possible, identify the high potentials in the industry and track them or, at the very least, have a recruiter who has their finger on this. In addition, don't take a resignation of a high potential as a permanent decision; they may come back for the right opportunity so keep that relationship going.

- *Supporting the transitions.* The succession planning process is not successful unless the new leader is performing in their new role. The toughest part of this is the transition – which can be a particularly stressful period in a leader's career, particularly where a vertical move is involved. Organizations are placing greater focus on helping leaders make these transitions as smoothly as possible.

CHAPTER 57:   TOTAL REWARDS PROGRAMS

"Take [an] enterprise approach to HR. Total compensation as a percentage of overall cost should vary if your company is growing, declining or staying the same."

Geoff Beattie, Board Director

People work for many different reasons: they have skills and talents they enjoy using, they want to contribute to society, or they would be bored sitting at home, but at the root for almost everyone is a need to financially support themselves and their families.

Employers use a variety of tools to provide rewards for work, including: base pay, overtime pay, special premiums, commissions, short- mid- and long-term incentives, profit sharing, recognition awards, benefit plans, pension and other savings plans, learning, and development. There are many interesting aspects to the design, funding and administration of these rewards vehicles. Two specific aspects of rewards program management have a particularly strong impact and should have prime focus in a total rewards strategy – differentiation and communication.

(a) Differentiation

You would never expect all shareholders to receive the same total dividend payout, regardless of how many shares they hold. Clearly, it makes sense that shareholders who contribute more money to the pool, and who own more shares, receive a higher total dividend payout. The same logic holds true with employees. It makes sense that employees who contribute greater performance to the company, and who have greater impact, should receive greater rewards.

It's logical yet it can be difficult to do. Managers tend to want to reward effort and attitude, and have difficulty giving "bad" news. Many managers would rather give all their employees a raise, because it's all good news, or give the same raise to all employees because it's easier to manage. It's not easy to make hard decisions on how to spend a salary increase budget – to give some employees no increase because they are paid appropriately for their role and contribution, and to give other employees high increases because they are low to market or their contribution is exceptional. But with limited dollars to spend it's imperative to show leadership and make the hard decision to differentiate.

Differentiation in pay will reinforce other messages you are giving your employees. When you tie the amount of an employee's raise to their annual performance, you reinforce your performance feedback messages. You remind the employee of the impact that their performance had on the organization, and how their particular results and behaviours help the organization to succeed. When you provide special learning and development opportunities to stronger performers, especially those with the potential to advance their careers with the company, you reinforce your career potential messages. Positive reinforcement through rewards to your highest performing employees will provide an incentive for them to continue to strive for high performance.

Similarly, incentive pay programs need to differentiate level of payout based on the level of achievement. Your shareholders rightfully demand a clear performance payout linkage, and will hold your Board and your leaders accountable to meet this expectation. However, there is nothing harder than telling your employees they won't get a bonus payout when those employees worked hard and had good results but fell short of targets. It's imperative to design incentive plans properly to measure the right things, and to set the targets properly to ensure there is appropriate but achievable stretch. But once the plans and targets are in place, we need to accept that there is risk to the payout, and the level of payout will differ based on performance.

To have integrity and to be fair, you can't reward effort; you need to reward results. And you can't be afraid of giving factually appropriate news, even if it feels like "bad" news.

(b) Communication

Rewards programs are very powerful communication vehicles. When there is money or perks behind what you want to say – they grab attention. Together they tell a better story than either on its own.

In the vast majority of cases the level of base pay is virtually invisible as to motivational impact on a day-to-day basis. An obvious exception is when base pay isn't sufficient to cover basic individual or family needs – then there is active motivation to get a new job. But if you are paying appropriately or are high on base pay, employees adjust their lifestyle to fit the level of pay, and pay flies below the radar. However, one thing will raise base pay to the forefront as an issue – the perception of a lack of fairness. If an employee feels that he is not treated fairly, as compared to people with similar jobs in other companies, or as compared to internal peers, base pay turns into a dis-satisfier that can significantly erode engagement. This can lead to reduced productivity or an active search for a new job. This is where communication plays a crucial role. Companies build trust with their employees through open communication about the processes involved in benchmarking pay to market and in determining internal pay of individuals.

Don't take this to mean that employees want everyone doing a similar job to be paid exactly the same. Employees can understand differences between industries. Oil and gas companies pay more than retail grocery companies. The difference makes sense because it's built on facts about profits earned and ability to pay, and is fair. Employees can also understand differences between individuals if those differences are built on facts about performance and contribution to the company, and feels fair. Employees need to clearly understand the factors that determine varying levels of pay or varying merit increases.

When you tie the amount of an incentive or profit sharing plan to the company's performance, you create a communication platform to educate employees on the company's goals. At the beginning of the measurement period you can frame why the goals are important to the business strategy. During the measurement period you can provide regular updates on how the company is tracking against those goals, and discuss why there are variances. And most importantly, both at the start of and throughout the measurement period, you can explain how employees can influence the achievement of the goals through focusing their time and energy on high impact areas and actions.

There is a lot of power in providing total compensation or total rewards communication to help employees pull together all the elements. Base pay is invisible once it's in place – every week or month when employees get their pay deposit they don't thank the company and feel rewarded. Similarly, pension and benefits are invisible until used, and then are an expectation with no real understanding of cost. Incentive programs have annual or longer time frames and are not top of mind on an ongoing basis. But an annual total compensation statement educates employees on the total value and reminds them how the company compensation package supports them and their family to enjoy a certain lifestyle. Broadening this beyond compensation to a total rewards statement that integrates learning, development, perks, and other work-life elements can be an explicit reminder of the overall return the employee enjoys for sharing his or her time, talents and energy with the organization.

(c)   What Leading Companies Do

Your HR team can drive higher value from your rewards programs by building manager competency in pay decisions and communication, and using compensation administration technology.

Since differentiation is a key strategic element of good compensation practice, managers need to be competent and comfortable making tough decisions to differentiate, and need to communicate those decisions to their employees. This certainly doesn't come naturally to all managers. Your HR team is responsible for building manager competence and for coaching managers through to a level of comfort using the skills. The base is one of well-designed programs, structures and processes. This includes a base pay structure with a clear methodology for assessing jobs and assigning pay levels, and a defined process for addressing geographic differentials and hot skills. It includes incentive plan designs with clearly defined success measures that link to business plans, and a defined process for updating employees on progress. With these structural elements in place, the HR team can educate managers on the mechanics of the tools and processes and can focus on building the judgment required to effectively use the processes.

Judgment is required to properly pay for performance; a necessity in finding the sweet spot where the company isn't overpaying for the employee's results and impact and the employee feels fairly compensated for his or her contributions. Once a market-based, internally equitable salary range is established, we know what the right compensation zone is for a given role. The mid-point of that range is generally the target for a fully competent performer. Employees who are developing in the role should be positioned lower in the range. Employees who are delivering exceptional results on a regular basis should move higher in the range, especially if the employee has the potential to move to a higher level role in the near future. Managers need to be smart in how they spend their salary budget and not over-inflate the salaries of the majority of performers who should be positioned around the mid-point. This requires the manager to tell employees that they are getting average raises, or even in some cases no raises. The latter scenario could come in where an employee is hired into a company at a higher salary level, but after a period of time has proven themself to be a competent, but not exceptional performer. The right message is that pay is appropriate for the job and the performance and no further adjustment is required. It's the right message, but potentially a tough message. HR coaching prior to the manager-employee conversation can help the manager have confidence in the integrity of the data, believe that the pay is fair, and understand all the other ways to provide the employee with positive recognition and growth opportunities along with how to increase engagement. This, coupled with coaching on how to have fact based, direct conversations and deal with conflict, will equip the manager to make and carry out appropriate pay decisions.

Similarly, where objectives defined at the individual or team level play a role in the calculation of an incentive payout, managers need to have the skills to set stretch goals for their team members which are specific, measurable, and linked to key business deliverables. Managers who allow soft, poorly-defined objectives are not fulfilling their responsibility to the company to extract high performance from their teams; there may be a sense that they don't trust their employees to be able to deliver against meaningful goals. If the starting assumption is that employees can't deal with well-articulated stretch objectives, the manager is neither giving employees the credit they deserve nor the proper opportunity to over-achieve. Your HR team can help in this area by providing templates of objectives that are linked to business objectives, guidelines for appropriate targets, and training on how to write clear and specific goals. The team can then help managers build skills in tracking progress against goals, coaching employees through the year to keep on track and manage gaps, and assess the final results in a fact-based fair way.

Bringing technology into compensation processes helps managers spend more of their time on the thinking, the decisions, and the conversations, and less of their time completing paperwork, doing calculations, and managing approvals. Technology to simplify administration of base pay decisions can make information easily available. It allows managers to view their teams' current salary levels, performance and potential information, and past salary increase history. It then allows for dynamic modeling, where the manager can allocate a salary increase budget by inputting salary increase amounts for team members and continuing to adjust and fine-tune until the proper differentiation is achieved. The technology typically provides a workflow process to forward the recommendations to the appropriate approvers, who are able to consolidate information from multiple managers in their team to see the big picture. At the end of the process the approved increases pass to the HR or payroll master database to execute the salary changes.

Technology can also support the administration of incentive pay programs. The primary beneficiary of incentive pay technology is typically the HR team, since the tool can perform calculations at various achievement levels, whether modeling for budget or forecast purposes, or determining final payout amounts. Where objectives defined at the individual or team level are involved in the incentive calculation, technology can allow managers to record objectives, with their weighting, targets and, eventually, actual results. During regular one-on-one meetings the manager and employee can then discuss the objectives and the manager can provide the appropriate coaching and feedback. Positive feedback to reinforce good progress provides recognition to employees and increases motivation to continue down the current path. Where gaps are identified, the manager and employee can identify any need for extra effort, resources, or other course correction supports.

The company will benefit where technology provides information at the manager's fingertips and makes it easy to execute processes, and where HR professionals build up the manager's ability to make smart decisions about linking pay to performance and discussing compensation matters with their employees. Dollars spent in the right place, in the right amounts, provide the highest return. It's just good business.

CHAPTER 58: EMPLOYEE COMMUNICATIONS

> "It's all about the people, folks. When you unleash the power of
> people, it's amazing what you can do."
>
> Hunter Harrison, CEO, Canadian Pacific

The role of the CHRO in leading employee communications differs across companies depending on their size and complexity, but in all cases the CHRO and HR team must be deeply engaged in the process, given their direct accountability for building a strong workplace culture.

Most large companies will have their own communications department, which leads the management and development of internal and external communications, and works with functional leaders and business units. In my experience, internal communications was part of my mandate and it was often difficult to get the resource support from the internal communications department. It was not a lack of skills that was the problem; the main issue was that employee communications were the lowest priority for the Vice President, Communications. They were usually immersed in other higher profile events like investor relations or new product introductions. As a result, I never felt there was joint ownership between the two departments for effective internal communications.

However, this all changed when I joined Maple Leaf Foods. When I met Lynda Kuhn, the SVP, Communications, my perception of employee communications changed forever. Not only was she my partner on employee communications, she became personally engaged in all forms of critical employee communications. When I asked her what the key drivers for effective employee communications were, she answered with the following principles:

1. At Maple Leaf, communications is seen as a critical enabler of business strategy and implementation. [We u]se the process of developing communications to drive alignment and clarity about the subject or change being communicated. Well prepared communications drive ownership among leaders, a shared sense of purpose and reflect clear thinking. If the leaders can't clearly, simply and with conviction frame their thoughts about what is happening and why, it's a given that employees won't understand it or support it.

2. Maximize involvement of leaders in delivering the communications. The Communications team helps develop the plan and materials, but the message needs to be delivered by people that are accountable for the change – people employees know and trust. A very detailed communications rollout is an

important means to drive engagement from shaping and reviewing materials through to delivering the communications.

3. Be fact based and transparent. If you don't know all the answers, at least provide people with an understanding of the process and timing to determine the end state and get them the answers. This is not about "spin" – which is the definition of bad communication.

4. Don't assume that communications will automatically deliver acceptance and support among stakeholders. Communications is only part of the journey – people need information but their experience, before and after the communication, also needs to support what they hear. Communications + experience are required to drive engagement.

Lynda indicated the company values are critical to enhance the credibility of employee communications. For example, one of the six Maple Leaf Foods values is "Dare to be transparent." This particular value has enabled leaders to deal with sensitive and difficult issues in a very open manner. As a very practical demonstration, the CEO provides a weekly message to employees describing his activities during the week. These weekly e-mails describe business results, critical activities that are consuming the CEO's time and some personal reflections. Through these notes, the CEO champions and models the importance of open communications in breaking through organizational hierarchies.

When I am working with Lynda in developing an employee communication, she is very fact based, has an independent focus and provides an analytical framework to describe the truth. She is looking to capture the essence of what I am trying to communicate. She really avoids any form of "spin-mastery." Lynda has a real gift in developing the message; she has the ability "to put ourselves as an employee."

Lynda takes a very disciplined change management approach to all of her communication strategies. She describes change management as follows:

> In the first instance, change management lives or dies by the extent to which leaders have a shared view of what is needed, the changes required to get there, and visibly model that belief with their people. Maple Leaf utilizes the communications process to drive this alignment. There is nothing like requiring leaders to support and champion a common view of the problem, the solution and how we get there to crystalize differing perspectives and build alignment. This is what a great communications strategy should deliver. The next step is clear communications that resonate both from a logical and emotional perspective, that ensure that the right information is shared, at the right time, with the right people. The third is matching people's experience with what they have heard. If there is a disconnect, people will not believe or engage.

I am blessed to have a partner like Lynda to help me drive effective employee communications. I hope every CHRO has the same opportunity to work with a real communications professional. They earn their equity each day and have a real seat at the business table.

CHAPTER 59: DIVERSITY AND INCLUSION: DOING THE RIGHT THING DELIVERS COMMERCIAL REWARD

> "The CHRO needs to be diversity focused."
>
> Claude Mongeau, CEO, Canadian National

It has been 50 years since Dr. Martin Luther King stood on the steps of the Lincoln Memorial and shared his Dream. How things have changed since then! How things have remained the same! Slowly, in the subsequent decades, the edifice of discrimination has been dismantled across North America and Western Europe. It has taken heroic sacrifice and tenacious struggle for equality to emerge as the dominant assumption in civil society.

But the reality of corporate life is far from equal. In the mainstream business world there is legal compliance and risk avoidance but there is not a heartfelt embracing of diversity. The ranks of upper management are still predominantly white, male and ostensibly straight. Most measures of diversity have not significantly shifted in the last 30 years other than in those few North European countries which have taken on a legal code of direct intervention. Discrimination has been replaced in the main with a subtle resistance to change. The pre-conditions required to develop into a candidate for a senior job remain unaltered. The relationship networks, the encouragement from above, the sponsorship and mentoring still flow from like to like across the leadership generations so that executive teams recruit in their own image. By the time it gets to an actual selection race it is already too late: the "best" candidate (which is itself culturally defined by the current elite) may well get the job without any discrimination because of the talented people who never got to the start of the race. There is a moral cost to this aversion to change.

But ironically for a corporate world steeped in the profit motive there is also a commercial cost. Talented people take their skills elsewhere. And they take with them their different views, insights, and knowledge. Innovation and possibility are lost. A senior leadership team that does not look like the people it is leading or the people it is selling to is a team already struggling for leverage as well as for legitimacy. The standout individuals who have broken through to senior positions attract all the headlines: Carly Fiorina, Marjorie Scardino, Sheryl Sandberg. But the progress of the few does not disguise the statistical reality that the old order has been very reluctant to hand over the keys to the C-suite to those not drawn from their own narrow community. If we just stay with gender inequality and use data from the United States, the numbers demonstrate the scale of the challenge:

- Women as percentage of the workforce: 47% (one of the lowest in the G8 nations)
- Women as percentage of university graduates: 56%
- Women as percentage of senior management positions: 19%
- Women as percentage of Corporate Boards: 15%
- Women as percentage of CEOs (Fortune 500 companies): 3%

The statistics for Canada are similar:

- 48% of the workforce is female
- 60% of university graduates are female
- 18% of executive positions are female
- 4% of the CEO population is female

There has been no major shift in these numbers for the past 25 years.

The "why" argument for greater diversity and inclusion in recruiting into the senior corporate ranks is therefore both moral and commercial. The "what" and the "how" of diversity and inclusion is more complex. It can best be summarized as, "Diversity awareness needs to be woven into every large and small Human Resource process." There is no single magic wand that will address the imbalance. Unconscious and accidental consequences of doing things as we have always done them will continue to deliver the same outcomes without any overt discrimination. The HR professionals responsible for recruitment, for performance management, for employee engagement, for learning and development, and for compensation all need to be aware of where the hidden biases slip in. They also need to be aware of the many small positives that can be built into systems to make them more inclusive.

Thanks to the struggle since that hot summer's day in 1963, we have equal protection under the law for all to be free and to strive for achievement. But if Martin

Luther King's dream is to be real for all minorities in the corporate world then a new effort is required. It will not need oratory or heroism to succeed: it will need awareness and systematic diligence to design HR processes that deliver inclusive outcomes from all our people decisions.

CHAPTER 60:   COACHING AND PEER MENTORING

> "I am not an avid book reader, I prefer to engage with inspiring people, never stop listening, allow sufficient time to reflect and ultimately always be ready to learn."
>
> Peter Goerke, Group Human Resources, Prudential PLC

Coaching and mentoring take the form of a conversation between two or more individuals. Although often referenced interchangeably, the nature of these two types of conversations can be very different:

- Coaching. The facilitation of problem solving to arrive at a solution. Coaches do not provide solutions to problems, but rather facilitate the process so that the coachee discovers a solution from within. Through this, coachees also build their own problem-solving skills.

- Mentoring. The transfer of knowledge (culture, skills, network contacts, experiences) from one person to another in a direct approach. Typically the mentor is two or more levels senior and not in the direct line of management within the organization.

Both of coaching and mentoring are leveraged as leadership development vehicles in many organizations as part of an integrated program or as a standalone. In most organizations, this is targeted towards executives and high potentials in the work place to help them achieve higher performance in a current role, to groom them for their next role or to facilitate their transition in a new role (it is used much less frequently for coaching against derailing behaviours). Often the coaches are external to the organization, implying a cost, and there is a greater ROI on this investment with these stakeholder groups.

There is a pull for these resources at all levels of the organization and companies are looking to expand their practices. This is occurring through the following vehicles:

- Building coaching skills into line management. Organizations are proactively building coaching skills (which include inquiry and active listening skills, conversation frameworks, and building trust) into their manager population. This has a number of benefits: it enables wider-reaching coaching from people who interact with the coachee day-to-day and who know their development needs. It builds crucial coaching skills in leaders, skills that are necessary to engage and lead teams that thrive under a collaborating, nurturing, two-way leadership style. It also helps managers learn to self-coach, that is, to work out their own challenges and issues as needed.

- Peer coaching (also known as sideways coaching). Peer coaching or mentoring is an area gaining momentum in the developmental field. The upcoming leaders learn best with and through others and love to share what they have learned. Peer coaching involves bringing leaders from similar career stages (often from different functions or even different organizations) to discuss and share experiences, lessons learned, problems and challenges in the work place. Typically, this format requires some light structure (so problems are being solved, not just discussed) and an experienced facilitator to keep the conversation moving. Through this, leaders have a forum to build their leadership skills, solve workplace problems, and build their coaching skills through coaching their peers.

- Reverse mentoring. Often mentoring is thought to be top down, but it can also go the other way. With the rise of social media and technology, organizations are pairing young employees with executives to help build the executives' technical savvy. Objectives and topics include, among others, learning more about the Internet, smart phone applications, or how to jazz up blogs and online communications. There is mutual benefit as the junior mentor gets visibility with the top leaders and experience in how they function. Another way these relationships are leveraged is the inversion of expertise as leaders at the higher levels often lose sight of what is happening at the lower levels. The junior mentors keep leaders versed in how the big moves have played out below, which can feed into better decisions.

"It is difficult to position an organization for the future without fully understanding how the organization operates. Since finance is the universal language of business, any discussions of business literacy must be grounded in finance. HR professionals should be able to interpret an income statement, balance sheet, and financial analyst's report on their organization. They should know how their company creates wealth and how to track wealth creation. Increasing business literacy, like learning a new language, includes many small steps:

1. Start every staff meeting by reviewing financial performance data, not just to review the data but to subtly enhance financial literacy among the HR staff. It is also useful to review competitor financials in detail.

2. Share the annual industry and competitive presentation presented at the board of directors meeting with the HR team so that team members can master the same information as company leaders.

3. Develop a course on "finance for the nonfinancial manager" and invite the HR leaders to teach this course so that they become more comfortable with financial information.

4. Record and play the quarterly investor call for the HR staff meeting and other HR professionals.

5. Place HR professionals on the distribution list for financial reports and industry trends sent to business leaders.

6. Ensure that HR professionals master the logic of their particular business so that they know its core technical requirements.

7. Require all HR professionals to enroll in financial training courses and then certify them at least in finance and accounting standards.

For 25 years, we have been somewhat confused by the way HR professionals tend to shy away from mastering the language of logic of business. Like those who move into a new country but avoid learning the local language and logic, these HR professionals will always remain isolated within their own enclave."

D. Ulrich, J. Younger, W. Brookbank, and M. Ulrich, *HR from the Outside In: Six Competencies for the Future of Human Resources* (New York: McGraw-Hill, 2012), pp. 70-71

CHAPTER 61: UNIVERSITY GRADUATE DEVELOPMENT

"As a CHRO, your key HR metrics should be around leadership development, bench strength and pipeline."

Katy Barclay, SVP, Human Resources, The Kroger Company

University graduate programs are a means to seed organizations with early talent. These programs identify and recruit high potential young talent and nurture and accelerate their development to become future leaders in the organization, essentially feeding the pipeline early. An added benefit is that these programs provide a great preview of the next generation of leaders – how they work, what motivates them, and their preferences (for example, how they learn and develop) – these insights can feed into various talent strategies.

These programs can be general in design or tailored to particular functions; they best operate within the company's existing people infrastructure, including performance management and talent management processes.

These programs should also connect with other development programs in the organization to ensure the talent gets picked up once they graduate and move into a more permanent leader's role.

Typical key features of these programs:

1. *Recruitment.* Experience, fit and potential can be more difficult to gauge for new graduates when their resume is not particularly long. Leveraging assessment tools, involving multiple interviewers and looking for leadership examples beyond the workplace environment can help minimize this risk.

   Despite the news on high unemployment for new grads, the competition for strong university talent is fierce, which risks for a zero return on effort. This means that organizations need to look for ways to recruit smarter, not harder. Some tactics for beating out the competition include: leveraging summer student/co-op work terms as a feed to the program; supporting targeted, strategic schools; and getting in front of their talent early through sponsorships, course activities, and case competitions.

2. *Rotation paths.* Most of the development occurs on the job. For this reason, most graduate programs offer defined rotations, that is, a series of roles that the employee moves through during their tenure with the program at an

accelerated pace and that equip them with the experiences for their graduating role. These rotation paths and associated roles are vetted and selected with business leadership and HR in order to provide participants with different functional and leadership experiences throughout the program.

3. *Mentoring.* Mentoring, from a leader at least two levels up from the graduate, is a mutually beneficial feature of a graduate program. Mentees leverage this relationship to learn more about the company and their profession, to build their network, and to get advice.

4. *Leadership programming.* A final feature is a leadership learning curriculum targeted to young talent that wraps around the rotations in the form of performance support. These can include formal techniques such as workshops, as well as informal methods such as peer coaching, knowledge portals, Webinars, and discussion boards in a blended format. Best practice organizations recognize the social learning needs of the organization and are reflecting this in their approach to development.

Instrumental to the success of this program is business support. The business needs to view the talent as its own (versus that of the program) so its involvement in the program is essential. This includes setting the recruitment targets, selecting the candidates, monitoring and reviewing their progress, and actively participating in their development.

One-up managers are also critical as they will remain the number one support resource for the graduate when on the job. Managers need to be strong coaches, nurturing in nature, and well educated on their role within the program, particularly with respect to their role in the young leader's development.

The largest risk with this program is that young talent may leave the organization after completing it. In fact, this is a risk with Generation Y in general. Organizations are trying to figure out how best to engage and retain these employees within a graduate program and all through the talent pipeline. Ways that organizations can differentiate themselves:

- Work/life balance. Approach to work/life balance is important. Young talent is accustomed to balancing many activities, such as teams, school, jobs, and philanthropic activities, and are attracted to organizations that respect this "work to live" philosophy. They also seek roles where there is flexibility with respect to work hours, working from home, and sabbaticals. They can be resentful of roles that requiring extremely long hours and weekend effort; this will lead to turnover.

- Community focus. Leaders are looking for meaning and are attracted to jobs and organizations that have a direct positive impact on society – careers in education, health care, and not-for-profits are all examples of this. A philanthropic strategy for core organizations goes a long way to support this; activities such as community days, volunteering on company time, and fundraising help to feed this.

- Ongoing mentoring and coaching. These leaders are looking for coaching and mentoring, more so than previous generations, but this does not mean a professional coach. Rather, coaching can take the form of a one-up manager who is a strong coach, or participation in a peer coaching group. Ongoing feedback is important.

5. Variety. This generation has a reputation for job-hopping. In reality, they are looking for a portfolio of experiences and want to have a say in what those experiences will be, otherwise they will go external to find it. Larger organizations have a benefit here, and are collaborating with these leaders to equip them with the experiences that are mutually beneficial to them and the organization.

"Your HR metrics should be focused on your ability
to attract, assess, develop and retain true talent."

Bill Conaty, former SVP, Corporate Human Resources, General Electric

---

CHAPTER 62:   PERFORMANCE MANAGEMENT – AM I DOING A GOOD JOB?

"A word to the wise: if you are not creating, making, or selling our products, you had better have a good reason for being here."

D. Ulrich, J. Younger, W. Brookbank, and M. Ulrich, *HR from the Outside In: Six Competencies for the Future of Human Resources* (New York: McGraw-Hill, 2012), p. 9

I don't think I'm going too far out on a limb to suggest that any person who has ever worked for someone else asks themselves, "Am I doing a good job?" on a regular basis; the key word being "themselves" because the last thing any of these same people would do is ask their boss – even if they were sure the answer would be positive.

From the employees' perspective the need to know how they are doing affects everything from their comfort level about job security, to pay increases, to work/ life balance issues, to their relationship with their peers and supervisors. Even their relationship with the company overall and external contacts, like suppliers and customers, can be affected.

In the absence of data, employees will construct their own answer; some will be overly critical of themselves and others overly complimentary, but either way the guesswork is costly to the company. It is de-motivating to be working hard without any feedback and it is inefficient to have no guidance about where to focus for improvement or for the company's best interest. In the absence of data, employees may have difficulty distinguishing between negative and positive behaviour; it isn't always so black and white.

Despite the evidence that employees are greatly concerned about their performance, many organizations fail to give their employees this information in a constructive way. Some employees receive no performance feedback at all, while others are subjected to a mechanistic process that neither guides nor motivates.

Many employees fear, and many managers avoid, the difficult conversations about performance. The fear is based on the negative connotation of "Performance Management", which usually means managing poor performers and is most closely associated with disciplinary and exit processes, as opposed to pathways to improvement.

To be sure, there are a number of obstacles to providing a good performance review. The examples below illustrate that this can depend on what kind of employee is in question.

Many hourly workers get limited or no performance reviews, yet their ability to contribute can be significantly enhanced through straightforward and regular feedback. Sometimes bad blood created by adversarial collective bargaining can inhibit a good performance review, but these obstacles can be overcome, for example, by giving line supervisors skills training and a clear framework to use – such as a scorecard – as well as the time required to have the conversations on a regular basis.

For salaried staff, clear objectives are the starting point of a constructive conversation about performance. For many salaried staff there is a significant qualitative element about performance and so any assessment has to be carefully supported by facts. Managers who are unskilled in behavioural observation and feedback are unlikely to participate in detailed conversations. Instead they resort to generalities that give no clear guidance.

This is why many staff feel let down after their performance review. They describe it as demotivating, as being a non-event, that the manager was awkward and seemed embarrassed or was just checking the boxes on the form. It requires skill and contact to engage in a conversation about performance. The architecture of the review system can help those conversations – but it is not a substitute for a manager and a direct report sitting down and having a detailed and example-based dialogue on the individual's performance. All too often the review slips across into a conversation about the most urgent task or current project because that is safer territory.

Another obstacle for the unskilled manager is performance-related pay because this key performance motivator can actually undermine good conversation about performance in a low-contact or low-trust setting. If there is a combative mindset, then the parties are jostling to influence performance assessments in order to earn or save money. The skilled reviewer is usually able to arrive at example-based consensus before performance-related pay is discussed.

Planning and preparation are key parts of a quality performance review – particularly in a matrix organization where the data on an individual does not originate from the line manager conducting the review. The reviewer has to reach out and gather data in advance of the review. Failure to prepare can leave the review taking place in a data-free zone. Again, it is the employee who feels frustrated and de-motivated at the end of such a meeting.

C-suite executives and the CEO are the most expensive employees in a company and have the most elaborate compensation plans tied to their performance, yet they seldom get high caliber performance reviews that focus on their individual behaviours. Senior staff members are assumed to be too "senior" to need behavioural performance feedback; company performance becomes a proxy for how well they are doing. Ironically enough, sometimes the best feedback they ever get is during their last walk to the door.

Part of the issue described above is that there is no management consensus about the value and efficacy of performance management processes. Management types typically see performance management in one of two ways and adherents to each usually see little common ground among them.

As the group tasked with operating the performance management processes, HR's challenge is how to get consensus on the value of the outcomes; it's almost guaranteed that HR is going to come under fire from some managers.

Here are the two competing views about performance management:

1. *It's a mistake.* People in this camp reject the process completely; they believe people do not like receiving feedback on their performance and that any feedback, good or bad, is a negative experience and is neither wanted nor needed.

2. *It's a good idea when it's done properly.* People in this camp believe that both the employees and the company benefit from a properly administered performance management system. They believe that even feedback about poor performance can be made into a positive experience and will result in better productivity and lower turnover, to name just a couple of benefits.

Of course the question is, what about a poorly administered performance management system? My view in that case is that many managers who might otherwise think it's a good idea, will believe that the concept itself is flawed and put themselves in the first camp; they may unable to see that the problem is with the execution and not the theory. My view is that if done properly, performance management will work wonders, even if it's unpopular with some managers.

The debate about performance management is very much like the argument in psychology about the relative importance of nature and nurture. Of course through research and the application of a little common sense, that argument was resolved by recognizing that both were important in the development of an individual's behaviour. Once that deadlock was removed, psychologists were better able to understand human behaviour. In that same vein, one way to achieve greater clarity on performance management is to make a distinction between performance management as a concept, and the systems put in place to administer the program. Most organizations, however, expend more time and effort designing the systems and processes and forcing managers to use them, than they do designing the conceptual model and making sure managers understand its benefits.

So, in essence, it's not the particular configuration of any system that really matters, but rather understanding that with performance management, employees are given insight into how their work efforts are valued by the company. The mistake most often made is that this insight is provided just once a year and in a format that is both intimidating and an intrusion into the daily work life of both employee and manager. The value of the concept is lost in the stress and distaste caused by the method in which it is applied, and the value of the outcome is mitigated for the exact same reasons, not to mention the employee gets the feedback just once a year .

Depending on how and when the performance feedback is presented, the employee may very well choose to reject it, making it moot, and so the performance management system should take certain realities into consideration.

For example, the best performance feedback will naturally be accurate – something the employee can readily see for themself – but it will also be timely and actionable. If any of the feedback is grossly inaccurate, the employee is likely to reject all the feedback entirely. If the feedback references something that was relevant 10 months ago, but not on the day of the review, then there is the same risk of rejection. And finally, if the feedback is presented as a disciplinary complaint, rather than as a roadmap to improvement, the only action taken will be what the employee chooses – which may not be much, given the likelihood they are p*&#@-ed off and making their own list of complaints about the company and management.

Underneath the divergent views about performance management is a common theme: it's tough to evaluate the benefits. It's been around for a long time and there is a question about whether it is beneficial or just a tradition.

However, there is solid evidence it makes a contribution. I had the opportunity to introduce performance management within a large unionized workforce and discovered some intriguing outcomes. What the project showed, beyond doubt, was performance management can work. Both employees and supervisors gained a better understanding about business needs and standards, and how to meet or exceed expectations. People who worked at different jobs in the same location could see connections between their roles, which improved teamwork. Development plans were put into place and supervisors saw the benefit of leading people whose skill levels began to improve. Employees liked receiving feedback and many of them said, "It's about time."

It was clearly the performance management system that triggered these benefits and improved communication between levels on a daily basis. It is, after all, day-to-day performance management that counts, whether it is feedback on the fly or more targeted coaching.

Figuring out how to free performance management from the confines of an annual evaluation is indeed tricky; but it's clear that performance management as a concept is valid; where it breaks down is management's failure to successfully translate the process into daily use. Additionally, it seems clear that most people like getting feedback, as long as it's perceived as being for the purpose of making improvements, as opposed to meting out punishment or recrimination.

To summarize, here is the case for performance management.

Before performance management:

- Positive feedback was rare and had little meaning.
- Negative feedback was the rule, encouraging people to avoid leaders.
- Performance standards were not understood by supervisors or employees.
- Supervisors were unaware coaching was part of their job.

- Supervisors were seen as not listening.

- Employee participation in the stock purchase plan was 30%.

After performance management:

- Positive feedback was explained, and shaped further good results.

- Negative feedback came with a remedial plan.

- Performance standards became well-known and people wanted to meet them.

- Supervisors learned how to coach and get the best from their people.

- Supervisors opened communication lines.

- Employee participation in the stock purchase plan went to 70%.

Is performance management perfect and does it always work? Unfortunately, the answer is "no" and some of the concerns about it are valid; but the preponderance of evidence makes it clear that done correctly, performance management will result in significant benefits for both management and employee.

> "Unfortunately, very few CEOs get evaluations from both the Board Chair and the HRCC Chair."
>
> Claude Lamoureux, Board Director

CHAPTER 63: EMPLOYEE TERMINATIONS AND FACILITY CLOSURES

> "You must respect the voice of the employees. Be humble. There are thousands of people who make a difference."
>
> Peter Goerke, Group Human Resources Director, Prudential PLC

For most industries there has probably never been a more competitive environment than the present in terms of what it takes to run a successful business. The intensity of the competition is getting fiercer, and the pressure on profitability continues to build.

Changing markets, social trends, technological changes, leadership shakeups, acquisitions, divestitures, and expansions are regular occurrences that lead to significant, sometimes massive, change. One hallmark of successful organizations is a culture of continuous improvement intended to drive increased levels of cost-effective performance improvements and to sustain competitive advantage.

This is a classic example of much easier said than done. Today's workforce continues to weather challenging times regardless of sector or industry. Downsizing, layoffs, hiring freezes, cost cutting, renegotiated union agreements, wage and benefit reductions, as well as changing job and skill requirements are a few of the effects generating the most significant HR challenges the profession has ever seen.

Thus the pressure increases on companies' HR teams to create a competitive advantage in the area of employee terminations and facility closures. By making a greater contribution much earlier in the process, HR can not only partner with the business, but can in fact lead in the conception of strategy, particularly when an organization is contemplating optimization initiatives and people changes. In addition to HR assisting with implementation after the decision has been made, it can seize the opportunity to deliver in early strategy and planning stages, shaping better decisions and outcomes, for example:

- Maximizing employee engagement and retention during a facility ramp down.

- Forecasting closing facility operating risks related to people and setting mitigation plans (e.g., solutions to minimize layoffs and reinforce employee loyalty, offsets to increased operating costs, contingent workforce options).

- Identifying ways to manage and reduce one-time and future operating costs (e.g., accessing government funding, navigating legal requirements, setting innovative compensation systems, managing severance costs).

- Setting people metrics that track operating performance and costs to ensure proactive identification and management of trends (e.g., absenteeism and turnover).

- Increasing profit margins by maximizing effectiveness of people and organizational design (e.g., performance management and reward systems, less bureaucracy and faster decision-making).

- Doing broad stakeholder analysis and setting plans to overcome resistance.

- Developing disciplined implementation plans that are tightly integrated with the overall project plan.

- Being part of the project governance team.

- Being part of the communications team and contributing to development of key material for internal and external stakeholders.

- Being part of a "community adjustment" team that works with external stakeholders to minimize effect on the local community and enhance outplacement efforts.

- Understanding what the Executive Committee and Board of Directors thinks it should know relating to people and what it thinks is important, then providing appropriate reporting (e.g., proposals for major capital or reorganization projects, people strategy implementation costs, talent management around top performers and succession candidates, governance and risk management).

One stark reality of today's globally competitive environment is that employees are terminated and facilities closed for many different reasons. In these circumstances HR has a unique and critical role to play in ensuring the performance expectations of the organization are met, while at the same time ensuring affected employees are treated fairly according to legal requirements and the organization's values and culture.

It is important to remember such events can have a material effect on an organization's reputation not only among employees who remain, but also across a wide variety of external stakeholders. The perception of the reasons for restructuring, how people were treated, and what it means for the organization's future has implications for such areas as organizational anxiety, decreased productivity, reduced customer loyalty, and even decreased share value. The increasing speed and penetration of social media will increase the breadth and importance of effectively managing these aspects going forward.

Thinking bigger picture: HR can help solve the issue of people without jobs and jobs without people across multiple industries and geographies; for example, layoffs in one region while another has labour shortages, unfilled skilled job openings while new graduates look for work, and unemployed domestic workers while there is a need to bring in off-shore labour.

Many subscribe to the view that skill and labour shortages in a number of professions are a material threat to future competitiveness, while others prefer the view that we are facing less of a labour shortage and more of a skills mismatch.

In any case, HR can lead for the future in areas such as:

- Enabling competency and skills forecasting prior to development and training so organizations are investing money in the right areas.

- Providing for on-the-job training and apprenticeships that are funded consistently, even when the economy isn't booming.

- Ensuring efficient use of today's labour pool to address cost and productivity gaps so organizations will be convinced they need to invest in R&D and growth infrastructure rather than cost cutting and people reductions.

- Using accurate forecasting of future skills demand to encourage required training that is supported by government dollars and infrastructure and in partnership with private business and education stakeholders. For example, many companies have long lamented the lack of availability of skilled trades, health professionals, and people in advanced manufacturing, but have they stepped up even at the school guidance counselor level to pitch these career options to students?

- Engaging unions to actively contribute as a means to deepening their representation of workers, addressing membership decline, and offsetting the impact of automation and movement of jobs to cheaper labour markets.

- Helping employees adapt to the shifts in skills and work patterns (e.g., from manufacturing to services, or up-skilling of typically lower skilled jobs due to introduction of technology) and considering creative solutions (e.g., work sharing, reduced or reconfigured work hours and pay systems, core versus contingency workforce models, diversity strategies, and international recruitment approaches).

- Analyzing increasingly global competitors, including those from lower cost countries, and those producing more with less people, to ensure proactive responses.

Thinking about the longer term health of the industry in which an organization operates, provides an opportunity to offset shorter term needs to eliminate people who don't fit the skill and competitive profile for the future. This has broader spinoff impacts, for example, reduced unemployment support infrastructure and an increased tax base, and it can address the demographic shift of older workers retiring and younger workers funding this continued tax and infrastructure base.

"As a former SVP, Operations, I found closing a factory to be very painful for everyone involved. Fortunately, I have worked with great HR people who showed genuine compassion for the affected employees. They added great value by creatively helping these employees find new employment and the communities getting public recognition for handling a difficult situation the "right way"; beyond my highest expectations."

James Olson, Board Director

CHAPTER 64:   PLANT LEVEL HR MANAGEMENT

> "Companies must find new work/life balance for employees."
>
> Hunter Harrison, CEO, Canadian Pacific

Today's complex and dynamic global business environment demands that organizations develop people solutions that yield bottom-line results. HR must foster an engaged, capable, and aligned workforce that can anticipate the market and deliver business objectives. Plant-level HR is on the forefront of this mandate, and is typically a faction of HR closest to the action in terms of generating an organization's key outputs; this is true regardless of industry.

There are five key performance areas where plant HR should be driving value within an organization:

1. Talent Management

   a. career management

   b. assessing, identifying and developing high potential employees

   c. identifying key positions and building succession pools

   d. managing retention risks

   e. supporting career planning and development

   f. employee learning and development

   g. identifying priority development based on performance assessments and career scenarios

   h. matching appropriate training and learning solutions to development needs (e.g., supervisory and leadership development)

2. Employee and Labour Relations

   a. Employee relations

      i. managing within various legal parameters (e.g., employment standards, human rights, health and safety)

      ii. operating within HR policies, compensation and benefit structures, and positive relations best practices

      iii. maximizing diversity and inclusion strategies

b. Labour relations

    i.   establishing effective relationships with, and between, managers, employees, and union representatives

    ii.   interpreting and managing within a collective agreement or employee handbook

    iii.   supporting the grievance/complaint process (e.g., proper policies in place with consistent application and thorough investigations)

    iv.   participating in the collective bargaining process

c. Conflict resolution (e.g., working with others to arrive at the right decisions following a rigorous fact-finding process, and employing adversarial problem-solving approaches to resolve issues)

3. Workforce Management

a. Planning

    i.   forecasting demand and supply and planning to meet staffing needs (e.g., availability, skills)

    ii.   employing a robust recruitment and selection process

    iii.   advising on talent movement decisions (e.g., promotions, terminations)

    iv.   building change management plans

b. Organizational design (e.g., advising on organization structure that provides the highest performance, increased development opportunities, and the least amount of people, cost and administration)

4. Organizational Effectiveness

a. Performance management and engagement

    i.   ensuring achievement of work objectives through a robust employee and team performance assessment and management system

    ii.   reinforcing key leadership competencies and behaviours that align with performance expectations and organizational culture

    iii.   advising on the best motivational techniques (e.g., rewards, recognition, feedback) for various situations

    iv.   supporting employee engagement initiatives (e.g., surveys, employee events)

    b. Coaching

        i.   coaching others as well as enabling others to coach around individual and team performance and behaviours

        ii.   applying appropriate coaching tools and techniques that encourage desired behaviours and discourage undesired behaviours to get results

5. Professional Practice

    a. sustaining a working knowledge of an organization's strategy, plans and financials in the context of industry and competitor data

    b. actively linking business plans to HR plans and vice versa with relevant metrics, and ensuring effective work planning for disciplined execution

    c. building credibility and influence to establish and maintain a strong network of working relationships inside and outside the organization

    d. supporting internal and external communication initiatives as they relate to employees

    e. acting as a key proponent of organizational values and culture

    f. being an effective functional leader of an HR team as well as a strong contributing member of a plant leadership team

    g. maximizing HR service value through continuous improvement

Keeping in mind that value is in the eye of the receiver, it is a well-known mantra that talent is an organization's most valuable resource, and that high performance organizations recognize that a strong HR function is necessary to develop people solutions that yield competitive advantages.

Organizations that utilize their HR function in this way can benefit greatly in terms of future talent and people planning by:

• improving understanding of how business works and what levers truly improve performance;

• anticipating required individual and organizational capabilities;

• anticipating the future drivers of employee behaviour and motivation;

• addressing the exigencies of an aging workforce;

• linking social responsibility to corporate culture and success; and

• understanding external trends and stakeholder expectations to build aligned internal action plans.

HR will also need to become a greater proponent of technology, for example, in improving the utility and speed of HR operations and administration, connecting people through technology and using social media effectively.

CHAPTER 65:   HR TECHNOLOGY SOLUTIONS

"Analytics: The Future of HR"

"The job of a leader is to define reality and give hope. The reality of HR is that the role the function plays in achieving business goals has changed dramatically. The time of the solely reactive HR department is gone, and it is not coming back. HR must now function as a full leadership member of the senior strategy team. We have more influence now than in the past, but also more responsibility for achieving superior business results. What gives us hope in the face of these new challenges is knowing that new technologies are providing us with the ability to quantify HR's capabilities and achievement."

P. Wright, J. Boudreau, D. Pace, E. Sartain, P. McKinnon, R. Antoine,
The Chief HR Officer: Defining the New Role of HR Leaders
(San Francisco: Wiley, John & Sons Inc., 2011), p. 21

HR technology solutions have really exploded onto the scene in the last 25 years. In the early days the payroll system was often the system of record for employee information, with the most sophisticated output for HR purposes being employee lists with basic data. Coupled with no-tech solutions like paper files and index cards to record and track employee changes and non-payroll information, this was a time when information management wasn't even on the radar for HR professionals.

Jumping forward to 2013 we have robust technology designed specifically to manage HR information, processes and decision making. It's a brave new world and the HR profession has only scratched the surface of what these new tools can do to drive value through people processes.

At the base of HR technology is a system that houses core employee information. This includes basic information like name, ID numbers, address, job, manager, status, pay level; it enables the employee to get paid. For employee groups where pay varies by hours worked, time and attendance technology is also available to track and integrate this information with core data for payroll processing. The core employee information makes it easy to do basic reporting on numbers of employees, to pull out basic budgeting and costing information, and to calculate tenure, turnover, and other straightforward metrics.

Once the core employee information is available in a system though, the real power and potential comes from the additional functionality can be layered on, or linked in – such as recruiting, learning management, compensation or the categories outlined below.

(a) Performance Management

Performance Management is one of the first people processes which integrates into the HR technology used in an organization. We all know that the primary benefit from performance management processes is the ongoing conversations between manager and employee regarding expectations for the role, progress, challenges, ideas, aspirations, and plans. HR professionals help ensure these conversations go well by training managers to be open and clear with expectations and feedback, and to use coaching to develop employee capability.

HR technology then provides the framework for the assessment and development planning conversations to occur. The system provides the common competencies and behaviours for assessment, with definitions, examples, and rating scales. Where different competency profiles are used for different populations, technology manages this by mapping the competency framework to employ information, such as level, function, and job. Using a technology solution for the performance management process allows multi-rater feedback to be consolidated in a single place, integrating input from the employee, the manager, peers, project leaders, two-up managers, and others. Annual objectives can be cascaded through the organization, creating alignment to business priorities, either through reporting lines, or through use of objectives libraries created by function or business or some other logical grouping. Similarly, creating personal development plans can be made easier using libraries that suggest ideas on how common development areas can be strengthened.

An overarching benefit of using technology to manage the performance management process is easy access to this important information going forward. The information is accessible to the employee and manager to track and manage progress against goals, to future managers as the employee moves positions in the organization, and to the HR team to provide additional insights. Insights can come at an individual level when coaching the employee or when helping the manager prepare for performance and development conversations. Insights can also come at a macro level when pulling out assessment ratings to ensure an appropriate distribution of ratings and when assessing highest need development areas to focus training and development efforts. Linking performance assessment information into other processes, such as compensation management, also creates more efficient and integrated processes.

(b) Succession Management

Beyond annual performance assessment processes and information, there is a significant opportunity to expand the depth of information about an employee to better assess and manage the overall strength of the talent pool. Succession management technology has been on the market for years, although many organizations still manage their succession processes with PowerPoint, Excel and Word documents, and binders on shelves. The clear and immediate benefit of using technology for succession management is taking the information off the shelf and making it real-time and interactive.

Succession management technology works best when integrated with performance management technology, bringing forward assessment and development information. The succession management platform adds information on employee potential and readiness for positions in the organization, along with assessment of retention risk and other relevant data points. The result can be interactive organizational charts showing the successors for roles with their readiness, and an ability to click and drill down into the development needs and capability assessments for any one of the successors. HR and business leadership teams can then review the depth of the succession pool for key roles and identify gaps that could lead to business risk, and work to develop internal successors and/or hire in new employees to fill skill and experience gaps.

The most sophisticated succession management technology allows the HR team to create competency profiles for roles, and then search the employee database for matches – to ensure that people aren't left out of consideration because they aren't on the radar for some reason. This helps to combat gender or other biases that could otherwise skew the identification of potential successors.

Creating performance/potential charts to support talent and succession conversations is then a matter of minutes of work rather than the days of effort required when preparing manually. In addition, metrics to monitor the strength of the talent pool and effectiveness of the succession planning processes are easy to create and report on, for example:

- number of key roles with two successors ready in 2 years;

- turnover of successors to key roles;
- gender mix of successors to key roles;
- percentage of replacements chosen from succession pool.

It is easy to create succession charts, but only by monitoring metrics such as those listed above can the HR team really assess effectiveness of the succession management processes. The number one purpose of doing succession management in the first place is to manage organizational risk. Lack of depth behind key roles poses the risk that the organization may not be able to execute on business plans if employees in those key roles leave the company. Assessment of the talent pool depth and identification of risk areas allows HR and leadership to put plans in place to manage those risks. Technology to enable this strategically aligned process is a huge enabler of quality work.

(c)   Self-Service Tools

The world around us has changed significantly in the past few decades with regard to how people interact, access information, and conduct transactions. Online research, chatting, invitations, banking, shopping, dating, gaming – they are all "just how it's done" now. And if employees are familiar with a self-service world outside the workplace, it's natural that organizations should provide self-service solutions to employees for information and processes inside the workplace. Not only is it how people expect to operate – especially those who grew up with the Internet – but it's also more efficient for companies. Putting information on a company portal ensures that employees accessing the information get only the most recent version of the information. Allowing employees to conduct processes online eliminates the low-value requirement for multiple people to handle paperwork. We no longer see processes where, after the employee or manager authorizes a change, HR professionals spend time filling out paper forms, getting signatures, and keying information into systems.

Employee self-service tools can empower employees to execute a wide variety of personal activities, including submitting benefit plan claims, changing pension investment choices, changing personal addresses and banking information, signing up for in-house training courses, submitting expense reports, and making travel arrangements.

Manager self-service tools can empower managers to execute a wide variety of employee-related activities including hiring new employees, processing pay increases, changing positions, changing from part-time to full-time, processing leaves of absence, and terminating employment.

Where additional approvals are required, automated workflow tools will forward on the request to the approver's in-box for review and sign off. For example, after an employee submits an expense report it can be forwarded to the manager for review and approval. After a manager initiates a change to an employee's position it can be forwarded to the HR leader and the two-up manager to review and approve the change. The business can define the required approvals and then build this into the technology solution, and increase adherence to review processes in a simple way.

(d) Summary

It's not really about technology; it's about information. Business information has real value in an organization and organizations manage their information to minimize gaps and errors, and to maximize their ability to identify issues and support business decisions.

Manufacturing professionals have always understood the importance of using business information to manage production, resources, and waste. Sales professionals have always understood how to use product cost, price, and volumes to set strategy and goals, and to reward results. Finance professionals excel at using information about income and expenses to model the impact of business decisions, to set goals, and to track performance.

HR professionals have been late to the information management game, but this is our new frontier. We need to use people information to make fact-based decisions that will lead to stronger talent pools, optimal use of reward and development dollars, and more effective organizations. We need to be as conversant with core metrics and how to interpret them as manufacturing or sales, in order to add successively more strategic value to the organizations we lead and support. We need to be as comfortable with statistics, charts, and graphs as we are with coaching or assessing employees.

CHAPTER 66:   HEALTH AND SAFETY

> "If you genuinely care about your people, then health and safety
> is not an aspiration it is a principle and value. In one of my early
> jobs as a construction manager, a worker died because no one was
> monitoring or insisting he used basic safety equipment. I have never
> forgotten that and never walked by anyone working in an unsafe
> manner since."
>
> James Olson, Board Director

One of the more under-valued or at least under-exercised opportunities in the area of employee Occupational Health and Safety (OHS) is the balance between employer and employee interests, however, these interests should be common and connected.

The typical relationship begins with the company striving for high levels of engaged employees who are vitally interested in the success of the employer; this engagement is manifested in their promotion of the company's safety record, higher product quality, reduced waste, more efficient production output, higher profitability, among other things.

Much less typical, however, is any significant reciprocal expression of interest in the employee's personal success; specifically the employee's personal health and well-being outside the workplace, continuing education, family urgencies, and/or financial education. From an OHS perspective, the employer's efforts and interest may range from minimal compliance (as a means to manage the employer's liability) to the employee's complete wellness inside and outside of the workplace.

On the wellness front, multiple studies suggest three or more return multiples for every dollar invested; and yet even with the known unfavourable trends of personal stress, smoking, and obesity, employer participation is modest.

The obvious opportunity here is an employer investment to at least assess the mutual benefits of an active employee wellness program. To start, an employer could offer personal health risk assessments and self-help education materials and references. This could graduate to personal health counselling and group wellness activities.

The discussion surrounding safety in the workplace is often couched in terms of a "culture of safety," as a prerequisite to safe work practices, just as there are similar discussions of a "cultural" requirement for high product quality, or continuous improvement, or other corporate values or objectives. Although different levels of maturity within selected areas may create the illusion that there are multiple cultures within the same team or department, the reality is that there is but one culture and the quality of that culture is typically a direct reflection of the company.

So with that being said, we must look again at the question of the employer's sincere attention to the employee's interests. We must examine those factors that create its "cultural" component; examples would include the opportunity for the employee to engage in how the work is executed (management with "ears"), reasonable employee scheduling practices (even flexible where possible), attention to workplace conditions (i.e., planning and mitigation efforts to address periods of high ambient temperatures), stress reduction, and fair compensation. These are all factors that contribute to the workplace culture and, therefore, to the company's performance.

The bottom line is this: where a company is looking for improvements in employee OHS performance, the best place to start is with a self-assessment.

7

Working with the CEO

"The CEO marries the strategy and people to execute it. Strategy execution should be on every HRC agenda meeting."

Dr. Chris Bart, Principal and Lead Professor, The Directors College

CHAPTER 67: LES' CEO PICKS

"Working with Jack Welch was intense but totally exciting and invigorating."

Bill Conaty, former SVP, Corporate Human Resources, General Electric

Working closely with the CEO has its special rewards and special challenges to be sure, but there's no doubt that one of the most incredible opportunities associated with the CHRO role is being able to meet and learn from some of the brightest, most talented and most interesting personalities anywhere.

I've had the tremendous opportunity to work with some of the best CEOs out there, and through study and osmosis I've also come to know about many others. I thought I would start this new section about working with the CEO by telling you about some of my favourite people who are, or were, CEOs.

CEO Guru: Jack Welch. You're probably not surprised to see this name at the top of my list – Jack Welch is probably one of the most well-known CEOs of all time and turned General Electric into a global powerhouse.

I chose Jack not because he is a respected and well known celebrity CEO, but instead because before he turned GE around, he turned himself around; changing his leadership practices mid-stream to became an advocate for talent management. He was the first CEO to properly position the CHRO as equal to the CFO in terms of a confidante to the CEO and his focus on talent acquisition and development made the HR function a best practices group. His books on business leadership are incredibly thought provoking and educational and his passion and encouragement of talent has led to a remarkable pipeline of talent at GE. His track record of profitable growth and exceptional stock price appreciation will be tough to match.

Railroad Industry Legend: Hunter Harrison. CEO at Canadian Pacific Railroad and former CEO at Canadian National, Hunter is clearly a legend in the railroad business having worked at four different railroads, leaving each of them in better shape than he found them.

In my opinion, Hunter's secret to success is his ability to not only develop a winning formula for making money in a tough industry, but also coaching and developing his staff to execute that formula flawlessly. His gift of storytelling allows him to educate his management team and lower level employees effortlessly and memorably and with unanimous buy-in. As a CHRO working for him, he pushed me hard to ensure we had a pipeline of talent at CN. Also, he single-handedly drove a management talent program called the Hunter Camps which had a significant cultural impact. Hunter's 10-year record of success at CN will not be easily repeated in the short term by any other CEO in the railroad business.

Fertilizer Industry Legend: Mike Wilson. The most unassuming CEO I have ever met. His ego is non-existent, but his presence is felt throughout the company he leads – Agrium, a huge Canadian potash company that has expanded globally over the last 10 years.

Mike is a successful CEO who has a winning record with shareholders, management, Board directors and employees and he receives incredible loyalty from his leadership team. I worked with Mike during my consulting days when I was hired as an executive coach to a number of his senior people and I found his desire to create a strong leadership foundation to be very evident, and admirable. I know that when he retires from Agrium in 2013, Mike's legacy will be a strong strategic plan and a wonderful internal successor.

(a)   The New Breed of CEOs – Young Players Leading Big Companies!!

The transition from the old guard to the new breed of CEO is well underway. I would like to highlight two superstars on the CEO playing field today. These individuals will lead differently from their predecessors and I am proud to have played a part in their development.

New Generation CEO: Joe Jimenez. Although Joe has been CEO at Novartis for less than 2 years, I predict his track record over time will equal those of the superstar CEOs mentioned above. I was involved in hiring Joe at Heinz and I predicted then that he would one day become a CEO. My 2 years working for Joe gives me the insight to confidently describe him as a superstar leader with great intelligence, strong business acumen, and someone who brings out the best in his team; people who work for Joe will go out of their way to deliver above average results. Joe made the transition from the Food industry to the pharmaceutical business without missing a beat. Here's how he describes the experience:

Building Novartis – Joe Jimenez

It is a privilege and an honor to be selected to lead our company as CEO. I'd like to thank Dan Vasella for this great opportunity. I look forward to continuing to work closely with him, seeking his advice when appropriate and engaging in a good debate from time to time!

During our Chairman and CEO broadcast last week, I commented on my first visit to Novartis. I arrived at our Basel campus and counted 13 cranes scattered across the landscape. In fact, I also almost got hit by a cement truck backing up as I walked toward the Forum I building for my interview. Nearly four years later, our campus has almost completed its transformation and is now one of the best places to work in the world. Like the cranes, we each have the opportunity to be a transformative force in shaping the future of our company. But only together can we reach our goals of strengthening our portfolio, driving innovation, expanding into high growth markets, improving productivity, and developing our talent.

My vision for the future of Novartis is consistent with Dan's: to be the most respected and successful healthcare company in the world. To do this, we will need to improve our execution, and deliver on our commitments. There is no long-term without realizing our short-term performance goals. Innovation is a core driver of our business, so we will keep this front and center to ensure that it becomes best in class. Streamlining our core processes and improving productivity was key to our success in Pharma over the last two years, and we will work together to make this part of our everyday life across all divisions.

During our Chairman and CEO Broadcast earlier this week, Farooq Abbas, BPA Head in Pakistan, sent in a question asking what my top motivators are as CEO. It was a great question and I had to stop for a moment to mull over what really makes me excited about coming to work in the morning. There are three factors that really motivate me. One, is wanting to win. As former captain of Stanford University's swim team, I learned that to be successful you must have a winning mindset, set goals and work in a self-disciplined way to achieve them. Second is making a difference in people's lives. I gained great insights from running consumer businesses internationally, which taught me how to stay close to consumers to deeply understand their needs. It was however, my role as a board member of a competitor pharmaceutical company that made me realize that I wanted to work in the healthcare industry. I have invited patients to join our management meetings, and it is most moving to hear how our products have improved their quality of life. I think Dan Vasella said it best when he commented that a pill itself may not look that spectacular, but it is magic. It represents the knowhow of so many people coming together to change a patient's destiny. Finally, I want to build something that will last beyond my time, to give to future generations of Novartis.

We are in control of our future, if only we have the courage and the determination to act. How are you transforming the future of Novartis? How are you working to create "magic" for patients and our customers? I want to hear from you. Leave me a comment below.

New Generation CEO: Claude Mongeau. Claude has been CEO at CN Rail since January 2010 and is knocking the ball out of the park. From the moment I met him I knew Claude would become a CEO, and I consider myself fortunate to have worked with him during my time at CN. What convinced me he was star CEO material is his incredibly intellectual and strategic mind, combined with a drive to succeed. What makes Claude so unique is his clear vision and common touch. He is a dedicated family man with a humble perspective on life and yet he will show the world how to deliver results in a Q4 manner. In Appendix 5: "More Notes From Claude Mongeau" are a number of examples of Claude's communication style, and here is an example of how Claude communicates with his team:

A note from Claude

Intensifying our sense of teamwork

Dear fellow railroaders,

It's often been said that railroading is a team sport, because so much of our work is interdependent. We couldn't get a single shipment to destination safely and efficiently without having a large number of people involved, from every function of the company, from the workblock to the shop floor to the locomotive cab, and every place in between. So on January 25 when I announced CN's senior Leadership Team it wasn't simply a list of people who report to me.

The sense of teamwork I want to encourage throughout CN is more than having everyone take care of their piece of the puzzle. It's about truly working together collaboratively and looking at our collective goals alongside our personal ones. And that attitude has to start at the top. The people on our Leadership Team do more than handle their individual area of responsibility. We meet face to face often and engage in debate about our common goal of serving customers well, efficiently and safely.

Many companies use sports metaphors to describe their business goals, and I've been using one lately that reflects my feelings about teamwork, which is rugby. I know that rugby is not the most popular sport in North America, and even some of our colleagues seem a bit perplexed by my example, but rugby has some very intriguing qualities. For one, there is generally no one player who can win a game on his or her own the way a hot goalie can in hockey or soccer. It has to be a full team effort if you're going to move the ball towards the goal. There's no waiting for your individual turn, as there is going to bat in baseball. There are football players who have been in a league for 10 years and have never touched the ball.

But in rugby you have to be alert, agile, tough, and react quickly all game long, because at any time you might be required to carry the ball. That implies a sense of accountability as well, which I value. Every one of us needs to carry the ball at one point or another, and we have to be accountable for the time we carry the ball; and know when it makes sense to give the ball to someone else for the good of the team. A great rugby team passes the ball, not the buck.

Now I realize that writing you a single message about teamwork is not going to magically revolutionize the company. In fact, we're already a solid team, and we don't need a revolutionary change. But we have seen CN people best pull together as a team in urgent situations and I want us to tap into that sense of teamwork more consistently without waiting for a crisis or an emergency. As we aim to constantly improve our performance, further developing our teamwork and getting everyone focussed on the bigger picture will help us move CN to the next level. I know we can become a great team that serves our customers, helping protect the communities in which we operate, delivering responsibly and providing a safe and stimulating workplace.

Claude Mongeau

President and CEO

So, who wants to bet on the future success of Joe and Claude? I do! I am so convinced about their capabilities that I am buying shares in their companies. I own a $1-million worth of CN shares alone and I am adding to my share ownership in Novartis. Big bets on big talent!!

Stand up CEO: Michael McCain. The year 2008 might very well have been the last for Maple Leaf Foods except for the incredible leadership of Michael McCain. That year 23 Canadians died after eating Maple Leaf products and what followed was by far the largest food recall in Canadian history. By all rights this should have destroyed the brand and it should have resulted in huge losses of revenue and profit – and to be sure Maple Leaf took a big hit – but it didn't fail. Michael immediately became the public face and voice of Maple Leaf and his amazing stamina, grace under pressure, candor, transparency, and accessibility is what made the difference. There was no doubt in anyone's mind – consumer, press, employee, shareholder – that Maple Leaf accepted full responsibility and was utterly committed to making things right, at the topmost levels of the company. For this book I interviewed Michael and asked him about working with a CHRO – his answers provide a number of tangible recommendations I think you will find most interesting.

During my interviews with the five CEOs, I asked each of them to comment on what they expect from their CHRO and what skills they look for. Naturally their answers are quite varied, but one thing they do have in common is a focus on talent. Here is a list of their specific comments.

Expectations:

1. HR functional excellence. (Claude Mongeau)
2. Plugged into "authentic truth" in people and organizational awareness. (Michael McCain)
3. Develop culture with CEO and gain alignment with everyone. (Claude Mongeau)
4. Development plans are executed with excellence. (Joe Jimenez)
5. Deliver HR services in an efficient and cost effective manner. (Michael McCain)
6. Partner with the CEO on people decisions. (Joe Jimenez)
7. Chief talent scout – assess & develop. (Hunter Harrison)
8. Develop relationship with C-suite executives. (Hunter Harrison)
9. Trusted sounding board for management. (Mike Wilson)
10. Seasoned arbitrator on employee issues – right vs. dead right. (Mike Wilson)
11. Keep the CEO grounded. (Mike Wilson)
12. CHRO needs to be an advocate for the CEO. (Hunter Harrison)

Skill Requirements:

1. Courage to push back and walk the talk. (Mike Wilson)
2. Unique ability to pick and choose great people. (Hunter Harrison)
3. Chief negotiator for union contracts. (Michael McCain)
4. Great alignment skills. (Claude Mongeau)
5. Strong emotional intelligence, empathy and toughness. (Joe Jimenez)
6. Know how to stroke – be flexible, and when to choke – be firm. (Mike Wilson)
7. Convince the organization to reward key talent. (Hunter Harrison)
8. Execution discipline, strategic contributor and psychology major. (Michael McCain)
9. Ability to be diversity focused. (Claude Mongeau)

10. Above all else, the ability to tell me the truth, as brutal as it may be. (Joe Jimenez)

Combined, these CEOs have decades of high-level experience. For more biographical information, see Appendix 8.

CHAPTER 68:   WHAT MAKES A GREAT CEO FROM A CHRO'S PERSPECTIVE?

> "Advice for new CEO – think about your vision, agenda and direction (ahead of the parade)."
>
> Claude Mongeau, CEO, Canadian National

If you follow a sport you are probably familiar with the coach phenomenon, where a hugely successful coach moves to another team and becomes an instant and persistent failure. So what happened? Did he forget how to coach; did he get stupid all of a sudden? The answer, of course, is that success isn't solely due to the person – circumstances and environment have an impact too. The same is true of the CEO role.

A great CEO in one company could be a bad CEO in another company. Sometimes it is the company's culture or environment that can derail a CEO's success. Having said all of the above, however, it is my contention that most great CEOs can succeed in many different situations and that the attributes that make for a good CEO, are the same characteristics that help a good CEO to migrate their talent, skills and success to another circumstance, another company, even another industry or another country.

There are many leadership books published that strive to describe what makes for a great CEO, but I'm not going to reference them here. What follows is my own personal assessment of what makes a great CEO based on my own experience as CHRO working for them, and being hired as a consultant to them. Here is my assessment:

A great CEO has:

1. A complete understanding of the business model.
2. A strong vision for where to take the business.
3. The ability to attract and retain a strong team.
4. The humility to listen to and engage all levels.
5. A stakeholder focus and understanding.
6. Inspirational leadership skills.
7. The courage to change the business model and team players.
8. The wisdom to know when it is time to move on.

As a people expert, working closely with a number of CEOs, I was eventually able to create an image of the ideal CEO for that particular company, but much like the ideal wife or husband, the truth is the one you currently have is probably not it, and as for the ones "out there", you're lucky if you can even get close.

That's not to say, however, that creating the image of the ideal CEO for your company is a fruitless exercise, because the CHRO's job is to also enhance the strengths of the CEO and leverage their positive attributes and to also mitigate their weaknesses. Comparing the flesh and blood CEO to the image of the ideal helps put things into perspective and make this task easier to understand in terms of the desired outcome and what path to take to get there.

Of course one of the challenges associated with finding or creating the ideal CEO is the fact that new times and new circumstances create new challenges and new skills requirements. I asked our CEO panel for their perspective of what challenges lay ahead for future CEOs and here is what they said:

Future challenges:

1. Must position their companies for future growth. (Joe Jimenez)
2. Manage at higher speed – timely access to data. (Claude Mongeau)
3. Take more calculated risks; for example, commodities. (Mike Wilson)
4. Customers are becoming more knowledgeable/demanding. (Hunter Harrison)
5. Higher level of strategic volatility/complexity and speed of commerce. (Michael McCain)
6. Interpret outside world to set vision and shape priorities. (Claude Mongeau)
7. Manage multiple bosses/stakeholders. (Joe Jimenez)

8. Avoid short term focus – need strategic vision. (Mike Wilson)

9. Managing employee demographics and quality of life. (Hunter Harrison)

10. Right balance between shareholders and business. (Michael McCain)

I also asked our CEO panel about what new skills might be required for future CEOs. Several interesting insights were noted.

Future skills required:

1. More personal resilience – financial, strategic, organizational and operational.

2. More leadership abilities and knowledge of the business.

3. Standing up to short-term activists.

4. Empower your direct reports more.

5. Ability to know what you can/can't do in the future.

"Lafley (CEO at Procter & Gamble) turned the strategy process into a powerful coaching tool by introducing a novel practice – one we recommend other companies to adopt. He reviews each leader's strategy document ahead of time and provides handwritten comments to the presenter before the meeting. The feedback might be, "I don't understand how this will address our number one competitor killing us on pricing" or "Boy, I think you really hit a critical item here." It is a way of coaching the leader, and the CEO learns something about the person from how he or she responds."

B. Conaty and R. Charan, *The Talent Masters,*
Why Smart Leaders Put People Before Numbers
(New York: Crown Publishing Group, 2010), p. 133

CHAPTER 69: STRATEGIC PARTNER AND CONFIDANTE
TO THE CEO

> "Outside and inside: As we have discussed, a primary challenge for
> HR going forward is to turn external business trends and stakeholder
> expectations into internal HR practices and actions. This will require
> that HR professionals simultaneously understand and operate in the
> marketplace and the work-place. HR professionals will likely spend
> time with customers, investors, and community leaders, and they
> will turn those experiences into HR innovations. To ride this paradox
> successfully is to be a strategic positioner who not only knows the
> business but can shape and position the business for success."
>
> D. Ulrich, J. Younger, W. Brookbank, and M. Ulrich, *HR from the*
> *Outside In: Six Competencies for the Future of Human Resources*
> (New York: McGraw-Hill, 2012), pp. 21-22

The HR professional in the C-suite is naturally the go-to executive in terms of the people strategy, but that isn't the same as being a strategic partner to the CEO. For that to happen the CEO first needs to believe that you are in fact their partner, and secondly, they need to understand that you are strategic in your business thinking and not just HR focused. It's difficult to imagine becoming the CEO's strategic partner without the ability to contribute to the wider business strategy.

Being their partner involves trust in the relationship and an understanding that in all situations you have their back – without that, everything else is moot.

On the business side, the acid test for most CEOs is if they would appoint the CHRO to run a business unit based on their leadership and business acumen. In my case, I have been told that my action/results orientation, combined with my leadership skills, would have been a great combination to run a small business unit. In truth, I never felt compelled to take on an operating role; I always thought I could add more value by being a strategic partner with the business unit presidents and the CEO.

The bottom line is the CHRO needs to earn the right to be a strategic partner and the best way to do this is to learn the business from the bottom up and become an active coach to the business unit leaders. They will value the leadership coaching from the CHRO and at the same time they will make the effort to educate the CHRO on their business strategy and tactical plans. It becomes a win-win proposition.

Today, most CHROs are still more comfortable as the people strategist than they are as a business strategist, but the good news is that this dynamic will change due to the caliber of individuals entering the CHRO ranks today.

So, how different is it being a strategic partner to the CEO vs. being their confidante? Some might say it is essentially the same thing, however, I would argue they are distinctly different. Being a confidante means being prepared to share all aspects of your working relationship and personal lives with each other. In other words, the CEO wants an in-house advisor who they can talk to about any issues in their life – anything such as a death in the family, tax or regulatory problems, a difficult divorce, drug-addicted family member, or the CEO's concerns about his relationship to the Board chairman. Nothing is out of bounds.

In my various positions as CHRO, or as an external executive coach, my role often evolved into that of both strategic partner and confidante to the CEO, but they weren't necessarily weighted the same each time. In one case, I was able to put everything on the table and really provided intimate personal advice to the CEO; it was testament to the stress my CEO was experiencing that they came to tears discussing an issue, and I felt a lot of gratitude that they trusted me that much to share so much, even with the heady responsibility that trust came with.

On the other side of the coin is the CEO that listens, but in the end ignores your advice. It can be supremely frustrating, especially when the chickens come home to roost. Sometimes being the CEO's confidante can literally mean putting your job on the line; for example, sticking to your guns on a stance you know is right even to the point of engaging in a shouting match to get their attention. For me that sometimes actually meant "shouting" in my emails, but being calm face to face.

I don't want to suggest that the CHRO becomes the amateur psychologist with the CEO, though it is very close to this reality. However, you must be very secure in knowing yourself before you can deal with someone else's issues. When you are a true confidante to the CEO, you can look into their eyes and know there is an incredible trust relationship. But, it is not for the faint of heart since someday you might have to assist in terminating the CEO. It can cut both ways.

> "HR professionals should play four roles with CEO: architect who
> frames ideas, designer/deliverer who implements ideas,
> coach who personally advises the CEO, and facilitator who
> manages organization and team processes."
>
> Dave Ulrich, Professor at the Ross School of Business,
> University of Michigan, and Partner at The RBL Group

CHAPTER 70: THE EGO OF THE CEO

> "CEOs and top executives feel they are underpaid but
> CHROs provide objective data."
>
> Mike Wilson, CEO, Agrium

Hundreds of books have been written about the human ego, but the one thing that seems certain is that we are not born with it. Instead it develops as we become socialized as human beings. According to Freudian theory, the ego is in fact the "reality check" on our id which is that part of us that is only intent on satisfying our every need and want. By age 5 or so we begin to develop our superego, which adds a social and moral overlay to the control of our id. In a healthy person, according to Freud, the ego is the strongest of the three so that it can satisfy the needs of the id, not upset the superego, and still take into consideration the reality of every situation. Now I remember why I took marketing in school.

For the purpose of this chapter, however, I am using the more common "street" definition of ego, which is to say an exaggerated self-confidence, often approaching arrogance, and often characterized by a disinterest in other people's needs, opinions, or rightful expectations. In this case, someone with a "small" ego would be humble, unassuming, and thoughtful and respectful of others. Someone with a "big" ego, on the other hand, would be none of those things – and picture a sliding scale in between. And just like Freud's ego, this one too is developed and can change over time.

To become a successful CEO requires a certain level of self-confidence or ego that enables one to perform at a high level under pressure and in the spotlight.

Both accolades and criticism presented publicly, and often strenuously, can have an exaggerated effect on the target – just look at sports figures and see how most change with years of adoration and astonishing incomes. It is the rarest of super-star who does not develop a "big" ego during their time on the public stage.

To a lesser degree I think the same can be true of CEOs, although I do think that most CEOs have their egos in check, even if they are bigger than when they first started out. In my opinion, one of the key responsibilities the CHRO has is to help the CEO remain "grounded" in the business while they are enjoying the benefits that accrue to high performing CEOs. To say that this role requires a high level of tact and diplomacy is an understatement of the highest order.

As with superstar athletes, there is the risk that a highly successful CEO's ego will grow to the point that it is impacting their personal and business relation-ships and having a negative impact on the business. When that happens, it is the CHRO's responsibility to tactfully and diplomatically put a mirror in front of the CEO for them to see the reality of the supreme confidence they are feeling about themselves.

For example, the CEO who experiences great success and as a result comes to truly believe they are smarter than everyone else and infallible. They may be a narcissist by nature, but add "big" ego behaviour and it can get to the point where the emperor has no clothes – that is to say they are unaware of the effect of their egotistical behaviour and no one is prepared to tell them the truth about it. That's when the CHRO is required to step in and attempt an intervention. That's not to say, however, that the CEO is prepared to listen to even the CHRO.

I can think of one instance where my CEO changed over time and became increas-ingly arrogant; engaging in behaviour that to me and many others was borderline embarrassing and risked tarnishing the company's reputation. I tried on many occasions to let the emperor know that he was naked and everyone was noticing, but without success, and so I stopped holding up the mirror.

Finally, as I knew would happen, there came a situation where the CEO risked being personally embarrassed if they acted in the egotistical way that had become their norm. Sure enough, he embarrassed himself, which really hurt people's opin-ions of him. Afterward he asked me why I hadn't prepared him to better handle the situation, to which I replied, "I've tried for weeks to talk to you about this but you wouldn't listen; maybe you'll listen now."

Today, most CEOs are being coached on how to better manage their personal and business image, including this "ego" stuff, and I believe that over time this issue will be less of a concern for the CHRO.

Points Scored

As a Canadian author and hockey fan, it behooves me to touch upon the analogy between our national pastime and business. When the NHL players union is not striking – also a national sport (I jest) – the game of hockey offers great parallels to business and leadership.

A hockey team is comprised of players that perform one of four roles: the "center" is the play maker responsible for directing the offense; the "wingers" – left and right – are also primarily offensive, but also have defensive responsibilities when the other team has the puck; the "defense," not surprisingly, is primarily responsible for preventing the other team from scoring, but also has an offensive role to play; and the "goalie" is purely defensive, with the ultimate responsibility for stopping the puck from going in the net.

So to continue the analogy, I see the CEO as the center in hockey; they set up the strategy and are directly involved in executing it. The rest of the C-suite are like the other players on a hockey team – they are either offensive in focus (i.e., grow the business) or defensive (i.e., control costs) and the goalie might be analogous to the CFO who has ultimate responsibility on the defensive side.

This is the point where you are probably wondering, "What the heck does this have to do with the ego of the CEO?" This is the point where I tell you that comparing two of hockey's greatest centers – Wayne Gretzky and Eric Lindros – offers a unique insight into two different "styles" of CEO. Despite playing the same position, Wayne and Eric execute their responsibilities with completely different methods.

And by the way, for this analogy to work, you must first know that in hockey, scoring a goal is worth 1 point in terms of the player's personal record, so is assisting in the scoring of a goal; scoring a goal *or* assisting = 1 point. And for every goal there is the possibility of 2 assist points being given.

At 6'4" and 240 pounds Eric Lindros used his size to his advantage; he parked himself in front of the opposing team's net and battled the other team's defense to stay there, waiting for a teammate to pass him the puck and score. He would also wait for the opposing goalie to give up a rebound, and score that way too. And score he did – often. In an NHL career shortened by injury, Lindros amassed almost 900 points – with more than 40% being points from scoring a goal.

Physically Wayne was at the other end of the spectrum. Much like me he is smaller and lithe and played best when he avoided the other team and moved to clear ice – which he was a master at doing. His favourite offensive spot was behind the other team's net, where he could spot the teammate in the best position and feed the puck to them so they could score – which they did often. In a 20-year career, remarkably free of injury, Wayne Gretzky accumulated an astonishing 2857 points, with over 70% being assists.

Although there has been much written about the comparison of a talented hockey player who used their brawn to succeed (but at the cost of an injury-prone and short career) versus a talented player who used their brains to succeed and not only achieved a higher point total, but also enjoyed a long, and injury-free career. But that is not where I'm going here.

In Eric's case, the team strategy was to wait for Eric to get in front of the other team's net and then keep passing the puck to him until he scored. The defense against Eric Lindros' style became readily apparent – if you could knock him down, his team was much less likely to score. The team's success was directly tied to his personal success – i.e. "CEO-centric."

In Wayne's case, however, although he was the key playmaker, executing the play and scoring was left mostly up to the other four skaters on his team. Wayne's approach was much more difficult to defend against – he could operate from anywhere and even while moving to avoid the other team. Plus, the opposing team still had to worry about the other four skaters on Wayne's team as any one of them at any time could be the goal scorer. Wayne Gretzky's approach was "team-centric." To read a more detailed account of the differences between Gretzky's approach and Lindros', please see Appendix 1.

Similar situations can be found throughout the business world; some company's rely so heavily on the individual skills of the CEO that they become bound by the CEO's personal success and their personality, while others seem to operate efficiently with the CEO in the background, directing the contribution of the other members of the team.

The moral of the story is that the CEO does not need to be the superstar goal scorer on the C-suite team, but rather a superstar playmaker ready and willing to leverage the talents of everyone on his team. When every person on the team contributes fully, the end result will be discretionary exceptional performance.

CHAPTER 71: HOW TO PUSH BACK WITH CEO WHEN
NO ONE ELSE WILL

> "My relationship with the CEO was extremely close. We discussed
> any issue on the table. He had trust and confidence in me."
>
> Bill Conaty, former SVP, Corporate Human Resources, General Electric

Inherent to each of the last three subjects–strategic partner, confidante, and deal-ing with CEO's egos, is the notion of being diplomatic, but brutally honest with the CEO – or "pushing back". As difficult and risky as this might sound, and to some degree it is, I am pleased to tell you that I think CEOs today are much more accepting of constructive push back from the CHRO. One of the reasons for this is the special role the CHRO could play in the career of the CEO and the reliance the CEO must place on the CHRO to cover their back, none of which can happen if there is any distrust between the two, or if the CHRO is afraid to be frank and honest in confronting the CEO.

Shortly after I started at CN, Hunter Harrison became the CEO. I knew very little about the railroad industry at that time and, in stark contrast, not only was he an industry giant, figuratively speaking, but also a commanding presence in person. I couldn't have imagined a more intimidating circumstance to begin the process of becoming the man's strategic partner and confidante.

So in the early days of our relationship, I must confess that there was a situation I observed where I believed he could have done better in handling a people issue, and I initially hesitated to give him my input. Later, after some reflection about what I had done – or not done really – I decided that if I was going to earn the right to be his strategic partner and confidante, I needed to start immediately, and so I called him on the phone and broached the subject.

"Were you happy with the situation with Joe?" I asked. The question was met with silence, followed by, "No." He understood the reason for the question and anticipated my feedback. I told him I thought my role as his CHRO was to give him direct unfiltered feedback on his performance, and asked him if he would like me to do that on an ongoing basis. Again silence. Then he said something I will always remember because of its turn of a phrase and because of the trust it implied. He said "I will tell you when to stop giving me feedback." For the 5 years we worked together he never told me to stop. There were a few times when I thought he would throw me out of a window, and he did not always agree with my feedback, but he never said stop, and he never stopped listening. He is one CEO who understood the value of hearing the unvarnished truth from someone able to push back, when others could not or would not.

> "It is not just the CHRO but the entire team needs to push back and be accountable for other people's performance."
>
> Mike Wilson, CEO, Agrium

CHAPTER 72: HUNTER CAMPS/CEO WORKOUT SESSIONS

> "Gary, you are absolutely right. I am going to have to cloud up and rain on some people to help you. It seems that sometimes you need rain to wash away the mud in the middle of an organization."
>
> at a Hunter Camp with Hunter Harrison

From a people and talent perspective, one of the most important value-added roles a CEO can undertake is to be personally active in the formal training of both the senior and lower levels of his management team. Accordingly, one of the many roles of the CHRO and the HR team is to organize and facilitate the CEO's involvement in management training, and to design a format and medium most appropriate to the company and the CEO. There are probably dozens of ways a CEO can personally participate in management training, but here are two examples that I can share from my own experience.

The first example is from my tenure at CN Rail during the time that Hunter Harrison was CEO. Hunter had created his 5 Guiding Principles for a profitable railroad company (how we work, and why) and he wanted to infuse them throughout the company in as short a time as possible. The issue was how to do that in a company as large and spread out as CN, without spending huge amounts of the CEO's time.

The solution we came up with was a series of intensive 3-day, off-site training sessions for a small group of managers, which Hunter would lead, with me playing a supporting role – the Hunter Camps.

Invited to the first few Hunter Camps were high potential managers and supervisors below the VP level, from operations and sales, with the idea that they would meet Hunter, be trained and engaged in his five guiding principles, and we would get to know the company's future stars better.

The concept proved so successful for the participants that we were conducting 18 of these 3-day sessions each year; and not just for high potential employees, but for all leaders from all functions in the company.

Six years, and 75+ Hunter Camps and 1500 participants later, the results were astonishing. The company enjoyed a pervasive and thorough understanding of our leadership values, our business strategy and most importantly, everyone understood how and why to execute the five guiding principles. Not only did we increase the competence level of each manager, we truly changed the culture of leadership at CN. The Hunter Camp got industry-wide exposure when it was profiled in 2007 by Pat Foran in "Progressive Railroading" magazine's article, "Postcard from the Hunter Camp" – a great story on a typical Hunter Camp experience which is reprinted in Appendix 6.

The second approach to involving the CEO in management training is a concept that we put to good use at Maple Leaf Foods – the Leadership Academy – with CEO Michael McCain being personally involved in its design and execution.

The program includes multiple training events at the IVEY School of Business at Western University, with Michael attending each program to introduce the content and in some cases actually teach a portion of the curriculum.

In 2012, we introduced an additional CEO-led training initiative called the "CEO Workout" – an intensive 2-day session led personally by Michael McCain. Participants are immersed in the MLF strategy and a review of the food industry, and then taken on a deep dive into the subject of the leadership skills and values required to be successful at MLF.

The participants are nominated by their business unit and come from all levels and functions and they are expected to bring "real business and leadership" issues to the session. One of Michael's favourite tactics is to turn to the participant and ask them "If you were the CEO what would you do in this situation?" The participants love the interaction with the CEO and leave the session tremendously proud of their company, with greater insight, and truly motivated to work even harder at their job.

Some experts would argue that the CEO should not spend their valuable time out in the field training the troops, and yet if you consider the value of a management team unified in their culture, pride, motivation, and awareness of the company's objectives, principles and strategies, it's not hard to understand why some CEOs choose to participate in this aspect of management training.

In my opinion, direct CEO involvement in management training is a core responsibility with benefits to the company that far outweigh the cost; not to mention the return benefit the CEO receives from seeing the positive influence they are having and the difference they are making. It's the kind of CEO ego boost most CHROs are happy to see.

> "How much time does a CEO at P & G spend on people?"
> Somebody once asked A.G. that question, Antoine says, he thought about it for a minute and said, "About 40 percent". I was sitting there thinking that sounds a little high, but I didn't say anything. I went back and looked at his calendar over a six-month period and found he was not far off. It was 38 percent.
>
> B. Conaty and R. Charan, *The Talent Masters, Why Smart Leaders Put People Before Numbers*
> (New York: Crown Publishing Group, 2010), p. 135

CHAPTER 73:   CEO'S WEEKLY NOTE

> "CEO needs to be resilient and tough – not let the criticism get to you."
>
> Joe Jimenez, CEO, Novartis

Another key accountability of the CEO is to communicate with the employees about where the business is going and how the company is progressing. The intent, of course, is to not only convey information, but to also engage employees emotionally and intellectually in the company's mission, vision and values.

Many CEOs believe that quarterly newsletters and formal earnings statements can do that job – and while it's true they may be enough to convey information, they do nothing to connect directly with the hearts and minds of the employees – and at that point, I have to ask, "Why bother?"

Some CEOs, however, take a different approach and communicate more often and more intimately. At Maple Leaf Foods, for example, CEO Michael McCain wrote his first weekly e-mail to employees, *What's Happening at MLF,* in his first week on the job, and has continued throughout the 12 years since.

Once a week, he discusses what he did during the week and its implication to the company and its employees. The emails are broad in nature, informal, and personal – including, at one time, the story of a customer dropping in on an employee training course that he was leading, and in another email he provided some colourful stories about his children. His style is engaging and heartfelt, and when he mentions specific employees it is always a badge of honor amongst their peers. And finally, with his characteristic honesty he discusses the state of the business; it's successes, and its failures.

Immediately following one of the company's worst moments, a food recall in 2008, Michael sent one of the most memorable weekly messages to MLF employees.

> From: McCain, Michael H
>
> Sent: Saturday, August 30, 2008 10:48 AM
>
> Subject: What's Happening At Maple Leaf
>
> "Success is not final, failure is not fatal: it is the courage to continue that counts."
>
> > Winston Churchill.

For many of us this has been one of the most gruelling weeks of our careers. Our products have been linked to illness and loss of life, and we've had to face those facts straight on. It's been stressful to say the least. Many of us have done jobs outside our area of expertise. Some have literally worked around the clock.

As difficult as these days have been, there have been some invigorating aspects of working through this crisis. Above all, we have become a closer and stronger team, knowing that we can count on and lean on one another in tough situations. It has also been inspiring to read the endless emails and messages that we – as a company – have received for the way in which we're handling the situation. Here is one small example:

"This is the first time I have ever witnessed a company step up during such a serious incident. I truly believe that Maple Leaf, as a whole, is genuinely saddened by the loss of life. In my view, Maple Leaf has gone over and above taking responsibility and promptly acting to notify the public to prevent any more serious incidents. This fast acting and responsible conduct has impressed me and has not discouraged me to buy your product but has encouraged me to support you. I know now that Maple Leaf cares more about their customers than the loss of revenue this has caused. Maple Leaf products it will be my number one choice in the future! Thank you for caring!!!'"

There have been literally hundreds and hundreds of such comments. We feel remorseful about the situation. But, this will heal and we have to move on. We have to focus on rebuilding.

Focus on our base business. We have and will continue to have Destination 2010 in our sights, but right now that is simply not what we need to pay attention to. This week, I intend to examine as you may also, the things we need to do as an organization to find stability again – to rebuild – our base business. Forget change for a moment; we have to stabilize our base business.

Complete the recall. We published this ad in the papers today. It was important to announce to consumers that it is our expectation that it is complete. The remaining work is additional verification activity as well as disposal of the product, and capturing lessons learned.

Get Bartor Road Re-Opened. I have been very specific about what I need to personally see from that facility before it opens its doors again. They are making excellent progress, but it's not complete yet.

Document Lessons Learned and Go Forward Plan. We have to accept what happened here and learn from it. There are many. We have to challenge ourselves to, on one hand, not be overly critical of ourselves for what has been an industry-leading track record, and systems, but on the other hand, be able to critique ourselves to find the path forward. Being the best just will NOT be good enough going forward!

Recover Brand and Customer Confidence. This will take minute by minute attention, and the Marketing, PR and product teams are focused on this. We have done a North American search of what other major brands – and MANY (if not most) have endured such pain and suffering. A key lesson is not that we made a mistake, it is how we handle the mistakes we make that counts.

Obviously, I've devoted virtually 100% of my week to this issue. Since my last weekly note, I've held two media briefings, held our employee call on Monday with around 3,000 of you, and had innumerable phone calls with so many people, including government officials, health authorities, customers and other industry participants!

As you know we retained a technical advisory team to give us the best advice possible. Their scope was to assess the condition of the Bartor Road plant and its ability to re-open. And then, to give us the very best advice possible on the path forward as a company, and as an industry. I would like to thank Rory McAlpine (VP, Government & Industry Relations). He has done a masterful job chairing this group.

Rory has really stepped up to the plate to lead this with clarity and objectivity, and we all appreciate that. Also on the advisory panel was Dr John Webb (Director of Emerging Sciences), and they drew on the expert knowledge of Peter To (Six Sigma) to lend his world class intellect to find answers to some of the most complex aspects of the improved safety program.

I am told that the volumes in the consumer affairs hotline are slowing down rapidly, and certainly the media appears to have abated somewhat. They can be very, very frustrating as they are now at the stage of trying to "dig up" stories that really don't exist.

HUGE appreciation on behalf of the entire company, for the "take charge" approach of MaryAnne Chantler, leading us through all of this activity with precision, attention to detail and leadership. MaryAnne…it always seems you are the "go to" person when we need things done, and done right….thanks for taking this on – and to your support team – and thank you for your commitment!!!

This has been exhausting to virtually all engaged, and stressful to those not directly engaged. I have received hundreds and hundreds of supportive emails – I will answer them all, but will need a little more time than usual. Please know, I appreciate each one of them.

I am hoping to be able to spend some of Sunday with my family for a breather on this long weekend. Please don't miss an opportunity to be a Maple Leaf Ambassador. I'm sure our company and our products will be the topic of many conversations! You can find all the materials you need, in both English and French, on portal, under the Product Recall banner.

Take care…..

Leadership Edge

Michael

In my experience, this weekly approach is one of the "best practice" communications in a CEO's playbook, despite the need for discipline and frankness. Some CEOs worry that one of their weekly messages gets picked up by the media, but the reality is virtually any kind of communication has the potential to go public, and that doesn't even factor in the rumours that abound in social media. Providing the factual message will only help your reputation and the benefits are huge from an employee engagement perspective.

For additional examples of McCain's weekly notes, see Appendix 12.

CHAPTER 74: STATE OF THE NATION UP-DATES

"Meaningful Purpose"

"This means that sometimes a CHRO has to put his or her own interests aside for the good of the firm. Once I had to take a hit for a CEO on an issue that wasn't mine. He later said, "I know you took one for the cause." One of our board members had given me some good advice. He said sometimes you have to be willing to stand in harm's way and take the hit. It wasn't easy, and it didn't feel natural. But I did it and realized at that point how much I cared about being part of the company's success."

P. Wright, J. Boudreau, D. Pace, E. Sartain, P. McKinnon, and R. Antoine, *The Chief HR Officer: Defining the New Role of HR Leaders* (San Francisco: Wiley, John & Sons, Inc., 2011), p. 135

"Information" – it's one of those words we don't think much about because we use it so often and we intuitively understand its meaning, or at least we think we do. Information is good, more information is better, and the best decisions are "informed". Do you remember the information highway? That's what they called it when information went digital and travelled at the speed of light. We had access to much more information, much faster, which was a good thing.

To my way of thinking, one of the hallmarks of a good CEO is the ability to process a lot of information quickly, parsing out the actionable insight and tossing the rest; and so to that end I felt my role as CHRO was to provide a weekly update, or as I called it, "SON" – State of the Nation. Truth be told, however, it was nothing more than a lot of important, relevant information.

Most CEOs I worked with welcomed this information (interestingly not all did) and I believe it is a characteristic of the best CEOs to want to be as fully informed as possible with an unfiltered view of the organization's state of health.

Because of the nature of the information and because of my intent for sharing it with the CEO, I purposely delivered SONs verbally – putting nothing in writing. This wasn't the kind of information that required any action on the CEOs part. It was in the strictest sense FYI – just to be informed.

Occasionally I would use these SON sessions as an opportunity to plant a few "seeds" with the CEO regarding a potential issue and, in other cases, I would simply state the issue is happening but is likely to be resolved without any action from the CEO – again, just a "heads up" to be informed.

For me, the most critical purpose for the State of the Nation update is to position an issue for resolution in advance of it becoming an emergency concern. More often than not, the issue would get managed without direct CEO involvement, but nonetheless most CEOs appreciated just being informed.

Another benefit of delivering the SON sessions verbally, and in person, is that it gave me the opportunity to gauge the reaction of the CEO to the information I was presenting, giving me the opportunity to better anticipate what I needed to keep an eye on.

The CHRO is the most objective executive to give the CEO an assessment of what's happening in the company, no matter how it might be presented. If the CHRO doesn't, frankly I would be concerned that no one is – and that would potentially mean the CEO isn't getting all the information they need.

CHAPTER 75: FIRING THE CEO

> "Only 10% of company failures are due to bad strategy development. 90% is due to bad strategy execution.
> The board can help management to create focus
> and culture required to execute the strategy."
>
> Dr. Chris Bart, Principal and Lead Professor, The Directors College

In North America, the average tenure for a CEO is between 5 and 7 years depending on what survey you read. Most of the turnover is caused by the CEO being shown the door. Ironically, it is not just poor performance that leads to the sacking of the CEO. It's a big factor, but the reality is it takes a lot for the CEO to get the pink slip.

In most situations when the CEO is fired, the CEO has not met performance targets, has blamed others for his failures and has significantly alienated their Board enough to be put in their sights. Even then, the Board will typically procrastinate before they are forced to pull the trigger.

In my experience, the successful CEOs never let themselves be put in a position to be fired. Even the average CEO is savvy enough to negotiate an employment contract that provides a financial safety net in the event they are terminated for something other than "for cause". Poor performance, for example, is typically not a "for cause" scenario.

For these reasons, a CEO is usually confident enough to aggressively lead the company without fear of being financially crippled should they be sacked for poor performance or some other egregious issue, which means that it is typically something else, or a combination of other things, that will get the CEO into the kind of situation where they are let go.

I would classify the following CEO behaviours as reasons why they can get fired:

1. The CEO does not listen to others and ultimately gets blindsided.
2. The CEO is not technically competent or business astute – does not know the industry well.
3. The CEO is too arrogant in dealing with others.
4. The CEO is a weak leader and fails to inspire his staff to deliver.
5. The CEO has too many priorities and fails to deliver the critical few.

Having witnessed or been directly involved in a number of CEO departures, to me the most obvious sign that the CEO is on his way out is when their relationships with their staff and the Board has deteriorated. The CHRO has the best vantage point to observe these dysfunctional behaviours and so being the strategic partner and confidante to the CEO, the CHRO has an opportunity to repair the relationships and save the CEO's job. If that's not possible, and the CEO loses the confidence of their team, then the CEO needs to leave quickly and the CHRO needs to manage the termination process with the Board so as to mitigate the impact on the company.

CHAPTER 76: WRITING BOOKS TO EDUCATE
YOUR WORKFORCE

"The 80/20 Paradox: What Matters Most Gets the least Attention. In the business world, here's the problem: Most organizations invest 80 percent of their time, budget, and attention on getting things started (projects plans, communications, training, etc.) – in other words, on the antecedents that have only 20 percent influence on behavior change. They invest much less on setting up truly effective consequences to strongly encourage sustained behavior change. Thus they fall prey to what we call the 80/20 Paradox."

S. Jacobs, *The Behavior Breakthrough: Leading Your Organization to a New Competitive Advantage* (Austin: Greenleaf Book Group Press, 2013), p. 51

In 1998, when CN Rail acquired the Illinois Central Railroad, they also inherited its president, Hunter Harrison, who became CN's COO. It was an auspicious moment for CN and, as it turns out, for my career as CHRO.

Hunter's career at that point was legendary in the industry. Beginning in 1964, while still attending University in Memphis, Hunter worked as a carman-oiler for the St. Louis-San Francisco Railway and was later promoted to an operator position. When Burlington Northern (BN) acquired "Frisco", he entered a period of regular promotions, eventually being appointed Vice-President, Transportation, as well as Vice-President, Service Design.

Harrison left BN in 1989 to join the executive team at the Illinois Central Railroad (IC), first as Vice-President and Chief Operating Officer, and culminating with his appointment as President and Chief Executive Officer from 1993 to 1998.

By the time Hunter joined CN he was regarded as an expert in the area of precision railroading – an expertise that CN needed badly. And so during his first few years at CN he toured the length and breadth of the company sharing his railroading principles.

At one point during an informal conversation with Hunter, Paul Tellier (CN's CEO) said to him "You know, you really should write this stuff down – get it on paper." With this off-hand remark, Tellier put in motion a special project that turned into a 2-year long journey to document Hunter Harrison's railroading philosophies, business practices, and success stories. Peter Edwards, CN's VP,

Leadership & Development, started working with CN's internal communications department to document Hunter's concepts. In 2005, we published the final product, a 146-page glossy hardcover book published in full colour and in three languages, called simply, "How We Work and Why". Although it was intended just for internal employees, we printed 25,000 copies for existing employees as well as for future hires.

To say the book was an instant hit, would be an understatement. We received tremendous feedback from not only the managers and employees at CN, but also the union management, who appreciated the frankness and transparency of Hunter's approach to railroading and the simple fact that he was willing to so openly share the secrets of his success.

For us, the book's success was really driven home when we started to get requests for copies from other railroads – and financial analysts – and even from our customers. Eventually it got to the point where we had to produce an additional 10,000 copies just to meet the immediate demand.

Obviously, the content was the primary reason for the book's widespread acceptance, though as we found out later, a big part of its success was the medium – people simply liked the fact that it was a book.

If you're reading this book in sequence, then you already know about the Hunter Camps – 3-day, face-to-face sessions for employees with Hunter Harrison himself. To satisfy the demand for a lasting record of these sessions we produced a DVD and sent out thousands of copies. But as successful as the Hunter Camps were, and as informative as the DVD was, managers and employees continued to ask questions about the change of the leadership approach at CN – questions that were best answered in writing. And so the second book came to be.

We called it "Change, Leadership, Mud and Why," and it received the same kind of positive response as the first. "Thanks for telling us about your leadership approach – we get it" was a common refrain. For managers, it became the blueprint for their efforts to engage and inspire their employees. Once again, we received numerous requests for copies from outside the company.

An interesting side effect of publishing the books was the impact it had on Hunter's personal profile (or should I say, celebrity) within the company. Employees would stop him in the hall to ask him to sign their personal copy of the two books; and I had to laugh when managers brought their books to meetings for him to autograph. He always seemed a bit uncomfortable about the whole "celebrity" thing and seemed genuinely humbled by the attention.

It was never our plan from the outset to produce two CEO books. The idea of putting Hunter's ideas on paper just snowballed into the book project. The idea may not have an application for every company. On the other hand, if you want to ensure employees truly understand "how to make money" and "how the CEO leads people", you might find that publishing your CEO's expertise in a book is the same kind of cultural game changer we experienced at CN.

CHAPTER 77: COACHING THE CEO

"A CHRO should develop a contract with the CEO – there should be a high level of trust and transparency, but an understanding that they will not share everything. The CEO must trust the CHRO to protect others' confidentiality while giving him/her critical feedback. In the end, it's all about a high level of trust and judgement."

Katy Barclay, SVP, Human Resources, The Kroger Company

Throughout this book I have advocated a number of different though equally important roles for the CHRO – coach, mentor, people expert and confidante to the CEO to name just a few. Mostly, my thinking is that the CHRO should aspire to be all these things and more because that's what is needed by the company, by the HR team, and by the other members of the C-suite, especially the CEO.

But there are a couple of roles that might, in fact, be best handled by being mutually exclusive. For example, being a coach to the CEO and being the CEO's confidante. This might seem like an odd exclusion to those who think that coach and confidante is the same thing. I assure you, this is no exercise in semantics.

There's no doubt that both roles – CEO coach and CEO confidante – require a high degree of mutual trust and frankness. However, it has been my experience that trying to be both at the same time presents some risks that may cause failure at one or both of these important roles because they have different objectives that at times can be in conflict with each other.

The CEO's coach must focus on the CEO's job performance and professional development as a manager, as a leader, as an administrator and often as the face and voice of the company.

The CEO's confidante, on the other hand, may be required to help the CEO find their way through turmoil at home, or difficulties in relationships at work or outside the corporate world, and may be required to know and keep confidential very intimate details of the CEO's life. Details that the CEO will share only with the most trusted of intimates; a sharing that often goes two ways.

The role that is, of course, most difficult to cultivate and grow is CEO confidante, simply because of the extreme level of personal trust that is required, and the time required to achieve it. It's not that this role is harder than that of coach, or even more important, but it is certainly more personal, potentially more emotional, and more difficult to engender. It is for those reasons that I think the CHRO should aspire to be the CEO confidante first, and, if needed, to forego the role of coach.

This choice also has some practical implications, such as where do you find a CEO coach, or a CEO confidante? The confidante relationship can only be developed over time and with someone the CEO trusts implicitly – there is no yellow-page category for this role. On the other hand, there are excellent CEO coaches who can be hired from the outside. Coaches with tremendous ranges of relevant and applied experience who can do an outstanding job with virtually no prior relationship with the CEO.

My recommendation is for the CEO to have their own personal coach, hired from outside the company, and working in tandem with the CHRO, to help the CEO develop into their role.

Over the years, I have worked with several seasoned and successful CEO coaches; Sandro Iannicca from SICG Consulting, Ned Morse from Boston Consulting Group, and Steve Jacobs from the Continuous Learning Group. These men are very skilled at working with CEOs and know how to build a strong relationship with the CHRO. In addition, I have seen the CEO's coach provide coaching for several of the CEO's direct reports. The coach becomes a team coach as well as a personal coach to the members of the C-suite, including the CEO.

For more about executive coaching, see sections 4, 6, and 11.

> "As the CHRO, you need to build enough trust with the CEO
> to be a truth teller without turning the CEO off."
>
> Ferio Pugliese, EVP & President, WestJet Encore (and former CHRO)

CHAPTER 78:   CEO SUCCESSION PLANNING: BE READY!

> "The internal CEO successors don't need to leave the company if they get turned down. Give them more accountability."
>
> Purdy Crawford, Board Director

If there's one good thing that "hard times" can deliver, it's great insight (a.k.a. 20/20 hindsight) into Board practices in the areas of executive compensation, risk management, and succession planning. This latest recession is no different.

As much as executive compensation and risk management make the headlines when questionable practices are exposed, they do fade over time – especially when the economy or the company's performance improves. Take a look at Wall Street, where Morgan Stanley, not long ago on life support from the U.S. federal government, is now giving out millions in bonuses and the news barely makes a ripple. CEO succession planning, however, will remain under the spotlight because it is the most critical Board task, and failures are front and center with the shareholders, with employees and sometimes with the press. It is also the one Board decision that failure reflects solely on them.

Despite the nature of the job and the characteristics of the typical candidates, CEO succession planning is, for the most part, a straightforward process.

The search for the incumbent's replacement should start long before they leave. In order to make that feasible, the Board must put in place an effective, predictable process to identify and to develop high potential leadership talent that, well in advance of the CEO's departure, begins the process of learning to fill the CEO's shoes.

As always, the best conclusions come from gathering data from as many sources as possible. CEO succession planning steps should include the following:

- Identify potential successors within the organization.

- Determine if executives are really interested in the role – not everyone is.

- Have an outside agency perform an assessment of all candidates to ensure objectivity.

- Put in place appropriate development plans for potential candidates against the estimated timelines for succession.

- Review development plans and measure progress against them on a regular basis.

- Provide high level feedback to candidates on their progress to shape their behaviour in the right direction.

- Always allow, without penalty, the opportunity for candidates to opt out.

Collins, in his book, *How the Mighty Fall*, demonstrates that if a Board chooses the wrong CEO, disaster may only be a short time away. He also reveals a correlation between internal succession into the CEO role and organizational success. To him, the prime sin of leadership is unpredictable, discontinuous change – the graveyard of many once successful companies. Internal candidates may bring change, but with a knowledge of organizational capabilities and values that allows it to be calibrated effectively.

Given the importance of the CEO succession planning and process it is useful to look at some areas where it can go wrong.

(a) The "Friendly" Board

It is not beneficial to have a CEO and Board with a constantly antagonistic relationship,.nor is it advantageous to have a Board that has been stocked with directors who are friendly to the CEO, which is more likely to happen when the CEO and the chair positions are held by the same person. The combined role tends to create a Board which lacks the necessary independence of thought in providing oversight.

For example, in a large packaged goods company that shall remain nameless, the charismatic CEO hand-picked faithful followers to head business units, and the Board rubber stamped his decisions. When health issues and pressure from institutional investors forced the CEO out, the Board at the nod of this individual, appointed his chosen successor. It was a blind decision, as the Board had never taken a hard look at the successor as a potential CEO. Mediocre business results were the outcome.

(b) When the Founder is the CEO

There is a variable track record of success when a CEO is the founder of the company. Not all entrepreneurs can adapt to leading a public company, or accept the limitations it places upon their need for control.

A mid-sized pharmaceutical company had a founder CEO who refused to consider an evaluation process for his role, a reconfigured compensation tied to results, or any succession planning to replace him.

The Board, nervous about alienating him, gave in to his demands to replace the directors who wanted to make such changes to bring the company into line with industry competitors. As a result, there was no successor in the wings, which left the company ill- prepared for continued future success.

(c)   The CEO Who Loves the Job

CEOs who thrive on the challenge of running a company and achieving success with it are often ambivalent about retirement. It is not easy for some CEOs to leave when they are having so much fun! Having a strong, successful CEO in place is an asset to a company, but boards can be swayed to delay succession planning by a CEO's current performance and desire to stay.

One notable company had exactly that situation. When a new Board chair arrived, who insisted on succession planning, the stage was set for a political battle that ran for several years, which ironically delayed proper succession planning. When the CEO retired suddenly, the Board hastily chose a candidate they were not convinced had the potential to be successful; in the "self-fulfilling prophecy" cycle nor did that individual have the advantage of being mentored during an orderly, planned transition.

(d)   Life Happens

Organizations can do everything right with succession planning and selection, but even then the reality is that they can face unpredictable situations at any time that may put their plans in question. One company found itself in that position when the CEO left suddenly before his agreed-upon retirement for a challenge that he could not resist.

While inside candidates had been identified and were in the process of development, they were not yet ready. An internal solution was found to bridge the gap, but this case is a good illustration that efforts at succession planning need to be matched by constant awareness of what can still go awry.

(e)   A Common Theme

A theme common to most of these real life stories is that CEOs are rarely in a hurry to see their successor named and all too often Boards share this lack of urgency, particularly if business seems to be going well. Success however can turn into challenge very quickly (another lesson this recession has taught); much quicker than it takes to put an effective succession plan in place.

There is also another factor to consider. Some recent research from CLG Consultants indicates that while new CEOs are highly confident that they will perform well, the job often turns out to be more complex than most of them had anticipated. A significant percentage of CEOs have reported that a phased transition and a period of mentoring from the outgoing CEO would have been of great value.

The message behind these stories is that it is never too early to begin the process of identifying potential CEO successors and developing them for the role. No matter how successful a CEO is or was, and no matter how reluctant they may be to leave, the inescapable fact is that one way or another they will.

The change to a new CEO can either be a minor blip on the company's timeline or it can be a disastrous failure with extinction-level implications. Either way, success or disaster, the Board and the CHRO will own the outcome.

Reference:

J. Collins, *How the Mighty Fall: And Why Some Companies Never Give In* (New York: Jim Collins Publisher, 2009)

CHAPTER 79:   INTERESTING CEO CHALLENGES

> "As the CHRO, my role was to take stuff off the
> CEO's desk – never dump on it."
>
> Bill Conaty, former SVP, Corporate Human Resources, General Electric

Although some of us find it difficult to accept, the truth is we cannot win every argument. This is especially true for the CHRO role given the nature of their relationship with the CEO and the rest of the C-suite.

In various roles and capacities I have worked with at least ten CEOs who, without exception, were very strong willed and in most cases very determined to do things their way – understandably so, given their success in reaching the big office. I have no doubt that CEOs everywhere exhibit the same strong will, and so in this chapter I am including stories from a number of different CHROs, CEOs and Board directors, and not just my own experience.

(a) Paying Merit Increases

In this particular case, the CEO wanted to ensure his direct reports were not demotivated and insisted they receive annual merit increases regardless of their current position in the salary range. When the CHRO of the company suggested that these executives were paid well above market, the CEO refused to accept the data. He was then shown that the salaries were above the salary range maximum – to no avail. He said they were top performing executives and deserved to get annual increases and his solution was to give them cost-of-living adjustments regardless of their performance levels and market comparisons. Even the HRC and the executive compensation consultant could not persuade him to change his mind. In order to pacify him, everyone relented and the CEO got his way and gave the merit increases.

The CHRO walked away from this argument feeling very frustrated with the outcome, but gratified that the facts supported their assertions.

Scorecard: CEO-1, CHRO-0

(b) Setting Unrealistic Goals

You expect the CEO to set stretch goals for the organization – that's part of their job. In some circles, however, it is considered counterproductive to have both a top-down and a bottom-up process in setting company goals. The top-down goal-setting process is the best approach since the CEO must link the goal setting to the shareholder expectations.

In this case, the CHRO was working with one CEO who believed that the goal-setting process was his opportunity to position himself with the Board and shareholders as a strong leader, by setting very aggressive goals. Unfortunately, his goals were so aggressive as to be essentially unattainable, and his management team, who had bonuses on the line, and who had a more realistic view of the company's prospects, were totally demoralized.

When the CHRO pushed back, his answer was "this is what the shareholders expect from us," ignoring the argument that the goals needed to be realistic or his management team would not work hard to reach them. "If that's the case," he said "then they are not being leaders."

When the Board questioned whether the goals were realistic or not, he told them that "they were in line with shareholder expectations ... aggressive but attainable." The Board eventually accepted his stretch goals, but did make the comment that he was "setting himself up to over promise and under deliver."

The CHRO, however, did not give up and continued to push back with the argument that the performance bonuses were intended to be motivational, and that their motivational value was being destroyed by the unrealistic goals required to earn them, with the ironic upshot being that the goals would be even less likely to be achieved. The CEO was unmoved by the argument and went on to say, "You and I are not on the same page on this one."

The story ended with the company not making their goals and no bonuses were achieved. The CEO was undaunted. "We always set aggressive goals – that is our culture."

Scorecard: CEO-2, CHRO-0

(c)   No Performance Reviews

It is commonly known that most CEOs do not like to give written performance reviews to their subordinates. As one CEO put it, "My people know daily how they are doing – I give feedback every day."

In this example, the CHRO suggested that perhaps a summary in writing would be a good idea. That balloon was shot down with, "This is too much bureaucracy."

In one instance, the CHRO even volunteered to write up the performance reviews. Although the CEO liked the idea (why not?!), at the end of the day they still didn't want to sit down with their staff and discuss the feedback.

Undaunted, the CHRO actually went ahead and met with his peers to review the written report, but as you can imagine the reaction wasn't all that positive. They wondered out loud why the CEO wasn't there. Who could blame them? They were right; the CEO should have been there.

On another occasion, when the CHRO asked the CEO about documenting the poor performance of one of his direct reports, the CEO responded, "Let's make this simple – just cut him a severance cheque." The thought of personally confronting his direct report was so distasteful, that this CEO preferred to write a sizeable cheque and cut his colleague loose.

Since most Board's do not enforce written CEO performance reviews, it is not surprising that most CEOs don't feel compelled to do the same with their staff. This is not to say, however, that no CEO is willing to provide performance reviews. There is the rare one that does it willingly, and then there is the equally rare CEO that gets pushed into it by the Board of Directors.

Although it may not be right away, I am optimistic that a younger generation of CEOs will be more committed to giving performance reviews, and so I'm going to claim partial victory on this one.

Scorecard: CEO-3, CHRO-1

(d)   The Impregnable CEO Inner Circle

Depending on the size of the business, most CEO's have between 8 to 12 direct reports, but that doesn't mean that all of them are involved in the high-level decision-making process. Some CEOs prefer a smaller group of executives – an "inner-circle" of decision-makers often called the Operating Committee or "OC."

In one example, the CHRO worked for a company that was run by the CEO and his OC. When the CHRO asked to be included in the inner circle, he was told "sure", but it never happened. Old habits are hard to change and the CEO was comfortable with the smaller group and the members of it.

You may not be surprised that the CHRO continued to push back – presenting the argument that the rest of his executive team, all direct reports, felt like second-class executives because they were excluded from the OC decision-making process. The CEO's answer was fairly blunt and didn't leave much for room for discussion: "This is how I want to run the company – the OC runs the business and I will inform the rest of the team on key issues."

Sometimes the OC process worked for the CHRO and sometimes it didn't, but he had no choice, he had to work with that structure to get things done even though it was highly inefficient. Eventually the CEO relented, however, and opened up the ranks of the OC to the CHRO.

Scorecard: CEO-3, CHRO-2

(e)   Too Fat Organizational Structure

When the CEO is the architect of the organizational structure, suggesting changes to it is something that you take on at your own risk. That's exactly what the CHRO did in one situation. He advised the CEO that his management infrastructure was too heavy and too costly, and showed him how they compared to other companies with similar profiles; they didn't compare favourably with many more VPs and Directors.

The CEO was unmoved. He said, "Our business is much more complex and requires this extra level of management." The CEO's opinion was pervasive and persuasive. Other senior leaders in the company expressed tacit support for what the CHRO was trying to do, but none would take action alone. If the CEO wasn't for it, they would not openly do anything or even offer their support. So, the intrepid CHRO would have to "go it" alone.

When he told the CEO that he was going to reduce the HR structure to become more competitive with industry counterparts, the CEO didn't stand in his way. But neither did he give his ringing endorsement. It wasn't until the CHRO had finished re-configuring the team and saved $3 million dollars did he receive any positive feedback from the CEO. Even then, the CEO did not insist that other departments should follow the CHRO's lead. Eventually, however, when faced with the realities of a recession, and the logic of the CHRO's business case, he simply could not refuse to make the CHRO's cost-cutting example policy for the rest of the organization.

Scorecard: CEO-3, CHRO-3

(f)   Sticking with Loyal but Underperforming Staff

Most reasonable people agree that loyalty is a good thing. Like most good things, however, too much loyalty or unquestioning of loyalty can be a bad thing – especially in the hands of the CEO.

Most CEOs have one or two players on their team that they turn a blind eye to. They have usually been with the CEO for a long time and are very loyal to them – sometimes even sycophantic – and as often as not they have also been promoted beyond their true capabilities; loyalty standing in for ability and performance. The result is a CEO that has to make unreasonable compromises so that these people can stay on the team; and the balance of the team finds fault with the CEO for doing so and criticizes them behind their back. Not me, mind you, I prefer to levy my criticism by way of a frontal assault.

In one instance, the CHRO confronted the CEO about one such individual and suggested they be demoted to a position more in line with their ability. The CHRO did not get the result he was looking for. Instead of assigning a new position, the CEO reduced the loyal individual's workload by assigning some of their responsibilities to other members of the team. The rationalizations ranged from

"Joe has been very loyal to me and I won't penalize him for a few mistakes" to "Joe is critical to me since he knows how I work – I need him on my team."

Despite the CHRO's misgivings, and regardless of his straight talk with the CEO, this situation continued until the CEO retired. "Joe" left the company shortly thereafter.

Scorecard: CEO-4, CHRO-3

(g) Values Trumps Results

As consumers, we all want the businesses we patronize to operate within a set of high moral and ethical standards which drives their business practices and the way that their employees behave and interact with their clientele. We expect that their internal company values will support these standards and when they don't we punish that business by taking our patronage elsewhere. Values are important to consumers.

As employees and as HR professionals, we can all agree that a proper set of values is essential to the growth and prosperity of the company culture and its business. This set of values is generally developed and extended throughout the company from the top down, and even though they might not be formally written down, employees usually know the behaviours expected of them and know the consequences of going outside the lines.

Having said that, some CEOs are not always consistent when it comes to balancing the requirement for employees to adhere to the company's values versus the drive to achieve positive business results. Often, we see the imbalance in favour of getting good business results, and the company's employees find themselves in the uncomfortable position of having to break the "values" rules in favour of revenue or cost cutting or profit.

Sometimes the imbalance goes the other way.

In one situation, the CEO had done a great job in outlining the required leadership values for the organization, even insisting on a set of supporting actions like training and rewards and recognition to ensure leaders understood these values. The performance review program had the values embedded into the process and, over time, meeting the company's values became the paramount metric for success.

When the CHRO first joined this company, one of his first observations was just how prevalent the corporate values were within the company. When he asked one senior executive what it was like to work there, they said, "We are very values based."

Shortly afterward, his next observation revealed the camouflaged fly in the ointment. Although virtually all of the leaders received high ratings for meeting the values requirements, fully 25% of them were not meeting their business objectives. The question was: why?

When the CHRO posed that question to his peers, the answers received ranged from "too new on the job" to "our performance standards are very high." Well, okay – I can understand someone new to the job taking some time to ramp up their performance, but based on all evidence the company's performance standards were totally realistic. It was highly unlikely that "too high" objectives was the answer.

Eventually another truth began to emerge. The reality was that if a leader consistently achieved high scores on their values assessment, they did not have to deliver business results in order to keep their job or maintain their standing. One person there put it very succinctly "Values trump results in this company."

When the CHRO talked with the CEO about it, however, he was surprised to hear about the leeway granted poor performers because that was never his intent. Yes he wanted an emphasis on company values, but never at the expense of business results.

Accordingly, the message to refocus on the proper balance between the two was cascaded to the senior team; that his expectation is, and always was, high performance in both values and business results.

Scorecard: CEO-4, CHRO-4

(h)   Using Job Titles to Motivate People

There is no doubt that there is a certain motivational value to giving out VP and Director titles to reward good performance. In most companies, the CEO is part of this approval process and as befitting the responsibilities that usually go with these titles, they are not quickly or frivolously handed out. There are some CEOs, however, who see the job title as a simple perk and hand them out like so much candy, stirring up a boat load of trouble for the CHRO.

In this example, the CEO who did this was questioned by his CHRO about the appropriateness of handing out a lot of VP titles; the CEO's response was, "We don't mind having more VP's in the company. The job title is cheaper than giving out big raises and bonuses." For further justification he referenced the banking industry and their predilection for handing out titles. When the CHRO countered that their industry was different and did not use titles that way, his response was "I want us to be different."

It was soon apparent that this CEO saw no risk in giving out titles in this manner. To him it was an easily-managed, cost-effective and highly motivational process. The CHRO had more concern with the possible downside than he did – possible dilution of the role, creeping compensation expectations and resentment from the other, "more legitimate", VPs on the team. If the CEO actually recognized these risks, he was obviously willing to take them.

Scorecard: CEO-5, CHRO-4

(i)   Asking for Bonus Exceptions

Despite the lurid headlines to the contrary, a CEO's bonus plan is most often tied to the achievement of their performance goals, and so typically when a CEO does not meet their annual performance objectives they do not receive a bonus payment. On the other hand, most CEOs meet their goals and the bonus approval process in that instance is usually very straight forward.

There are circumstances, however, when some external factor beyond the CEO's control can disrupt the company from achieving their annual performance object-ive, and in these situations it is not unusual for the CEO to go to bat for his management team and ask the Board for a bonus payment exception. It is also not unusual for the Board to be predisposed to grant the request.

In one such case, the company came very close to meeting their objectives, but just missed due to a once-in-a-decade circumstance that was unpredictable, uncon-trollable, and impossible to mitigate. The CEO was well aware of the unusual circumstances behind the company's failure to make its numbers, but when the CHRO asked him if he was going to request a bonus exception, he said this, "No, we set aggressive goals and when we meet them, we get paid very well. When we don't, we don't get a bonus."

The CHRO was expecting a different kind of response, and so he continued the discussion, presenting the option of requesting a partial bonus in light of the exceptional circumstances. If anything, the CEO's position seemed to harden, "I am *not* going to ask for relief – my credibility will be called into question if I do."

The CHRO took out his last arrow, notched it into his bow, and shot back, "The team worked exceptionally hard against difficult circumstances and even then, fell just short of the minimum; and what's more the HRC Chair is amiable to this recommendation – can we reconsider?"

The rock finally moved and the CEO relented and accepted the input from the CHRO and his peers and allowed a partial bonus payment in light of the exceptional circumstances.

The CEO and the CHRO relationship was strained for many weeks after this event; however, the CHRO felt the gratitude of his peers for leading the charge.

Scorecard: CEO-5, CHRO-5

"The key skills that I value in a CHRO are strong emotional intelligence, empathy, toughness, yet with the humility to listen and change course if there is a good reason. Above all, it is to be able to tell me the truth, as brutal as it may be."

Joe Jimenez, CEO, Novartis

Supporting the Rest of the C-Suite

> "The CEO and CHRO have a special relationship beyond other
> C-suite interactions, notably the level of intimacy."
>
> Michael McCain, CEO, Maple Leaf Foods

CHAPTER 80: EXECUTIVE COACHING: IF TIGER WOODS NEEDS A COACH, DO YOU?

> "It is a massive change to go from a business unit head to the CEO's
> role."
>
> Joe Jimenez, CEO, Novartis

The popular understanding of the nature of "coaching" and "coach" is that of an older, wiser, more experienced mentor imparting new understanding to the younger, less experienced, less wise student. In a lot of cases, perhaps most cases, this is the true nature of the relationship. We see it all the time with sports teams and in our schools and all sorts of activities. But if this was an absolute relationship, how do we then explain the fact that Tiger Woods, arguably the best golfer the world has ever seen, needs a coach? Why does any sports figure at the zenith of their career, for that matter, need a coach? And yet many have one. Conversely, one could legitimately ask the question, "If the coach knows so much about the subject, why are they a coach and not actually doing the very thing that they are teaching?"

The answer to both these questions is the same, and it has two parts to it.

The first part is the assumption that everyone at the top of their game is fully developed, complete, and incapable of improvement; and the second is that the process of coaching is the same as doing the activity. In other words, the assumption is that to be a golf coach, you have to be a good golfer.

Both assumptions are incorrect, especially as it applies to executive coaching.

No matter how complete and accomplished an executive might be, the environment in which they compete is always changing. Entry into a new role, or a change in business demands, for example, can reveal opportunities for change or improvement. Additionally, executives often find themselves isolated, without any source of objective feedback on their performance, as work associates may tell them what they "want" to hear, rather than what they "need" to hear.

Under some or all of these circumstances, executives often encounter barriers to achieving maximal business results. Barriers that only an objective expert observer might recognize. Enter the executive coach.

There are a host of good training programs on the market, but they may not be calibrated well to the needs of executives. The better solution is to provide executives with a coach to assist them with their specific individual issues to help them perform to their full potential. The key is to ensure that the executive and the coach are well matched and have good rapport.

Being an executive coach is not the same as being an executive. Executive coaching entails different processes of objective observation, discovery, analysis and solutions-development that is not the same as being an executive.

Every coaching assignment can differ, but some of the main steps remain the same:

Feedback. While work associates may not give direct feedback to an executive, they will to a coach. Under a confidentiality agreement, they are free to describe the individual's strengths and limitations. Other forms of assessment may also be used.

Job shadowing. While feedback from others is highly useful, an experienced coach will want to observe the individual in action. That observation gives a context to feedback.

Development plan. Feedback from all sources and the coach's observations are aggregated and delivered to the executive. From the discussion around this report comes an agreement on what to work on, and a development plan with specific steps and timelines.

Execution of plan. Coaching is likely to take the form of an ongoing dialogue with the executive, although specific skills training or knowledge acquisition may be included. The emphasis is on real business challenges and handling issues as they arise.

There are many benefits to coaching and a coach's role is varied to the specific needs of the client.

A coach serves as:

- a third-party objective advisor, whose focus is on the needs of the individual executive;

- a sounding board for ideas and problem-solving, who can ask the right questions to clarify issues, as well as counsel and caution;

- a provider of ongoing feedback on leadership and strategic behaviours, as well as support, encouragement, and any needed reality checks; and

- an information source for benchmarking and current practices across industries.

CHAPTER 81: JOINT ACCOUNTABILITY FOR COMPANY RESULTS

> "You can't be just supporting the CEO –
> there are 15 other peers who must be satisfied."
>
> John Lynch, SVP, Corporate Human Resources, General Electric

In terms of who is accountable for meeting which company objective, my philosophy is that as a group, all the C-suite executives are equally responsible for meeting all the objectives. Together we were charged with developing the strategy and executing the business plan and we built and designed the incentive plan which was designed to reward the team's efforts. Our bonus plan was based on company metrics like revenue and profit, which we all owned.

In order to put this philosophy into action, in one company we eliminated the executives' personal goals from the bonus plan so that we were all measured on the same company-wide metrics. This company-centric focus really encouraged the executives to take the high road when dealing with issues. It was easier to focus on what was good for the business rather than any individual function.

For example, in one situation, the executive team was confronted with taking a strike to maintain our labour relations strategy. The team knew the strike would be very costly and that ultimately we would miss our company profit target which would result in no bonus for the year. The CEO and his executive team knew that the right thing to do was take the strike, and no one had an individual motive to disagree. This joint solidarity allowed me as the CHRO to negotiate the right labour agreement rather than being subject to pressure to compromise so the bonus plan would not be affected.

When you have joint accountability for company results, the C-suite team acts more like shareholders. In one situation, I complained to my C-suite peers that they were not acting like common shareholders. We were expected to own lots of company stock, but we were not acting like joint shareholders in maximizing the company's performance. This shareholder reference was an "ah ha" moment for the team.

CHAPTER 82: TEAM BUILDING

> "As a new CHRO, you need to spend time with the C-suite to see how they tick, what matters to them and assess the current impact of HR."
>
> Peter Goerke, Group Human Resources Director, Prudential PLC

There are many pages in this book dedicated to the merits and the risks associated with performance management and in particular the annual review and other feedback mechanisms – mostly related to employees, both unionized and not. Most sizeable companies today have a process in place that provides employees with some sort of understanding about their performance and their standing within the company. But what about the senior executive team? Even in companies with sophisticated performance management programs in place for employees, the members of the executive team typically do not receive a formal review from their boss, the CEO.

There are many varied and historical reasons for this, usually revolving around the notion that the CEO's relationship with his direct reports are intimate enough and strong enough that this information is presented almost on a daily basis and therefore the executives are aware at any given time how their performance is being perceived. This is often stated as, "You will know if you're not doing a good job." So the understanding becomes, "No news is good news.Additionally, there is the idea that senior executives are perceptive enough, self-aware enough, and responsible and accountable enough, that they will know their performance is lagging even before their boss does – and self-correct. Depending on the individual, this may or may not be the case, but, in any event, the lack of CEO feedback does impact the teamwork of the C-suite members. If the CEO does not explicitly state that "team-work' matters, the team will operate as silos; working together enough to get things done, but not in a way that leverages the full benefits of a strong team. The concept is pretty simple; rather than being accountable to just themselves for their perform-ance, C-suite executives need to be accountable to the entire team, and that can only happen if the CEO makes them accountable in a formal and transparent way.

In most cases, the CHRO has the opportunity to take on the role of "team coach" if they believe in teamwork and have the courage to coach and confront other mem-bers of the team. I remember in one situation, my peers were afraid of the CEO and, as such, developed a strong bond to protect themselves. Not necessarily by upping their game, but rather by creating a multi-lateral "cover-your-a*s" (CYA) pact – in essence becoming each other's apologists. As the CHRO, I was tasked with the job of convincing the CEO to tone down his intimidation approach so the team would do the right things versus avoiding the CEO's wrath. At the same time, I had to get the team to be more open to feedback and dialogue.

My advice to any CHRO is to take on the role of facilitator for all team meetings. This will allow the CEO to participate and make decisions without worrying about "owning the pen". As well, it will give you the opportunity to control the flow of the meetings.

And finally, as the CHRO, think about increasing your value to the CEO by pro-viding other team members with feedback about their behaviour in team settings; by offering congratulations where appropriate, and by confronting those acting like "jerks" when needed, especially when you know it's likely that the CEO won't. Do everyone a favour and step in as the talent manager and do it yourself.

CHAPTER 83: WORKING WITH THE CFO

"Next to the CEO, I have come to value the CHRO together with the
CFO as the indispensable players in a performing organization.
If the CEO drives the bus, these two key advisors manage the fuel –
both human and financial resources. I must admit that this was not
always my view as I held a deep skepticism over the contribution
of staff officers who were all too often self-aggrandizing and over-
compensated. As I became more deeply involved in the HRC functions,
however, I came to appreciate the role that a truly capable CHRO could
play – and the damage that could be done by one less competent."

Gordon Ritchie, Board Director

Of all the members of the C-suite, the CFO is the one role where I had the biggest
relationship challenges. In some cases, it was because the CFO did not value my
office's contribution to the business because it couldn't necessarily be measured
in dollars. It was all too common to hear the CFO say, "We can't measure the
return on these HR programs – you're spending money on a prayer versus real
facts." This is a serious issue when you look at it from the CFO's perspective
because their role is to challenge any expenditure that cannot be justified in terms
of return on investment.

Therefore, the CHRO must know the numbers and work with the CFO to develop
a business case for each initiative. I found that when I asked the CFO to co-spon-
sor an initiative, we were an incredible team. In particular, the CFO is always
interested in designing the executive compensation program. This is helpful since
the CHRO must have the CFO's input on these types of programs anyway. In one
case, I brought the CFO into a Board presentation to help sell a new compensation program and he did a fantastic job including taking most of the Board's
questions – much to my delight and the Chair of the HRC.

The other challenging situation that I've encountered in a relationship with a CFO
is when they believed I was replacing them as the CEO's confidante.

Historically, the CEO works most closely with the CFO as their go-to "numbers"
person and often there is a unique bond that develops between them. With the rise
in importance of the people strategy, the CEO is now relying more on the CHRO
as their go-to "people" person and coach on critical issues. As a result, there is
tension created between the CFO and the CHRO.

In a related example, I was coaching the CEO on his decision-making approach and the organizational processes, and the CFO was incensed that he was not part of these discussions. Unfortunately, the CFO was used to my predecessor taking a back seat on these issues and he was the direct advisor to the CEO. We ultimately reached a truce and ended up meeting jointly each week to discuss issues and essentially tag-teamed the CEO on controversial matters.

This love/hate relationship between the CFO and CHRO can also be influenced by the CFO's ambition to be the primary successor to the CEO. Having a CHRO with influence in deciding not only who the successor is, but having an active involvement in assessing internal candidates for the CEO succession, could be seen as a major threat to some CFOs.

In my experience, the best CFOs understand the role of the CHRO in CEO succession planning. The best example of a great CFO in my experience has to be Claude Mongeau at CN. I worked with Claude for 7 years before he took over as CEO. Claude was a pleasure to deal with as a peer – he gave me direct feedback on the merits of my business cases and he looked for active feedback from me on his personal development. He was a CHRO's dream partner in the C-suite.

> "The CHRO must have a great fit with the CEO and CFO.
> I had wonderful relationships with CFOs."
>
> Bill Conaty, former SVP, Corporate Human Resources, General Electric

CHAPTER 84: CONFRONTING A POOR-PERFORMING EXECUTIVE

> "Chemistry is key between CEO and CHRO –
> they need to make "gut calls" together."
>
> Joe Jimenez, CEO, Novartis

Of all the roles I played as CHRO, the one that I felt I really earned my salary the most was in working with one of my C-suite peers as they were struggling in their job.

In my experience, most C-suite executives get promoted to their jobs through a combination of their technical skills, their results orientation, and their leadership skills. Unfortunately, a C-suite role also requires strategic thinking and the ability to fit with the CEO and the rest of his team, which is more difficult to acquire. C-suite leaders are rarely fired due to a lack of results or unethical/unlawful behaviours.

When I think about C-suite executives who I have exited from the company, I find the reasons for their failure typically fall into one of three categories. First is not being a good "fit" with the CEO or the team; second disagreement with the CEO on strategy; and third, the executive does not collaborate well with their peers.

Fit is such a difficult thing to describe and even more difficult to fix. As one CEO explained, "You know it when you have it." This is true, but not beneficial in helping someone fit into a team. In some respects, it's easier if people can see the "odd duck" or "loner" behaviours of the executive before they are place in a C-suite position. Most executives can adapt to their new CEO or their peers, however, there are instances where no chemistry exists between the executive and the CEO or the C-suite team members. This is usually when an outsider is hired for the role.

Internal promotions will tend to mitigate the chances of a bad fit, but when it happens, it's usually no one's fault and typically, as CHRO, it's up to you to take care of the situation. Personally, I would sit down with the executive and ask how they are feeling about their "fit" with the CEO or the team. In most cases, they'll indicate that they're not happy and we'll discuss an exit strategy. In the unique circumstance of their not being aware of their impact with the CEO or team, I would be more direct with specific examples. Unless this blind spot can be easily corrected, an agreement to a transition period to exit the company will be worked out. Fit is so hard to fix in the short term and if the CEO is not patient, showing the executive the door is often the outcome.

When the executive and the CEO do not agree on the company strategy or how the function should be run, a major knock-out blow to the relationship is the result. Sometimes, this situation is caused by the CEO who is too domineering in their point of view or it may be that the CEO is a micro-manager who wants to run everything. In my own experience, I worked for one CEO who literally wanted a say in all HR program design and execution. On the one hand, I was impressed with his interest in HR, but I was totally frustrated by his intrusion. He would sometimes say "there are two CHROs in the company." This did not sit well with me. We ultimately worked out a compromise and I stayed with the company. However, if the CEO and the executive are butting heads on the company's strategy, it is unlikely their relationship will get much better. If the CFO or the Chief Marketing Officer is in violent disagreement with the CEO on the business strategy, one of them will have to leave and it is unlikely to be the CEO. In cases such as these, I would try to mediate a successful resolution to the disagreement or sit down with the executive and discuss their exit strategy. I was never really successful in resolving these major strategic differences.

A C-suite executive who does not collaborate well, or at all, with their peers presents another problematic scenario. The individual may be a great person to have a drink with or to go out to dinner with, but the issue is that they are fundamentally wired to do their own thing without working across the organization. Since the C-suite is most effective as a "team sport", this independent operating style will quickly become dysfunctional with the other team members.

The cause for this dysfunctional behaviour could be that the executive has a blind spot or simply that they feel they know best for their function. I believe collaboration can be encouraged and coached by the CHRO and all is not necessarily lost. In most cases, I have been successful in turning around the behaviour with the executive. However, in cases when the individual is more like an "Attila the Hun" leader and is very unlikely to change enough to be a legitimate collaborator, I have had to ask that they leave the company .Team building is a critical skill that all successful CHROs need to have. Occasionally, bringing in an external team coach is a great solution especially if the CHRO is part of the problem. As the saying goes "you can win as a team and you lose as individuals".

CHAPTER 85:   WORKING IN A MATRIX STRUCTURE

"You influence the CEO and C-suite peers without authority.
Need to be mature enough to handle issues and back off
when you are unable to influence them."

Ferio Pugliese, EVP & President, WestJet Encore (and former CHRO)

In large companies, we often find multiple business units combined with stand-alone functional leaders (i.e., CFO, CHRO, CMO, etc.); a matrix structure designed to leverage the functional expertise within each business unit, such as marketing, finance or HR. Like most organizational designs, however, the matrix comes with its shortcomings as well as its strengths. The president of each of the multiple business units will want to control all functions to achieve their business goals; marketing, sales, finance, operations and human resource departments, for example. Since this has great merit, the corporation needs to avoid duplication of efforts, hoarding of talent, and different processes and systems.

To maximize the autonomy of the business unit structure while maximizing the use of people and resources, large companies often create centers of excellence with functional leaders. The best way to make this work is to have highly respected C-suite executives who are technically sharp in their functions, are great collaborators, are strong talent masters, and are incentivized to deliver on total company goals. These functional centers of excellence must be small in staff and not be too involved in the tactical part of the business. Their primary focus can be centered on strategy development and the strategic movement of talent so that some functions can be removed from the business unit and run as centralized functions. They can include corporate functions, such as Information Systems, Human Resources, Legal, Logistics, Procurement, Engineering, and Corporate Affairs. In some large companies, the business units are primarily sales and marketing functions and are supported by functional groups including manufacturing.

My own take on the matrix structure is that it must be kept simple. Executives need to be able to navigate the structure to get things done; processes need to be common to avoid confusion; systems need to be leveraged across the company; and talent must be carefully managed to maximize retention.

Additionally, incentive programs need to be team-based and performance metrics made clear to all employees. On a personal level, I have seen matrix structures turn into major bureaucracies and power struggles. On the other hand, a well-run matrix structure can harness the critical talent and develop great leaders. The bottom line is that you must work smarter to make a matrix structure work and the rewards will be greater.

In some organizations with matrix structures, the CHRO is the focal point for C-suite harmony. In other companies, the CHRO is the facilitator for C-suite rhythms.

In my own case, I felt the CEO was the quarterback for the C-suite. He consulted with everyone but ultimately made the key decisions and orchestrated the business strategies. The CHRO role that I played involved ensuring the C-suite had performance goals that supported the CEO's strategy and were aligned across the various functions in the company. In addition, I would ensure the C-suite members were working together to efficiently get things done.

In some circumstances, I would facilitate the team's meetings to guide the team and the CEO to a resolution of issues. I felt the C-suite members needed to be aligned on organizational structures (spans and layers) along with collaborating on budget setting. There needed to be some give and take on how we spent our monies throughout the year.

When we met, I would emphasize the following four types of meetings:

1. *Problem resolution*: you have an issue that requires a fix (i.e., sales miss for the month).

2. *Decision to make*: the team has gathered all of the information needed to select an option (i.e., hiring a manager).

3. *Develop a plan of action*: the team has decided on a strategy, but now needs to develop an execution plan (i.e., launch a new product).

4. *Status updates*: the team needs to be informed on the status of the business (i.e., monthly executive meeting).

In all of the afore-mentioned meetings, the CHRO can be the meeting facilitator. This role can add value to the team by allowing each of the meeting participants (including the CEO) to actively be engaged in the session. In addition, the CHRO will learn more about the business as the meeting facilitator.

A command center view provides the CHRO the ability to guide the C-suite team on critical aspects that need to be managed. They include:

1. *People*: do we have the right players?

2. *Strategy*: do we have the vision and strategic plans to win in the marketplace?

3. *Structure*: are we organized to execute our strategies and tactics?

4. *Systems*: do we have the information systems to track our progress and identify shortfalls and opportunities?

5. *Processes*: do we have the most efficient processes to get work done in the company?

6. *Rewards*: are the incentive and recognition plans in place to reward the right behaviours and results?

7. *Culture*: do we have the right leadership approach in place to reinforce the employee behaviours that will drive business results?

CHAPTER 86:   CHIEF OPERATIONS OFFICER

> "I can buy a lot of CFOs and corporate lawyers but what I can't find is a great operating person who knows the business."
>
> Hunter Harrison, CEO, Canadian Pacific

The Chief Operations Officer is sometimes called the Chief Supply Chain Officer or the Chief Manufacturing Officer. Regardless of the title, this role encompasses the manufacturing, logistics, procurement, distribution, and engineering functions of most companies. It is also the role that manages the largest number of employees and managers in the company. Not surprisingly it is also a role that, as the CHRO, I have paid a lot of attention to.

Of all the different ways we can look at complex businesses, one of the most simple is this: in any company there are only two critical roles, those who make the product and those who sell it. The people who make the product ultimately work for the Chief Operations Officer. In every company I've worked for, they were my biggest customer. Because this function makes products every day, sometimes 24/7, the COO often measures performance in units per minute or hour; compared to most other functions that measure their progress over a much longer time frame. As far as the COO is concerned, the role of the CHRO is to help him make his numbers each hour, each day, each week, and each month.

The COO is usually a leader that has a more predominant "command and control" leadership style which is more conducive to the typical "assembly line" processes, and so they are typically not inclined to value HR solutions that are longer term in nature. Having said that, even though they look for more immediate results, if the CHRO can demonstrate a solution that can transform the entire organization and result in a steep change in performance, you can usually get their attention.

My favourite COO was Jim Krushelniski at Heinz. Jim was a university graduate who started in the agriculture department, moved into procurement, then distribution, and ultimately transferred into the direct manufacturing function. Based on his broad supply-chain background, he knew a lot about how all of the functions needed to work together, but his major strengths were his results orientation and his ability to hold people accountable.

His direct reports nicknamed him the "Krusher", in part from his name and physical size, but also because of his leadership style and high performance standards. In reality, his bark was worse than his bite and he had a tremendous following amongst his team. I was the HR person supporting Jim and he pushed me hard on many fronts to support his key goals. When we did a good job for him, he was great at recognizing my team. He was also quick to recognize and reward the top performers on his team, and it was always an easy thing to help out there too.

One of the toughest situations we encountered together occurred when one of his top performing managers harassed a female staff member. At that time, in the mid 1990's, the company might have simply reprimanded the employee; however, I believed very firmly that the offense was egregious enough to justify dismissal. Understandably, Jim was conflicted in making the decision – this was a loyal manager with a record of success, and he felt a strong sense of loyalty to anyone who was loyal to him. The tide turned, however, when I suggested to him that the female employee could have been his daughter. That seemed to focus his thinking solely on the issue and the manager was let go.

Jim later became a group president responsible for multiple companies around the world. He eventually retired from Heinz and I wish him nothing but the best.

I have enjoyed working with the COO role and their team. They work at a high pace and are always demanding clients, but they also make the product, and there is nothing more fundamental to doing business than that.

CHAPTER 87: CHIEF MARKETING OFFICER

"You need to interpret the outside world, move in a fast paced world and have timely access to relevant data."

Claude Mongeau, CEO, Canadian National

If you started this book at the beginning – and of course, you did – then you know that my post-secondary education was in marketing, and so wherever I have worked I've had a "soft" spot for the marketing function.

In some companies or some industries, the Chief Marketing Officer is the dominant, most powerful role in the C-suite, while in others it is more of a neutral staff function. In the consumer products world, for example, the CMO is very influential because of their accountability for new-product innovation and consumer insights, both of which are critical to success. On the other hand, in a railway company, for example, where the focus is on operational excellence, the CMO is combined with the sales management portfolio.

My experience with CMOs has been mixed. The best ones are people who have a real commercial sense (versus a strong technical orientation) and a strong general management focus. This makes them the glue that combines the cost side (supply chain) with the consumer focus and the retail customer perspective. And although they know the numbers well, their real strength is in creating a vision for the product portfolio and motivating all functions to strive to achieve the business goals. In a sense, the CMO is the perfect training ground for the next CEO since their general management focus is like a mini-CEO role.

The worst CMOs in my opinion, are those who are focused on the *mechanics* of marketing. They love advertising, and relish the thrill of consumer research and writing crisp marketing plans. Don't get me wrong, these are all valid and necessary activities to be sure, but their contribution to the bottom line should be the priority and not the activity itself.

Another personal point of contention regarding some CMOs is their tendency to focus unduly on job titles and levels, combined with a lack of awareness about spans of control or the need to have fewer organizational levels. They want to give their people fancy titles and pay them at the P75th salary level (perhaps part of a need to be the *prima donna* – always in the limelight). From a CHRO perspective, these CMOs can be most difficult to deal with and usually garner the most complaints from their peers – the charge being arrogance and a pompous attitude. [End mini-rant.]

In my opinion, the CMO must put the business first ahead of the fun mechanical parts of marketing. The best CMOs I have worked with could do this. Doug Tough, currently CEO with International Flavors & Fragrances, was one such CMO I had the pleasure of working with. Classically trained in marketing Doug was hired directly out of university to work at Procter & Gamble, where he stayed for 12 years. When I was with Cadbury Schweppes, we recruited Doug to be the top marketing executive in our Canadian candy business. We found out soon enough that even though he was steeped in the marketing discipline, he was first and foremost a business man. He successfully ran several businesses with Cadbury and moved internationally. He subsequently left Cadbury to become CEO at Ansell, and, as I noted above, is now CEO with International Flavors & Fragrances. What struck me most about Doug was his fantastic combination of intellectual horsepower, people development orientation, and great business acumen – a great role model for all CMOs.

CHAPTER 88: CHIEF SALES OFFICER

> "Future CEO's will be confronted with more educated and discerning customers with more choices. You will want more strategic partnerships with them."
>
> Michael McCain, CEO, Maple Leaf Foods

In contrast to the Chief Marketing Officer, the Chief Sales Officer is a relatively new C-suite role. In the past, the sales head typically worked for the CMO. Today, with the sophistication of retail customers in the consumer packaging industry, the CSO is becoming more valued and respected as the retail trade in North America and in Europe consolidates its power over consumers, manufacturers and suppliers.

The Chief Sales Officer usually manages a large "trade" budget consisting of listing fees, volume discounts, etc., to fight for sales to major customers like Wal-Mart, Kroger's, Costco and Target. These customers have very strong buyers who are analytical and aggressive negotiators and they know how to leverage their company's weight in the market to extract all kinds of monetary and non-monetary consideration from their suppliers.

In order to compete in this environment, manufacturers have had to redefine the sales function and strengthen the quality and expertise of the person occupying the top sales office. No longer is the head of sales just the relationship person who entertains the customer. Now, in addition to being relationship-oriented, they also have to understand the full financial picture of their own company and the profit and loss story for each of their customers.

In my view, today's CSO role is much like the CMO and CFO roles – a new competitive environment has necessitated a very different and much higher caliber of talent as the new minimum qualification.

Like a lot of companies, Maple Leaf Foods doesn't have this role in its structure, relying instead on sales executives to lead the function in the bigger business units. Nonetheless, looking at the skills needed for a great Chief Sales Officer, one of the Maple Leaf sales executives is a good example of what it takes – Adam Grogan.

Adam graduated from York University with an MBA and went straight to work at Maple Leaf Foods, starting as a management trainee. He worked in various parts of the business and spent a considerable period in marketing; and so when the MLF Consumer Foods business established its Customer Business Teams, he became the CBT VP and General Manager for the Loblaws account. Loblaws, as you know, is the biggest food retailer in Canada. Adam's success with Loblaws led to his promotion to run the entire sales function at MLF Consumer Foods. He is clearly an excellent role model for the top sales role in the new era.

CHAPTER 89:   CHIEF INFORMATION OFFICER

"Become current on technology and information. The technology proponent competencies are among the more intriguing and potentially powerful findings of this study. Effectiveness in this domain may not have the same impact on personal effectiveness as in the credible activist domain, but it has considerably greater impact on business performance – as much impact as any other area of HR involvement, in fact. However, technology is changing how work is done in dramatic and unexpected ways, and it is essential that HR have both knowledge and expertise in understanding the effects of new analytical and social media technology. The new HRCS suggests that automating administrative and transactional work is the tip of the HR iceberg. HR needs to go beyond using technology to do HR work more efficiently and use technology to drive knowledge and relationship inside and outside the company. For example, HR professionals need to be more adept at connecting people and work through technology. Today's work is not only defined by geographic or functional boundaries, but it is also defined by common interests."

D. Ulrich, J. Younger, W. Brookbank, and M. Ulrich, *HR from the Outside In: Six Competencies for the Future of Human Resources* (New York: McGraw-Hill, 2012), p. 253

There was a time, not that long ago, when the term "nerd" was considered a derogatory reference to people who are obsessed with highly-technical things. In recent years, like a lot of pejoratives, the term has been reclaimed and is now considered something of a badge of honour and pride, and group identity.

As an interesting side note, if you started this book at the beginning, you know that my HR career started at Nortel, a Canadian high-tech giant that, at its zenith, employed almost 100,000 people around the world and could trace its origins as far back as Alexander Graham Bell. One of the earlier iterations of the company was called the Northern Electric Research and Development Laboratories, or, "N.E.R.D." as it was often referred to. There are some who believe that this was, in fact, the origin of the term in use today.

When I joined CN Rail as the head of HR, I inherited responsibility for the Information Services department (IS), thus completing the circle from my beginnings at NERD's successor company, to being the head NERD at CN. At CN, the IS function was the glue that kept all functions wired together. It was a very large unit with over 600 people and it had a huge operating and capital budget. I was stoked.

At first I thought this would be a great combination – people and systems – what could be better than that? The VP who ran the shop day-to-day, Fred Grigsby, reported to me, so it didn't matter much that I had no real IT education or training; but, nonetheless, I relished the thought of making a difference. Eighteen months later, however, I had changed my mind. Not only was Fred running the shop well, he was running it well without any practical help from me. I wasn't qualified to head IS and I wasn't adding any value to the relationship with Fred. I made up my mind what I had to do, and it was going to be controversial.

I booked a meeting with the CEO and made my case: "Fred should be promoted to CIO and report directly to you." What?! – Indeed, he was surprised – as was Fred. When I explained why I would give up this accountability, he had to agree that it was in everyone's best interest. So the CEO agreed to the move and the new C-suite role was created, quickly becoming one of the most critical C-suite contributors at CN.

Hunter Harrison, who became CEO after Fred's promotion, really leveraged the IS team to create a competitive advantage and while other railroads tried to replicate the CN systems, they never could. Fred Grigsby was an engineer who worked hard to bring value to the IS group – due to the nature of the business his job was basically 24/7.

The irony of Fred's success was that in one conversation with Hunter he could be praised mightily for his group's creativity and hard work in bringing new systems to CN, and then scolded for how many passwords Hunter was required to remember.

The CIO in today's world has become much more business savvy and is no longer the weird guy who is hard to talk with. Many companies have a greater turnover rate for CIOs than other C-suite roles because they are in great demand as companies make major changes to IT systems and processes. Another potential factor in this high turnover rate may be the system itself. SAP seems to be the favourite enterprise system out there, however, not all CIOs are compatible with it. I know of one company that turned the CIO over three times before the SAP system was finally installed.

From an HR perspective, supporting the CIO and his department is an on-going challenge, especially during a SAP installation. Finding qualified talent for the IS team is the major issue. Fortunately, with many more companies having SAP or related enterprise experiences, the talent base is growing.

CHAPTER 90:   WORKING WITH A SIX SIGMA FUNCTION

"Everyday behavior is so important—and so neglected—that in the years ahead, competitive advantage in any industry or geography will flow as much from behavioral leadership as from new strategies, processes, or technologies. In fact, behavioral leadership techniques will get your existing strategies, processes, and technologies working to their full potential by reducing the hidden human barriers that so often scuttle them."

S. Jacobs, The Behavior Breakthrough: Leading Your Organization to a New Competitive Advantage (Austin: Greenleaf Book Group Press, 2013)

The improvement process known as Six Sigma was actually created by Motorola in 1981, but few people outside of Motorola knew about it until Jack Welch at GE made it famous in 1995.Outside of what I had read about it in terms of GE's experience, I had no direct exposure to Six Sigma and although we considered adopting it at CN Rail, we chose not to because we felt the organization was not ready for the level of work that would have been required to install it.

All that changed for me when I joined Maple Leaf Foods, and now I am very familiar with the Six Sigma function, especially as it applies to a manufacturing company. I would describe the SS tools as performance enablers that are particularly effective in a manufacturing environment. From my CHRO perspective, the best approach to leveraging the Six Sigma methodology is to ensure C-suite endorsement; but an endorsement as an enabler for continuous process improvement, not as a focus of the culture.

Many companies have evolved their use of the SS tools; where at one time they started with a small core of a centralized group of Black Belts, they now have a very large number of BB's and these people have taken on senior positions throughout the company, with the result being that Six Sigma processes in many ways have become the norm for doing business.

My caution to companies who are considering implementing the Six Sigma approach is to keep it simple and initially grounded in areas such as manufacturing where continuous improvement is a necessity to survival. Stepping straight into the Six Sigma world in a marketing or sales environment can be a tricky introduction to the Six Sigma tools, and perhaps better suited to a later launch once it is up and running in other areas of the company.

CHAPTER 91: CHIEF STRATEGY OFFICER

> "In the future, CEOs will face a higher level of strategic volatility in business – technology, globalization and environmental disruptors."
>
> Michael McCain, CEO, Maple Leaf Foods

"Strategy: attaining and maintaining a position of advantage over adversaries through the successive exploitation of known or emergent possibilities rather than committing to any specific fixed plan designed at the outset."

When you consider what strategy really is, versus tactical execution, I'm hard pressed to think of anyone in the C-suite who doesn't have the responsibility for developing strategy – especially the CEO, CFO, and CMO. Depending on the industry and the size of the company, however, there may be a need for a dedicated Chief Strategy Officer with a small dedicated staff focusing on the longer term future of the industry, the market, and/or the company. The challenge with this role is to differentiate the output from the role versus what other executives would typically have on their plate; for example, a business unit president, or a CMO, or even the CEO, all of whom would normally expect to own direct responsibility for the development of strategy.

From an organizational design perspective, as the CHRO, I would seriously question the need for a chief Strategy Officer if you already have a Chief Marketing Officer or a very strategic CEO or CFO. Make sure you can clearly see a line of sight in terms of who really owns the Strategic "pen".

CHAPTER 92: SHARED SERVICES FUNCTION

> "Rugby is a great analogy to how business teams perform. There is no star quarterback in the scrum; everyone has to play strength to strength."
>
> Claude Mongeau, CEO, Canadian National

With the emergence of shared services centers in many organizations, a new exec-utive is entering the C-suite ranks. Their titles may vary from VP Shared Services to President, but the role is clearly growing in importance and impact on large to medium sized companies.

A shared service function usually encompasses all of the transactional work in a company including payroll, accounts payables and receivables, employee pension, benefits and compensation administration, facilities, recruiting, training adminis-tration, help desk and customer service, workers compensation claims and other related transactions.

Some companies have added logistics, supply chain, purchasing, information services, and customer facing functions like pricing, category management, and customer service. Going from a decentralized company to one with a shared services focus is not easy. There will be a lot of executives who don't want to give up control over the work., Some executive roles will even be eliminated or combined and the concept of outsourcing or off-shoring work creates high anxiety

The implications for the Human Resources function is simple – you will transfer all your HR transactional work into a Shared Services group and focus your time on value added HR work like coaching, performance improvement, succession planning, and talent management. We finally have a place to send our less value added work – a long-time wish for most CHROs.

The Shared Services concept has become a well-respected function and they are using their leverage to reduce costs and streamline work to allow internal and external customers to feel it is easy to do business with your company.

CHAPTER 93:   CHIEF LEGAL OFFICER

> "Apart from the CEO, there are three substantial C-suite roles that are directly linked to Board committees: the CFO, CHRO and the General Counsel/Secretary to the board."
>
> Yvonne Jackson, Board Director

I restarted this chapter half a dozen times because the temptation to begin with a lawyer joke was too great. In the end, good sense prevailed and I took the high road – after all, many CLOs go on to take CEO positions, and the one thing I know about lawyers is they tend to have long memories about who does and who doesn't tell lawyer jokes. For the record, I don't – at least not in my books.

The CLO is the third C-suite executive who typically has a dual relationship between the Board and the CEO. Similar to the CFO and the CHRO, the Chief Legal Officer must remain independent enough to provide sound advice to the CEO and the Board, and there will be times when the CLO is caught in between the CEO and the Board Chair.

The CLO is often described as the "cop" on the C-suite team, and indeed in some companies this reputation might be deserved if they take a "command and control" approach to their role. But to be fair, the legal governance standards have been dramatically increased in recent years and maintaining corporate "checks and balances" is now a full-time focus on checking all of the boxes. For example, companies have CEO and CFO sworn statements each quarter, and this is pure non-value added work.

In my view, the level of scrutiny is considerably more than what is truly required to run a business. The most effective CLOs work with the CHRO to determine the best controls that do not burden the business with lots of bureaucracy. They work with the team to streamline processes while ensuring the company has adequate safeguards. However, the CLO adds the greatest value when they put on their business hat to analyze business issues. I feel the CLO brings an incredible analytical mind which can be used to tackle strategic and tactical issues in the company.

To be successful, the CLO is required to have the same skill set that makes for a good CEO, and therefore not surprisingly the CLO often moves into the CEO position as a natural evolution of their career development. One excellent example of this career evolution is Todd Stitzer who rose from the legal ranks at Cadbury Schweppes to become the CEO. He successfully guided the company into a global leader in confectionary and beverage products which attracted the attention of Kraft Foods.

9

Leading and Interacting with Employees

CHAPTER 94: EMPLOYEE ADVOCATE OR NOT?

> "Have the personal independence, self-confidence and courage to push back or challenge the system when necessary."
>
> Bill Conaty, former SVP, Corporate Human Resources, General Electric

One of the more traditional opinions of the role of the HR function is that of employee advocate. This opinion assumes an adversarial relationship between employer and employee within an environment whereby the company objectives and the well-being of the employee are mutually exclusive. Consistent with this view point is the notion that the HR functions do not understand the business realities of the organization and do not contribute measurably to the strategic success of the business.

In my opinion, this view is antiquated and counterproductive to the interests of both the company and employees. As it applies to employee advocacy, my preference is for a definition of HR as the department that seeks to balance the interests of the employees with the well-being of the company.

As the people experts in the company, the HR team must be sure to advocate for the needs of the employees. Quite simply, it's good business sense – in order to maximize employee productivity, HR has to know and manage the expectations of the employees, although with the combined view to ensuring that the company is financially successful.

The company needs to provide a competitive range of employee services and programs in order to retain people, but at the same time each industry has a cost profile for their employee expenses and investment that must be considered. If your company has more people than your competitors and you spend more money on a per employee basis, you will need to ensure you are getting a significant return on this employee investment, otherwise, you simply have a higher employee cost basis.

On the other hand, if senior management has the attitude that employees are too expensive, they will not have employee interests in mind and there will be work challenges (retention and productivity losses). Also, there will be times when the employee needs an advocate because they have been lost in the system (medical or financial hardships). The HR department, in conjunction with local management, needs to rescue good employees who have been harmed by the bureaucracy.

I have a very simple philosophy- if an employee delivers their part of the bargain (good work), the company must deliver its part – fair and equitable treatment.

CHAPTER 95: EMPLOYEE ENGAGEMENT

"Many companies seek to build employee engagement throughout their organizations, but behavioral leaders go further. They do this by fostering the discretionary performance of their people, usually by targeting the high-impact behaviors that directly improve business results and competitive advantage."

S. Jacobs, *The Behavior Breakthrough: Leading Your Organization to a New Competitive Advantage*
(Austin: Greenleaf Book Group Press, 2013), p. 81

Long gone is the notion that employees are "owned" by an organization, fortunately, so too are the attendant attitudes of servitude, autocratic supervision, capricious dismissal, and general lack of transparency in the employee/company relationship.

So if employees are not the chattel of a company, and if they're not a "human asset", how exactly do we describe the employee/company relationship and how is that description manifest in the practical day-to-day operations of the company?

One way to think of the relationship is two parties making a trade – time and effort for monetary and other compensations. What's missing from this model, however, is any sense of a rich and mutually committed relationship. My preference is to think of the trade as a bi-lateral investment – almost like a share swap – with both parties exchanging investments in each other's health and well-being. Consider it a mutually beneficial engagement that delivers a return that transcends the cost to either party.

The hallmark of such a relationship is two parties fully engaged in the well-being of the other. So what does employee engagement look like, does it really make a bottom line difference, and what does it take to create it and maintain it at a high level?

There has been so much written about employee engagement that there are many, many different definitions of it and just as many different views on how to maximize it. My definition of successful employee engagement is simple:

> "An employee is engaged when they are self-motivated
> every day to happily do what's in the company's best interest."

In a group setting, employee engagement can be defined as the group taking accountability for their work and delivering consistent performance. The ultimate expression of this is when a group becomes a self-directed team – no direct supervision is required. In a manufacturing setting, this would mean the plant was run by the employees with minimal management intervention.

In a white-collar environment, the definition of employee engagement can be a bit more complex, but generally it revolves around the same theme of autonomous dedication and personal accountability.

Of the number of viewpoints regarding measuring employee engagement, there are two of which I'd like to make mention. One holds that measuring employee engagement is more art than science, while the other asserts that there is, in fact, a scientific way to measure employee engagement.

In the "art" category there are a number of soft measures that together can be used to deduce the level of employee engagement; for example, consider the cumulative answers to these questions:

1. Employee productivity – are employees meeting their goals?

2. Employee safety – are employees working safely?

3. Employee attendance– are employees working every day?

4. Employee suggestions– are employees suggesting new ideas?

5. Employee complaints– are employees getting their issues resolved?

6. Employee stock purchases– are employees buying company stock?

7. Employee retention– are employees staying with the company?

8. Employee referrals– are employees referring friends to the company?

9. Employee promotions– are employees getting promoted at the company?

10. Employee wellness – are employees taking care of their health?

If you are getting good scores on the above measures, I believe you have an engaged workforce.

In terms of a "scientific" measure, there are various methods in the industry to measure engagement. The Kenexa organization, a partner of Maple Leaf Foods, uses the following four elements and questions as their "engagement index":

*   Pride – "I am proud to be an employee of this organization."

*   Commitment – "I rarely think about looking for a job with another organization."

*   Advocacy – "I would gladly refer a friend for employment at this organization."

*   Satisfaction – "I am extremely satisfied with this organization as a place to work."

Similarly, the Gallup organization has a 12-question index. But at the heart of all engagement measures are a few key questions that sum up how much the employee cares for and feels connected to the organization. And regardless of whether there are four questions in the index or twelve, all of the firms that measure and analyze engagement have studies upon studies that show a strong correlation between employee engagement and organizational performance.

The Gallup organization periodically does a deep dive into this correlation, using data from all the organizations that use their services in this area – their "meta-analysis". In their 2012 analysis, they confirmed the connection between employee engagement and nine different performance outcomes, including: customer ratings, profitability, productivity, and quality.

Gallup researchers also found that "those [companies] scoring in the top half on employee engagement nearly doubled their odds of success compared with those in the bottom half. Those at the 99th percentile had four times the success rate of those at the first percentile." (*Gallup Business Journal*, June 2013*)*

The Kenexa organization publishes similar findings from their analysis. When they looked at "Organizations on Engagement", the Top 25% fared much better than the Bottom 25%:

- Organizations with highly engaged employees achieve twice the annual net income of organizations whose employees lag behind on engagement.

- Organizations with highly engaged employees achieve seven times greater 5-year Total Shareholder Return (TSR) than organizations whose employees are less engaged.

(Kenexa Research Institute's *2008 WorkTrends™ Annual Report*)

There can be little doubt now that a high level of employee engagement has a direct and substantial effect on the company's bottom line; which begs the question, "How do we get it and how do we maximize it?"

Ironically, the most important thing an organization can do to increase employee engagement is the first step to understanding how to increase engagement – listen to them.

Employees will increase their affiliation and caring for an organization when that organization shows it cares for the employees in return. And nothing shows caring more than asking someone how they feel and what they're thinking, really listening to their answers and then doing something to actively respond to the feedback. No matter what answers the questions get in response, the asking is itself a means to increased engagement. The only time to worry about asking is if you get little or no response – engagement has to be incredibly low that employees don't care enough to even complain.

Research indicates that there are some common elements that consistently drive employee engagement; across employee groups, across organizations, and across industries. The exact order of the elements may change from study to study, and the wording used to express the element may change, and there may be some overlap, but the themes are generally consistent.

Communication: If there is only one thing an organization can invest in to improve the level of employee engagement, a robust strategy and plan for ongoing communication would be at the top of the list.

Confidence: In the organization's future and the organization's leaders is consistently shown to be amongst the key drivers of employee engagement. Employees will affiliate themselves with organizations they believe in.

Pride: The company needs to make it clear to all employees what the purpose of the organization is, and what there is about that purpose to be genuinely proud of.

Connection: The communication needs to put a human face on the leadership of the organization, to increase the likelihood of connection and loyalty.

Trust: In the leadership, in the company strategy, and in how the organization is evolving into the future.

Teamwork: A sense of common purpose and mutual accountability and support.

Access: Employees feel more connected to an organization that puts in place feedback mechanisms that actually work and generate a response to the employee.

Recognition: At its most basic this is just another form of communication. When an employee is recognized for what he or she does at work, it shows that someone is paying attention or "listening" to them, and is responding back. It's a validation that they are not just a cog in a machine, but rather a valued individual, and that the organization cares about what they do.

People managers are critical to building engagement and need to consistently watch for positive results and behaviours and provide appropriate recognition. Recognition does not need to mean large salary increases or special awards. It *can* mean that, but it can also mean saying thanks for a job well done. As a very simple example, "I saw how you handled that tough situation. Your patience made a huge difference in our ability to settle the problem quickly. I am so pleased you're on my team. Thank you." You probably felt good just reading those words and they weren't even directed at you. Imagine how the employee who earns them would feel and imagine how they would feel about the person saying them and by proxy, the company. Think of the cost of this "investment" and think of the probable return – does it get any better?

HR professionals can help build the recognition culture within the organization, since people managers may need training or coaching to understand how to effectively provide feedback and recognition.

The overwhelming majority of people want to do a good job, and want to contribute. They want to feel good about themselves and the place they work, and they want to feel they belong. Because these are natural desires, and this kind of connectivity leads to highly engaged employees, it should be easy right?

The truth is reality bites. In the real world things get in the way – companies struggle with business issues and don't spend enough time communicating with or listening to their people – leaders don't understand how human behaviour works and they tend to look at people as "assets", there just to do their jobs. And other factors such as pay or work life balance, if not managed properly, can also become mere roadblocks to increased employee engagement.

The good news is that an increased focus and effort on the drivers of engagement can significantly improve employee caring, affiliation and passion. And the proof is in the numbers – there is a return on investment in improved organizational performance. It won't solve all the issues that an organization faces, but it can make the most of the most important investors that the organization has … its employees.

"A leader must engage and energize the workforce through extensive local empowerment, while at the same time keeping close control of the direction and critical points of the enterprise's competitive advantage."

Rose Patten, Special Advisor to the CEO,
(former CHRO), BMO Financial Group

CHAPTER 96:   THE IMPACT OF POSITIVE LEADERSHIP

"The CEO is like the boat captain with the rudder – setting the tone and pace – it is exhilarating. A small turn of wheel has a big impact."

Claude Mongeau, CEO, Canadian National

In the chapter above, on employee engagement, we examined the nature of the employee- employer relationship and its effects on employee happiness and the business bottom line – specifically, engaged employees have a direct, substantial and positive impact on the company's net income and total shareholder return.

Engaged employees are the product of company values and processes that create an environment of mutual respect, pride, trust, and confidence within a framework of effective communication, reward and recognition.

Within this construct leadership is the key contact and delivery mode connecting the employee with the company, responsible for conveying the company's message and putting into action its values. *Positive* leadership is organizing a group of people to achieve a common goal using positive reinforcement to reinforce desired behaviours. The result is a workplace and daily activity that becomes a source of positive emotions and positive associations for the employee.

Leaders create positive meaning by focusing on the value of an organization's outcome beyond just personal benefit and they are attuned to the different orientations towards work – job, career, and calling. Leaders build a positive climate through acts of compassion, collective forgiveness, and gratitude so that employees feel they are cared for and supported.

Elements of positive leadership:

- Focus on what is working; our strengths.
- Be grateful for what we have.
- Take personal responsibility; "no one is coming" to save the day.
- Get the balance right; it's not "either/or", it's "and"'.
- Make time for recovery from stress.
- Ritualize and build habits that will put good things in your life and those of the people around you.

Reference: Tal Ben-Shahar, *Happier: Learn the Secrets to Daily Joy and Lasting Fulfillment* (New York: McGraw-Hill, 2007), pp. 8-11.

With regard to this last point – the following list is a series of tips about some behaviours and habits that you can build; rituals that you can add into your life as a leader that will make both you and your team happier. And since employee happiness is an investment in business success there is a solid business case to be made for investing time and effort into maximizing it.

Tips for being a positive leader on an organizational level:

- Be clear about the destination, and describe it in a way that is meaningful to people across the business.
- Publicly show support and belief in the plan – and support each other on the plan.
- Refer to the Power of Consistency (17 out of 17) – chapter 27 in *Switchpoints* book.
- Be accountable when you see negative behaviour creeping in.

- Watch for finger pointing, blaming, giving up, looking backwards at mistakes instead of forward on solutions.

- Call out these behaviours with each other when you see them.

- Shift the balance in broad-based communications to the positive – AND – don't shy away from the negative.

- Don't sugar-coat or mislead people; this causes confusion and distrust.

- People can understand that strengths and effort don't always translate to results.

- Focusing on the long-term destination and progress and celebrating stories along the way will help keep people engaged.

- Ensure clear lines of accountability to remove overlapping accountability and decision rights.

Tips for being a positive leader for your team:

- Celebrate progress and success.

- Make team meetings more energizing by building in rituals to share and celebrate wins.

- Start team meetings by having everyone share what they are personally proud of – "30-second success sharing".

- Every month identify and share the top three successes in the team:
  o Have people explain what led to the successes; how did it happen?

- Make time in all team meetings to talk about what is working well.
  o Have team members recognize each other for what they observed and appreciated.

- Create a monthly/weekly newsletter sharing best practices, wins and fun.

- Collect from team members and share:
  o Proud moments, what was learned, what was enjoyed.

- At every meeting focus on positive examples of high impact behaviours.
  o These are behaviours that have the strongest direct tie to results.
  o This will help direct people to care about the behaviours that matter most.

- Provide the context for how the team fits into the big picture.
  o Make sure everyone knows how they're helping the company get to the desired destination.

Be Present and Have Fun

- Celebrate milestones – small, low (or no) cost events can go a long way.
- Schedule time to be present with the team, who need to see and talk to you more than ever.
    - o Do it, even though you may feel less and less available due to competing urgencies.
    - o Spend unstructured time with a different person each week, ensuring that communication is open and transparent.
- Schedule regular lunch-and-learn sessions so the team can get together.
    - o Teach each other, it's also positive recognition for individuals.
- Build fun rituals and events into regular team meetings.
- Set up a new ritual to carve out some creative time – using small collaborative teams.

Have Positive Personal Energy

- Focus on your own energy level.
- Take time to think through how to balance the negative AND the positive for yourself and in your communications with your team.
- Don't be too hard on yourself, be accountable, but focus on solutions rather than failures.
- Ask the right, positive questions to bring out the right energy and focus in others.

Help Your Team Reframe Negativity

- Help reframe negative emotions that come with missing a target or not succeeding in the moment.
    - o What did we learn?
    - o How can we make sure we don't feel this way again or repeat this problem?
    - o How are we now better for having this experience of failure?
    - o How can we push forward even stronger?
- Don't forget to acknowledge how people feel, and help them work through negative feelings.

Make Sure there is Time to Recover

- Encourage better work/life balance for everyone in the team .
- Ask the team to set aside time for reflection, and set time aside for your own personal reflection.
- Organize lunchtime walking groups – getting out of the office for 30 minutes is sometimes enough.
- Consider formalized "quiet times".
    - o No e-mail/meetings at a consistent time each week.
- Tell staff it is ok to decline optional meetings.

<u>Tips for being a positive leader to the individual people around you</u>

One of the more important elements to employee engagement is recognition;. Employees who are doing a good job need to be recognized by positive consequences on a continuous basis. Additionally, leaders will need to periodically offer constructive feedback to good performers when they are derailing on a particular task.

In order to ensure good performers continue to deliver, they must receive a balance of consequences that is positive in nature. The most commonly referred to balance is 4:1 (5:1 or higher for certain people or circumstances). Positive consequences consist of a variety of activities including non-compensation recognition/feedback and compensation tools. In most cases, cash compensation is a relatively low proportion of the reinforcement actions that are utilized (positive consequences).

Negative consequences serve to discourage behaviour and can include everything from personal feedback to termination of employment. As a formal consequence, employment termination is used in less than 5% of these situations.

Here are some tips for leaders to apply in providing a 4:1 balance of consequences:

Applying positive consequences/feedback:

1. A Positive consequence is "in the eye of the performer". Each person has different "hot' buttons for encouragers such as recognition, but the more valued and timely the consequence is in the performer's eyes, the better.
2. A positive consequence is best delivered in person.
3. Consider feedback that is shared broadly within the organization, if valued by the employees.

4. Positive feedback has more impact when it calls out specific behaviours/ actions that clearly led to a favourable outcome.

5. Try not to combine positive and constructive feedback at the same time. In creating a feedback rich culture, it's important to deliver the positive feedback, describing impact, etc. and walk away. Avoid the use of the word "but".

6. Don't forget the power of constructive feedback. A common trap when using 4:1 is to over-emphasize the positive and forget the power of the "1".

7. Delivering constructive feedback provides the opportunity to "catch people doing things right", thus providing the opportunity to increase the positive feedback.

8. It's worth mentioning that the ratio of 4:1 consequences is delivered over time, not all at once.

9. In times of change, i.e., when people are learning something new, they need a 10:1 ratio, or more, because the new ways of doing things may be hard.

10. As with most behaviours, when someone steps up to providing 4:1 consequences, this automatically encourages others to do the same, and creates a wave of reinforcing higher performance.

When leaders hear 4:1, they typically think of feedback only, however, it is the balance of consequences that people receive from all sources. 4:1 is the ratio of encouraging and discouraging consequences.

In addition to feedback, other consequences might include:

Tangible

*   Items that can be physically touched or held including items that can be enjoyed by the employee's family.

Activity

*   Opportunity to participate in a rewarding activity.
*   Homework then play.

Work process

*   Many natural reinforcing consequences.
*   The next step in the work being performed.
*   Job gets easier, task is completed earlier, avoid unpleasant task.

The following excerpt from *The Behavior Breakthrough* includes a helpful tip:

A Big Buy for Pocket Change

As the leadership team applied DCOM to strengthen its business unit, key leader Sean drove action plans forward in exemplary fashion—until the team committed to increase use of positive encouragement to employees for doing the right things. Clearly uncomfortable, Sean acknowledged being raised under a command-and-control leadership style by his military father. He saw "positive encouragement" as unnecessary coddling and a sign of weakness. Asked how often he recognized someone for a job well done, Sean replied, "I guess never."

Sean agreed to try giving more frequent encouragement, and he devised an ingenious trick. He began each day with four quarters in his right pocket, and his goal was to go home with them in his left pocket. To move a quarter from one pocket to the other, he had to give someone positive feedback for something meaningful—four times a day, every day.

Within days, Sean found it easier to encourage people. Within weeks, his efforts were making a difference. He spent less time following-up on deliverables and resolving operational issues. His direct reports were anticipating needs and generating ideas for improving the organization.

One direct report received a complimentary voicemail from Sean, which the employee then played for his family. Another said she had planned to leave, but decided to stay because Sean was now appreciating the difference she made. Within months, Sean no longer needed the quarters. He actually enjoyed providing daily encouragement. Quite a buy for a little pocket change—that he didn't even spend!

Next steps: creating a habit of 4:1 each day

For the next two weeks, try to document your interaction with your staff. Specifically, write down the name of each person and note each time you provide feedback to someone.

Over a two week period, try to hit a 4:1 ratio with each person. The following types of feedback count as positive consequences:

1. Positive e-mails

2. Phone calls or messages

3. Public recognition

4. Hand written letters

5. Face-to-face feedback

6. Peer recognition

7. One up feedback

8. Project assignments

9. Asking for their opinion

10. Customer recognition

After this two week period, your leadership behavior will start to change. There is a built in positive consequence to the leader when you give positive consequences. For example, when you give positive feedback to an employee (in person), the employee will feel you have made their day. They will smile and may be a little embarrassed. When you make someone smile, you will automatically feel better yourself – it is psychologically rewarding to make someone else feel good. Therefore, your recognition behavior will provide a positive consequence to yourself. It is a reinforcing cycle.

Reference: Steve Jacobs, *The Behavior Breakthrough: Leading Your Organization to a New Competitive Advantage* (Austin: Greenleaf Book Group, 2013), pp. 87, 88.

CHAPTER 97: EPS – EMPLOYEE PERFORMANCE SCORECARDS FOR UNIONIZED EMPLOYEES

> "When it comes to evaluating employee performance, Les Dakens gets it right. Unions and workers are always suspicious of any evaluation scheme. If employers followed the steps of the Employee Performance Scorecards, I see nothing but positive outcomes. Workers need to know that their contributions are recognized and valued."
>
> Bryan Neath, Assistant to National President,
> United Food & Commercial Workers

The following passage is reprinted from *Switchpoints: Culture Change on the Fast Track to Business Success*

Les Dakens had always been bothered by the lack of formal recognition for unionized employees at CN. The vast majority are great people who contribute a lot to our success. Yet we didn't take time with them individually to discuss what they achieved, nor did we take time to thank them for their efforts. In some cases, we knew that a number of employees had been given very little if any feedback for years.

The scope of this neglect was staggering. Of our 22,500 employees, 18,500 were unionized. This meant 80 percent were without any type of formal review! So the vast majority of our employees who were good contributors went without specific thanks and the small percentage who needed to improve their performance went without coaching. Clearly, this was no way to move our culture.

It was time for action. We were going to make improvements and sweeping change. There would be no phase-in or multiyear rollout. It would happen this year.

For the first time in CN's 90 year history, every single employee was going to get a review. Thus was born the Employee Performance Scorecard (EPS).

Many found this revolutionary idea unthinkable as well as undoable. No one else in the rail industry – or most other industries – used scorecards for unionized employees. Reviews for unionized people were unthinkable because the employees were covered by a collective agreement. This tends to make leaders believe that straight talk about performance is risky.

Doing the Unthinkable

Yet, it's funny how thinking the unthinkable can lead to change. As Les and Hunter flew to New York for an analysts' meeting in 2005 to celebrate the tenth anniversary of CN's IPO, they spoke again of Les' dream of Employees Performance Scorecards for unionized workers.

Even though it had not been done before, it was easy to see the value in EPS:

- Most unionized employees work hard and do a good job. It was right to recognize their contribution and thank them for it.

- The lifeblood of successful companies and the fuel for future change is inclusion of shared understanding of goals, expectations, and priorities. Having another 18,500 people engaged in making us even more effective couldn't hurt!

- We have a big appetite for leaders and the unionized ranks sported many bright able employees. Performance reviews could be a vehicle for supervisors to further coach their people for their current job and towards future promotions.

So Hunter and Les decided that during the analysts' meeting, Les would announce that in 2006 every employee would receive a performance review, including unionized people. It was all part of helping employees do a good job which would translate into improved company performance which analysts always want to hear.

So Les addressed the analysts: "The new performance evaluations will be called EPS. To you in this room, that means earning per share. But when you think about it, the individual performance of our employees is what adds up to make the company successful. So our new EPS stands for Employee Performance Scorecards. These scorecards will produce the other EPS earnings per share. By growing one, we'll grow the other."

Executing EPS

Promising EPS was one thing, making it happen for 18,500 people within a year was quite another. It was not a scheduled Human Resource priority for the year. There was no staffing, funding or detailed plan for design or delivery. HR bought the concept, but pulling it off would take a miracle.

When Les arrived back in Montreal, he went to Peter Edwards' office to break the news. Peter wasn't shocked by the concept. He had experience in the area, and he and Les had talked about it many times. But he certainly was startled by the timeline. It suddenly had been moved up two years earlier than planned! However, it had already been announced to the analysts, so we were off to the races.

Peter assembled the team and charted the course. Led by Christine Joanis and Susan Seebeck, they developed the scorecard and metrics, trained supervisors, and planned the rollout logistics. Although CLG had not been involved in developing the EPS, their consultants assisted with implementation.

By the time EPS was finished, it would directly touch about 90 percent of CN's people. Of course, we anticipated that the unions would be concerned, so we needed a communication plan to give people the heads-up on EPS.

Communicating EPS

We wanted employees to have a good experience with EPS. Our goal was to start a meaningful conversation between the supervisor and employee on performance. Here are a few of the points we covered with each employee:

- We thanked them for their contribution to a successful organization. (EPS is a vehicle that can help supervisors take time to say thank-you.)

- We discussed their progress to date.

- We discussed the impact of their performance on the business.

- We discussed their opportunities to improve and advance.

So we needed to train the supervisors. They needed to be clear on EPS's purpose so they could explain it to employees. They would need some help with the feedback part, as not everyone had attended an ABC workshop. We put a training program together that piloted it in the field.

Then Come the Problems

Any change initiative will have problems, but this one was really asking for it.

- Pushback from the unions. As the buzz about EPS grew, the unions grew curious. Their chief concern was the EPS was going to be discipline in disguise and they had strong and negative initial reactions.

- A lack of common definition on measurements. Senior operations leaders all identified their most important metrics. However, CN is actually an assembly of many different railways with multiple legacies of culture, union contracts, and leadership style. So while measurement might all have the same label (like absenteeism), they had different numerical values in each legacy railway.

- Finding accurate performance data. EPS required accurate data to track individual performance. But CN had multiple data sources, very few of which talked to each other. We had to find ways to get accurate data so the scorecard would prompt a discussion about individual performance instead of a debate on data accuracy.

- Different version for different needs. Operations wanted to own the scorecard. There were many different jobs in the system, and opinions across the regions varied about what was needed. Demand mounted for multiple versions. So 48 unique styles of cards were developed for use across the organization, some in English, some in French.

- Printing colour scorecards. The scorecard was to be given to employees as a tangible reminder of their EPS review. Supervisors would actually print the scorecards at their desks. But the scorecard needed the right look and feel, which led to doing it in colour. With few colour printers in the field, that meant planning ahead to print and ship from corporate.

The biggest surprise was the way so many supervisors viewed their jobs. To them, their job was getting the work done by assigning tasks – not supporting, developing and coaching employees.

We planned to roll out EPS very soon and we fixed the problems fast. We revamped the training, with more emphasis on developing and motivating employees. We defined each measurement and added an explanation to each scorecard package. Where needed, we scrambled to identify each direct report for the supervisors.

Rollout for Success

The rollout happened on schedule. As is typical for CN, EPS was an idea developed centrally, then deployed regionally. Our small team, with other looming priorities at the start of the year, pulled off the massive undertaking in less than one year. We were done in December 2006. Our promise to the analysts was kept.

The employees' reactions opened many supervisors' eyes. The feedback held real meaning to employees. It was positive recognition that their contributions were important and appreciated. Some employees took their scorecards home and taped them on the refrigerator!

For those supervisors who had the ABC training, EPS was the next logical step. Using the ABC's methodology, they were having discussions about performance and giving feedback to employees day to day. Now, with EPS, supervisors could pull together performance data and their observations from the year to have a meaningful conversation.

Supervisors learned that people needed to hear the details and were actually hungry for them. The supervisors could also see the need to be clear in setting expectations, exact in defining measurements, and precise in choosing the right consequence for behavior.

After EPS was instituted at one rail yard, employees exceeded their goal of handling 340 railcars per shift by hitting the 360 mark. Intrigued by this productivity gain, Terry Corson, a Senior Mechanical Officer, asked yard supervisors what had changed. What new process had they instituted? The answer: "The only thing changed at this location was the Employee Performance Scorecard."

Supervisors: I Didn't Know That!

EPS enabled supervisors to know their people in a different way because it required conversation. Supervisors asked employees how it was going, discussed issues, and gave their perceptions about the employees' performance.

They got employees to talk about their experiences on the job, about the company, and what they thought about working there. And this enabled supervisors to learn some things:

- That some employees knew the customers and their needs better than they did.

- That employees had ideas about how to make the work more efficient, but often were afraid to share.

- That there were some practices that employees didn't understand well or maybe just didn't like.

- These conversations helped supervisors rethink how to do things. They were getting upward feedback for the first time.

Consultant Steve Quesnelle has a remarkable story about what one supervisor learned while conducting a one on one EPS session with a veteran employee in a mechanical shop in Winnipeg:

When they came to the section on attendance, the supervisor congratulated the employee for having zero absences. The employee responded. "That's right. I've never had an absence." To which the supervisor replied. "Hey, that's great. You went the entire year without an absence." The employee smiled wistfully. "Actually I haven't ever had an absence – not one in 30 years." The supervisor nearly fell off his chair – partly from the enormity of this fact and partly from embarrassment at not knowing this stunning fact and how dedicated this employee was.

EPS Was Another Switchpoint

EPS was coming on the heels of major cultural changes: the Five Guiding Principles, the ABC methodology, and the introduction of the Q4 leadership framework. EPS was a layer atop that existing foundation and it was an informal test of how well CN had learned to put Q4 into action.

We saw a difference in how people responded to EPS. Of course, we got the usual comments from those who dislike change. But with the EPS – a huge change that came from nowhere – we got some new reactions. "What do you need from me to make it work?" "Sounds like a plan, let's do it." It was obvious that our resiliency with change had grown.

We'll give the last word on EPS to our employees. Here's what they said:

- "For the first time I feel like I'm being heard."

- "This was a good discussion. Supervisors are changing. Previously, I always wanted to stay out of the superintendent's office. Now supervisors have their door open."

- "I've been here 30 years and no one's ever thanked me before."

- "It's about time."

And although not a CN employee, French dramatist Victor Hugo perhaps said it best. "An invasion of armies can be resisted, but not an idea whose time has come."

...

Buzz Hargrove, former President of the Canadian Auto Workers Union, said this about *Employee Performance Scorecards*:

"This book provides a great example of how companies should lead versus direct their employees, to make them feel more engaged and part of a team. This definitely results in greater productivity and employee satisfaction. The book also shows that a union will support these programs as long as they understand what the company is trying to accomplish. I enjoyed reading the story about Employee Performance Scorecards."

Reference:

J. Johnson, L. Dakens, P. Edwards, and N. Morse, *Switchpoints: Culture Change on the Fast Track to Business Success* (New York: Wiley, 2008), pp. 173-178.

CHAPTER 98: HIGH PERFORMANCE PEOPLE SYSTEMS

"In reality, when employees are allowed to question authority, they are more likely to feel invested in their jobs and therefore more likely to perform them well. And when they are actively encouraged to question the status quo – when their viewpoint is sought out and valued – they are more likely to think innovatively and come up with the sorts of ideas and feedback that help move an organization forward."

A. Lang, *The Power of Why*
(Toronto: Harper Collins Canada, 2012), p. 51

Back to the Future: High Performance People Systems (HPPS) were in vogue for much of the 1980s and early 1990s. After much fanfare, things quieted and it seemed that organizations moved on to other things. What happened?

HPPS approaches had much potential and led to some notable successes. That said, they were often bundled with beliefs and practices that became unnecessary deterrents. Some of these gaps between the operating premises and what actually happened in practice included the following:

The Premise ... In Practice

- "Organizations are perfectly designed to get the results they are getting", so new results require a new design.

- If you change the organization design, the right behaviour will naturally follow.

- Organizations must design and align the "whole system".

- "Self-managed teams" are essential to high performance organizations.

- Since there are a number of "systems" to redesign, interim structures such as dedicated design teams and steering committees are needed so that the rest of the organization can "get the washout".

- Skillful transition planning and "roll out" are vital.

- There was a tendency to overlook other, at times more practical and direct, influences on performance, such as day-to-day leadership practices.

- Often, desired behaviour did not naturally follow or sustain, primarily because organizational levers are not automatically strong influencers of new behaviour.

- "Whole system" sometimes translated into "whole enchilada" approaches rather than focusing on "minimum critical" changes.

- Overlooked that self-managed teams are merely one means to the end of ensuring that those who do the work have the direction, competence, opportunity, and motivation to perform at sustainably high levels.

- Resulted in low organization change readiness, staff-led rather than leader-led deployment, and compliance rather than commitment.

- The HPPS is important, indeed, but what happens "Monday Morning" after rollout is much more important. New and lasting behaviour requires consistent and skillful ongoing reinforcement.

HPPS 2.0

Integrating the science of behaviour change with whole systems redesign methods (and a dose of practical experience) can provide a powerful platform for achieving the potential of High Performance People Systems without falling prey to the pitfalls of the past. For instance, Applied Behavioural Science's focus on skilful pinpointing of the new behaviour that will truly drive new results greatly sharpens focus at the design table. The precise analytic approaches shed different light on the current drivers of behaviour, which in turn clarifies the range of alternatives for achieving performance breakthroughs in both the design and execution phases. Understanding that very timely and highly probable consequences are by far the most important influencers of discretionary performance re-balances the focus for organization levers to leadership and peer levers. And so on.

One example of this integrated approach to HPPS design is taking place at Maple Leaf Food's state of the art Heritage Plant. Led by Dave Harman, and supported by CLG, the organization's people systems intentionally leverage learning of the past with the behavioural best practices of the present to build for the future. Heritage Plant leaders aim to create a common and consistent suite of practices which gives people, leaders and team members alike, a predictable, repeatable system upon which to drive continuous improvement (see Figure 1). In effect, they are taking unproductive and de-motivating people variation out of the system, so focus can be fully placed on business performance. Over time, everyone will know "how things work" and "how to make improvements" in the facility.

Figure 1

 People System Program Architecture

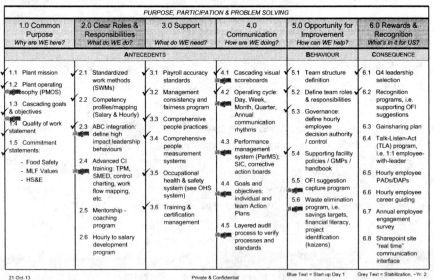

PURPOSE, PARTICIPATION & PROBLEM SOLVING					
1.0 Common Purpose Why are WE here?	2.0 Clear Roles & Responsibilities What do WE do?	3.0 Support What do WE need?	4.0 Communication How are WE doing?	5.0 Opportunity for Improvement How can WE help?	6.0 Rewards & Recognition What's in it for US?
ANTECEDENTS				BEHAVIOUR	CONSEQUENCE
1.1 Plant mission 1.2 Plant operating philosophy (PMOS) 1.3 Cascading goals & objectives 1.4 Quality of work statement 1.5 Commitment statements: 　- Food Safety 　- MLF Values 　- HS&E	2.1 Standardized work methods (SWMs) 2.2 Competency profiles/mapping (Salary & Hourly) 2.3 ABC integration: define high impact leadership behaviours 2.4 Advanced CI training: TPM, SMED, control charting, work flow mapping, etc. 2.5 Mentorship - coaching program 2.6 Hourly to salary development program	3.1 Payroll accuracy standards 3.2 Management consistency and fairness program 3.3 Comprehensive people practices 3.4 Comprehensive people measurement systems 3.5 Occupational health & safety system (see OHS system) 3.6 Training & certification management	4.1 Cascading visual scoreboards 4.2 Operating cycle: Day, Week, Month, Quarter, Annual communication rhythms 4.3 Performance management system (PerMS); SIC, corrective action boards 4.4 Goals and objectives: individual and team Action Plans 4.5 Layered audit process to verify processes and standards	5.1 Team structure definition 5.2 Define team roles & responsibilities 5.3 Governance: define hourly employee decision authority / control 5.4 Supporting facility policies / GMPs / handbook 5.5 OFI suggestion capture program 5.6 Waste elimination program, i.e. savings targets, financial literacy, project identification (kaizens)	6.1 Q4 leadership selection 6.2 Recognition programs, i.e. supporting OFI suggestions 6.3 Gainsharing plan 6.4 Talk-Listen-Act (TLA) program, i.e. 1:1 employee-with-leader 6.5 Hourly employee PADs/DAPs 6.6 Hourly employee career guiding 6.7 Annual employee engagement survey 6.8 Sharepoint site "real time" communication interface

21-Oct-13   Private & Confidential   Blue Text = Start-up Day 1   Grey Text = Stabilization, ~Yr. 2

Key dimensions of the approach at this writing include:

- Designed for results; not merely to be different.

- Explicitly anchoring decisions about people systems design decisions and expected leadership practices to four cornerstones of sustainable high performance: Direction, Competence, Opportunity, and Motivation.

- Intentionally focusing on "minimum critical" design improvements rather than "boiling the ocean".

- Defining and using ongoing "management rhythms" and operating leaders in lieu of artificial structures and interim personnel.

- Preparing leaders to consistently demonstrate deliberately selected leadership practices from day one, including provision of expert coaching to accelerate new leadership habits where they are most needed.

- Balanced aim for team autonomy and accountability that leverages the power of peer reinforcement for collective performance, without taking on the added challenges of "self-managing teams".

- Designed for scalability to other plants in the system.

The real purpose of designing a Maple Leaf Food's Heritage Plant HPPS is to drive continuous improvement behaviour where all employees have the opportunity to participate in problem-solving and opportunities for business improvement. The intent is to create an environment in which employees become vested, engaged partners in their own employment relationship. To accomplish this, highly detailed leadership and team member competencies and behaviours need to be developed, embraced, and practiced by all site leaders. This objective is systematically shaping HR practices such as talent selection, training against standardized work instructions, level of maturity or team/performer autonomy, communication rhythms, and rewards and performance feedback.

CHAPTER 99: THE POWER OF CONSISTENCY –
"17 OUT OF 17"

> "Leadership does not require official authority. As I said before, many of us are waiting to be in a position of influence before we influence. The opposite is more representative of reality. The more we influence, the more we will get the opportunity to influence."
>
> J. Izzo, *Stepping Up: Why Taking Responsibility Changes Everything*, (San Francisco: Berrett-Koeler Publishers, Inc., 2012), p. 156

The following passage is reprinted from *Switchpoints: Culture Change on the Fast Track to Business Success*

Armed with the ABC Toolkit and a deeper knowledge of the Five Guiding Principles, our leaders were ready to change the culture – except for one thing. To truly drive culture change, we needed to provide consistent consequences from consistent leaders. This realization became a switchpoint in our cultural change.

In a relay race, it doesn't matter how well three runners do, even if they are the fastest on the track. If the fourth runner drops the baton, the race is over for the whole team. For the same reason, consistency in culture change is essential to winning.

While consistency seems like an obvious requirement, it took a small group of managers 12 hours of discussion to really grasp its impact as revealed in this story from our recent history: We slumped in a meeting room late one night amid empty pizza boxes and soda cans, tired to the bone. We had been at this since 7:30 that morning, and had been on the grueling schedule for weeks. We were desperately trying to change the out of control elements of our railroad – early quits, theft, low productivity. That night it finally dawned on us. We, the leaders, were the problem. Too many of us were inconsistent in our expectations of employees. Some of us let people leave early, overlooked theft, or didn't ask people to do their best. We thought we were being good guys. If we didn't stop overlooking these actions, then and there, CN was headed for a dead end. There would be no need to continue, as there would be no way we could change the culture.

So we took a simple oath: No one dodges responsibility. We accept our role as leaders, and this is what we signed up for. And we still hold each other accountable for doing the right thing. There were 17 of us on that table. Some said. "We all must agree – all 17 of 17 must align." That phrase stuck. From that point on, whenever the going got tough, we'd look at one another and say "17 out of 17."

The mantra 17 out of 17 was catchy – an icon for consistency, performance, accountability. It spread like wildfire through the organization.

Every leader had been in a situation that created inconsistency and knew the pain it caused. The leader might have been the bad guy, the good guy, or even stuck in the middle. It didn't matter – they all recognized the issue. Through the ABC workshops, they saw the confusion that inconsistency brings to employees. We identified two kinds of inconsistency: inconsistency in the rules, and inconsistency in applying them.

Inconsistency in the Rules

We knew from the ABC methodology that antecedents (rules, expectations, policies) must be clearly aligned with the right consequences if they are to work. Employees are smart – they can see when the consequences they receive don't align with managers' expectations. When employees see the inconsistency, they decide it's all right to ignore the rules. We found this to be true on several occasions, including the following:

- Antecedent: Our rule says "Arrive at meetings on time."

- Behaviour: People drift in later each week – first two minutes late, then five, then ten.

- Consequence: Nothing was said about it. In fact, sometimes we waited for latecomers before we started meetings.

- Result: The consequence didn't align with the antecedent, so employees made their own rule. "Show up when you feel like it."

- Antecedent: "No entry" signs were posted in hazardous areas.

- Behaviour: People ignored the signs and took shortcuts through the areas.

- Consequence: Nothing was said about it. And those who took the shortcut usually got where they were going faster than if they had obeyed the signs.

- Result: "No entry" signs were ignored so often that it became common practice to walk right past them. Employees made their own rule: "Those signs must not apply anymore – no one bothered to take them down."

To make things worse, when we hire new employees, we pair them with experienced, old hands to give them on the job training. The old hands tell them. "Forget the handbook that's not how we do it – let me show you the real way."

Once a culture creates this second tie of real expectations and rules, you have lost the battle. You have widespread inconsistency between antecedents and consequences, meaning that you have lost control of behavior – people will do things their own way. At CN, this inconsistency was another switch we needed to spike.

Inconsistency of Applying Rules

Sometimes the consequences are clear, but they aren't applied in the same way every time by every leader. This is where 17 out of 17 comes in. If even one leader bends the rules for someone, he is creating inconsistency that can multiply and bring progress to a halt.

Employees see these inconsistencies (you do, too) and try to figure out when the consequence will be in their favour (you do, too). Do you have to do something only when Joe is on duty? Or only in the north side of the rail yard? Or only during day shift? Many companies have tales of how lax night shift is, compared to day shift, or how lax one supervisor is compared to others. All these observations get tucked away in employees' heads as they try to make sense of their unclear work environment.

These inconsistencies are bad enough, but there's more. Employee time spent in figuring out the system is lost time. Often, inconsistency drives so much grumbling and discussion among co-workers that employees lose many hours of productivity. These employees are not bad – they are normal people trying to make sense of their inconsistent work environment.

Inconsistency Breeds Opportunity

When things are inconsistent, the negative leaders step up – they smell an opportunity to make their own decisions about expectations and rules. This is where 17 out of 17 comes in again. If even one manager is lax, people who work for the other 16 begin to resent the special treatment they see some employees receiving. The negative leaders pounce on the opportunity to spread dissent.

The neutral majority who struggle to follow the rules but don't see their value will see this as an opportunity to take advantage of the system. They will take the opportunity to get away with what they know is the wrong thing to do.

If you have one manager who allows just one employee to break the rules, the floodgates open. "Hey, if Sally can do it, then so can I!" "And me, too!" The flood races forward and the management team is left to deal with managing rules instead of managing performance.

Leaders who fail to consistently enforce the rules create lifelines for bad actors, enabling them to get away with breaking the rules. Here is an example, told by one leader:

Inconsistency provides shelter and encouragement to negative leaders. For example, negative leaders often find one manager they can get along with. Such a manager then becomes a life-line to that negative leader, one who listens and even helps them when they need a favour.

Here is a simple test I use to discover who is serving as the lifeline for a negative leader. When we have a culture problem, I gather the managers and ask. "Okay, who's the negative leader among our employees?" Pretty quickly, everyone agrees that it's Sue – everyone except Pat. He says, "I don't know why the rest of you are having problems with her. Sue's okay with me." A-ha! Pat is likely the lifeline for Sue.

So if you are the only person in the room that Joe seems to be okay with you might be Joe's lifeline. You're the person Joe keeps for when he needs things. Joe probably doesn't work directly for you, but he's figured out that he can have everyone else angry with him, be a terrible employee and co-worker, and it doesn't really matter – he has you.

The real ability to get a negative leader to do the right thing comes when the lifeline manager truly embraces the concept of 17 out of 17 and tells the negative leader. "We have a good relationship, but I'm no longer going to be your source of help and favours in the future. You treat me well but you don't treat the other managers well. You sneak out early on them, and you don't treat your job with respect. When you don't do right for them, you don't do right for me either."

Now the negative leader has no lifeline, no shelter – and just as important, the recognition and positives are reserved for employees who do the right thing, not those who abuse.

The negative leader no longer gets undeserved rewards. He now must make a conscious choice: Am I willing to change, or live without someone to help me? Good employees see that we are serious about what we say. Over time, we create a consistency of consequences that people can count on us.

So consistency on rules, policies, and procedures is the basic foundation for a strong management team. Once you have consistency, you can focus on performance – and helping employees maximize their abilities. Without consistency, leaders are wasting time dealing with basics that never give them time to deal with greater things.

Does size matter? Regardless of how big our management team became, or how spread out we were, we drove 17 out of 17 on every dialogue with them. It was just as critical for two people sitting in an office as it was for the team of 12 managing rail lines between Chicago and Memphis.

Be Consistently Flexible

One Caveat: Consistency doesn't mean being inflexible. Being inflexible means thinking has stopped and that policy is being used as if it were set in stone, or is being used as an excuse. If someone suggests a change, you can discuss it with others and approach the person: "I've heard your request and I talked about it with the others, and we collectively agree that it's okay."

That's part of the common sense approach we are building across CN. Our good people should be able to expect recognition and that we will deal with those who choose not to help.

This is why we ask each manager to behave in a 17 out of 17 manner. As Hunter noted, some have said they can't. These people can still work for us – they just can't lead.

Reference:

J. Johnson, L. Dakens, P. Edwards, and N. Morse, *Switchpoints: Culture Change on the Fast Track to Business Success* (New York Wiley, 2008), pp. 191-195.

CHAPTER 100: THE SUPERVISOR TO EMPLOYEE RELATIONSHIP

> "Perhaps the most important lesson that the science behind behavioral leadership teaches us is that, whether we know it or not, we are making a difference in others' work lives every day. Helen Keller once remarked, "The best and most beautiful things in the world cannot be seen or even touched. They must be felt with the heart." What we reinforce or discourage, intentionally or quite unintentionally, makes a difference. A difference that others feel. The question is, "Is it the right difference? Is it the difference that you want to be remembered by?" So, choose well the difference that you want to make in the workplace."
>
> S. Jacobs, *The Behavior Breakthrough: Leading Your Organization to a New Competitive Advantage,*
> (Austin: Greenleaf Book Group Press, 2013), pp. 215-216

Sometimes, ironically, the best feedback we get from our employees about how things are going for them is during the exit interview following their resignation. I guess the idea that they don't have to face their colleagues the next day grants them the freedom to be completely forthcoming. In some ways, I see this as being similar to a death-bed confession – it's probably about as accurate and true as you can imagine any workplace feedback to be – and, accordingly, I think it should be taken into consideration in that light.

There are a lot of good reasons why employees leave their current employment – they are getting a better paying job, or it's enhancing their career development, moving to a different part of the country. All of these can be considered "positive" reasons to leave, and cast no negative light on the company. On the other hand, based on statistics derived from exit interviews, one of the most prevalent reason employees leave the company is due to a bad relationship with their boss. Think about it – most of us spend more time with our boss than we do with our spouse, and so if that relationship isn't working, it has a huge effect on every other aspect of life; and so leaving the company is tantamount to divorce – it's the last resort.

So, if we want employees to be really productive in their jobs, they need to relate to their supervisor in a positive way. They need a supervisor who knows and understands them – not in any kind of *Stuart Smalley* way, but in an "I know what makes you tick and what's important to you, so I can help create a positive work environment for you" kind of way.

In most companies, the front line supervisor role is the toughest job in the company; they need to balance the work demands from their manager with the needs of their employees, and yet rarely do they get the right kind of training to help them do this. Typically the front line supervisor simply becomes the supervisor one day after they were promoted from the ranks of the employees in the department; and the plans for developing the new supervisor are either non-existent or hit and miss – the assumption being that because they were good enough at their job to get promoted to supervisor in the first place, then obviously they will make a good supervisor. Murphy had a field day with assumptions like these.

Because employee productivity and happiness are intensely linked, and because employee happiness is intensely linked to their relationship with their supervisor, it only makes sense to make sure the supervisor a) knows this, and b) is selected and trained to do a good job being supervisor. Companies today simply can't afford to have bad bosses. Bad bosses can wreak havoc in their department, and any other department the unhappy employee has contact with.

I like to think of it this way: the supervisor might control as much as 80% of what goes on in their department, so I think of them as the department "CEO", with accountability to provide the right direction, the right training, the right tools, and the right motivation to their employees. If the supervisor is ill-equipped to do so, they must be re-trained or replaced. You can't afford to have a bad "CEO" in the department.

CHAPTER 101: DO EMPLOYEES WANT TO GET PROMOTED?

> "The case for change"
>
> "The world of work has fundamentally changed, and because of it, leadership has never been more important – or more difficult. The old models, which assumed obedience and loyalty and management having all the answers, are no longer up to the task. There has never been a greater need to develop leadership at every level of the organization."
>
> Rose Patten, Special Advisor to CEO (former CHRO),
> BMO Financial Group

Do employees want to get promoted? While most people would answer this question with a "yes", my experience tells me that, in fact, most people are not actively seeking a promotion, and that at any given time the majority of employees are quite content to keep on doing what they're doing. Apparently the concept of "The Peter Principle" is quite well known. Nonetheless, there will always be a significant portion of the workforce that does want to be promoted, or at least moved in order to broaden their experience base and enhance their career development.

There was a time where "up or out" was the career development mantra. If you weren't considered promotion material, then you better start looking for a new job – but that really isn't sustainable in today's flatter organizations. Accordingly, the new metric for career development isn't promotion, but instead, varied and broader experience and challenges.

For example, in the HR department, the organizational levels have been reduced to allow us to get close to our employees and managers in the company and as a result, most HR people are pursuing work experiences rather than levels on the corporate HR ladder. In one company, I reduced the number of VP's and HR Directors by 40%, and while some HR employees complained about the lack of HR Director roles, the others thanked me for eliminating the bureaucracy.

The bottom line is you need to help your employees manage their careers within the context of your company's size. If you consistently hire top talent for each job in your department, you will incur more turnover and resentment due to your inability to promote all of the top performers in your group. I would rather have a blend of A, B and C players than all A players. Remember, you cannot have too many Michael Jordans or Wayne Gretzkys on your team – they will fight each other for the ball/puck.

CHAPTER 102: REWARDING POSITIVE CULTURAL BEHAVIOURS

> "The great CHROs manage culture and alignment – they drive/ communicate values, rewards systems and employee engagement."
>
> Claude Mongeau, CEO, Canadian National

> Organizational culture: The behaviour of humans who are part of an organization and the meanings that the people attach to their actions. Culture includes the organization values, visions, norms, working language, systems, symbols, beliefs and habits. It is also the pattern of such collective behaviours and assumptions that are taught to new organizational members as a way of perceiving, and even thinking and feeling. Organizational culture affects the way people and groups interact with each other, with clients, and with stakeholders.

Although the Wikipedia description above is somewhat clinical and even dry, when a company gets the culture right and employees buy in, it is a thing of beauty and a pleasure to watch in action – I've experienced it myself, at Maple Leaf Foods.

At MLF, employees make a point of telling me how much they feel in touch with the company's six values, and new hires tell me that it was the values that attracted them to the company in the first place.

Maple Leaf's CEO was the architect of these company values and he is active every day in making sure that they are reinforced and that it's more than just a list, but a living, breathing code that actually drives behaviour.

Every year MLF has an Annual Awards event to recognize employees who demonstrate the company values. Employees are nominated by peers or their managers for an award based on one of these six company values:

1. **Do what's right** – by acting with integrity, behaving responsibly, and treating people with respect.

2. **Deliver winning results** – by expecting to win, owning personal and collective accountability to deliver; taking appropriate risks without fear of failure while challenging for constant improvement.

3. **Build collaborative teams** – by attracting only the best people, serving, recognizing and rewarding their development and success; fostering a collaborative and open environment with the freedom to disagree, but always making timely decisions and aligning behind them.

4. **Get things done in a fact-based, disciplined way** – by seizing the initiative with the highest level of urgency and energy; meeting all commitments responsively while being objective, analytical and using effective process.

5. **Learn and grow, inwardly and outwardly** – by being introspective personally and organizationally, freely admitting mistakes or development needs; deeply understanding and connecting with consumers and stakeholders globally as a primary source of learning and growth.

6. **Dare to be transparent, passionate and humble** – by having the self-confidence and courage to be completely candid and direct; willing to communicate openly in a trusting manner; acting with passion, conviction and personal humility, especially when delivering winning results.

The nominations come from all functions within the salaried workforce, and from that group about 50 employees are selected to receive rewards. A company paid trip for two for 7 days to a great international location. And, the CEO chooses to *not* join the trip winners – he wants them to feel free to enjoy their reward without any undue pressure from him.

These employees are very appreciative of this reward and become great ambassadors of the company, its products, and its people, and, of course, its values.; It's not surprising then that MLF enjoys an incredibly high level of support for the corporate culture based on these six values.

CHAPTER 103: LABOUR RELATIONS – WORKING WITH UNIONS

> "I tell my people you don't have to go on strike to bring the company to its knees. All you have to do is stop taking initiative. Let your supervisors make all the decisions. Let them solve all of the problems. Just do exactly what you're told."
>
> A union leader

In a company like Maple Leaf Foods, where almost all hourly employees are unionized, keeping an eye on labour relations is an important part of the CHRO's role. Interestingly, I was first introduced to Michael McCain by the Canadian Director of the United Food & Commercial Workers Union. The UFCW represents more workers at Maple Leaf than any other union and the relationship runs deep. A successful labour relations strategy includes maintaining working relationships with the union at multiple levels, from the stewards on the shop floor to the senior leadership of the union. In building these relationships, it is critical that the CHRO avoids becoming an extra step in the grievance procedure.

Interacting with the Chief Stewards whenever I visit a plant is a great opportunity to get to know the people who have important influence with the hourly workforce. Stewards often have great insight and ideas about how to make our workplace better and increase employee engagement. When speaking to a steward, be careful not to provide a forum to resolve issues which are already being addressed by plant management through the grievance and arbitration processes under the collective agreement. Personally, my ulterior motive when meeting a steward is to identify future supervisory candidates.

In many workplaces, the union owns the health and safety agenda and is highly visible as the champion of worker safety. The Maple Leaf Safety Promise is a core strategy embedded in the culture of the organization in how its plants are run, keeping the company highly visible and accountable for worker safety.

Central to the union management relationship is the collective bargaining process. Collective bargaining is not a single event. Success is largely determined by how you manage the union relationship and engage employees between renewals. This is one of the reasons why the Maple Leaf People Strategy included a renewed and heightened focus on engaging the hourly workforce. Front line workers are critical to business success and it's easy to take them for granted. Investing in the engagement of the hourly workforce increases the likelihood that the contract will be renewed without incident, notwithstanding the emotional and unpredictable aspects of the collective bargaining process.

Critical to the successful renewal of a labour contract is preparation. Initiating an audit process 12 to 18 months before an agreement expires allows an opportunity to identify problems which might derail the negotiations. Where possible, don't defer the resolution of grievances to the bargaining table. Avail yourself to mediation and arbitration processes to clear any backlog of grievances in advance.

As the CHRO overseeing collective bargaining, I ensure the mandate has been approved in advance so the lead negotiators can properly pace the talks. To have credibility, the Ccmpany negotiator needs to have the authority to make the deal, without having to check back with the boss. The CHRO can't be the white knight riding in to save the day, otherwise they run the risk of being dragged into every contract negotiation, undermining the management bargaining committee.

The bargaining mandate includes a financial modeling of the maximum cost of the settlement that the business can support. It becomes a "line in the sand" whereby you will take a strike before crossing it. The financial model is detailed and fact based. Understanding what you "can" afford, is as important as knowing what you can't. Deals rarely come together by simply saying, "No", and the union accepting it. My preferred approach is to say, "While I can't do that, here's something I can do."

Strategies to achieve concessions during collective bargaining are best crafted with surgical precision. Broad-based concessions impacting the majority of the workforce are typically only achieved following a lengthy dispute. Getting an agreement often requires compromise. Management cannot expect to achieve concessions without increasing the risk of a work stoppage. Managing the expectations of senior management is an important part of the CHRO's job. It often seems that when a deal is reached and a strike or lockout averted, everyone is happy for about 30 minutes. Then buyer's remorse sets in as other members of management, not at the table, realize they didn't get everything they wanted, or feel they spent too much. This is a part of labour relations that simply "is what it is" and you just have to get over it.

"Sacred Cows" are terms and conditions of employment which are of significant importance to the company and its ability to run a profitable business. They include things like the ability to contract out work if necessary and the management right to schedule work in a cost-effective way. A tough stance on these issues should not come as a surprise to the union. Having frequent conversations with the union leading up to the actual bargaining will help the union rep's understanding of the company's position and allow him or her to manage the expectations of the membership regarding "Sacred Cows".

The importance of having a contingency plan cannot be overemphasized. Maintaining good union relationships and high workforce engagement is not guaranteed insurance you will not have a strike. Despite the best efforts of the union bargaining committee, they cannot always deliver a deal to the membership that meets their every expectation.

As the CHRO, I coach negotiators to treat the leadership of the union and particularly those sitting at the table with respect. They have a tough job to do, representing what are often competing demands of the membership. They are often, perhaps always, criticized for not getting enough.

Operating safe plants, treating employees and their union with transparency and respect does not change the fact that collective bargaining is an adversarial process. The perception of power is a fundamental requirement to bring the bargaining to a successful conclusion. The company is placed in a weakened bargaining position if the union and their committee believe the company cannot afford or is not prepared to take a strike. The contingency plan must be credible and be highly visible to the union.

When communicating the company's final offer, be unwavering on the principle of never improving the deal after employees engage in strike action. To do so, establishes the consequence that employees will get a better deal if they go on strike, which over the long-term will likely result in more disputes.

It is not uncommon to have a tentative agreement rejected by the membership and then result in the parties getting back together to find a way to salvage it. Trickier still, is if the rejected deal *was* the company's final offer. Improving the offer at this point suggests that you get more if you vote the offer down the first time. That said, it would be a rare situation where the union re-voted the same deal, resulting in the opposite outcome. The way out is often to "change two nickels for a dime" or "move the flowers around", resulting in a repackaging of the original deal in a non-material way.

Changing a final offer or maintaining a position that increases the likelihood of a dispute are critical events in the bargaining process. In both cases, the CHRO's involvement changes from being trusted and removed, to hands-on participant. In these situations, the importance of having maintained relationships at multiple levels within the union is revealed. Having the senior leader of the union and the CHRO both removed from the often emotionally-charged atmosphere at the table, is often a key ingredient to coming up with a solution that will work for both parties.

CHAPTER 104: PLAYING HARDBALL WITH TOMATOES

> "The CHRO usually knows the pulse of the employees.
> In one company, the CHRO accurately predicted the vote
> outcome on a decision between a pension plan versus the
> current employee profit sharing stock plan. The employees
> voted 90% to keep the stock program. The CHRO was right."
>
> Edward Lumley, Vice Chair, BMO Nesbitt Burns

In 1994, I was negotiating a collective agreement at the Heinz's Leamington Ontario factory. At risk was the entire workforce of 800 hundred employees. It would have been very easy to close the factory and move all of their production to various U.S. facilities that had excess capacity. The factory produced a large number of products that ranged from baby food to ketchup. At the end of the bargaining process, we reached a settlement that resulted in wage and benefit rollbacks for employees, but provided them with a more secure future. We had to play hardball with the employees in 1994, but saved the facility.

In November 2013, almost 20 years later, the Heinz Company announced the closure of the Leamington factory. The factory employs over 700 employees and their production volume is very large. A variety of circumstances have led to this closure announcement including a new owner of the company.

I am saddened by this news and extend best wishes to all of my former colleagues at the facility. To read more about the 1994 transformational labour relations story, please see Appendix 4 – Playing Hardball with Tomatoes. It was written by Suzanne Craig of the *Financial Post*.

10

The CHRO and the Board of Directors

"As an HRC chair I have always been extremely fortunate in the CHROs with whom I have worked. Without exception, we have enjoyed a great relationship, including incredibly frank discussions of the inner workings of the organizations involved and the strengths and weakness of the key people. I cannot say how typical this experience has been. Perhaps it goes with the territory as both the chair of the HRC and above all the CHRO are selected for their experience and judgment in such matters. But in talking with other chairs I have found that this is not always the case and some of these relationships border on the counter-productive."

Gordon Ritchie, Board Director

CHAPTER 105: CHRO ROLE AS DEFINED BY THE NATIONAL ASSOCIATION OF CORPORATE DIRECTORS

"The HRC Chair needs unfiltered access to the CHRO and needs their opinion about the CEO's skills and execution."

Peter Gleason, Managing Director & CFO, National Association of Corporate Directors

Founded in 1977, the U.S. National Association of Corporate Directors' mission is to advance exemplary board leadership, and they do a great job of providing knowledge and insight that board members can use to successfully navigate complex business challenges. They have more than 13,000 members who are directors and key executives of private and non-profit companies.

The National Association describes the CHRO role on its website as follows:

Position Description

Introduction

The role of the chief human resources officer (CHRO) is to serve as a member of the executive team with key responsibilities of linking the "people strategy" to the business strategy, and developing and driving human capital programs and processes that both align with the overall objectives of the business and to ensure regulatory compliance. As a part of the leadership team and a named executive officer, the CHRO can be expected to have a broad business background and to be knowledgeable about the company's governance, strategy, operations, finance, sales/marketing, and products/services.

Purpose and Scope

With the charge of making sure that all levels of the organization have the required talent for the short and long term to support the business, the CHRO develops and leads an end-to-end talent architecture including: talent acquisition and recruitment, diversity and inclusion, training, leadership development, employee relations, performance management and evaluations, total rewards and executive compensation, organizational development, HR analytics and information systems, and even succession planning. In addition, the CHRO often serves as a trusted advisor to the CEO and the executive leadership team while overseeing a generalist team that provides similar support to divisional or other functional parts of the company. Depending on the needs of the company, the CHRO can also oversee internal communications, corporate social responsibility, and/or payroll, and actively participate in due diligence in any mergers, acquisitions, or other significant corporate events.

The CHRO works closely with the compensation committee of the board and its advisors on compensation philosophy, executive compensation, and incentive and equity compensation with emphasis on pay for performance. There may be times that the CHRO, along with other executives, will interface with the audit committee on other aspects of compliance, ethics, and/or risk issues, and with the nominating/governance committee on succession discussions.

As the leader of the human resources function, the CHRO will typically have a team of technical experts in areas such as compensation, benefits, training, leadership development, organizational development, HR information systems, and operations. In addition, the HR executive will have a team of "generalists" who support and advise various functions or divisions of the business, ensuring a consistent implementation of practices and policies to support leaders and employees in driving business outcomes.

In some cases, the CHRO or senior executive managing the function might report to the COO, CFO, CAO, or general counsel rather than to the CEO. CHROs who report to the CEO indicate that they are more effective in this reporting structure, with other named executives as their peers.

The role of the CHRO has evolved over the recent decade. CEOs have increasingly recognized the importance of the human capital function as a critical lever in the success of the business. In the past, the CHRO was an administrative functionary focused on "personnel." Today, top CHROs are key business partners in driving strategy, performance, accountability, culture, and change.

Talent management, executive compensation, and risk/ethics are at the forefront of the CHRO's agenda. Additionally, the rising costs of healthcare, regulatory changes, new technologies, and the challenges created by an increasingly global, multigenerational, and mobile workforce receive priority.

Information and Reporting Expectations

In general and at a minimum, the board should expect information, metrics and performance data, competitive information process support, and guidance from the CHRO. Mainly, this information allows the board to evaluate and appropriately compensate the CEO and ensure leadership succession, as well as to ensure its own effectiveness. Thus, the principal information provided is related to the following items:

- Executive compensation.
- Compensation discussion and analysis.
- Compensation program design and philosophy.
- Market data.
- Performance measures and results.
- Legal and regulatory compliance requirements.
- Succession planning.
- CEO and executive team competency requirements.
- Assessments of top talent including readiness levels.
- Development and identification plans for top talent including individual and organizational gap analysis.
- Workforce plan, talent management, and workplace environment.
- Assessment of workforce's capability and commitment to execute on business strategy.
- Environmental/code of conduct and legal risks.
- Productivity issues, gaps and opportunities, along with plans to address issues.
- Diversity and inclusion.
- Crisis management planning.

> **"Time for a Change"**
>
> "It is time for CHROs to change their role and respect to boards.
> They need to go beyond simply providing input to the board with
> respect to compensation and succession decisions and enter into
> a strategic support and advice relationship with the board. Human
> capital management and business strategy decisions are too important
> to be left to board members who lack expertise and data on talent
> management and organizational effectiveness."
>
> P. Wright, J. Boudreau, D. Pace, E. Sartain, P. McKinnon, and R. Antoine,
> *The Chief HR Officer: Defining the New Role of Human Resource
> Leaders* (San Francisco: John Wiley & Sons, Inc., 2011), p. 191

CHAPTER 106: BOARD DIRECTORS' EXPECTATIONS OF THE CHRO

> "There is a trend to put more CHROs on Boards.
> They would bring good judgment."
>
> Stan Magidson, CEO, Institute of Corporate Directors

One of the more interesting dynamics in any CHRO's career will be their inter-action with the Board of Directors, especially the HRC Chair. This dynamic can be filled with great learning, great rewards, and, to quote Dickens, "great expectations".

Sometimes it's difficult, within the framework of the day-to-day CHRO role, to discern what these expectations are. I interviewed a distinguished group of experienced Board Directors from Canada and the United States to find out what they generally expected of their CHRO. The list included Sarah Raiss, Yvonne Jackson, Geoff Beattie, David Emerson, Gordon Ritchie, James Olson, Edward Lumley, Stan Magidson, Peter Gleason, Claude Lamoureux, Chris Bart, and Purdy Crawford.

When I asked them to describe key accountabilities of the CHRO from a Board perspective, they offered the following comments:

- Hire, retain, and evaluate great people. (Claude Lamoureux)

- The CHRO must have a real opinion on the talent in organization. An objectively driven process from CHRO can reduce subjectively of CEO and Board. (Geoff Beattie)

- "Brave" person to give feedback to CEO and team. (Sarah Raiss)

- Overall responsibility for the health of the human organization. (Gordon Ritchie)

- Provide individual coaching to CEO and others. (James Olson)

- Become the Chief Strategy Execution officer. (Chris Bart)

- Build capacity for talent. (Yvonne Jackson)

- Provide independent and frank advice to the HRC. (Gordon Ritchie)

- Must be on top of CEO succession planning. (Purdy Crawford)

- Steward of talent portfolio to execute corporate strategy. (David Emerson)

- Provide balanced advice to the Board. (David Emerson)

- Accountable to the whole Board and CEO. (Stan Madigson)

- Interlocutor – has the trust of various partners who make decisions. (Ed Lumley)

- Partners with the executive team on talent management. (Peter Gleason)

- Trusted confidante to CEO and HRC Chair. (Ed Lumley)

- Role is dynamic and changing – must look at the future for talent decisions. (Geoff Beattie)

- Develop the right culture for success. (Claude Lamoureux)

- Keeper and co-definer of culture (values expected of people).(Sarah Raiss)

- Must be on top of leadership and ethical behaviour. (Purdy Crawford)

- Manage the social costs of running the business. (Geoff Beattie)

The second question I posed to the distinguished panel of Board Directors was "what are the skills needed for a future CHRO?" Their responses were both inclusive and insightful:

- The ability to see the business in a 5-10 year horizon. (Geoff Beattie)

- Understand CEO/Board personalities -- be dispassionate and objective. (David Emerson)

- Skill to serve several masters at once – CEO and Board. (Gordon Ritchie)

- Math and accounting skills combined with operating experience. (Stan Madigson)

- Ability to assess talent and provide coaching. (James Olson)

- Be passionate – lead by example, lead from behind the scenes. (Chris Bart)

- The savvy to push and pull the CEO. (Purdy Crawford)

- Understand compensation program and other motivational programs. (Peter Gleason)

- To be trustworthy and candid. (Ed Lumley)

- Compensation in their DNA – know the levers for incentive programs. (Yvonne Jackson)

- Business understanding and knowledge of strategy formulation. (David Emerson)

- Strategy execution focus – eat, sleep, breathe, and talk strategy execution. (Chris Bart)

- Change management practices in transformation situations. (Yvonne Jackson)

- Must be, and be seen to be, a straight shooter. (Gordon Ritchie)

- Role model for leadership behaviours – i.e., ethics (Sarah Raiss)

- Management skills appropriate to managing the administrative aspects. (James Olson)

- Knows how to identify weak players and take action. (Purdy Crawford)

- Strong negotiating skills – manages conflicts with management, Board, and unions. (Ed Lumley)

- Relationship building and communications skills. (Sarah Raiss)

- Strong financial skills to understand the total cost of operating a business. (Geoff Beattie)

- Know how to manage by walking around. Plugged into rest of organization. (Claude Lamoureux)

For biographical information about the Board Directors referenced here, please see Appendix 7.

CHAPTER 107: HRC CHAIR AND CHRO: A DELICATE RELATIONSHIP

> "As the HRC chair, I relied heavily on the CHRO to re-negotiate a CEO contract. The process was very time consuming and the CHRO helped shaped the thought process. He was strategic and independent from the CEO."
>
> Yvonne Jackson, Board Director

"Should you decide to take the senior vice president, human resources job, please be aware that you will report to two people: the CEO and me. You will require great skills to make this relationship work well."

Purdy Crawford made this statement to me when I was hired as the Senior Vice President, Human Resources (SVP, HR) at CN Rail in 2001. He was the Chair of the Human Resources Committee (HRC) at CN, and he wanted me to know in advance that our working relationship was going to be just as important as my connection with the CEO.

In today's fast-paced business environment, the relationship between the HRC Chair and the CHRO needs to be a solid partnership. The relationship is the same as that of the Audit Committee Chair and the CFO. In both cases, there is a need to work effectively together to balance the interests of the company and its shareholders.

In this chapter, I identify eight key challenges that the HRC Chair and the CHRO can encounter. How successfully they can meet these difficult issues depends to a large extent on the relationship the two are able to develop.

(a)   Challenge 1: The Overpaid CEO

In one large company, the chair of the Board was preoccupied with the proposition that the CEO should be the highest paid executive in his industry, as the organization was a benchmark for performance in its sector. For the Chair, having the highest paid CEO in the industry was a badge of honour. The Chair got his way. Subsequently, however, the company's performance began to slip. Market analysts started to comment on the overpaid CEO, and their pronouncements were beginning to create a negative public perception towards the company. To deal with this unintended outcome, the HRC chair and the CHRO agreed to confront the Board Chair and to insist on coming up with a strategy to correct the situation. While the Chair and the CEO were not pleased, they agreed to take action.

The lesson learned: Leadership compensation must be carefully managed.

(b)   Challenge 2: When Management and Board Philosophies Differ

Management and the Board do not always see things the same way. In some cases, this can broaden discussion and lead to positive outcomes. However, when differing philosophies result in heated conflict, there is the potential for considerable damage.

The decision to pay an annual performance bonus to the CEO and senior executives is usually straightforward as it is based on established factors. The following is an example of this potential for damage when policies are not set and followed:

When a very successful company missed its targets due to some unusual business challenges, the Board decreed there would be no bonuses. Members of the senior management team disagreed; they proposed to award a nominal bonus for middle managers to reflect their extraordinary efforts in a difficult year and to encourage their further initiative and engagement.

The HRC Chair refused, concerned about external criticism and setting a precedent. It became an argument about who was right and who was wrong, which damaged the working relationship between the HRC chair and the CHRO.

The lesson learned: It is important that policies be clear and respond to real life circumstances. The solution is to craft policies that can be applied with some flexibility to support the priorities of the organization. Keep in mind the advice from Jack Welch, the former CEO of GE: "Even in a bad year, the best performers deserve rewards."

(c)   Challenge 3: Dueling Compensation Consultants

The increased focus on governance has encouraged Boards to pay more attention to executive compensation. As a result, there may be two separate consulting firms hired to advise the HRC and management on appropriate Compensation strategies. While in theory the two sources of advice can be "aggregated", it does not always work out that way.

A global company was faced with a situation where the HRC and management's compensation consultants gave very different recommendations. Rather than end up with a fight between the dueling consultants, the HRC chair elected to bring in a third consultant to break the tie.

The lesson learned: Having consultants duelling for executive compensation is a waste of money and time. The solution is to let the HRC own the process, since the Board is ultimately responsible.

(d)   Challenge 4: The HRC Chair and CHRO do not Get Along

It is important that the HRC Chair and the CHRO develop an effective working relationship. In most cases, these two individuals do not get to pick their respective partners, and personal differences can wreak havoc.

In one company, when the Board Chair chose to replace the retiring HRC Chair with a long standing Board member, a cold war ensued. The new HRC chair and the CHRO lacked mutual respect due to prior disagreements. A relationship based on shared dislike does not progress well. The result in this case was that they each spent more time trying to block each other than on anything else, and an exasperated CEO had to be the mediator.

The lesson learned: The HRC chair and the CHRO do not have to admire each other, but they do need to find a way to co-exist. The easiest solution is to make sure that if the incumbent is the HRC Chair, that person gets a voice in selecting the CHRO. Alternatively, if the incumbent is the CHRO, the CEO and the Board Chair need to ensure that there will be some chemistry between them when the HRC Chair is selected.

(e)   Challenge 5: Certain Members of the HRC do not Understand the Basics

A disruptive element in the HRC committee can occur when one or more of the members do not have the required basic knowledge to understand key recommendations. Since the HRC has some very serious mandates, this lack of critical knowledge will decrease the effectiveness of the committee.

In one such example, the Board Chair wanted to give two new Board members experience on the HRC. Unfortunately, these individuals had no direct business experience and lacked any knowledge of executive compensation. These members were slow to pick up on essential concepts and their numerous questions became annoying to the other members of the HRC. While they wanted to contribute, their proposals were so off base that the HRC chair had to overrule suggestions from them.

The lesson learned: The HRC is not a place for Board members to learn what they do not know. One way to avoid this is by establishing knowledge and skills criteria that prospective candidates for the HRC must meet before their appointment. An alternative solution is to put in place a plan for the development of such inexperienced members prior to their joining the HRC so that they can acquire the necessary expertise. Both the HRC chair and the CHRO have a role to play in coaching and supporting new members.

(f)   Challenge 6: The HRC Chair and CEO do not Get Along

There is an argument to be made that a CEO has multiple bosses: the Board Chair, the HRC Chair and the Board as a whole. The quality of the working relationship between the CEO and these multiple bosses varies. If there is a poor connection at any point, it can be a distraction for everyone involved.

For example, in one company, the CEO and HRC chair were like oil and water. It seemed that they each went out of their way not to get along with each other, and their disputes were well known in the boardroom and within the senior ranks of the company. The irony was that both of them were very talented and strong contributors. It fell to the Board Chair and the CHRO to leverage their existing relationships with both individuals and in order to broker deals to get business done. Eventually, the HRC Chair decided to retire, which allowed the Board Chair to find person that would be more compatible with the CEO.

The lesson learned: Arguments at the top can stall progress. The solution is for the Chair to engage in a careful selection process in order to find the right person from the Board to work with the CEO.

(g) Challenge 7: A Lack of Agreement on Internal CEO Successors

One of the big challenges for a Board is to get close enough to internal executives to assess their candidacy for the CEO role. Many boards find this to be a difficult task, and it is not unusual for members to disagree on who are the best internal candidates. There will always be partisans and detractors for each candidate. These differences can help to bring all information to the table. On the other hand, disagreements can go too far and split the Board, which leads to a stalemate in making a decision. When this situation occurred in one large company, the HRC Chair and the CHRO were united in their insistence that external assessments had to be done for the prospective candidates.

The lesson learned: To break an internal impasse, new information from outside sources is often useful. Gathering data from a variety of sources, including objective and independent sources, helps to identify the best internal CEO successors. After this is achieved, the necessary consensus can be reached to support ongoing development for possible succession into the CEO role.

(h) Challenge 8: Everyone is a Human Resources Expert

There is some confusion over the nature of the responsibilities in the HR area. A common erroneous idea is that HR is "just about people". This idea leads to the assumption that it is easy to be an expert in the field. Many individuals feel that they could easily fill the role of HRC chair or CHRO. In reality, HR is about putting in place policies and processes to support an organization's present business goals and future needs. While the end outcomes affect people, so do all of the organizational policies, systems and procedures. People without a background in finance, do not normally believe they can automatically be experts, but this is not so for HR.

For example, in one situation, the entire Board was very insistent on questioning all the recommendations from the HRC. Valuable Board time was consumed and the HRC Chair lost authority. Eventually, the Board Chair had to replace the incumbent HRC Chair. The new HRC Chair insisted on limited interference from non-HRC members, which lead to a more effective decision-making process.

The lesson learned: The issues that the HRC handles are of compelling interest and attract everyone's attention. Ensuring that the HRC chair is both grounded in HR and a savvy leader will inspire confidence in other Directors and will lead to a more efficient decision-making process.

(i)   Conclusion

Many organizations are likely to face one or more of the challenges outlined above. The best way to deal with these is to ensure you have the "right" people in the roles of HRC Chair and CHRO, and to acknowledge that the "right" person may change over time. A basic requirement is that the CHRO have a broad general knowledge in HR matters and that they be able to apply this knowledge to business needs. Also, just as the Audit Committee Chair must have a substantive financial background, so too should the HRC Chair have broad human resources experience.

The HRC is becoming a focal point for many boards. The best companies realize the importance of having their people strategy aligned "from the boardroom to the factory floor". This focus on HR can attract new Board members who want to add value to the way the company manages its people. It is an exciting time to be part of the HRC.

CHAPTER 108: TRUTHS AND MYTHS OF CEO SUCCESSION PLANNING

> "The Board selects the CEO, approves the strategy
> and needs to constantly support the CEO."
>
> Hunter Harrison, CEO, Canadian Pacific

If companies were rated on their CEO succession planning process, many would not get much more than an average score. Why is this? The capacity to identify, develop and then appoint a CEO from internal candidates rests on the establishment of a high quality succession-planning process. Sadly, it seems to be missing in many companies.

Let's examine the truths and myths about CEO succession planning.

Truths

• CEO succession planning is the most important task of a Board.

• The current CEO is the best person to develop a successor.

- There are usually viable candidates within an organization for the top job, provided there is sufficient time to develop and prepare them.

- CEOs from internal ranks are usually more successful than external executives.

Myths

- Boards devote an inordinate amount of time on CEO succession planning.

- The CEO is fully supportive of developing potential successors.

- Company shareholders are strongly interested in the CEO succession planning process and will exert pressure to be sure it is done correctly.

- If there are no viable internal successors, finding a CEO is relatively easy since there are more executives than there are top jobs.

- The Chairperson can step into the CEO role on an interim basis if necessary.

These myths don't stand up to close scrutiny. Many boards probably spend less than 20% of their time on succession planning. As senior human resources executives tend to be excluded from such discussions due to a perceived conflict of interest, there may be very little expertise brought to bear on discussions and on the shaping of an effective succession process.

In general, current CEOs enjoy their jobs too much to want their successor in place. They are likely to give this task low priority. Nor is it unheard of for a CEO to see identified successors as a threat and attempt to undermine them.

Except perhaps for large institutional investors, most shareholders' prime interest is not in how company processes work, but in the value of their shares. Organized shareholder pressure, when it happens, is directed at CEO compensation practices.

Last minute sink-or-swim approaches to appointing a CEO don't work very well. Finding a CEO who understands the essence of the business and has strong leadership and strategic skills is very difficult. As for the Chair stepping in, most have been removed from day-to-day business leadership for years and lack the currently needed skills for the role.

It is unfortunate that the myths about CEO succession planning still seem to dominate the thinking on many boards. These myths seem to overwhelm the two critical truths; with time and patience good candidates for the role can be developed, and an internal candidate is more likely to be successful. While it can take years to develop the right candidates, it is one of the best investments that any Board can approve.

> "No company ever got to be a talent master without the wholehearted commitment and participation of an enlightened CEO: one who understands that building talent is the most important priority and will be their legacy."
>
> B. Conaty and R. Charan, *The Talent Masters,*
> *Why Smart Leaders Put People Before Numbers*
> (New York: Crown Publishing Group, 2010), p. 254

CHAPTER 109: DEVELOPING INTERNAL SUCCESSORS FOR THE CEO ROLE

> "When I appointed Bill Conaty our new senior VP for human resources in November 1993, I told him that our biggest job was to select the next CEO for the company. The thing you and I will both live with for a long time is getting the right person in this job."
>
> J. Welch and J. Byrne, *Jack: Straight from the Gut*
> (New York: Business Plus, 2003), p. 409

In 2001, a very large Canadian company informed two internal candidates that they were potential successors to the current CEO. Eight years later, in 2009, the company announced the appointment of one of these individuals to the CEO role. It had been one of the longest succession planning processes in Canadian business, but it worked well.

I would generally not advocate telling internal candidates 8 years in advance that they might become the next CEO. Too many things can happen in the interim to change the potential outcome. Fortunately, in this true story, the two candidates stayed with the company and supported each other until the final decision was made.

In this chapter, I will discuss a more realistic 3-year plan to develop internal successors for the CEO role. First, however, a question: "Is it better to promote from within or to hire an external candidate for the CEO position?" The research on the answer is mixed. Some studies show that the internal CEO successor produces better results over the long term. Another study disputes this conclusion and advocates hiring the outside person.

In my experience, if the company is doing well, promoting from within is more advisable. That decision provides stability and continuity in executing the company's strategy. The transition for the current CEO is easier, the troops know the new leader, and the market will reward the company for the Board's good planning. I would recommend going outside to find the next CEO only in cases where the company's performance and strategy are broken, or where discontinuous change is occurring in the organization's industry sector.

Let us suppose that it is known that the CEO is planning to retire in 3 years and that two or three internal candidates have been identified. What can the Board do to develop these potential successors so they are ready to take on the role? Below are my suggested steps and developmental recommendations for each year.

(a) Three Years Away

Tell the candidates. The Board should be open with the potential successors. Be direct: tell them that they are in the running and will be judged partly on how they perform in the race. Be clear that if anyone turns the race into a messy competition, that person will not get the job.

Undertake rigorous assessment. The Board should insist on an outside assessment of the skills of each candidate. Inform candidates that psychological testing, interviews, in-basket exercises, role plays, and 360 surveys will be conducted and that the assessment report will become the basis for each candidate's development plans.

Provide an executive coach – preferably the same coach for each candidate. The coach will help each person prepare for the CEO role and will provide a sounding board for each of them. In addition, the coach will report to the Board on the progress of each candidate.

Ensure the individuals have exposure to the Board. Each candidate should spend at least a day with the Board's human resource committee (HRC). The purpose of this day together is threefold: 1) to give the candidate an opportunity to discuss the business with directors; 2) to give Board members an opportunity to get to know the person better; and 3) to set the expectations for a future CEO role.

Encourage candidates to talk to each other. An honest and open discussion among candidates is desirable. They need to answer the questions: "How can we make the next 3 years successful for each of us and the company?" and "Will I stay with the company if someone else gets the CEO spot?" This discussion is critical so that the race does not become a deleterious battle.

Enlist the current CEO as a mentor. The CEO is accountable for the development of a successor. Most successful CEOs want to hand the ball to a successor in the best possible manner. They should be expected to play a significant mentoring role.

(b) Two Years Away

Provide the candidates with international experience. If the company has a large international presence and potential successors do not have this experience, give them a project (linked to their current position), which allows them to build a better understanding of the company's international business.

Consider providing the individuals with media and financial training. The candidates need to become good spokespeople for the company. In addition, they must have a solid understanding of the financials of the business. Specialized coaches can be brought in to help in these two areas.

Arrange visits by Board members. Members of the HRC should spend a day with each candidate in their workplace. This will allow Board members to see the candidates in action with their team as they face their business challenges.

Meet the shareholders and analysts. The candidates need to be profiled at the annual shareholders meeting and to make presentations at various industry conferences.

Seek an outside directorship. Getting Board experience is a wonderful way to develop an understanding of the CEO-Board relationship. It provides an opportunity to be involved in developing another company's strategic plan and its execution.

Benchmark against external candidates. The Board should engage a search firm to assess the talent in the industry or in related businesses. This is the time to determine if the internal candidates stack up well against outside talent.

(c) One Year Away

Obtain feedback from the management team. They will know the key successors and will be able to provide observations on each of them. The Board needs to encourage the retention of the candidates during the transition and the other members of the management team can be helpful in this regard.

Control the egos. Being promoted to the CEO is a "big ego event". Once in the CEO role, the successor will need to engage people. Displaying a large ego will not help in this task. The HRC needs to carefully monitor the candidates' egos and rein in those that are becoming excessive.

Retain the other candidate(s). The Board Chair needs to meet with each candidate to encourage them to stay with the company if another candidate is selected for the CEO position. It is important not to assume that unsuccessful candidates will leave the company. Retention is achievable if the process is handled well.

Undertake a personal health and family check. The HRC chair may find it valuable to meet with each candidate to discuss individual health and fitness plans, thereby forming an opinion of each one's readiness to handle the stress of the CEO role. In addition, it may be useful to meet with each of the spouses to discuss the demands of the CEO position and perhaps discuss possible strategies to manage these demands.

Communicate with employees. Most employees in medium to large companies do not get to engage with the CEO on a first name basis. However, they are very interested in knowing about the process of selecting the new CEO and the candidates being considered. Keep them posted on the process.

Create an internal MBA Program. Three months before the decision on who will become the new CEO is made, it may be useful to remove the candidates from their current roles and send them on a "mini" internal MBA program around the company to assess the current state of the business, meet critical customers, visit key company sites, and spend time with non-HRC Board members. This move can pay dividends in preparing the new CEO to get a "running start" on the first day. It can also build the knowledge and skills of the other candidates who will thus be encouraged to stay with the company.

(d) The Announcement of the New CEO

A carefully considered communications plan will put the final touches on your company's successful succession planning process. About 3 to 6 months prior to the exit of the current CEO is the best timing for an announcement. The Board

Chair should inform each potential successor of the Board's decision regarding the new CEO before any public announcement is made.

If the succession planning process has been well constructed, the other candidates will remain with the company. The Board and the current CEO will sleep better at night knowing they have done their best to create a smooth transition to a new CEO.

> "In-camera sessions can become so extensive that they dominate board deliberations to the detriment of the relationship with the CEO and management."
>
> David Emerson, Board Director

CHAPTER 110: THE ROLE OF THE BOARD IN ASSESSING THE PEOPLE STRATEGY

> "As HR professionals contribute to strategy discussions, they need to master competencies that will overcome these challenges and enable strategic work. Our research has identified specific be, know and do insights that HR brings to strategic dialogues. The chief contribution to business strategy formulation involved helping shape the vision of the future of the business. HR professionals spot opportunities for business success, framing complex ideas in simple and useful ways. In the process, they help identify and manage risk and provide alternative insights on business issues. They translate business strategy into a talent (workforce) or culture (workplace) set of initiatives."
>
> D. Ulrich, J. Younger, W. Brockbank, and M. Ulrich, *HR from the Outside In: Six Competencies for the Future of Human Resources* (New York: McGraw Hill, 2012), p. 79

It was a recipe for chaos. Start with a large institutional shareholder deciding to sell their shares. Mix in a new, somewhat critical hedge-fund shareholder. Stir gently to avoid a proxy battle between the hedge fund and the majority shareholder. Fold in ongoing recovery from a food-safety crisis two years earlier that had rocked the company to its core. Add in a major transformation to reshape the supply-chain footprint, and spice it up with an enterprise-wide SAP implementation.

With all this going on, one could say that the last thing Maple Leaf Foods needed was to create and implement a new People Strategy. On the other hand, it could be said that that was exactly what was needed. I certainly fall into the latter camp, since I joined Toronto-based Maple Leaf Foods in January 2011 specifically to develop and implement a new People Strategy. The rationale was simple.

It goes without saying that a business needs a well thought-out strategy that defines why the organization exists and how it will compete in the marketplace. The strategy dictates which paths to follow and creates focus for the organization. Much has been written about the importance of having an operational plan to translate the strategy into action. As Morris Chang, Chairman and CEO of Tai-wan-based Taiwan Semiconductor Manufacturing Company (TSMC) has put it, "Without strategy, execution is aimless. Without execution, strategy is useless."

Often, however, organizations are also in need of an enabling People Strategy. Plans are executed by people, and they are executed with excellence only when the right people, with the right abilities and high desire to perform, are in the right seats at the right time. This doesn't happen by accident. A well thought-out People Strategy is critical in order to enable and drive the execution of the oper-ational plan and, ultimately, achieve the business strategy. Given the situation at Maple Leaf Foods last year, it was exactly the right time to review and reshape the company's People Strategy.

(a)   What is a People Strategy?

A good People Strategy is built on a deep understanding of what the company needs to deliver, and the subsequent translation of those needs into the right enabling people programs and processes. It's relatively easy to "mirror" your com-petitors by copying products and services, or by buying similar equipment. But it is much harder to duplicate a People Strategy. At Maple Leaf Foods we define the four core elements of a People Strategy as the necessary culture, leadership, engagement, and talent base to run the company and deliver results. A People Strategy looks at the people systems in place within the perspective of these four core elements, and then determines what should be changed, added, removed, or emphasized to ensure business success. Specific people systems examined should include: organizational structure, performance management, rewards, talent and succession management, and development systems. Next, action plans and tactics must be defined to execute the People Strategy.

Like any strategy, a People Strategy makes choices for the organization and creates focus. People Strategy is never a plug-and-play solution. Benchmarking to other companies can prompt new ideas, but it can't provide the answers for what it is that a specific organization needs to succeed.

(b) Why Should the Board Care about the People Strategy?

The Human Resources and Compensation Committee (HRC) needs to be confident that there is a People Strategy to support and enable execution of the operational plans. People Strategy takes the HRC beyond CEO succession and Named Executive Officer (NEO) compensation, although these can certainly be elements of the strategy.

The committee should ask to see the organization's People Strategy, and make sure it is aligned, focused, and forward-looking. Alignment with the business strategy is demonstrated when the more critical operational plans are clearly and fully supported with solutions to ensure the right people and the right working environment are in place. Focus is demonstrated by having a few critical people areas highlighted as having the highest impact on business success. The strategy is forward-looking when it anticipates the business's operation's needs, both for today and for tomorrow.

(c) How Should the Board Assess the People Strategy?

There are three key ways in which the HRC should assess and support the People Strategy:

1. Ask questions to understand, and provide feedback. HRC members should actively ask questions to understand the elements of the People Strategy and to provide feedback, drawing on their experiences in other organizations. Most importantly, members should question in order to ensure that the strategy is aligned, focused, and forward-looking.

2. Monitor progress through regular updates. On an ongoing basis, the HRC should receive updates on how the key initiatives of the strategy are progressing. To make these reviews effective, the HR team needs to put in place specific, clear and actionable metrics against the strategy and its key initiatives. The HRC should ask questions to pinpoint areas where the strategy may require modification, based on both the People Strategy updates and on the progress of the business plans.

3. Meet with and observe people. HRC members should have the opportunity to spend time with the leaders responsible for execution of key business plans

in order to observe their work environments, alignment, and engagement. Unlike other areas of the business, where "nose in, fingers out" is the order of the day, I believe the HRC needs to get close enough to key talent to watch them in action in order to provide the right level of oversight to the People Strategy.

(d)   HRC Involvement with the Maple Leaf Foods People Strategy

In late 2010, Maple Leaf Foods defined its new Value Creation Strategy, which created a blueprint for organizational success. The HR and executive teams took a deep look at existing people systems and determined that a new People Strategy was required to drive the successful execution of the business strategy.

Cheryl Fullerton, Director of HR transformation, was selected to drive this project for Maple Leaf Foods. She recognized going into the project that there was a solid foundation to build upon: "We have a very strong culture supported by some excellent performance and development solutions. Our opportunity was to build on this solid base and identify how to reshape and refocus for the next stage in our company's evolution."

It took about 6 months to create the strategy, and the creation process included conversations with all senior executives in the organization, and involved detailed reviews with many executives (including the CEO and the business unit presidents). These conversations were critical to ensuring that the direction of the strategy and the key initiatives defined under the strategy would be accepted and supported by the business team.

In the summer of 2011, a new People Strategy was approved by CEO Michael McCain and other senior executives. The strategy would ensure that the right people and the right people solutions were put in place to deliver results under Maple Leaf's new business strategy. McCain noted that: "Our prior People Strategy was heavily focused around establishing and building our values-based culture, and on leadership development ... But one thing we need now is increased focus on our hourly employees, to engage all employees fully in our business success."

Maple Leaf's HRC assessed their People Strategy through review and feedback, and will continue to assess and support the strategy through monitoring and observation.

(e) Review and Feedback

Maple Leaf Foods' HRC reviewed the People Strategy in detail and actively discussed the overall strategic focus, as well as the specific tactics identified to execute the strategy. Of particular interest to the HRC were:

- Culture and employee engagement
- Employee share purchase plans
- Leadership style
- Incentive plans
- Executive stock ownership
- Succession planning
- Gender diversity in leadership

The company's new People Strategy includes a new definition for great people leadership, and maps out initiatives to build new capability within the organization's people leaders. This new definition of people leadership is described through a model that looks at both "what is delivered" (results) and "how it's delivered" (engagement behaviours). Drilling deeply into this model helps leaders understand how to influence behaviour and, more importantly, the consequences that follow behaviour. A review of this model generated active discussion at the HRC on various leadership styles, and on the elements of great leadership.

(f) Monitoring

On an ongoing basis, the HRC will receive updates on the progress of the strategy, provided through a dashboard that includes key success measures, and updates on the various initiatives in progress to achieve the strategy.

HRC chair Gordon Ritchie is particularly interested in monitoring the depth of the talent pool behind key leadership positions. In a recent meeting, Gord emphasized, "We need to go deeper into the organization to identify the next generation of leaders, and then make sure they get the right developmental experiences so they'll be ready to step in and take us to the next stage in the company's evolution."

(g) Observation

Each year, as part of a "Board Connect" program, every Board member spends one day in the business with a senior leader. This gives Board members an opportunity to assess the leadership talent in the business, which in turn enhances future succession-planning conversations and provides insight into the execution of key operational plans. In 2012, Board Connect visits will include a day with the senior Vice-President of Manufacturing, to gain insight into the progress of the supply-chain transformation, and a day with the senior Vice-President of Marketing for MLF's meat business, to gain insight on its growth plans. On these visits, Board members have the opportunity to observe the leadership, engagement, and alignment of the teams they meet.

Director Jim Olson, who joined the Maple Leaf Foods Board in 2011, didn't wait for his Board Connect visit to observe and provide input on some key people elements. Jim has global experience in the consumer packaged-goods industry, specifically in manufacturing and supply chains. He recently visited some Maple Leaf plants and offered valuable thoughts on supervisory training and increasing the engagement of manufacturing employees, which are two key elements of the new People Strategy.

(h) Conclusion

The HRC is ultimately responsible for ensuring that the organization's people, HR processes, and culture align with its chosen business strategy. The best way to create shared understanding between the committee, the CHRO, and the CEO on how this alignment will be achieved is to conduct a strategic analysis of the people implication of the business strategy, and then to define a formal People Strategy.

The process involves both inputs and outputs. The input is a clear business strategy and well-developed operational plans. The output is an aligned, focused, forward-looking People Strategy with actionable execution plans. The key objective of the People Strategy is the same as that of the overall business strategy: superior business results.

CHAPTER 111: CORPORATE CULTURE AND THE BOARD

> "Every company has its own tapestry."
>
> John Lynch SVP, Corporate Human Resources, General Electric

What is corporate culture and why is it so important? A company's culture is important because we are all looking for meaning in our work and our lives. The more clearly we can connect our values to our work, the more alive we feel and the more engaged we are at work. The greater our engagement at work, the more productive and successful we and the company can be.

Board governance experts advocate that Boards set the "tone at the top" to create a company culture of integrity and honesty. But what does culture mean?

How do we define company culture, measure it, drive it, and hold management accountable for it?

(a) Company Culture Defined

What does "organizational culture" mean? Essentially it boils down to how things get done within a company. As I explained in *SwitchPoints: Culture Change on the Fast Track to Business Success*, "Culture is the patterns of behaviours and actions that are encouraged or discouraged by people or systems over time."

Behaviour is what you see people do or say every day. When these behaviours are aligned and effective, organizations tend to be more successful. Within any one organization, especially larger ones, there may be micro-cultures, where things get done a little differently. As long as these differences are not too great or too visible, they are tolerated, and sometimes even encouraged.

There is no such thing as a "perfect" culture. Every organization creates the one that works for it, based on the stage of the company and its business.

A start-up company will have quite a different culture from a long-established one. Things get done one way in a culture that is driven by innovation, and another way in a culture that is driven by precise repetition in operations. Some cultures are adaptive and change over time, while others are frozen in place.

Culture is not a set of common values or aspirations in an organization. Rather, culture shapes the values within an organization.

(b) Great Companies Contrasted with Bankrupt Companies

Does culture play any part in the success or failure of companies? Indeed it does. Consider some of the recent large bankruptcies in North America. Many of the companies that went bankrupt were leaders in their industries at some point in time. Some shaped and drove their industry. One reason companies lose their way is that they fail to shift behaviours in their cultures to meet changing external environments. When competitors start doing the right "new" things, some companies are slow to adapt and change. It is hard work to admit you need change, and even harder work to make change happen quickly. Great companies are very ready to change their culture when their customers expect new products or services. They usually have a pulse on what is needed in the marketplace and can translate this knowledge into new behaviours in their company culture. For these companies, the ability to change their behaviour set is a touchstone of continuous improvement. Sometimes, it's also a necessity for continued existence. IBM is an example of a company that had to undergo a culture revolution to survive, and came through the experience with distinctly different behaviours in its new culture.

(c) Who Drives the Company Culture?

Employee behaviours in an organizational culture are driven from the top. Realistically, Boards cannot be expected to drive daily changes in employee behaviours. This is not the job of a Board. Rather, it is management that drives what happens in a company's culture. The leadership style from the CEO and executive team is the greatest influence on the company. If the CEO wants lots of innovation and risk taking, he or she will rewarded these behaviours directly or indirectly through compensation and reward programs. If the CEO is more bureaucratic or conservative, these types of behaviours will pervade the culture.

(d) The Board's Role in Company Culture

The Board's initial opportunity to influence culture is during the strategic planning process. When management presents its strategic plan, the Board can ask for a precise definition of the critical behaviours necessary to execute each step of the plan. For example, if the strategic plan calls for significant organic growth, and innovation is identified as a critical behaviour, the Board can ask for specific clarification on how innovative behaviours will be fostered.

Once the strategic plan has been set in motion, it is possible for the Board to verify the presence or absence of identified critical behaviours in the culture. The Board can track if these behaviours are present in management communications, and to what degree they are measured in the performance-management processes, included in the reward system, and supported by training. Access to employee-survey results gives the Board a view of the company culture at a high level. As well, Board members can attend company events, visit locations, and meet with key managers at different levels of the company from time to time.

With their accountability to shareholders, it's important for Board members to have an accurate read of a company culture, as this contributes directly to the effectiveness of the leadership team and to profitability. Understanding the culture also helps the Board detect undesirable behaviours, such as undue risk-taking or reckless decision-making, and to put the brakes on them.

Who is the scorekeeper on company culture? The chief human resource officer is the guardian of company culture, and is responsible for monitoring, nurturing, and supporting culture. Corporate culture can be monitored, tracked, and recorded in many ways; the most common methods being employee surveys or town halls.

An employee survey can highlight trends and identify risks. Examples of risks are retention of top talent and performance issues that could result in liability problems down the road. Tracking and monitoring performance using an employee survey can act as a barometer of culture and enables HR to put in place coaching, training, and performance-management systems to manage issues before they become liabilities.

(e) How Do You Measure Culture and Hold Management Accountable?

The everyday behaviours of employees (including management) produce results for the company. If the organization's leaders are clear on what critical behaviours are required to produce the desired results, and they communicate and reward these expectations throughout the company, they are likely to achieve their goals. For example, in an industrial setting, safe work behaviours are required to prevent loss of life or injury. If supervisors do not train their employees properly and hold them accountable for safe work practices, the company's safety goals will never be achieved.

A culture is measured by identifying the critical behaviours desired in the work environment and the measurement of how often these behaviours are successfully demonstrated. In the safety example, in addition to the company's accident rate, the rate of employee compliance to safe work behaviours would be measured. If a company's goal is predictable steady sales growth, the critical behaviours associated with the successful sale of products (such as the ability to sell product benefits or make use of customer-assessment profiles) would be measured. Measuring the critical behaviours in the culture will lead to better company performance.

Where some companies fall off the rails is by having reward programs that are misaligned to the critical behaviours being measured. Even though their behaviours are being measured, employees are nor feeling the impact in their wallets.

(f) Why Should You Evaluate the CEO on the Company's Culture?

Most CEOs can achieve short-term results; they can charm, harm, or overwhelm people to deliver short-term performance. The best CEOs recognize that to deliver long-term sustainable results, everyone in the company has to be doing the right things. The required behaviours from each employee must be clearly articulated and reinforced through consistent communication throughout the company. In addition, the CEO has to ensure that management and workers are recognized and rewarded for these behaviours, and confronted when they are not delivering them. The Board should evaluate the CEO and the senior leadership team on how well they foster desired behaviours in the culture. This assessment needs to be incorporated into Board meetings on a frequent basis, with sufficient time reserved for a full discussion and debate.

(g) Boards and Behaviours the Secret Sauce

There are many ingredients to a successful company. Boards can help management by focusing on the critical behaviours necessary for the company to achieve sustainable long-term success. A focus on how management is leading the company and on strengthening the culture may be the best predictor of future success.

> "The CHRO can be very helpful in managing a harmonious relationship between the Board and management."
>
> David Emerson, Board Director

CHAPTER 112: LINKING STRATEGY AND EXECUTIVE PAY

> "The CHRO is the steward of the talent portfolio to execute corporate strategy. They have the respect of the key players, are familiar with all aspects of the company and have strong business acumen."
>
> David Emerson, Board Director

The recent economic crisis may prove to have a silver lining if organizations pay attention to the lessons it has taught. Consider, for example, the recent public outrage over executive compensation. While the furor has diminished, it hasn't disappeared. Looking ahead, a proactive way for boards to manage executive compensation is to more closely link compensation to company strategy.

Let's start with the following considerations:

- The current pay and performance system is getting more complex, and it isn't working. Adding more metrics to compensation procedures is intended to make them work better, but it really only adds more complexity and better chances to "game" the system. Also, these metrics tend to be tied to lagging measures of performance rather than future strategy, which encourages short-term thinking.

- A majority of strategies fail because of organizations' inability to convert their strategies into actionable, executable plans. Some companies do a great job of developing strategy, but fail to communicate the strategy clearly or to set actionable metrics against it. When compensation is not linked to the execution of strategy, there is a fundamental disconnect between what executives are asked to do and what they are rewarded for doing.

- Companies fail to understand the relationship between the personal values of individuals who will be executing the strategy and the strategy itself. As a result, some employees will either reject the strategy or won't engage. Companies like Southwest Airlines, Apple, and Zappos are examples of successful companies that have built a culture around specific values and goals, hired people whose values align with that culture, and developed strategies that brought together individual and company values.

- Good strategy development requires an in-depth understanding of the business. The majority of Board members must have an understanding of the industry and know the true drivers of financial performance and results. This is particularly critical when the Board examines the linkage of senior-level pay and performance.

The following are some ways to apply the ideas above.

(a) Build the Strategy First

Most organizations build their strategies based on external market factors, and don't consider the relationship between the strategy and the personal values of the individuals who will be executing the strategy. As a result, even the best plans may fail because the people in the company are not putting a full effort into their roles.

A contrasting approach that is being applied in many organizations and taught in leading MBA schools is the "new leadership model". This model provides a way to better align values and culture with strategy. The core concept is to build strategy by taking into account a senior team's aspirations along with external influences such as product life cycle, technology advances, and market demographics. (See D. Logan, et al., *Tribal Leadership: Leveraging Natural Groups to Build a Thriving Organization* (New York: Harper Business, 2011).)

The first step in the model is to ask "why?" and "what?" What is our purpose? Why are we here? For example, Google's purpose is to provide information 24/7. Southwest Airlines' purpose is to provide customers with a fun, friendly flying experience. Employees who join these companies presumably do so because they believe in the cause and what the company stands for. The "what" takes into account the competencies that enable a company to achieve the "why".

After the "why" and "what" have been determined, the next question is "which?" Which products, services, partners, and assets are needed to bring the company's competencies and purpose to life? These questions should be asked and answered by the team responsible for executing the strategy. As noted above, when strategy is aligned with the team's aspirations, there is greater commitment, engagement, and passion from the team.

In this approach, leaders continually ask their teams the following questions:

•   What's working well?

•   What's not working well?

•   What do we need to do to fix any problems?

•   What else should we be considering?

This ongoing re-evaluation of strategy keeps the team focused and engaged on working together to solve specific problems. Board members ask similar questions to pinpoint areas where the strategy may not be working or where it may require modification.

These leaders attempt to align individual's intrinsic values with work assignments that will create economic value for the organization. The strategy is developed in collaborative fashion within the senior team, and includes specific, actionable, and clear metrics, both for the long-term and the short-term.

(b)   Link Compensation to the Strategy

Traditionally, compensation programs provide three components: base salary, annual bonus and some form of longer-term, performance-linked compensation. The annual bonus plan is usually based on financial results achieved within a yearly business plan. It may also include individual performance goals that have been linked to specific, near-term strategic goals.

Longer-term performance rewards have typically been equity-based. Historically, stock options were favoured, but now restricted share units (RSUs) have become common. Generally, RSUs are granted without performance conditions and vest in a specified period of time (generally 3 years), for tax reasons. On vesting, the executive receives a payout equal to the number of units vested, multiplied by the share price at the date of payout. In cases where performance conditions have been attached to the equity grant, they have most often been based on financial metrics or total shareholder return; results which, for the most part, are lagging indicators of performance. It is rare to see performance conditions linked to strategic objectives.

The following are some ways in which boards can achieve the linkage of pay, performance, and strategy.

(i)   Keep the Compensation Program Simple, Clear, and Focused

Compensation programs have become complex for numerous reasons, including tax effectiveness, regulations, and the perceived need to find more perfect metrics. The only real result of this increasing complexity has been to add more work for Directors and shareholders in understanding how executive compensation impacts organizational risk and in the additional reporting required to explain the programs. It is questionable whether executives and the broader management group can see any link between their personal accomplishments and organizational success based on current compensation programs.

(ii)   Use Performance Metrics that are Wide-Ranging, Relevant and Hard to "Game"

As the strategy is developed and action steps established, the team responsible for executing the strategy should be asking the following questions:

- how will we know when we are successful?
- how will we know we are doing the right things?
- how will we know we are executing the right strategies?

Asking these questions will lead to measureable outcomes that can be linked to both short-term and long-term compensation. Consider the following examples:

1) Assume your strategy is to grow your business in Asia by a certain percentage over the next 5 years. The chosen metrics could be a specific number of viable leads in Asia, global growth targets, and completed acquisitions. In order to link pay with the longer-term business strategy, you might decide to include a specific number of viable leads as a metric under the annual bonus plan, with the other metrics being tucked into the longer-term incentive plan.

2) Assume a product-innovation cycle is part of your strategy. Your purpose is elegant design and short-term execution. A metric to consider in your annual bonus plan could be the number of design ideas accepted, while the number of product launches and adoptions would be included as metrics in the long-term incentive plan.

3) If a company is considering a large IT expenditure such as SAP implementation, SAP milestones can be included in a longer-term incentive plan design.

4) If a company is consolidating its operations, important strategic considerations could include the speed and cost of consolidation, level of staff engagement, retention of customers and suppliers, and community impact. Specific metrics around each of these outcomes could be factored into annual and longer-term incentive plans.

(iii)   Use Compensation as a Mechanism for Building Collaboration Across Groups

Successful companies encourage and build collaboration rather than competition between groups. As the authors note in *Tribal Leadership* (D. Logan, et al. New York: Harper Business, 2011 p. 32), as organizations develop stable cultures, they attract people who respond to the values of the culture and thus tend to be more engaged in their work: "setting and implementing a successful competitive strategy becomes easy as people's aspirations, knowledge of the market and creativity are unlocked and shared." Compensation strategy and design can support this movement by rewarding collaboration and knowledge sharing.

People want to do work they find meaningful. They want to be successful in their efforts, and to work within a successful organization. Devising a specific strategy along with clarity about what the organization expects of its people on the individual level are key to that success. Once the strategy is conceived, boards can focus on compensation plans that will link and support the strategic imperative.

> "The CEO and the HRC chair need to be aligned philosophically on succession planning, talent review and compensation. The day to day working relationship is with the CHRO."
>
> Sarah Raiss, Board Director

CHAPTER 113: WHO REALLY DRIVES CEO COMPENSATION?

> "Say on pay is dangerous – shareholders do not have the information."
>
> Geoff Beattie, Board Director

(a) Coping with Complexity and Perception

Executive compensation remains a hot button issue. While there have been many attempts to resolve the continuing debate around pay and performance, none of these have worked satisfactorily over time. Compensation remains controversial because of a tricky mix of complexity and false perception.

The complexity arises from companies having multiple compensation programs, all intended to align with overall business strategy and to link pay to performance. Perception problems arise largely because one key part of executive compensation is equity (usually restricted share units (RSUs), and less frequently, stock options). These reward instruments are not well understood. For instance, when the equity component is realized at some future time, those gains may not appear to correspond to the company's current financial performance. Then false perception takes over and emotions run high, as executives are seen to be realizing a "windfall" that is not deserved.

Despite increased Board governance and greater public and media scrutiny, the compensation conundrum is not getting any simpler. Today, compensation is policed by the Chair of the Board, the Chair of the HRC, the audit committee Chair, the Board's external compensation consultants, and in some cases, the company's shareholders. The target in their sights appears to be the senior executive team, which can give rise to an undesirably adversarial climate.

How did we get to this point? Let's start by taking a look back at the process for determining compensation for the CEO and the senior team.

(b) Before 2002: The CEO-centric Era

There was a time when the CEO was the dominant figure in the executive compensation discussion. It was this individual who determined salary increases and bonus awards for the current year, and set out next year's bonus plan design and metrics. Often, performance metrics were not reviewed by the CFO or evaluated by the Board.

External advisors were used largely for market data and trend analysis, and the chief human resources officer (CHRO) would submit the CEO's recommendations to the Board for approval. In most cases the Board rubber-stamped the recommended salary increases, bonus plan, and stock option grants. Plan designs were relatively straightforward and were approved without much debate.

Typically, option grants had no performance conditions attached to them. Since options were not expensed, they were the "candy" given to executives as a motivator for performance. With few strings attached to these grants, any measureable appreciation in stock price resulted in handsome gains for the CEO and his or her executive team. When stock prices rose because of market conditions rather than improved company performance, there were real windfalls to be had.

Proxy statements on executive compensation were mandated in 1993, but provided few details to shareholders. Data on compensation was considered proprietary information and a matter of competitive advantage.

(c) 2002 to 2007: The Governance Trend

With the dot-com bust and high-profile company scandals coming to light in the U.S., public outrage fuelled growing interest in corporate governance. The Chair of the audit committee became "top dog" on the Board. The *Sarbanes-Oxley Act of 2002* was enacted and the accounting of stock-based compensation was introduced in Canada and the U.S.

CEOs were still able to get what they wanted from the Board, but pay for performance developed traction and executive compensation design became more complex. Shareholders and the press started asking Boards more questions about CEO performance, executive compensation, and risk management. With this increasing complexity, many members on the HRC had to rely on company management and compensation consultants to provide the answers, and those answers didn't always match up.

(d) 2008 to 2012: The Governance Police

With the recession, and its headlines about executives receiving huge bonuses and equity payouts while their companies received taxpayer support, most Boards "got religious" about governance. Boards emerged as the drivers of executive compensation, and the HRC Chair grew to be equal in influence to the audit Chair.

HRC Chairs hire external compensation consultants to advise them, with higher consulting costs. CHROs are relegated to minor roles in the executive compensation discussion, and must clear any recommendations with the Board's consultant before they go to the HRC. The roles of the CFO and the audit committee chair in executive compensation are to review risk issues and to push for cost controls.

With this shift, the design of the executive compensation program is now owned by consultants and the HRC chair. Ironically, some of these consultants lack proprietary databases and instead rely on management's compensation consultant for data. Lawyers prepare proxy statements to provide transparency, but the actual documents are very complex and exhaustive to read for the average shareholder. More CFOs and lawyers are being recruited to become Directors, with the emphasis on risk management and liability.

Executive compensation components have gravitated to more conservative instruments such as RSUs, which better control reward levels but do little to encourage executive innovation, collaboration, or creativity. Short-term cash bonus plans have become the key reward vehicles to minimize complaints regarding long-term incentive plans. If stock options exist, they have become increasingly linked to performance.

Today there is certainly a more elaborate process around executive compensation decisions. It is still difficult, however, to find compensation plans that clearly link performance with the critical factors needed to succeed in the global marketplace.

(e)   The New Tomorrow: Emerging Pragmatism in 2013

The core purpose of executive compensation programs is to improve productivity, boost personal engagement, and stimulate innovation. But these behaviours have to start at the top of the house. This shift requires a new way of thinking, involving collaboration and co-creativity. This new culture needs to permeate all dealings between management and the Board, including the determination of executive pay. Below are a number of items to consider in planning for this brave new world.

(i)   Relationship among Management, Consultants and the HRC

These relationships, currently adversarial, will benefit from becoming more collaborative. The result will be a more open and transparent dialogue in the boardroom. The external consultant will act as more of a facilitator, building consensus between management and the Board.

(ii)   Board Composition

Boards need members with relevant HR expertise to join their HRCs. The HRC Chair should have the equivalent expertise in HR as the audit committee chair has in finance. Only then can the HR chair truly leverage the skills and knowledge of the company's CHRO in the areas of executive compensation and succession planning.

(iii)   Compensation Decision-making

To find out what motivates people, you have to ask. It's important to re-engage the CEO in executive compensation design, and to involve other internal stakeholders, including the CFO, CHRO, and business-unit heads.

All perspectives need to be heard in order to align compensation programs with business strategy and to produce the desired behaviour. To anchor decisions in rational analysis, back up those perspectives with a hard look at industry comparisons and talent reviews. Give the Board flexibility to exercise discretion when compensation decisions may be impacted by unique circumstances in the marketplace.

(iv)   Compensation Consultants

Boards and management have to rein in the cost of compensation consultants and the way they have been used to date. Bringing this expertise in-house, with firewalls in place for governance purposes, will enable both management and the Board to share this resource. Fortunately, this expertise is likely to become more commoditized through technology and online information sources.

(v)   Pay for Performance

Performance metrics will become more standardized based on industry comparators and relevant stock market assessments. Also, the ratio between executive pay and average employee earnings needs to be tracked and reported, which should reduce complaints from unions and other critics of executive compensation.

(vi)   Compensation Design

The types of rewards used in the executive compensation mix will continue to be both short-term and long-term oriented. However, long-term incentive plans must have a minimum 5-year horizon to reward long-run strategic planning and execution.

(vii)   Shareholders Say on Pay

Shareholder input should be solicited at all publicly traded companies. Upset shareholders need a vehicle to express their views, and Boards should meet with shareholders on executive compensation policies.

(viii)   CEO Evaluation

CEOs have to receive more focused feedback from their Boards on their short- and long- term effectiveness in the areas of strategy and execution, results delivered, people development, and risk management. The process must include comparisons to the performance of other CEOs in the same industry.

(ix)   Rethink External Rewards

It's not just money that drives performance. The culture of an organization can do much to motivate people when it offers autonomy and a sense of purpose, and encourages them to develop their expertise. The challenge for Boards is to start at the top to reduce the focus on pay as the primary motivator, and rethink how to bring innovation and creativity into the workplace.

Organizations that understand these needs will have a competitive advantage in attracting the right people, and in keeping them engaged and productive.

"In working with the HRC chair, I offered my
independent view of the CEO and other officers."

Bill Conaty, former SVP, Corporate Human Resources, General Electric

CHAPTER 114: TOP TEN TIPS FOR THE HRC CHAIR AND THE CHRO

> "There will be times when the CHRO has to prepare the HRC Chair to ask the tough questions of the CEO – not an easy situation."
>
> Yvonne Jackson, Board Director & former CHRO

1. Include the HRC Chair in the hiring of the CHRO.

2. Include the CHRO in the HRC in-camera sessions.

3. Jointly develop the HRC agenda and key priorities.

4. Ensure a "code of silence" is established.

5. Hold frequent meetings including the CEO, CHRO, and the HRC Chair.

6. Use the Board Chair and CEO to help resolve differences.

7. Ensure the HRC Chair knows the CHRO's staff.

8. The HRC Chair and CHRO should attend an HRC course.

9. Develop a relationship built on trust and respect.

10. Enjoy your work together!

11

Working with Strategic External Consultants/Partners

"Perhaps the funniest moment came when the head of HR had to report that a set of outside consultants had just presented a bill for an outrageous amount of money, at least twice what I had expected. The CHRO was thunderstruck. I assured the head that we would, of course, honor any contractual commitments into which he had formally entered, but suggested he use his negotiating skills to cut the bill in half, which he did. The incident did not diminish his credibility with the committee but, if anything, enhanced it further."

Gordon Ritchie, Board Director

The CHRO in most organizations has a roster of consultants that can be brought in to supplement the work of internal HR specialists, or to supply expertise not present on the HR team.

This may involve the ongoing services of pension, benefits or compensation experts, or labour and employment lawyers for specific issues, or a coach or trainer to assist with the development of people. Executive recruiters and outplacement firms are used as needed, as are outside experts in reorganization, strategic planning, or cultural transformation. Typically, when consultants are brought in the project is a large one, with cross-functional scope and the involvement of senior leadership, with HR tasked with its completion.

Competent consultants bring more to the party than simply technical expertise because they tend to have a much broader view, gained from working across multiple companies in different industries. While I may not have come across a given issue before, they likely have, and can express the problem succinctly and offer pragmatic, objective advice. The best ones identify the right path to follow in navigating a particular issue, and the determination of how to achieve the desired outcome.

On the other hand, hiring a consultant can present some drawbacks which need to be managed. Sometimes consulting firms put people on their project teams who are not experienced, with the intention of educating them and providing them with experience. Such education can come at the client's expense, so having an understanding of the different levels of expertise that are being brought to a project is important.

A second pitfall can occur if fees are not explicit and budgeting runs out of control, with the result being an unwelcome surprise at the end of the project. Preparing the ground by ensuring that HR staff and the senior leadership team are onside with the consultants' work is key, and be prepared to run interference if problems occur.

An effective way to work with consultants is to focus on developing a relationship of mutual trust. Start with an explicit contract and well-defined expectations on both sides with respect to the scope of the work, project steps, and timelines. Be sure that you have a clear understanding of what will happen if the scope of the work is changed, in terms of deliverables and billing, and make sure you know what has to take place in the organization for the consultants to do their work. Plan ahead for regular communications with them and above all else, monitor the billing.

"These are the major points to remember as CHRO when you manage the executive compensation function and balance the requirement of your company, the CEO and management, the compensation committee (and board), and shareholders.

Learn compensation details thoroughly (internal and external) – plans, programs, results and issues. Everyone needs to know you know this information cold.

Gain and maintain credibility with the compensation committee. Credibility is precious: it is hard to gain, easy to lose, and very hard to regain.

Compensation expertise is a mandatory for a CHRO; it's not a discretionary topic."

P. Wright, J. Boudreau, D. Pace, E. Sartain, P. McKinnon, and R. Antoine, *The Chief HR Officer: Defining the New Role of HR Leaders* (San Francisco: Wiley, John & Sons, Inc., 2011), p. 210

CHAPTER 115: WORKING WITH THE EXECUTIVE COMPENSATION CONSULTANT

Contributed by Luis Navas, Vice Chair, Global Governance Advisors

Without question, executive compensation is a hot topic throughout North America. As a consequence of the economic downturn, organizational mismanagement, increased government oversight, and media and stakeholder scrutiny, organizations are taking executive compensation very seriously. As a result, there is increased pressure on the shoulders of today's Chief Human Resource Officer (CHRO).

For years, compensation consultants worked in secret, protected their data and their benchmarking methodologies, and even developed complicated job scoring techniques that organizations had to trust at face value. However, today's environment has not only increased the expectation that organizations use external third-party compensation consultants, it demands that Boards and executives knowledgably communicate and defend the decisions that are made. Consultant secrecy is now a liability that organizations are beginning to recognize.

(a)   The New Reality

Executive compensation is one area that the majority of CHROs say provides them with the most challenges since its level of complexity in terms of design, regulations, accounting, tax, and internal and external politics has changed significantly. Although most companies use third party advisors, today's Boards and CEOs need to be able to look to their CHRO for advice in the same way that they look to their CFO regardless of having External Auditors. As a result, CHROs are spending more time studying and understanding the issues with a clear understanding that there is legal liability behind the decisions made within their organizations.

At the beginning of each of our training sessions for CHROs on executive compensation, we ask the participants why they have chosen to take the course and what they would like to get out of it. The typical response is that the evolution of their HR responsibilities now includes a greater focus on executive compensation. That focus brings increased pressures and liabilities to this part of their role, which can make them uncomfortable if they are aware that they know little about current market trends, technical assessment and design methodologies, and governance best practices. Thus, our typical participant tends to be strongly aware that they "know what they don't know" and are proactively doing something about it.

Strong CHROs recognize that the world of executive compensation is changing and that government, stakeholder, and public pressures are increasing. As a result, they look for ways to strengthen their knowledge and understanding of executive compensation governance. They appreciate that they are often considered a trusted advisor, and know that additional education, training, and confidence in their abilities further enables them to "lead from behind." They lead through their monitoring of decision making, performance management, and administrative processes as well as by providing timely and insightful guidance on whether or not their organization is on side with current governance best practices.

CHROs are not only expected to work closely with their Boards and fellow executives on compensation issues, they are also expected to work closely with external service providers. Educated CHROs possess the strength and knowledge that keeps external providers accountable. At no point should an organization be placed at the mercy of external experts and it's the CHRO who helps to ensure that their organization receives accurate professional advice. Realistically, the CHRO does not need to fully understand the technicalities of compensation and assessment work, but he or she does need to have sufficient understanding to ask good questions, confirm that methodologies are sound, and make sure that recommendations presented to their organization are based on strong, acceptable principles.

Overall, strong CHROs are proactive in managing executive compensation governance within their organization. With increased pressures, Board Members truly appreciate it when a trusted CHRO is able to keep them both on track and out of hot water. The more CHROs are able to do this, the more invaluable they become within their senior leadership team.

(b) Annual Compensation Reviews

Increasingly, CHROs are expected to assist Boards with regular executive compensation reviews. These reviews not only cover rank and file staff, but also include the executive reviews of the CHROs' senior executive colleagues and superiors, which can lead to some awkward moments. The key way to deal with this is for CHROs to be acquainted with objective assessment methodologies, understand the strengths and weaknesses of the methodologies and plan designs, and have the self-confidence to speak up when they feel their organization needs to revisit the way compensation plans are designed or managed. By being armed with this information and confidence, and by maintaining the compensation discussion on a fair and objective level, CHROs are able to avoid awkward situations while maintaining a positive rapport with their Board and C-suite colleagues.

Many organizations subscribe to, and regularly use, compensation survey data to assess the relative strength and market fairness of their compensation plans. Blindly accepting market survey data increases the liability associated with the potential of making misinformed decisions that result from faulty data. CHROs therefore need to be comfortable with assessing the overall strength and appropriateness of the data that they use.

Effective CHROs question and understand how the data was collected, know what organizations participated, and are aware of the importance of survey survivorship year-over-year. They also understand the importance of checking the size and the relevance of the organizations that are included in the data cuts they use. If the data includes compensation information from organizations that are significantly larger or smaller than their organization, relative comparisons will be incorrect. As well, strong CHROs check the job descriptions used in the survey to assure that the relative scope of responsibilities is consistent with the assessed positions within their organizations. CHROs understand that all comparisons made should always be on an "apples to apples" basis, as the use of mismatched peers increases the risk of establishing incorrect market benchmarks and increased associated financial liabilities.

(c)   Aligning to Performance

Pay-for-performance is a hot topic for stakeholders. Both the public and private sectors have struggled with this concept for years, and as a result, CHROs are consistently pressured to strengthen the linkage between executive compensation and performance.

Strong CHROs understand how to properly incent the right behaviours within their organizations. They also know that the use of the term "bonus" implies a different psychological meaning than the term "incentive." Effective incentive plans are easily articulated, include clear performance objectives, have appropriate buy-in from the plan participants, and include an appropriate level of objectives that enable the participants to stay focused on their goals and objectives.

Long laundry lists of non-negotiated objectives are never useful because they disperse the focus that should be strategically placed only on areas that are key to the success of the organization. CHROs are beginning to realize that performance expectations should be sufficiently narrow to truly maintain executive focus and incent behaviours that have the greatest impact on organizational success.

CHROs also are realizing that even the best designed plans can quickly become irrelevant if they are not constantly revisited and tested on an ongoing basis. Good CHROs follow a cycle and constantly test performance benchmarks against their organizations' evolving corporate objectives and business plans. Throughout the annual cycle, their Board members and executives should be involved to maximize buy-in and the probability of approval at each step. The last thing a CHRO wants is to work diligently on a plan design or modification and then have it fail if executives or Board members do not agree with the end outcome or feel blindsided when asked for approval. Successful CHROs make sure that all stakeholder interests are considered and heard. By doing so, they ultimately increase the probability of approval as well as their overall success in the eyes of their Board members and fellow senior executives.

The establishment and implementation of a scorecard process helps CHROs properly communicate the design and expectations of annual incentive plans, which enables plan participants to correlate the expectations with associated performance levels and incentive payouts. Using threshold, target, and superior performance levels allows organizations to minimize the consequences associated with sudden unforeseen shocks that deter executives from hitting their targets, but also incents executives to perform beyond established targets and strive to realize superior levels of performance. Typically, it is the Board that is responsible for approving such scorecards and benchmarks. However, it is the CHRO who is normally asked to work with external advisors to properly establish the performance benchmarks and associated payout levels on the Board's behalf.

(d)   Understanding Long-term Incentives

Long-term incentives are a common tool used by organizations to strongly align executive actions with longer-term success, sustainability, and stakeholder interests. As the use of equity tools such as whole shares, stock options, performance shares, restricted shares, etc., are becoming more prevalent and complicated, CHROs need to become familiar with the strengths and weaknesses of each incentive tool and to work with their Boards, executives, and external advisors to assess which tools are the most appropriate for their organization at that specific point in time.

By considering the objectives of the plan, current market practices, and the expectations of the executives and stakeholders, knowledgeable CHROs can work with all of the relevant parties and help their Board establish a plan that best suits the needs of their organization and can minimize any associated risks.

(e)   Compensation Risk Management

Since the economic crisis of 2008, the global community has become increasingly interested and aware of the financial risk associated with executive compensation plans. In April 2009, delegates of the G20 London Summit publicly recognized that one of the root causes of the economic crisis was the lack of compensation risk oversight, particularly the risk associated with the design of incentive plans.

As a result, organizations – and ultimately their CHROs – need to be vigilant in the monitoring of their incentive plans. Whenever new objectives or benchmarks arc established, all immediate or possible risks should be identified and fully understood. Strong CHROs are entirely aware of the risk profile of their organization and should be able to flag a misalignment of any of the incentive risks with their organizational risk tolerance levels to their fellow executives and Board. Realistically, all business activities include some level of risk, and some industries or sectors are more risky than others. Therefore, CHROs are now expected to make sure that incentive plans are appropriately designed, not to completely eliminate all elements of risk, but to make sure that they fall within the acceptable risk limits set by their Board.

(f)   General Sources of Compensation Risk

There are many sources where compensation risk can exist or emerge. Even though it is the ultimate responsibility of the Board to monitor and control organizational risk, CHROs are most often responsible for overseeing the compensation and incentive policies, processes and practices, as they are best positioned to monitor and control most of the aspects related to compensation risk.

Risk is an element that regulators and stakeholders take very seriously. As a result, additional pressures are now placed on organizations, which ultimately increases the pressures placed on the shoulders of CHROs. Strong CHROs understand and foresee the risks associated with compensation plan designs, get the expert advice they need, and then make decisions that are in the best interest of their organizations.

(g)   Special Situations

Organizations evolve in different ways, but ultimately evolution results in changes and stresses that CHROs are always expected to manage. Organizational growth is sometimes a result of mergers and/or acquisitions, and these mergers and acquisitions always require that adjustments be made to compensation plans. Strong CHROs anticipate growth curves and have compensation plans that easily grow with acquisitions and increased responsibilities. As well, they are able to see where old executive plans don't fit into new realities and are able to quickly work with their Boards and advisors to make appropriate changes or implement new plans that better align with their evolved organizational needs.

As mentioned earlier, knowledge of equity incentive tools is important, and this expectation is heightened when equity plans are merged, shut down, or bought out. In such situations, CHROs need to understand what equity transition or conversion methodologies exist, the taxation and security rules associated with the equity, and how to treat incoming or outgoing executives fairly.

The recognition of special incentive elements is used by CHROs to strengthen the retention of executive talent throughout a merger or sale situation. Such situations always make executives nervous and substantially increase flight risk and the loss of talent at crucial moments. Effective CHROs identify such flight risk, and know when a supplemental plan, such as a sale maximization plan, can both incent executives to increase the sale value of a company and create an acceptable reward that is substantial enough to retain executives throughout the sale or transition process.

(h) Executive Employment Contracts

Good CHROs truly understand that in most cases the devil is in the details. With the complexity of executive employments contracts increasing, CHROs must truly pay attention to the details. CHROs are now forced to become quasi-legal professionals when asked to manage executive contract negotiations. The media loves to cover situations when contracts were not properly tested, such as the 2007 exit of Robert Nardelli from Home Depot. Unfortunately, when the Board realized that Nardelli was no longer the "right fit" for the company, they were shocked to find out that his contract entitled him to leave with a total exit package of approximately $210 million. As you can imagine, mistakes like this are harmful to the reputations of Boards, and they consequently pressure their CHROs to help them make sure that costly situations like the Home Depot example are never a possibility.

Strong CHROs are prepared prior to the start of any executive contract negotiation. They have a good understanding of market trends in compensation levels, typical incentive designs, and are aware of the legal pitfalls of poorly designed contracts. If they are not responsible for making offers, they prepare individuals such as Board members or the CEO on how to make offers legally. Far too often, verbal offers are made informally over a coffee, lunch, or dinner, which can have the potential of causing problems in the near future when a formal offer is presented to the potential hire. CHROs make sure that the principal negotiators understand when offers can be considered legally binding, and when required, they have a legal professional walk the person(s) through what is and is not legally acceptable when making the offer. They then work closely with the lawyer to draft contracts that are legally sound and free of future surprises. Again, the devil is in the details, and as a result, CEOs and Board members are relying more and more on their CHRO to make sure the details are correct.

(i)   Pension Management

HR departments are most often the group tasked with the administration of employee pensions. The administration is normally done *en masse* for their organization, and once implemented the rules are pretty cut and dried as to how pensions must be administered and what Canada Revenue Agency (CRA) pertains to its management and payouts. Unfortunately, executive pensions are not as straightforward and often include substantial carry forward liabilities.

Many executives are entitled, under their employment contracts, to receive a regular pension similar to the other employees within their company. However, under the 2013 CRA rules, the maximum a company can annually put into a defined contribution pension is $23,820. This does not enable executives to retire with a pension that is remotely close to their pre-retirement levels. Therefore, many companies create Supplemental Executive Retirement Plans (SERPS), which are essentially pension top-ups which enable their executives to collect a retirement income that is closer to the relative percentage that regular employees receive.

The difficulty is that the funds required in this retirement pool need to be managed separately (meaning outside of the regular pension pool) and tend to be quite substantial. As a result, CHROs in these organizations normally have the added responsibility of managing the SERP plans and are required to be well versed in the CRA rules of how these plans can and cannot be managed. Yet again, this responsibility increases the pressure placed on them, as they are managing plans with large sums of deferred money that their boss and their fellow senior colleagues are counting on for retirement.

(j)   Talent Management

An increased corporate emphasis on executive talent management is a welcome change for CHROs, but it also presents new challenges. Beyond developing and maintaining the corporate talent bench amid an increasingly dynamic talent environment, the CHRO must also provide the company with an outside perspective regarding industry standards, ensuring that leadership, the talent bench, and the overall workforce remain on par with or superior to competitors.

Poor succession planning costs companies millions of dollars in lost productivity, increased compensation, and search fees. Succession planning is not an easy skill to acquire or an easy process to implement, but some of the world's best performing companies excel in this area in large part because of their CHRO. All too often, organizations that have not properly managed their talent succession find themselves paying on average two to three times the total annual remuneration of an executive position when they are forced to search and bring in an outsider. This means two to three times the position's salary, annual incentive, long-term incentive, pension, and benefits. Consider the $49 million Canadian Pacific Railway had to pay its new CEO, Hunter Harrison within the first 6 months of his start date. $45 million had to be paid to replace Harrison's former pension, which he had walked away from to accept the new position.

Too many organizations consider succession a soft luxury that gets in the way of doing their business. However, when a trusted CHRO explains the legitimate associated financial costs of not managing talent, other executives and Board members will pay more attention to the matter. And given the financial connection to the overall compensation budget, proper talent and succession planning is very much a vital part of any long-term executive compensation strategy.

Strong CHROs are able to work with their organization's short, medium, and long-term plans and properly anticipate and map the talent required at each stage. Gone are the days when human resources departments managed a steady state of consistent talent. Today's companies demand the right talent at the right time, and CHROs are expected to possess an understanding of their organization's current and future requirements, know what their current talent pool includes, and have an ongoing strategy as to how the requirements and talent pool will be matched. This is not a simple task, especially when corporate strategies dictate that different skill sets are required in other C-suite positions.

Organizations that are planning for a change in direction most often require different leadership skills. At the most general level, successful corporate expansion, ongoing management, and organizational downsizing all benefit from different leadership skill sets. The situation is further complicated when CHROs recognize that the skills required in future stages are not those that the current executive team possesses. In such instances, CHROs may be placed in very awkward situations where they could be viewed as "judging" the abilities of their colleagues and superiors. Strong CHROs avoid these situations by working closely with the Board and by managing discussions in a very factual, objective manor. Armed with their skill inventories, assessments and their organizations' formal business plans, CHROs are able to work with their Board members to develop strategies that are in the best interest of their organization and thus to avoid the "personalization" of strategic talent decisions.

(k) Compensation Governance and Oversight

Boards have many responsibilities and sometimes, unfortunately, there are items that are overlooked or pushed aside. With regard to CHRO responsibilities, general compensation governance and oversight is definitely where CHROs can effectively "lead from behind." Strong CHROs work with their Board or Board Human Resources and Compensation Committee to establish an effective annual plan or process by which their executive compensation plans can be properly managed. It is interesting to note that Boards most often cannot be sued for the amount of money they pay their executives, but there is, rather, a higher probability that they can be sued for the process by which they came to that determination.

Recent examples are the 2012 stakeholder lawsuits in the United States against Simon Property Group and Viacom. Viacom shareholders are suing for the return of past incentive awards for the top three executives and are claiming that the payouts between 2008 and 2011 were partly based on subjective actions taken by the Board. Simon Property shareholders are suing because the Board unilaterally granted the CEO, David Simon, a $120 million retention bonus that had no performance elements associated with it and that was granted without the consultation of any additional stakeholders prior to the AGM. In both cases it is the assumed arbitrary process that the stakeholders are challenging, and as a result, both Boards now have additional external pressures.

Effective CHROs help to manage the process by initially proposing formal schedules to Boards, reminding Boards of upcoming process events or deliverables, and keeping Boards on track. Once established and implemented effectively, an annual compensation governance schedule can be easy to manage and can effectively keep Boards focused and out of hot water with their stakeholders.

(l)   Increased Value of CHROs and the Future of the Profession

We are now starting to see more and more CHROs elected onto Boards. As Boards experience increasing pressures pertaining to executive compensation, performance, and talent management, it is easy to see why strong CHROs are not only considered valued and trusted advisors of a Board, but are also becoming more and more highly valued members of Boards later in their careers. It is a phenomenon that is increasing, and from what we have observed teaching senior HR professionals in the AECP, this phenomenon will only grow in its practice.

Our experience suggests that Boards often have a greater appreciation of the role of HR (of its relevance and value), than HR leaders themselves have. Boards see senior HR executives as crucial business partners to themselves and to the business. They want them to be coaches and sounding boards for the executive team, and to continue to act in the role of confidante with respect to other executive team members.

Boards feel that HR executives, more than other senior executives, should have the capability to build trust and to communicate and collaborate with others, with exceptional levels of diplomacy and discretion. These attributes must co-exist, however, with a deep understanding of the business and a strong grasp on the business's operations and financial realities, including its algorithms and Profit & Loss.

Boards expect their senior HR executives to apply their professional expertise with a focus on issues and trends that matter to the business. If there is one area where CEOs want HR to perform better, and would do things differently themselves if they were heading the HR function, it is in knowing what the real business challenges are and applying expertise to managing and solving these challenges proactively.

CHROs have the ability to be seen in the same light as CFOs by CEOs, shareholders, and Boards. Only the future will reveal whether the profession rises to the challenge.

> "Writing a proxy circular – take my life with a razor blade."
>
> John Lynch, SVP, corporate Human Resources, General Electric

---

CHAPTER 116: WORKING WITH THE EXECUTIVE COACH TO THE CEO AND THE C-SUITE

Contributed by Sandro Iannicca, of SICG Consulting.

(a)   When the Use of an Executive Coach Makes Sense

As a CHRO, it is your job to determine when it may make the most sense to suggest the use of an Executive Coach (EC) to your CEO or C-suite members. In many cases, it will require an understanding on your part of what needs to be accomplished, what success would look like, and if the target individual is amenable to the use of an EC. An assessment of what is expected from the EC and what is likely to be achieved is required on your part.

One of the more unique and interesting situations the CHRO may be faced with is when an Executive Coach works with the CEO or members of the Executive team. This relationship needs to be managed delicately on both sides. There are several aspects of this kind of engagement that require overview, direction, and insight from the CHRO:

- When individuals need personal attention, guidance, feedback, and reinforcement.

- Where benefits are realized through in-depth exploration of issues.

- During transition events.

- During high-change situations.

- When a confidential and "safe" environment is required for learning and growth to occur.

- When the CEO and/or the Board Chair and/or the executive team are not working well together.

- When "tough calls" need to be made and adhered to (for example derailing, inappropriate behaviour).

(b)   Selecting an Executive Coach

In some cases, an executive may want to have a choice of coaches while in other cases he or she may simply ask that you choose someone you feel would be appropriate for the engagement. One note of caution in the selection of an EC: there is evidence that suggests the "fit" between the EC and an Executive is the single most important criterion which dictates whether the objectives of the Coaching engagement will be met. This critical decision is one to which you have a direct line of sight and an important contribution to make.

Consequently, as the CHRO, you need to have a good understanding of the C-suite Executive in terms of his or her style, approach, preferred working conditions, and likelihood of receptivity to different approaches to Executive Coaching. This includes considerations such as:

- Gender.

- Coaching style (directive, participative, intellectual, motivational, exploratory, Socratic, didactic).

- Logistics (the frequency, nature, and duration of the coaching interaction).

It will be helpful for the EC to provide counsel on your understanding of the style of the C-suite Executive and what kind of approach might work best for him or her. In fact, one best practice is that the CHRO becomes the Coach to the EC during the engagement. This will be expanded upon later.

(c)   Contracting with the EC

Even though the coaching relationship is a personal and sensitive interaction between the two parties, as the CHRO you have a fiduciary responsibility to ensure that the goals and objectives of the engagement are met. To derive value from the coaching engagement, it is helpful to outline the overarching goals and objectives that will be the focus of the coaching, such as:

- Developing a more decisive style.

- Improving relations with the Board.

- Delegating more.

- Softening or hardening your approach according to the situation.

- Controlling inappropriate behaviours.

It is also very useful to state your thoughts on how success in the coaching assignment will be measured, and how you will know if the objectives have been met. Informal updates should be scheduled with the CHRO to relate what is going on, what is working, and what needs to improve. These conversations are an excellent opportunity for the CHRO to coach the EC in terms of suggestions as to what might work best with the individual being coached. A responsible and professional EC should be very receptive to the advice and counsel of the CHRO.

Be warned, however, that in some cases the individual being coached, usually the CEO, may wish to leave the objectives of the engagement somewhat vague. For example, in one case the President of a large multi-national company told the CHRO he would like to work with an EC, but did not mention any specific objectives he wished to achieve. When he met with me and was asked what he wanted to get out of the coaching engagement, he said things like: "I want to take my performance to the next level" and "I am not sure what that looks like, I will know it when I feel it." To combat this ambiguity, I pushed harder to have him clarify what he would see himself doing more of and/or less of as a result of the coaching experience. I wrote up the answers, shared it with the President and then asked for his approval to share it with the CHRO to ensure everyone was on the same page.

(d) Managing the EC Relationship

The CHRO should have a healthy working relationship with the EC. So healthy, that in best practice cases the CHRO is the internal coach to the EC. The EC should approach the CHRO on a reasonably regular basis to discuss aspects of the engagement (maintaining confidentiality where appropriate) and to seek insights, advice, and counsel on how to proceed. The EC can also use the CHRO as a "sounding board" to test ideas and approaches on how to engage with the client, and can solicit views on key relationships in the organization that may be the focus of the coaching engagement.

These discussions are an opportunity for the CHRO to alert the EC about any specific challenges which the Executive may be facing. In one case, I was advised by the CHRO that my client was to meet with the CEO to discuss some role modifications that were more in line with his current performance. We knew it would be a difficult situation for the person, and there was a high likelihood he would contact me to discuss the issue, which he did. Because I had been alerted by the CHRO (which I kept confidential), I was able to prepare for his strong reactions and suggest an approach for when he met with the CEO to ensure he stayed on track. He met the challenge and continued to develop a strong, positive working relationship with the CEO.

The EC should also have some formal mechanism to update the CHRO on the status of the engagement. It can take the form of a mid-term and final term report that outlines the goals of the engagement and the EC's assessments as to progress made and what remains to be done. It is an opportunity for the CHRO to review the progress of the engagement against the goals set out during the contracting phase. The CHRO can also use this opportunity to provide further support, guidance and advice to the EC to facilitate the achievement of the engagement objectives.

(e) Delicate Situations

There are many circumstances that may arise when coaching the most senior executives of an organization that require sensitivity, diplomacy, and effective leadership on the part of the CHRO. I have outlined a few examples below along with how they have been handled by the CHRO.

(i) CHRO Not Involved

I have run across situations where the President/CEO did not want the CHRO involved in the coaching engagement. This situation is usually the case when the CEO is being coached and he or she does not want the CHRO to know what is being discussed or what progress is being made. It tends to be a very challenging situation because it suggests one or more of the following:

- The two parties are not aligned.
- The CEO does not have trust or faith in his or her CHRO.
- The CEO is an inherently private individual.
- The CEO may be trying to hide something.
- The CEO does not believe his or her development is of any concern to the CHRO.

In any case, this situation will pose a challenge for the CHRO/EC relationship. At minimum, the CHRO should request to be a part of the process, given his or her mandate. It may be appropriate that whatever information is shared only focuses upon the goals of the engagement rather than on any specifics about what is discussed during the coaching sessions. It can become a tricky issue if the CEO is not aware that the CHRO and the EC have struck an agreement to share some components of the engagement.

This situation occurred when I was coaching the CEO of a very large national retailing organization. The CEO expressed concerns that his CHRO was very political, and he feared that the shared information could be utilized inappropriately. I asked the CEO if I could talk to the CHRO about the situation and share some of his concerns. After some cajoling, the CEO agreed. When I sat down with the CHRO I expressed the concerns of his CEO and explained that the CEO had agreed to share progress information and nothing more as a part of the tracking of the engagement. I was also able to express the concerns about the CHRO's apparent political behaviour, which was acknowledged and accepted by the CHRO. This became the focus of the relationship between the two parties going forward and also comprised some of the coaching process during my sessions with the CEO.

I have also been in a situation where the CEO was a reluctant participant in the coaching process, partly because he felt the CHRO had been providing information to the Board about some challenges he had in managing the Senior Executive Team. Indeed, the Chair of Board had been advised by the CHRO that the senior executive team was not operating effectively and that the lion's share of the blame lay with the CEO. As a part of the process I conducted confidential interviews with the members of the Senior Executive Team. Sure enough, the CHRO's concerns were warranted. As a part of the feedback process I was able to convince the CEO that by co-opting the CHRO in his development efforts it would help him to get back on track with the team and it would help him to effectively manage the views of the Board Chair as well as other Board members.

(ii)   *The Trojan Horse*

Perhaps the most common situation I have faced is where I have been approached by organizations to coach one member of the senior executive team, but the true intended target was the CEO. Generally, the one individual who is seeking coaching support does it with the full understanding that by involving the CEO in the monitoring and feedback process, it would present an opportunity to provide developmental advice and coaching for the CEO. In almost all cases I have been involved with, the CHRO has spearheaded the initiative or has been a willing participant in the process.

The CEO is reached by including him or her in the quantitative or qualitative 360 degree process which is a typical part of assessing an individual prior to active coaching. The consolidated feedback from this process is presented to the individual being coached, the CHRO, and the CEO. As a part of the feedback process, I discuss what the CEO can do to be more effective in managing the performance of the individual. Another opportunity may occur at the end of the coaching engagement when the final report is presented. At this point, the EC can give more directive advice to the CEO on how to lead or manage more effectively. This approach works best when the EC works closely with the CHRO to craft the messages to the CEO to achieve the intended behavioural change. Sometimes, a CEO will ask to undergo personal coaching after seeing the benefits to one of their direct reports.

(iii)   *CHRO Drives the Agenda*

Perhaps one of the more challenging situations an EC faces is when the CHRO has a very strong view as to what should happen in the coaching program beyond what the CEO or the EC have in mind. In these cases, it is very important for the CHRO to make any concerns known to both the CEO and the EC, and to share the rationale for a different suggested approach or desired outcomes. At this point, the EC needs to share the views of the CHRO with the CEO to determine if these should be part of the coaching engagement and contracted deliverables. It may be possible for the CHRO to participate in the formal feedback process, perhaps by receiving a copy of the summary report, or by soliciting feedback for help to guide the coaching program going forward.

In one situation, I was brought in initially to deal with some team issues, but my role quickly evolved to coaching the President to improve his openness to others' points of view and his general team leadership style. His CHRO had some very strong views about what I should work on and was very directive. It was a conflict for me, and I dealt with the situation by involving all the other members of the President's team by soliciting their views about the progress of their leader during the coaching program. This information was fed back confidentially to the President and the CHRO to validate what was working and what needed to improve. Sure enough, some of the CHRO's concerns were legitimate and required attention, and in some cases the CHRO's views were moderated by the feedback and changed.

"CHRO's at the U.S. 100 companies don't seem to be subject to a glass ceiling. Women hold 44 percent of the Fortune 100 CHRO jobs, and men hold 56 percent. This would indicate that the CHRO role seems to be the C-suite role that has the greatest representation of women among the largest U.S. based companies."

P. Wright, J. Boudreau, D. Pace, E. Sartain, P. McKinnon, and R. Antoine, *The Chief HR Officer: Defining the New Role of HR Leaders* (San Francisco: Wiley, John & Sons, Inc., 2011), p. 290

CHAPTER 117: WORKING WITH THE BOARD'S CEO SUCCESSION PLANNING CONSULTANT

Contributed by Helen Handfield-Jones, Helen Handfield-Jones Inc.

Though my work around CEO evaluations and succession planning is done directly with a Board, I often see the helpful hand of an effective CHRO contributing behind the scenes to the Board's thinking.

With CEO succession planning, I may be involved in a short burst of work to help through a crisis intervention, but most commonly I work with a Board for 18 to 24 months before the CEO transition occurs. I am always very clear on the fact that I am working for the Board, not the CEO. It is my job to help the Board do what is best for the organization, even if that might not perfectly align with the CEO's plans or wishes. My clients are the Chair of the Board and the Chair of the Committee that is leading the succession process.

The CHRO has a duty to do what is right for the organization and to help the Board effectively carry out its talent management responsibilities. One of aspect of this duty is to advise the HRC Chair on whether or not the current processes are adequate and on what kinds of improvements should be made. It is also useful for the CHRO to remind the CEO to put succession planning on the Board's agenda.

The CHRO has a front row seat to the relationship between the Board and the CEO, and is privy to the thoughts and concerns that the CEO and the HRC Chair may have regarding succession planning. It is the CHRO who helps the CEO present a candid and thorough annual assessment of the performance, potential, and development of each of his or her direct reports. Working closely with the CEO is necessary for the development of potential succession candidates, as is providing the Board with as much assessment information about the candidates as possible. This assistance means that the CHRO is very well placed to offer insights into possible internal candidates for succession and that he or she understands the dynamics within the executive team. Since succession planning is an HR process, albeit at the Board level, effective CHROs will track progress and work with the HRC on any issues that arise.

I counsel, guide, and support the Board all the way through the succession process. I help them gain clarity on the expected time to transition, provide some possible scenarios, and craft a multi-year work plan for the key activities and decisions. I help everyone understand the appropriate roles of the Board, the Committee, and the CEO. I facilitate the process of identifying, assessing, and developing possible internal candidates, and help the Board decide if, when, and how to conduct a search for external candidates. I also provide the "staff" support to this Committee all the way through the process. I bring best practices, frameworks, and tools to this work for every step along the way. The Board makes all the key decisions throughout the succession journey, while I facilitate, guide, and advise.

I also help boards with the annual process of evaluating the CEO's performance. There are a number of benefits for Boards and for CEOs when the evaluation is done well, but all too often the process used for the evaluation is incomplete and oriented primarily around deciding the bonus award. I work with Boards to develop and execute a more robust and meaningful process that will help the Board in its oversight of the CEO and that will help the CEO to develop and improve.

CEO evaluation is usually the responsibility of the Boards' Human Resource and Compensation Committee (HRC). My client is usually the Chair of this Committee, while the Chair of the Board and the CEO are also very involved. Sometimes I only design the process and the HRC Chair carries out this process each year. Other times, I design the process and help the HRC Chair conduct the process (at least for the first year that the new design is in place).

There may be some limits on how involved a CHRO can be in the CEO evaluation process. The CEO is the CHRO's boss, and that relationship may present some obstacles. It is helpful when the CHRO encourages the CEO to advocate for a thorough, robust evaluation process because it is in his or her best interest.

As well, the CHRO can prod, advise, and support the Chair of the HRC, the CEO, and consultants to ensure that every is performs their roles effectively. With knowledge on what an effective, robust CEO evaluation looks like, the CHRO can educate the HRC Chair and CEO. Having an understanding of what roles the CEO, the full Board, and the HRC should play is also important.

A critical part of designing the CEO evaluation is to develop a list of the responsibilities and objectives that succinctly captures most of what the CEO does. The responsibilities and objectives will be unique to each organization, to each particular CEO role, and to the strategic imperatives facing the organization at this time. You might think that CEO roles are all alike, but in my experience the key levers the CEO pulls and where he or she adds value vary a great deal from one organization to another.

After the performance criteria have been defined, I collect written and interview-based input from each of the directors. Sometimes I also collect input from each of the CEO's direct reports. Then I compile the data and synthesize the big themes and overall view that the Board has of the CEO's performance. I refine the report with the HRC and help him or her craft just the right message to share with the CEO. We discuss important implications from this evaluation, such as how much longer the Board might want the CEO to serve, how this will impact the CEO's pay, and how the Board can best support the CEO's development.

When the Board does engage a consultant, the CHRO should inform the consultant of anything germane to the assignment. If the consultant conducts interviews to gather input on the skills needed in the next CEO, the strengths and weaknesses of internal succession candidates, or the performance of the CEO, it is helpful for the CHRO to be included in those interviews and for them to be candid with the consultant. In my experience, CHROs can contribute a lot to the process through this quiet indirect channel.

How well a Board carries out its responsibilities for planning CEO succession and for evaluating the CEO's performance is extremely important to an organization's health. Most Boards find this work challenging. CHROs can promote improvements to these important processes by introducing a consultant to the Board who has expertise in this area and by encouraging everyone to commit more attention to these matters.

"Succession planning is the most important role of the Board Directors. The CEO is accountable for this process."

Edward Lumley, Vice Chair, BMO Nesbitt Burns

CHAPTER 118: WORKING WITH THE EXECUTIVE COMMUNICATIONS COACH

Contributed by Judith Humphrey, President of The Humphrey Group, a Communications Consulting firm.

No skill is more critical for leaders than their ability to communicate. These individuals must influence and inspire team members, customers, partners, senior management, and Boards. Whether in a brief elevator conversation, addressing a boardroom, or speaking to employees in a Town Hall, leaders must present clear, compelling, and inspiring messages.

The Humphrey Group works closely with Chief Human Resource Officers (CHROs) to ensure that leaders have strong communication skills. Sometimes C-level executives approach us directly. But often CHROs or their HR staff identify the need and come to us for help.

It is no easy task for a CHRO to approach a senior executive and say, "You need help in this area." But if you see a need, it's important to address it. In fact, I've seen some amazing CHROs who have a gift for articulating the need and working with us to create a solution.

What must a CHRO do to strengthen the communication skills of leaders in their organization?

Here are my recommendations:

1. Put communication skills on your radar screen

    As organizations become flatter, everyone needs to influence and inspire – from above, from below, and from the side. So CHROs increasingly need to be on the lookout for ways to help their leaders develop their communication skills. Weakness in this area can be career limiting even for the brightest, most talented individuals.

2. Develop communications skills in your up-and-coming leaders

    The ability to influence and inspire is a core skill – if not *the* core skill – for a leader. Why wait until your leaders are executives and well along in their careers to give them the ability to influence and inspire? In fact, when we work with executives, they often say, "I wish I had this training earlier in my career." If you are overseeing the development of a curriculum for emerging leaders, high potential leaders, or top talent, be sure to include a module on communications. My firm has provided such a module often, and participants are thrilled to have it.

3.   <u>Identify executives who need communication coaching</u>

As leaders move up the ladder, their communication skills must become finely tuned. Their entire job is to lead, and to lead they must motivate others every day and every moment. As well, they spend more time communicating with senior management and with their Board of Directors, and this requires strong communication skills. Inspirational leadership is really their mandate.

As CHROs, you'll want to be alert to the fact that many executives do need to strengthen their communication style. Look for the following indicators that suggest you need to offer help.

Be aware when the executive:

- turns the Board off when presenting;
- has poor engagement scores among their employees;
- presents or speaks too technically and overwhelms the audience with data;
- sounds garbled or unclear when speaking;
- is too casual in preparing and therefore rambles and often puts "foot in mouth";
- has a "command-and-control" style that turns people off;
- lacks the warmth that top leaders need to inspire;
- is boring, monotone, or too flat in their speaking style;
- lacks gravitas and sounds more junior than they are; and
- needs to develop executive presence.

This is just a sampling of the issues we see in executive clients who come to us for coaching. In many cases, an executive will face more than one of these challenges. All these individuals need your intervention. Approach them and tell them you will provide the support they need to become stronger, more persuasive communicators.

4.   <u>Have a vendor you can trust</u>

If you are going to work with your leaders to improve their communication skills you must have an outside firm that you can trust. Speech coaching is a sensitive area, and you must convey confidence in your vendor when you recommend training or coaching to any leader. What should you look for in a vendor? A track record is a starting point. Strong word-of-mouth is another. And finally, you want a firm that teaches leadership communications and not just public speaking or presentation skills. You want a firm that focuses on teaching leaders how to influence and inspire every time they speak. This is the approach we in The Humphrey Group take; our goal is inspirational leadership.

5.   <u>Stay connected and look for results</u>

You are the linchpin in these training/coaching relationships. Having introduced your leaders to an external firm, make sure you stay with the relationship. Check in regularly to see how it's going. Some CHROs, having made the introduction, opt out of the conversation, and just assume that the coaching is going well. But that's not always the case. Let's say a CEO has been told that he or she needs a communication coach because the CEO has a command-and-control style that turns off employees. It's likely that the CEO will have the same style toward the coach, and may even fire the coach. You'll never know this is the case unless you stay connected. You must provide leadership and keep the training on track. Arrange a three-way meeting, and restart the process. Don't be afraid to be forthright, even if the CEO ranks higher than you. He or she needs your leadership and conviction.

6.   <u>Know what success looks like</u>

The following examples illustrate successful communications coaching:

- A Chief Financial Officer needed our coaching because he was being considered for a more senior position where he would have to deal directly with the Board, the CEO, and the senior management. He was an introvert who kept to himself and avoided small talk. We helped him become more outgoing, and capable of engaging in networking at senior and Board levels. He did became much more effective at building these important relationships and became an extraordinarily attractive candidate for the CEO position, which he was offered.

- A Senior Vice President needed our coaching because he rambled on when he spoke and turned off key audiences. We helped him learn to frame his ideas, and to successfully convey clear messages. He learned to pause, organize his thoughts, and express them persuasively. People began to see him as the smart, savvy business leader that he was.

- A Vice President was being considered for the position of Chief Underwriter of a subsidiary company. She did not speak with sufficient polish, presence, or clarity. She used tentative language that made her sound weak. We worked with her in all these areas, and she gradually developed a more focused, confident speaking style. She impressed the Chairman of the Board, and was appointed Chief Underwriter.

As evidenced in the examples above, the CHRO plays a key role in shaping the communication skills of leaders. I have teamed up with some wonderful CHROs who have enabled The Humphrey Group to work with leaders at all levels. The results have been stronger communication skills and inspirational leadership. Building your talent pool in this way is critical.

> "The top 200 people must have Development Action Plans that are executed with excellence."
>
> Joe Jimenez, CEO, Novartis

CHAPTER 119: WORKING WITH THE EXECUTIVE SEARCH CONSULTANT

Contributed by Marty Parker, President, Waterstone Human Capital

As an executive search professional, I have seen the role of the Chief Human Resources Officer (CHRO) evolve significantly over the last number of years. Whereas CHROs once managed the inflow and outflow of human capital and its operations, today, CHROs are especially important in helping organizations navigate workforce issues on a much broader and strategic level. This work includes, but is not limited to, recruitment, retention, talent management, succession and workforce planning, training and development, compensation, labour and employee relations, engagement, human resource systems, and of course, corporate culture.

The strategic role of the CHRO in shaping and aligning human capital to corporate culture has grown significantly in importance as organizations are increasingly composed of knowledge workers. Furthermore, with an aging population of baby boomers, CHROs are recruiting in a highly competitive employment market. Therefore, CHROs today must concentrate on creating strong talent pipelines to both enhance organizational decision-making and secure future growth. These changes in the business landscape have required the CHRO to heighten the focus on recruiting for fit to ensure that new and existing human capital match company culture, as corporate culture is now commonly thought to be an organization's greatest asset and one that is critical to driving employee engagement.

The best CHROs today are the ones who are the keepers of corporate culture and who do everything to ensure that culture is well understood and that the organization's human capital systems and structure is aligned to the culture. This alignment will drive high employee engagement and significant business results.

The relationship between the CHRO and the executive search professional is very important to ensuring a successful outcome in recruiting a high-performance candidate that fits the organizational culture. The best CHROs provide the search team with as much access as possible to the organization in an effort to have the search professionals truly understand the nuances of the role, and most importantly, the culture of the organization.

Top CHROs understand that culture is created by the leadership's behaviour and that this behaviour is critical to driving success in an organization. By providing insights and access to the highest performers at the executive level (and often other levels), CHROs help the search professional see and experience the culture. This knowledge allows the search teams to best articulate the culture in both the candidate profile and in their pitch to candidates throughout the search.

The CHRO acts as partner and coach to the search firm to provide them with critical insights into the organizational culture, history, and future plans, and guides the firm through its meetings with the client team. CHROs are keen observers of not only what makes for successful candidates in a search process, but also, how the search firm can best work with the client team. Finally, the CHRO works closely post-recruitment with the search team to ensure successful integration and to provide post-search support to the placed candidate.

In short, the CHRO shepherds the search firm along and acts as coach, advisor, client, and partner through this challenging and critical work of finding candidates that fit the organization's culture.

In our Waterstone Human Capital's 2012 Canadian Corporate Culture Study, 85% of respondents indicated that cultural fit is more important than necessary skills when hiring. This is a stunning percentage, although in our world, not surprising. We noticed early on in our executive search practice that clients were placing more importance on fit (defined behaviours), when hiring. The successful candidate placements and longer tenures were far more common when the client focused on finding the right cultural fit, rather than relying solely on an exact skill set.

Essentially, when organizations focused on hiring people based on how they thought they would fit with their culture and how similar that person's behaviour was to the behaviours of their existing high performers, they tended to find a more successful hire in the long term. The reality is that all organizations have a culture. Understanding a given culture is critically important in recruiting for fit.

So how do you hire for fit? After years of experience working with high-performance candidates in our executive search practice and after having gone through thousands of interviews and submissions for our Canada's 10 Most Admired Corporate Cultures program, here is a critical starting point that a strong CHRO can help you with:

Find Your Key Success Behaviours; Know Thyself, Know Others

Finding successful people isn't enough anymore. What is really important is finding out *how* people are successful. Ask yourself this question: how do the most successful people in your organization behave? The best way to start the process of answering this question is to construct a culture index. Look at the most successful people in your organization, and identify five or six common behaviours. Spend some time with your high performers and find behavioural themes that are consistent among those high performers. The successful people that are currently in your organization are the key to finding the right kind of new talent. We see this proven time and time again in our search work.

I have worked with many successful CHROs in North America. Over the course of 10 years of working with Josée Dubuc, who is currently executive Vice President of Human Resources and Corporate services with Ivanhoé Cambridge (and formerly CHRO with Yellow Pages Group), I developed a very successful partnership with her.

For 10 years, Josée worked closely with me and with our team to execute over 90 leadership searches and consulting engagements as Yellow Pages Group (YPG) grew from a $300 million subsidiary of Bell Canada to an independent public company with just under $2 billion in revenue and almost $800 million in EBITDA. Not one of these engagements needed to be conducted a second time and over 25% of these candidates were promoted during this time.

Josée provided excellent counsel to our professionals and always gave open access to the senior team no matter what role we were engaged in. She was a key advisor to the YPG executive and chief executive officer Marc Tellier through many hires, acquisitions and talent reviews. Josée worked very closely with Waterstone to ensure we understood the mandate and could clearly and succinctly define the behavioural attributes required to fit the YPG culture.

> "This is all part of the development process at GE,
> and we never feel bad for long when one of our executives
> lands a big number one job outside the company."
>
> B. Conaty and R. Charan, *The Talent Masters, Why Smart Leaders Put
> People Before Numbers* (New York: Crown Publishing Group, 2010), p. 81

CHAPTER 120: WORKING WITH THE EXECUTIVE OUTPLACEMENT CONSULTANT

Contributed by Ralph Shedletsky, Chief Commercial Officer, Knightsbridge Human Capital Solutions

Knightsbridge's outplacement support for companies begins with our understanding of the business objectives of a staff change or reduction, and the policies, practices, and values that govern the way the change will take place. Most often, the CHRO provides this context, and gives our team the necessary insights to ensure we fully support the company's overall goals. Typically, CHROs delegate implementation of the change to members of their team working directly with the business units, who become responsible for ensuring the values, culture, and brand are safe-guarded through the change exercise. In the case of very senior leaders leaving the company, CHROs become directly involved to support the CEO or other members of the executive team, rather than delegating downwards.

The executive outplacement requirements and experience have changed considerably since the early days of our relationship with Maple Leaf Foods. The bar has been raised for today's leadership, which is no less true for those leaving an organization than it is for those remaining. Today more than ever, executives will benefit from specialized Executive Career Transition services made available to them.

While the planning for a release takes place well in advance of the event, the executive experience with Knightsbridge begins at the termination meeting, where our most senior and experienced consultants meet the executive immediately upon hearing the news. This meeting launches the relationship, which will move from immediate concerns such as breaking the news to family, to how to manage their message with others, to clarifying next steps and issues.

Mitigating risk at this sensitive stage of the process is critical for any organization. A key role for the Knightsbridge consultant is to help the executive talk about their reaction in a way that sustains the goodwill of their former organization and avoids erosion of the perceptions of those left behind.

No one remembers how someone joins a company. But everyone remembers how they leave and how they were treated as they leave. Knightsbridge can help the organization and the executive manage the exit and the time afterwards with dignity and with goodwill intact.

The objective with every new executive is to understand their starting point and bring all of our talent and tools to their advantage. If they are ready to hit the market running we start with communication coaching and market strategy. If they wish to reflect on their career options and leadership capabilities we start there.

At the initial meeting, our consultants will focus on the immediate needs of the client including financial, legal, personal, and tactical issues. Then, using a strategic career planning process, we identify our client's marketable strengths. Together we develop a focused and targeted approach to enable the individual to reach their career objectives, which may include re-employment or an entrepreneurial pursuit such as consulting, franchise ownership, or starting or buying a business.

For many executives at a stage in their career when they are free to make substantive directional changes in what they do, the service supports an in-depth exploration of the passions and life interests that would offer the most fulfilling career move. Once identified, a strategy and implementation plan for the change is created to allow the executive to launch the next stage of their career with maximum personal fulfillment.

One of my favourite stories of working with a CHRO exemplifies the importance of ensuring that our role supports the business outcomes the company has set. In this instance, the CHRO of a company in the energy sector engaged us to assist with a business transformation that would see the company exiting the retail segment of their business. The plan was to operate the outlets fully up to the announced close date, which required that the company keep employee retention and engagement at as a high a level as possible to ensure that there was no revenue impact during the months following the announcement.

Through joint planning, we developed a support program for leadership and employees which was launched months prior to the closure. The program began with helping employees manage their careers through on-site workshops focused on dealing with change, career planning, creating a resume, etc. Though the company initially feared that enabling employees to conduct a job search early would hasten their departure, the impact, combined with a responsible retention reward program, was the opposite. Employees were grateful for the help, felt empowered and confident about being able to find a job, and stayed and produced at levels greater than pre-announcement. At closure, revenue targets were exceeded, and the CHRO received appropriate recognition for not only delivering great results, but also, importantly, for demonstrating to the company's remaining employees how well those leaving felt about the support they received and the respect they were shown.

> "My experience is the CHRO has that unenviable task of serving two different constituents with the CEO and the committee, and within the committee perhaps different approaches/agendas by its members. That leads to many conundrums for the CHRO serving different masters and maintaining the integrity of not compromising what is right. They need great skills regarding persuasion, general business acumen, etc. My observations, having now dealt with 4 people in that role, is that the best know how to make their points and also know when they have done all they could on an issue and at least moved it in what they believe is the right direction. And, if it is really an issue of credibility, the CHRO was able in a non-disruptive way to get a full airing."
>
> James Olson, Board Director

CHAPTER 121: WORKING WITH THE LABOUR COUNSEL

Contributed by Israel Chafetz, QC, Taylor Jordan Chafetz

In matters of labour litigation and periodic labour advice, the solicitor/client relationship is somewhat unique. In most types of litigation, the solicitor/client relationship is focused and confined to a specific case that, once completed, more often than not ends the relationship. In labour litigation, the issue in dispute is usually one element of the ongoing labour relations relationship. The strategy or fact pattern of one case often impacts other cases and issues. Thus, the solicitor/client relationship is continuously evolving as a matter of strategic necessity, efficiency, and understanding of the overall labour strategy within the organization.

The issues within the relationship between counsel and the client are: the nature of the relationship, and how interwoven the counsel is within the fabric of the organization. The relationship depends largely on two factors: (i) the sophistication of the client; and, (ii) the continuity of management within the organization.

The extent and timeliness of labour advice more often than not depends on the sophistication of the client. Clients with experience and ability are subject to a different process when given advice than the less experienced or able client. In general, the client with more experience requires less detailed advice. For some clients a conversation about the issue will suffice; for other clients a detailed written opinion is required, and the lawyer must draft the appropriate letters to the union. For some individuals we detail every step in the logical analysis, while for others their understanding is such that not much detail is necessary. Also, some clients require lengthy memos to help them absorb the advice and pass it on, while others only require a discussion. In both cases we arrive at the same result but the route to get there can vary considerably.

The continuity of the participants in labour issues is an important factor both in the process and in the results. In labour matters issues tend to repeat over time. A long-standing client relationship provides a resource of continuity that is invaluable. Given management turnover, it is advantageous to have an individual that can provide a dependable corporate history to avoid repetition and learn from past mistakes. What worked or did not work in previous labour strategies is valuable information for both the quality and efficiency of current decision making. Past commitments made to the union and past responses by the union are valuable information. The continuity of counsel is one way to preserve such information as these matters are often found in the solicitor's files.

A long-standing counsel relationship lends itself to a more efficient process in the conduct of labour litigation. Counsels who have dealt with clients for a long time have a sense of their priorities and can often summarize complex matters more quickly because of this familiarity. Also, a long-term relationship is a foundation for a better understanding of what really matters to the client and what issues are nothing more than academic. Given the reality of turnover in management ranks, this resource of continuity in corporate culture and history that counsel can bring cannot be replicated easily and has considerable value.

Finally, there can be a downside to the advantage of familiarity. In spite of the positive aspects of a long-standing relationship with the client, it must be kept in mind that the organization is the client and not any one particular person in it. Familiarity with the instructing client, along with all of its benefits, can raise potential conflicts. Examples of such conflicts are becoming embroiled in internal corporate struggles or taking sides in resolving strategic direction. The best advice to counsel is to provide clear and competent advice no matter the inter-personal impact. The over-riding principle is that counsel is there to help solve the labour issue and it is not part of the decision-making process regarding who it will affect. Counsel's role is to help and bring energy to the work, which form the basis to of ensuring longevity and a meaningful contribution.

> "The CHRO needs to be plugged into the
> rest of the organization – managing by walking around."
>
> Claude Lamoureux, Board Director

CHAPTER 122: WORKING WITH THE SALES TRAINING CONSULTANT

Contributed by Art Horn, Founder of HORN

Most of us know sales training as a means to elevate performance in short- and long-term metrics like revenue, margin, market share, and productivity. But optimizing performance in these areas surely underlies all business initiatives – probably everything we do ought to be working towards long-term shareholder benefit.

Sales training is most interesting when viewed as a strategic tool. One of the most commonly cited motivations for sales training is to differentiate an organization by virtue of the consultative expertise of the sales force. Particularly in commoditized industries, sales training becomes a key method of marketplace differentiation.

There are other ways to use this tool. Sales training can be used to elevate change receptivity in advance of, or during times of, significant transition. It can be used to help modify the perceptions held by customers and consumers. It can be used to galvanize team selling, launch products, inspire growth, reward performance, reduce sales force attrition, reduce receivables, and improve recruiting efforts (people like to work on a sales team that invests in its people).

Sales training can change the culture of a whole organization. There is a growing trend towards training non-salespeople to think like sales people. Organizations that once self-identified as bureaucratic, perhaps because they were once government-run (for example the post office,), or massive in size (banks, for example), or highly risk sensitive (example, hospitals), often choose to provide what is essentially sales training to help individuals think like entrepreneurs, develop customer-centricity, generate leads, and influence internally. It should be clear that sales training is not just for salespeople.

Many organizations want their people to think the way that salespeople are considered to think. Sales training is often used to nurture an "optimal" attitude for success in business. After all, given that facing rejection is implicit in their job, salespeople need to be resilient, hopeful, optimistic, self-motivated, and courageous. A decade or two ago scientists weren't able to measure the traits listed above, and certainly had no idea of how to heighten a person's tendency toward them., Credible Human Resources departments were not inclined to invest in such intangible intra-personal nuances. However, with the advancement of technology that allows scientists to see the inner workings of the brain and to observe and measure human traits, and scientific evidence that individuals can self-manage these traits, the world of sales training has incorporated positive psychology.

Self-management (how to stay engaged and positive) is one broad sales training topic. The others are:

- *Tactical skills*: Ability to "sell" (how to negotiate, make an effective presentation, or conduct a meeting, for example)

- *Strategic skills*: Ability to see the big picture, make a plan (a territory plan or an account plan, for example)

- *Knowledge*: Knowing the products, company, and marketplace

(a)   Human Resources and Sales – the Shared Mission

External sales training providers tend to work with leaders from both Human Resources and Sales, and the amount of involvement or control of either group varies depending on the corporate culture, which department holds the budget, who instigates the initiative, and the nature of the topics being delivered.

There are, however, some consistent factors in determining which of the two departments has the most involvement a. Sales leadership knows what needs to happen in the marketplace while HR knows what constitutes effective training and how training must align with the overall corporate values and "people strategy".

Both groups generally collaborate over what other non-training processes and systems are necessary to support the investment in training. For example, you can teach salespeople how to sell customer service as a point of difference, but if their claims are not backed up with effective customer service, obvious problems will ensue. Similarly, if sales people are taught to develop their skills at selling profitable volume because that's the current mission, but their compensation plans focus on volume alone, the counter-productive dissonance will slow things down.

(b)   The Seven Keys to Successful Sales Training

For decades sales training was purely a classroom event: a couple of flip charts, a crowd of salespeople pulled from the field (some flown in) – a binder for each participant, a trainer at the front of the room, and go! Most people knew there were problems with this methodology. Only one or two learning nuggets would be gathered by each participant, costs were high, evidence of efficacy was low, and training binders ended up collecting dust on bookshelves.

However, this state of affairs is rapidly changing for the better. One of the reasons for this change is the significant research that has been done on what makes sales training stick. Academics now know that sales training will transfer to the workplace when:

1. There is a clear measurement strategy such that the behaviours to be taught in the program are clearly defined and used to dictate design, and their frequency is measured, pre- and post-training

2. The learning is genuinely important for the learners. Training has to get right at the nub of thing the learners crave to resolve (generic training has the significant disadvantage of being sweeping rather than targeted)

3. There is a strong sense of challenge (without significant accompanying anxiety) Salespeople face significant challenges on a daily basis and training should bring a certain level of intensity to the experience (through competition, for example)

4. Sales managers are intimately involved in design, pre-delivery meetings with learners, kicking off or attending (or even delivering) sessions, and one-on-one meetings with learners throughout the training initiative to monitor the application of the learning

5. Pre-work occurs prior to any classroom work (via e-Learning, for example)

6. During and after (in a teleconference, webinar, or web-meeting) the program participants are brought together to discuss and explore the application of learning

7. Attention is placed on the antecedents of historical behaviour so that the salespeople can recognize how desired behaviours represent superior choices for them to make back on the job (for example, when a customer asks, "can you improve on that price?" instead of saying "sure," say, "well, there are various ways to cut the price."

(c)   Leverage Technology

Technological advancement is another reason for the major changes taking place in the world of sales training. Technology has substantially reduced the cost of delivery. Why fly someone across the country when they can join a webinar from their own desk? Why take someone out of the field when they can do web-based e-Learning during their spare time (or even from home). Why put people through a whole course when key nuggets can be made available in a just-in-time mobile application while they are in the field?

Another gift brought by technology is increased effectiveness. In sales, the more hits, the better, and technology enables multiple touch points. Sure, classroom learning can't be replaced because sales training requires supervised, real-time role-playing of nuanced interpersonal skills and behaviours. But evidence shows that by reducing classroom time and supplementing it with some sort of technology-based learning (such as mobile apps, traditional web-based e-Learning, webinars, discussion groups for pre-work, mid-program work, and post-classroom session) will increase learning retention.

> "Most sales training programs are too generic. I have seen great training companies produce remarkable results through an academically sound, values-based, blended-learning approach. The training company focuses on creating a culture that drives the entire organization closer to clients as opposed to simply imparting stand-alone sales techniques."
>
> Tal Bevan, EVP, Sales – Canada, Ceridian HCM

CHAPTER 123: WORKING WITH THE LEADERSHIP AND PERFORMANCE BEHAVIOURAL CONSULTANT

Contributed by Steve Jacobs, consultant and Board Chairman with CLG

For two decades, a few select companies have been achieving breakthroughs in results and employee engagement by systematically managing a performance lever that most other companies leave to chance: behaviour. This trend has been called a "quiet revolution." It is a "revolution" in the sense that it is a powerful and transformative performance lever. It is "quiet" in the sense that pioneering companies are generally more interested in further extending this advantage than in telling the world about it.

What distinguishes these pioneering companies from others? First, they've adopted key operating principles, including:

- "People are the only sustainable source of competitive advantage." (i.e., Peter Drucker's enduring observation)

- New results nearly always require new behaviour. That is, people-based competitive advantage is about more than merely attracting superior talent; such advantage requires shaping what talented people throughout the organization do consistently and in concert every day. It's that simple, that important, and that difficult.

- All behaviour is rational, if you know what the drivers are.

- Discretionary performance of high impact behaviour is the aim. Mere compliance is insufficient, as are generally defined employee engagement goals.

Second, they execute these principles by applying the science behind behaviour change, and they do so using practical, reliable, scalable methods. This knowledge is crucial to the breakthroughs that they achieve.

And, third, they explicitly target and achieve significant measurable returns on their behavioural leadership investment. One example is Canadian National's decision in 2003 to strengthen its industry position by transforming its culture. CN's leadership defined culture as a pattern of behaviour that linked to explicit business objectives, and applied practical, science-based methods for systematically reshaping their culture. During this period, they achieved unprecedented results. By 2006, CN had tripled its stock value, increased its Operating Ratio advantage over competitors by an additional 10 points, and delivered nearly twice the industry average for Return on Revenue. In 2007, James Valentine, former

Morgan Stanley Dean Witter Rail Analyst, noted: "CN is to freight railroading what Michael Jordan is to basketball and Tiger Woods is to golf."

As of this writing in 2013, CN's dominance continues. Other companies have demonstrated similar impact, typically achieving between 5:1 and 30:1 ROI within 12 to 24 months.

(a)   From Performance Breakthroughs to Enterprise Advantage

One of the most interesting patterns that has emerged in the work of some of these pioneers is that, once they achieve the performance breakthroughs that they see, they don't stop. Instead, they set about extending their behavioural leadership capability to new areas and to new applications. As one executive remarked, "Just when you think that you've fully leveraged what's possible (with behavioural leadership), the penny drops and the world never looks the same again. You realize that you've just scratched the surface, and you will settle for nothing less than building a 'wall to wall' advantage that others can't touch."

These companies then adopt another guiding principle: build new advantage in every deployment cycle. They intentionally integrate their behaviour-change (and engagement-enhancing) acumen in a variety of ways, including:

- Annual business planning and deployment.

- Coaching for elite performance.

- Large-scale change leadership.

- Transforming culture.

- Taking talent acquisition and development strategies to the next level.

- Accelerating process excellence initiatives ("behaviouralized" lean sigma methods, for example).

Finally, the power of behavioural leadership provides an additional dimension to the unique role of the CHRO as a business partner in building people-based advantage. Key tactics for CHROs in these companies include:

- Think big, start small, scale fast.

- Build simultaneous capability for superior execution and winning culture.

- Guide progress with a multi-year, stage-gated roadmap.

- Require leaders to lead.

- Expect ROI, and use it to fund extensions.

- Align your talent systems to develop and leverage behavioural capability.

- Measure and reward sustained new advantage (over and above new results).

- Make sustainability an explicit accountability and measured priority. Really.

There is another important aspect of behavioural leaders that differentiates them. They seek to perform at the highest levels, individually and organizationally, and the fact that behavioural leadership demands a certain capability that others are unwilling to develop is part of the attraction. As John Sullivan, CEO of Cadillac Fairview, Canada's premier commercial real estate company, remarked, "Our industry competes on tangible things like physical assets, capital investments, and acquisitions. None of our competitors are thinking about behaviour as a source of competitive advantage. And even if they were, we have a head start that we don't intend to relinquish. Behavioural Leadership will put new distance between us and them for years to come."

"The New Mindset"

"Unless leaders really dig down and get deeper expertise in a number of different areas – to ask compelling questions, challenge the status quo, adopt new business models and relate to new talent mindsets – they will become irrelevant."

Rose Patten, Special Advisor to the CEO (former CHRO), BMO Financial Group

---

CHAPTER 124: WORKING WITH THE ORGANIZATIONAL/ RESTRUCTURING CONSULTANT

Contributed by Cliff Grevler, Partner and Managing Director of the Boston Consulting Group (BCG)

One of the CHRO's most important responsibilities is leading during times of organizational change. Reorganizations play a pivotal role in the business world; few other initiatives have as much potential to reinvigorate a company's strategy and strengths. They help make companies more effective and efficient by finding and fixing redundancies, suboptimal structures, and misalignments between strategies and designs. And, in industries where change is constant and unpredictable, reorganizations play a critical role in allowing companies to continuously adapt to the shifting landscape.

As elemental as they are, however, reorganizations are notoriously difficult to implement. Even the most well-coordinated transformations impose heavy burdens on a company's senior and middle managers, who – apart from trying to guide a massive change program, stay focused on strategic goals, and keep the business humming – often end up devoting a disproportionate amount of time to gathering, validating, and managing the vast amounts of data needed to make informed decisions about the new structure.

Recognizing the opportunity for technology to address this challenge, BCG developed a software tool called OrgBuilder, which helps companies gather and analyze the data they need to make critical decisions when developing and implementing a new structure. The tool does not make reorganizations painless, but – in the hands of a CHRO and BCG team that knows the ins and outs of reorganization – it does bring greater transparency, accuracy, and efficiency to an unwieldy process. More importantly, it frees up business leaders to spend more time on the issues that matter most, including managing talent, keeping the reorganization locked onto strategic goals, pressing ahead with existing business priorities, and maintaining employee engagement. OrgBuilder has become an indispensable part of BCG's broader approach to reorganizing for sustained performance.

(a)   Partnering with the CHRO: A Four-step Process

A close partnership between BCG and the CHRO is critical to success in any reorganization. Most often, our joint approach to reorganization begins with a comprehensive diagnosis of the organization, followed by a high-level view of the redesign. The changes necessary to implement the new design are then cascaded throughout the organization, from top to bottom, affording managers at all levels a clear, real-time view of (and responsibility for) how the transformation is unfolding. BCG's software tool brings order and clarity to each of the following four steps:

1. Assessing the opportunities.

2. Mapping out the new design.

3. Matching staffing needs and talent.

4. Hard-wiring the change.

1. *Assessing the opportunities.* A successful reorganization starts with a comprehensive HR balance sheet: an accurate database of a company's people and roles, along with such detailed information as each individual's title, compensation, tenure, and division. To generate this view, the team that leads the effort works with HR and business leaders to compile, clean, and validate information, ensuring that all the company's people and roles are captured. This undertaking can be daunting, given the labyrinthine structure and dynamic nature of many companies. OrgBuilder can make the process far more efficient, accurate, and timely.

   This fact-based view of the organization is then used to identify opportunities for improvement, which are typically related to efficiency and effectiveness. Common signs of inefficiency include duplicative roles and responsibilities and substandard performance relative to peers, as measured by benchmarks for specific functions. Inefficiencies often arise from excess layers between the CEO and frontline employees, which slow communication and stall decision making, and from narrow spans of control (managers with a small number of direct reports), which can inhibit empowered, ambitious leadership. OrgBuilder can quickly generate charts and graphs that help managers visualize many of these inefficiencies. By highlighting opportunities to improve the business, this first step provides a glimpse of what the target organization might look like. It also sets out a clear rationale for the difficult changes that lie ahead.

2. *Mapping out the new design.* In this step, the company translates the opportunities for improvement into a blueprint for the new organization. It comprises three discrete activities.

   • Set targets. Target setting provides guidelines for key aspects of the design, including structure, incentives, and performance management systems, and ensures that the new organization is aligned with the company's objectives. It is both an art and a science. The targets should be driven by data and analysis, but they ultimately need to be embraced by key stakeholders – they will mean little without adequate buy-in. Once set, the targets are disseminated to senior leaders, who communicate them to their respective parts of the organization and set in motion the initial wave of change.

   • Use scenarios to describe the future state. The targets influence the shape of the organization, but senior leaders still have an opportunity to develop and test different permutations of the structure in order to determine which will best fulfill their particular objectives. OrgBuilder is particularly helpful in this phase. It allows the company to understand how variations in the contours of the organization lead to different outcomes. What are the savings implications of melding division A and division B? Would collaboration be enhanced by redefining the reporting lines in division C and division D?

• Reinforce the company's culture and drive employee engagement. Companies must not lose sight of the design's impact on culture and employee engagement. Culture describes how things are done in a company. It goes hand in hand with a company's strategy and sources of advantage. Engagement, measured by employees' willingness to go the extra mile for the company, often wanes during reorganizations but is critical for change to take hold. With this in mind, the organization needs to reinforce the behaviours, structures, and processes that facilitate the desired culture and engagement level. Above all, the elements that are crucial to engagement must not be subsumed by the company's push to extract more efficiency or rationalize its structure.

At the end of this step, the company will have arrived, through a combination of analysis and iteration, at an agreed blueprint for the new structure; one that reinforces its strategy, strengths, and culture, and that preserves, to the extent possible, employee engagement.

3. *Matching staffing needs and talent.* Once the basic shape of the organization has been determined, it's then time to start matching people to roles. The CHRO typically leads a process that identifies the employees and positions that are most critical to strategic objectives. This includes top performers, along with the people who are indispensable to a specific strategic initiative or who have specialized knowledge or skills. The most important part of this process is to ensure that individual capabilities are matched to role requirements. OrgBuilder can help companies manage the complexity and breadth of this task. The tool can quickly provide an organization wide view of the capabilities required for each role and help match people's skills to current and future needs.

4. *Hard-wiring the change.* Throughout this process, there needs to be a dedicated focus on embedding change. In addition to having the right leadership in place to drive change and maintain the cadence of day-to-day operations, companies need to communicate the purpose and progress of the transformation early on, particularly among opinion leaders, people at risk of leaving, people who have critical skills, and people in positions that may be altered or eliminated. As personal as it is, communication, too, can benefit from the use of a software tool. By providing a real-time view of the transformation while linking actions to a broader strategic framework, OrgBuilder can help alleviate some of the anxiety associated with restructuring, which often stems from the confusion and the sometimes inscrutable logic surrounding key decisions. At a more practical level, the software can track which individuals

– including top performers or people at risk of leaving – have received certain communications.

(b) "A single source of truth"

A CHRO recently compared two reorganizations that he had led over the course of his career, the second of which was supported by BCG and the OrgBuilder tool:

> The first time round we had real difficulty managing the vast amounts of data which led to all kinds of issues. The same position was being offered to two individuals in different parts of the company, we could not keep track of our current employees who were unstaffed in the new organization, and had difficulty knowing the current state of communication to our high performers. With OrgBuilder, many of these issues were solved. We have a database that is both comprehensive and current – and a single source of truth to the often messy and iterative process of organizational redesign.

Reorganizations are rarely loved, but they are valued for the results they produce. Moreover, the ability to adapt is fast becoming a strength in and of itself. As the drivers of success in various industries continue to change (owing to a host of factors, including globalization, deregulation, digitalization, connectivity, deconstruction, and the shift from products to services), advantage will inevitably accrue to companies that have the foresight and skills to keep their organizations aligned with their objectives.

The CHRO will always be the leader through these periods of change. Being equipped with a tool that brings discipline and science to the art of reorganization greatly enhances the changes of success.

"Design the org chart to be as flat as possible, with blindingly clear reporting relationships and responsibilities."

J. Welch and S. Welch., *Winning*
(New York: HarperBusiness, 2005), p. 114

CHAPTER 125: WORKING WITH THE EXECUTIVE ASSESSMENT CONSULTANT

Contributed by Dr. Al Schnur, PhD, President of PCI Human Resources Consulting

Chief Human Resource Officers (CHROs) are in unique roles in organizations. Executives in these roles not only support the entire employee population, but also their peers at the "C-level", the CEO, as well as the Chairman and Board of Directors. They are ultimately responsible for the quality of the hiring decisions made by the organization and the development of all of its key employees. Hiring decisions on senior executives are especially critical in that they can shape future success. These key decisions, in addition to involving candidates, recruiters, and hiring managers, also involve other stakeholders, both inside and outside of the organization.

Candidates for key roles can come from many sources, including executive recruiters, previous employees of Board members and executives, and others. The referring stakeholder can feel very strongly about the skills and fit of the executive candidate in question. These candidates may have been quite successful in other organizations, but often at lower levels than that of the target position. While candidates can come in highly touted, perform very well in interviews, and "look good on paper", not all candidates have the potential to be successful as senior executives within the CHRO's specific organization. This is especially the case if there are key differences in terms of mental demands of the role, cultural fit, and level of position compared to roles they have held previously. In addition to trying to make the best decision for an organization, the CHRO is also often placed in the middle of political situations where the parties are not unbiased.

It is helpful to understand the motivations and perspectives of the key stakeholders in the hiring decision. We will take these in turn, beginning with the candidate and then discussing the hiring manager, recruiter, and other stakeholders.

(a) Candidate Perspective

From the candidate's perspective, he or she has likely been recruited actively for consideration, whether by an executive recruiter or referred by a Board member or a former employer. The candidate, especially if the target role would represent an increase in compensation and responsibility, is likely very motivated to try to get the job offer. Savvy candidates will study corporate websites and listen carefully to position and company descriptions to try to position themselves as the best candidate based on the organization's stated needs. The candidates can often talk themselves into roles that may not be the best fit for them, which then leads to sub-optimal results for both the organization and the individual. Therefore, it is important to note that, during the interview process, the candidate will be at the best he or she will ever be in terms of impression management and stated willingness to do the things that are required for success in the role. Whether the position is a good fit in terms of skills, motivations, and abilities needs to be closely considered from a variety of perspectives in addition to that of the candidate. The CHRO and others involved in the hiring decision need to realize that the candidate's ability to be objective about fit can be compromised by a desire to receive a job offer.

(b) Hiring Manager

The hiring manager typically has a very clear idea of what is needed in a role in terms of skills, abilities, and motivations. If the position has been open for some time, there is often a sense of urgency, or even desperation, to fill the role. It is this "selection anxiety" that is likely the biggest obstacle to making an effective hiring decision. Too often, candidates can tell hiring managers what they want to hear and consciously or subconsciously, hiring managers can be overly influenced by the schools candidates attended, their interests, or other factors. There is also an assumption that certain degrees indicate a certain level of cognitive capability, or that accomplishments in lower level positions will translate into success in expanded roles without considering the "Peter Principle", which suggests that often executives are promoted one level beyond their competence. The hiring manager will certainly benefit from objective data from a disinterested party, such as an executive assessor, who does not have a vested interest in the hiring decision or outcome.

(c) Recruiter

In the current HR consulting climate, executive recruiters often position themselves as assessors of executive talent, as well as sources of the same. A good executive recruiter has an expertise in finding qualified candidates, many of whom are not actively seeking to change jobs. Their ability to network, understand the position requirements, and to screen unqualified applicants out of the pool are valuable services that can support the CHRO and the organization. However, when the recruiter tries to play "judge" as well as "advocate" for the candidate, there is the potential for unintentional bias. It is this strong desire to make a placement to aid the organization, and the recruiting firm, that can lead to potential conflicts of interest or over-promoting of under-qualified candidates. It is not to say that these are intentional biases but, like good government, a system of checks and balances that has important data provided from a variety of perspectives will typically lead to better hiring decisions.

(d) Board Perspective

The Board of Directors is often involved in executive hiring decisions and will want to hire people who are not only credible in front of the Board, but potentially in front of investors and other stakeholders outside of the organization. A candidate's track record, presentation skills, or other interpersonal factors can easily overly influence a Board either positively or negatively, and impede them from fully considering the candidate's ability to make a long-term positive impact for the organization. In addition, Board members often refer people with whom they have worked previously, or know of, to try to help solve key hiring problems for the organization. In these cases, the Board member may be considering the relationship, loyalty, or other factors rather than looking objectively at how the candidate's skills and abilities fit the position profile. The Board of Directors, like other stakeholders, certainly can benefit from an unbiased and objective look at the candidates, especially in politically charged environments.

(e) The CHRO Dilemma

The CHRO must consider all of the stakeholder perspectives and try to make the decision that is best for all concerned. They must navigate the political waters, Board or hiring manager pressure, as well as pressure and influence from the candidate and recruiter – both of whom, as we already know, are highly motivated to obtain the job offer. The CHRO can expend significant political capital if they feel that a candidate is high risk or not a good fit for the organization and can risk hearing, "I told you so" if the candidate is then screened out and goes on to success elsewhere. An effective executive assessment can provide a solution and valuable input into the hiring decision for the CHRO's fiduciary responsibility to do what is best for the organization from a strategic HR perspective.

(f) Executive Assessment

A high quality, objective executive assessment is typically conducted by a professional with a Ph.D. or other advanced degree in Psychology. Assessment firms that use best practices develop a clear understanding of the role, the organizational culture, and the long-term vision for both. The assessor will spend time with the hiring manager, the CHRO, and perhaps other stakeholders (including Board members), to gain a full understanding of the position requirements and must/ must-not haves for the target role. A credible assessment consists of a battery of valid psychometric tests that measure cognitive abilities, communication skills, decision-making style, strategic abilities, as well as leadership capabilities and style. In addition, the assessment will look at interpersonal skills, peer relations, stress management, and other work style factors. Finally, key management "detailers", which are extreme aspects of personality that can derail executives inside and outside of the organization, will be noted.

Once the test data is collected, often remotely through the internet, the assessor will conduct an in-depth interview, with a focus on results that are of critical concern. Executive assessments that use best practices will provide feedback to the candidates on the results, as well as feedback to the hiring manager and other stakeholders. A written report, that covers all information relevant to the role, and an overall recommendation, should be provided. Finally, any data from interview and reference probes on potential derailers in terms of risk are provided as well.

(g)   Key Benefits of Executive Assessment

The greatest value that an executive assessment has is its data-based objectivity. The assessor is outside of the organization and has no vested interest in the outcome. While the executive assessment is not the only factor considered in the hiring decision, it is an important piece of data that, as the research clearly demonstrates, is ignored at the organization's own peril. Armed with this objective data, the CHRO can confidently advocate for or against candidates with the assessment results as support. When there are multiple candidates for a role, the assessments can be compared and contrasted to determine overall potential for success.

Regardless of whether the candidates are internal or external, or a combination of both, important decisions can be made using the data, including who to hire or promote, and what their long-term "runway" is. As no 360 degree feedback, interview or reference process can describe behaviour at a higher role than the person has ever held, the objective predictive data of the executive assessment uniquely allows the CHRO to look into the future. While interviews, reference checks, and education and track record are all important, the executive assessment is a key piece that represents a very inexpensive insurance policy to make sure everything is as good as it sounds from the candidate, recruiter, and interview perspectives.

(h)   Assessment at Other Levels

While senior executive hiring decisions receive the most scrutiny, hires at all professional managerial levels in the organization are of even greater importance to the long-term ability of the organization to be successful, grow its own talent, and remain competitive. Therefore, CHROs should ensure that all external professional and managerial hires, as well as promotions, have some level of objective managerial/executive assessment as part of the decision-making process. While these processes may not be as robust, having the objective data prevents hiring mistakes or promoting people beyond their level. The objective research shows that executive/managerial assessment is a strong predictor of job success and, on the flip side, of failure or under performance. Having objective data at all levels of management in the organization is a best practice, as well as a competitive advantage for the CHRO and the organization as a whole.

> "Jimenez's experiences in his first year at Novartis drove home for him the value of rigorous psychological assessments focused on enhancing leaders' self-awareness. "Other companies too often define leadership development in a cursory way without that deep up-front assessment of what will really make a person a more effective leader. They don't identify the root cause of the problem, if there is a problem, or the key opportunity that the leader has. The thing that Novartis does better than any other company I've seen is that up-front piece." "
>
> B. Conaty and R. Charan,
> *The Talent Masters, Why Smart Leaders Put People Before Numbers*
> (New York: Crown Publishing Group, 2010), p. 193

CHAPTER 126: WORKING WITH THE HRC TRAINING CONSULTANT

Contributed by Hugh Arnold, Adjunct Professor of Organizational Behaviour, Rotman School of Management

Two key generic issues in effective corporate governance have particular implications for the role and impact of the CHRO. The first is the importance of maintaining appropriate role differentiation between the Board and management. While all formal authority rests with the Board by law, organizations can only function effectively if significant authority is delegated by the Board to the CEO and senior officers, including the CHRO. Along with delegation comes the exercise of oversight by the Board. An important role of the Board is holding senior management accountable for their performance and ensuring that the interests of management are aligned with the interests of shareholders and other key stakeholders. At the same time, highly effective organizations are character-ized by high levels of trust between Directors and senior management rooted in shared values, a common vision for the future of the organization, and a mutual understanding of the strategies to be pursued in achieving that vision.

There is thus an inevitable tension involved in balancing the competing, and sometimes conflicting, needs for the exercise of effective and dispassionate oversight by Directors and the need for Directors and senior managers to be fundamentally aligned on vision, direction and strategic priorities for the organ-ization. The relationship between the CHRO and the chair of the HR committee is a key point of interface between Directors and management where this tension must be effectively managed. Success requires effort by both parties to establish and maintain a relationship characterized by:

- Collaboration.

- Mutual trust and respect.

- Shared values.

- A sense of common purpose regarding both overall corporate strategic dir-ection as well as key HR priorities to support the strategy.

- An appropriate degree of deference involving recognition by both parties that:

  - they are not peers;
  - ultimate power and authority rests with the Board.

A second perennial challenge for organizations is addressing the inevitable infor-mation gap (some call it a "chasm") that exists between Directors and senior management. Research indicates that Directors of large publicly traded organiz-ations devote on average somewhere between 200 and 250 hours a year to their duties. The members of the senior management teams of those same organizations will normally be investing on the order of 2500 to 3000 hours per year in fulfilling their responsibilities. In order for Directors to discharge their duties effectively the information gap arising from this huge differential in knowledge and information must be effectively bridged.

The CHRO and HR chair working together can help to address this issue. As in so many areas, the solution is almost never the provision of more data to the committee by the CHRO and staff. Instead, the solution lies in understanding the informational needs of the chair and committee members and then organizing, focusing, and editing the information in a fashion that can be easily digested and analyzed by the chair and committee members.

In addition to helping address these generic governance challenges, the CHRO is also in a position to provide some unique forms of advice and support to the HR Committee and the Board. The CHRO's role is unique within the organization in a number of ways, listed below.

The CHRO is almost always the repository of a large amount of highly confidential information regarding people and issues within the organization.

By virtue of this, the CHRO has the trust of all constituencies to maintain confidences.

The CHRO is often seen as an "honest broker" who is even-handed in resolving conflicts.

These characteristics of the CHRO and the role they occupy puts that person in a position to support certain functions of the Board and the HR committee in ways that other members of senior management cannot. For example, the CHRO is sometimes called on to facilitate resolving issues between the CEO and the Board regarding CEO compensation at contract renewal time (a situation that often involves the CEO and the Board having retained separate compensation consultants as advisors). Another example occurs when the Board is seeking potential new members. As a result of the CHRO's frequent experience working with executive search firms the Board may seek the CHRO's suggestions and advice to the Board Nominating Committee on firms with strong track records for director searches.

Moving in to the CHRO role presents the new incumbent with a whole set of challenges in effectively managing the relationship with the HR committee in general and the committee chair in particular. There is often little, if anything, in the previous work experience of new incumbents to prepare them for managing these new responsibilities and relationships effectively since they differ fundamentally from the responsibilities of HR roles below that of CHRO. Addressing this gap in knowledge and experience is an objective of Rotman's annual 3-day Board Human Resources Committee Program. The program attracts CHROs, senior HR professionals anticipating taking on CHRO responsibilities, as well as current and potential members of HR committees. It provides an opportunity for both groups to gain a fuller understanding of their mutual roles and how they can become more effective more quickly in those roles.

For details about three case studies used in this program, please see Appendix 10.

> "The CHRO is in a fiduciary role to the Board.
> They are accountable to the whole board and the CEO."
>
> Stan Magidson, CEO, Institute of Corporate Directors

CHAPTER 127: WORKING WITH THE PENSION CONSULTANT

Contributed by Bernard Morency, SVP, Strategy, Caisse de dépôt et placement du Québec

When CN did its first IPO in 1995, the pension plan had some 28,000 active contributors and 48,000 pensioners who received monthly cheques. If the IPO was a success, the expected market capitalization would be roughly $2.3 billion. At that time, the assets of the CN Pension Plan had a market value of about $8 billion. This contrast led to some jokes that the IPO was not about a railway company with 75 years plus of history and a dominant position in Canada, but rather about a pension plan with a rail operation on the side. Having a pension plan of that size, was a very serious matter for CN, one that the CEO, the CFO and CHRO always kept top of mind.

Pension plans, especially defined benefit ones like the CN Pension Plan, are like sea liners: they move slowly and it takes time, effort and foresight to change their direction. Just like huge ships that follow defined navigation routes across the oceans, you can pretty much predict where a pension plan is going next if you know its past history. So, to understand the challenges faced by Les when he joined CN in 2001, it is important to shed some light on the status of the CN Pension Plan at that time. Beyond its particular demography and its huge size relative to the market capitalization of the company, three other characteristics made the CN Pension Plan rather unique.

There was only one plan for both unionized and non-unionized employees, with identical plan provisions for both groups. While the plan was not a formal part of the company's Labour agreements with its unions, pension-related issues were regularly discussed with union representatives. That led to many interesting debates.

In 1989, the plan had adopted an innovative experience and risk-sharing mechanism which made post-employment indexation conditional upon the plan's ability to pay for it. This feature was known as the Escalation Account. The concept was expanded in 1998 to manage basic pension improvements for active employees through a process known as the Improvement Account.

Governance of the plan was overseen by the Pension Committee, with a membership which included six senior representatives from the unions, one representative from non-unionized employees, five company representatives and five pensioner representatives. The Chair of the Committee alternated between the company's CHRO and union representatives. The Committee had the power to recommend improvements to pension payments based upon how much money was available in the Escalation Account and in the Improvement Account.

As the new CHRO, Les was faced with the need to manage a hugely important organizational component with financial, Labour relations and managerial aspects. In 2001, the plan had some 20,000 active employees with roughly 45,000 pensioners, which yielded a ratio of 2.2 pensioners for every active employee. Its financial position was sound, with assets of around $12 billion, and a small surplus. It was also a task that had two components: a fairly cumbersome "management" process and a platform for co-operation among all stakeholders in the form of the Pension Committee. To make it a little bit more complicated, while it was a defined benefit plan, it had a rather unique experience/risk-sharing mechanism, and pensioners on the Committee also had a say on administration.

The plan's assets were managed by the CN Pension Investment division under the supervision of the Investment Committee of the Board of Directors. The President of the CN Investment division was Tullio Cedraschi, a well-known and respected investment professional who had been in that role since 1978. I had been the plan's actuary since 1984, and when Les arrived in 2001, I was the Executive Vice-President responsible for Mercer's Global Retirement, Benefits, Outsourcing and Investment Consulting practices. I had been a party to all of the major changes made to the plan since the mid-eighties and was well known, and hopefully, well respected by all parties: management, union, and pensioners.

Pensions, especially defined benefit ones, are a technical and complicated matter. When I first started working with Les in his new CHRO role at CN, I could tell that he was very surprised and a bit overwhelmed at the size and complexity of the pension plan and its governance process. Fortunately, CN had many pension specialists on staff including actuaries, and he could draw on their expertise.

I have had the chance to work with many great CHROs in my career as a consultant, and there are some common themes. The CHROs knew what they wanted to accomplish with their pension plan, invested time in understanding it, shared their viewpoint and objectives with me and their stakeholders, and surrounded themselves with experts internally. They made me part of their team, and I tried to understand their business so as to tailor my consulting to their particular circumstances. "What would you do if you were in my place?" wasn't a question that they had to ask, because with my help and the help of our respective teams, they would know what to do.

My objective was to work the same way with Les. We created a monthly schedule, with our respective teams present, to meet and resolve issues. We quickly agreed that trust and collaboration were needed between us and all of the parties. Full transparency was a necessary but not sufficient condition for success. An appropriate line had to be drawn between administrative and governance matters on the one hand, and negotiations and managerial matters on the other. We also needed to make sure that the interests of all parties represented on the Pension Committee were aligned and that they shared a common goal: a secure, affordable plan. It had to be a plan that could pay the promised benefits without unduly encumbering the company, allowing it to adjust to shifts in the market and outside economic forces.

Les and I can say that it worked. The plan withstood the "burst" of the tech bubble in the early 2000s, the challenges of decreasing interest rates throughout Les's tenure at CN from 2001 to 2008, and the 2008 financial crisis. The plan was able to pay the benefits and provide for some post-retirement indexation. Money was put aside for the rainy days; which arrived very abruptly in 2008. All of this was achieved at a reasonable cost to CN.

The ingredients of success were:

Collaboration: Collaboration not just between the two of us and the pension committee, but also between the various union groups, CN finance, HR and Investment divisions and, yes, pensioners.

Clarity: We had a clear delineation of powers with well-written plan rules.

Education: We put our focus on taking the time to discuss issues to get all of the facts on the table before decisions were made. Then, we spent time explaining the decisions to all of the parties involved. Tullio and I made regular presentations to the Pension Committee, with frequent discussions with the unions' and pensioners' representatives, and with CN's Board of Directors on pension issues.

Patience: It takes time to make effective changes to pension plans, especially when a CHRO wants to make changes that require thoughtful planning and discussion.

Forward Thinking: We made and shared projections of where the plan was going, including the impact of various economic scenarios.

Expertise: Not only external expertise, but just as importantly, internal expertise at CN. CN's actuarial staff worked closely with the Mercer team, and shared responsibilities based on each other's capabilities.

Trust and Respect: We were both strong-willed professionals who wanted to do the right things.

My administrative assistant once asked me why I worked so hard on CN's actuarial valuation. She said, "In the end, what difference does it make what you say in your report?" I remember telling her: "If we do our job well, the plan will be secured and affordable, making it sustainable. That means that the 50,000 pensioners who depend on their CN pension every month will continue to receive it. The active employees will be able to plan their retirement because the CN plan will be there when they retire. If we do our job well, these outcomes will be achieved without putting an undue burden on CN; allowing it to adjust to changing economic conditions."

> "Running a pension plan takes common sense. The challenge is to predict the future. Most people tend to wear rose coloured glasses when they do so. The role of the consultant is not to throw oil on the fire but to skillfully guide trustees and management to reasonable assumptions."
>
> Claude Lamoureux, Board Director

CHAPTER 128: WORKING WITH THE EMPLOYEE BENEFITS CONSULTANT

Contributed by Mark Dahlman, former Canadian Health & Welfare Leader, Towers Watson

It is the role of the CHRO to make sure that the company's employee benefits effectively support the company's broader strategic business plans, which is both a challenge and opportunity.

It's helpful to look back at the evolution of employee benefits. These programs developed over many years, and often were initially considered as add-ons to the employment relationship. They got their start during the Second World War, when mandated wage control programs limited employers' ability to adjust pay due to market demands. To attract and retain staff, new "fringes" were allowed. As a result, group medical, disability, and life insurance programs became recruitment and retention enhancements.

Subsequently, from the 1960s into the early 1980s, union bargaining strategies used employee benefit enhancements as lower-cost tactics compared to wage increases. Thus, the advent of dental benefits and retiree life and health coverage became competitive practices. Further, both U.S. and Canadian federal fiscal policies in the mid-1980s brought about changes to income tax laws, which permitted broader tax-favoured opportunities for employee benefit programs.

As workforce demographics shifted to include greater diversity, there was a need for different employee benefits such as child-care, and for more flexible work arrangements. Societal pressures for better work/life balance, better stress management, the acknowledgement that treatment for mental health must be treated the same as any other illness, and the expansion of the definition of "dependent" and "family" further expanded the programs offered. A growing focus on employee engagement as a strategic goal has also broadened what is now within the purview of employee benefits. We are also seeing changing patterns in retirement as economic pressures force many employees to work longer due to increased life expectancy and in many cases due to insufficient sources of financial support.

All of these factors mean that current CHROs have inherited a panoply of programs that emerged from unrelated business influences. While initially "low-cost" incidentals, they have evolved into a collection of expensive (both from a balance sheet and cash flow perspective), emotionally highly charged, and administratively complex HR programs that need to better support the organization's strategic business plan.

Organizations are addressing this issue through various approaches. Many are rationalizing their employee benefit programs, primarily driven by financial pressures. They often end up consolidating how programs are funded and budgeted and in some cases reduce or eliminate programs. Many organizations simply cannot afford to maintain what were past "entitlements."

However, this exercise is not necessarily easy. Legal or contractual restrictions can prohibit changes that would better meet company needs, not to mention the impact changes have on a corporate culture. Further, simply reducing employee benefits may be counter-productive to broader business goals. Therefore, determining the right balance (cost versus benefit) of employee benefits is where CHROs should focus their attention.

A method to evaluate and address this balance follows this four-step approach:

1. inventory current employee benefit programs;

2. understand the criticality of each program;

3. develop an overall "benefit strategy" and implement changes needed to fill the gaps between strategic goals and the current state; and

4. regularly assess the effectiveness of employee benefits both in the context of a single input to "total rewards" and as stand-alone programs.

(a) Inventory

Start by classifying each program by its cost and benefit to the organization, who manages each program, key stakeholders, and critical vendors. Determine how programs overlap and integrate with other programs, and how they support broader company strategic goals (how they attract/retain/motivate highest performing workforce, support low-cost provider objective, reduce risk exposure, enhance the brand, etc.) This step establishes your "universe" of programs, defining what your company's employee benefits are. Include programs that may traditionally fall outside of your formal definition of employee benefits. For example, some organizations have an occupational health group that performs an employee well-being role. Include such functions (with their consequent costs, management structure, expected outcomes, etc.) in the inventory. Now you can identify potential efficiencies or redundancies.

(b) Understand Criticality

Once you have categorized all programs, perform a cost/benefit analysis for each one. Beyond identifying a program's "cost", state in writing how each program supports broader organizational goals in quantifiable terms. Go beyond assuming that a program is sacrosanct and thus is beyond reproach.

This exercise forces you to recognize both the cost of each program and its broader organizational purpose. You may find that some programs are hard to link to goals or have duplicative roles. You may also find that it is simply too hard to define what either a program's costs or benefits are. This analysis may serve as an indication that rationalization is in order for that program.

(c)   Develop an Overall "Benefit Strategy"

An employee benefit strategy should state the general purpose of having each benefit and how each program links to broader HR strategies. This exercise sets forth the criteria programs must embody to justify their further continuance.

A common benefit strategy is often to assess programs based on industry competitiveness, with many companies wishing to maintain a "median" competitive position in their workforce market to neutralize the potential impact a large expenditure could have. If a company wants to define an employment value proposition that aspires to be unique in its market, but then states that wages and benefits are "competitive", it may undermine that goal.

Rather, in your employee value proposition, why not define how employee benefit programs support the value proposition, instead of just listing the programs offered through employment. Recognize the time constraints on staff and describe how your program is designed to ease employees' administrative requirements. The message here is that the company wants its workforce focused on the activities they should be doing to help the company be successful. This approach is an example of how a company can maintain "median" programs from a cost perspective, but also create a distinguishing brand attribute.

It can be helpful to communicate your benefit strategy to employees in order to make the entire package of benefits more understandable and valuable to them. It may also help you explain why, when broader company goals change, changes need to be made to specific employee benefit programs.

(d)   Assess Effectiveness

Regularly assess the effectiveness of employee benefits in the context of both a collective input to "total rewards" as well as stand-alone programs. Test your "criticality" analysis on a periodic basis. Ask yourself and your staff if the programs meet your stated goals. If and when goals change, should changes to programs also be made to meet new goals?

By using the "inventory", "criticality", and "benefit strategy" process regularly, it will help you avoid problems that can plague some CHROs. In doing your analysis, try not to be overly influenced by the effectiveness of managers responsible for individual programs. Assess each program using common metrics. Require the manager for each program to present facts that conform to the broader criticality analysis.

It will be necessary to look at collectively bargained negotiated benefits in the same way as non-negotiated benefits. If the analysis of programs does not meet your path for achieving broader goals, establish a plan for rectifying it.

Regularly justify vendor relationships. These relationships should be viewed against and meet the stated broader organizational goals.

Try not to get too involved in the technical details of programs. It may be tempting to insert yourself, but have the program manager address issues with you to determine whether they meet or do not meet broader company goals.

It is sometimes easy to rely solely on legal or "expert" advice about the existence, function, or consistency of programs. If the advice doesn't make sense to you or clearly contradicts your benefit strategy, push back on the advice.

(e) Conclusion

The ultimate determination of a program's usefulness to the company rests with you and your business judgement. Naturally, this does not mean wilfully breaking the law or ignoring common sense advice. You should, however, be able to sincerely answer any question raised about an employee benefit program's role in meeting your broader business objectives. Focusing on clearly stated objectives and having the support of a set of integrated and consistent facts will make you more successful in your role.

> "The CHRO helps manage data points.
> They coach the CEO on what is real versus perception."
>
> Ferio Pugliese, EVP & President, WestJet Encore (former CHRO)

12

Lessons Learned, Recommended Books and Best HR Models

> "The CHRO has to have a business mastery
> focus versus running a social work department."
>
> John Lynch, SVP, Corporate Human Resources, General Electric

CHAPTER 129: LESSONS LEARNED IN MY CAREER

> "CHRO's need to have an inherent strength at their core, and the
> ability to exercise tremendous courage – particularly in times of crisis."
>
> Katy Barclay, SVP, Human Resources, The Kroger Company

Now that I've been doing this job for almost four decades, I'm able to reflect back and see that there are all kinds of things that I did and didn't do well. What follows is something of a generic description of the lessons I've learned and the things I would do differently if I was doing them again – as well as those things that, in hindsight, I think I did right.

Things I would do differently

- Waiting too long to drive change – there are times that I fell into the trap of allowing the pace of change to be driven by the lowest common denominator (i.e., the weakest players).

- Getting too comfortable with the status quo – sometimes I took my foot off the gas when I should have continued to push for continuous improvement.

- Not benchmarking enough with external peers – I became too insular at times and lost the edge that comes with comparing to/with other companies.

<u>Things I think I did right</u>

- Being part of the HR profession's transformation – I started in Personnel and ended my career as Chief Human Resources Officer.
- Working with talented people – executives and HR staff inspired me to be my best.
- Getting business results through people leadership – it's all about how you optimize the talent you have in the company.
- Becoming a decent "talent master" – it's a lifelong journey.
- Never getting fired from my job – close a few times!!

Along the same lines as above, I've also had my share of success and failure as a functional HR leader, and so here are my observations in that regard:

<u>Things I would do differently</u>

- Not being on the leading edge of HR technology – I feel I didn't personally learn about and "role model" the use of technology.
- Unable to get more money for the HR budget – I wasn't as persuasive as I believe I could have been to convince senior management for the need to invest more in people.
- Visible leadership with the team – in hindsight, I feel I didn't spend as much time with my staff as I would have liked to.

<u>Things I think I did right</u>

- Providing the vision and strategy for my team – everyone knew where we were going.
- Providing training and development for the HR team – we sought out opportunities to develop our staff.
- Covering their backs – my team knew that I would support them in tough situations.
- Presentations to outside conferences – actively profiled our HR best practices.
- Restructuring the function to be efficient and effective – lean HR teams.

I've also had my share of successes and things I would do differently as a CHRO in developing successors. My lessons learned in that regard:

Things I would do differently

- Waiting too long to start the process – I was often too wrapped up in the daily grind.
- Not always seeing the big picture – sometimes I simply went too quickly into Ready-Fire-Aim mode.
- Not rallying my peers to help make it a team legacy – they were not at the same stage in life as me.

Things I think I did right

- Developing great CHRO successors – I had a plan for each one.
- Developing successful People Strategies with my staff – they bought into the plan.
- Empowering the HR team – they were more confident in their work.
- Showing executives that HR was a partner at the table – we earned the right to be there.
- External peers using me as their coach – I was humbled by their confidence.

Being a good leader isn't easy and there are tough lessons to swallow in the on-the-job learning experience. As I reflect on those tough lessons, there is more to categorize and so:

Things I would do differently

- Taking too long to replace under-performing staff – I sometimes didn't push individuals hard enough or fell into the trap of thinking I could fix them.
- Hiring too raw talent – there were times I made the mistake of thinking I could mould the talent, only to realize too late that they were too green to start with.
- Not connecting enough with my staff – as an introvert, I didn't always spend enough personal time with each staff member.

Things I think I did right

- Seeing my staff promoted – I found real pleasure in developing people.
- Hiring really smart and passionate people – they were great to work with and they inspired me.

- Creating opportunities for my staff to work with the CEO and C-suite team – they got better with this senior executive exposure.

- Working with young talent – they needed some guidance to get started.

- Rallying the troops to be a great team – we enjoyed and supported each other.

Working with the CEO can be a real challenge and, again, the on-the-job training can be tough; in terms of working with CEOs over the years, here are some lessons learned:

Things I would do differently

- No written performance reviews for C-suite staff – I should have convinced the CEO to own this process.

- The CEO set business goals that were not achievable, they demoralized the management team – I should have pushed back.

- Loyal but ineffective leaders – it was very difficult to get the CEO to take action on their direct reports. I should have pressed on this.

Things I think I did right

- Establishing the Hunter Camps and CEO workout sessions – they had a very high impact.

- Introducing Q4 leadership and the ABC's – these changed our leadership practices.

- Successful CEO succession plans – the CEO's took this very seriously.

- CHRO succession planning – the CEO's actively supported the process.

- Being the CEO's confidante and part-time coach – they respected my feedback and support.

Working with the other members of the C-suite was, at times, both extremely rewarding and extremely challenging and there certainly was never a dull moment:

Things I would do differently

- Having major conflicts working with most CFO's – possibly as a result of my style; maybe not.

- Not breaking into the club – one executive team did not want another person in the inner circle.

- Prevent end running to the CEO – some executives would not take "No" for an answer.

Things I think I did right

- Providing coaching to my peers – they felt I filled a void that the CEO did not cover.

- Enjoying the company of my peers – on a professional and personal level.

- Celebrating my peers' successes – both individually and as a team.

- Helping peers find better career opportunities – not always with the same company.

- Restructuring to make the team more productive – doing the right thing for the company.

I've always enjoyed meeting with employees, despite my introverted nature, and so in terms of how I interacted with employees here are some observations:

Things I would do differently

- Not being able to connect with every employee – this is especially true with plant employees.

- Not having sufficient touch points between HR and the employees – HR is still not really understood by the average employee.

- Convince some unions to become strategic partners with the company-they see themselves as the only advocates for the employees.

Things I think I did right

- Introducing the EPS process into a unionized workforce – one of my proudest moments with my team.

- Visiting plants to meet the employees – I enjoyed talking with them about their jobs and recognizing their accomplishments.

- Working with the employees and union to save the Heinz Leamington Ontario plant in 1994.

- Identifying talented employees and helping them get their first management position.

- Ensuring long-service employees receive recognition for their tenure.

Working with the Board of Directors, much like working with the other members of the C-suite, has its great challenges and great rewards. The following lessons learned pertain to more specific instances in my career.

Things I would do differently

- Getting the Board to approve a special Bonus payment – the CEO and I did not use the right approach to convince them.

- Not connecting with certain Board Directors – I did not respect them and I let it show.

- Having allowed a major conflict with an HRC Chair to get beyond mendable – I left the company as a result.

Things I think I did right

- Changing the executive compensation programs – making it more management and shareholder friendly.

- Supporting CEO successions – working with the HRC chairs to make it happen.

- Working with very gifted Board Directors – they took the time to help me be a better CHRO.

- Being recognized for my contributions – the Board of Directors respected my point of view.

- Getting appointed to various Boards – the CHRO has a contribution to make.

In terms of working with external consultants and lessons learned:

Things I would do differently

- Prevent end running by certain consultants – they wanted to influence my thinking by getting others in the debate.

- Giving inexperienced consultants too much autonomy – they needed more of my support.

- Being too "big picture" sometimes and not controlling costs as a result – I didn't always have proper financial expectations and controls in place.

Things I think I did right

- Being introduced to behavioural science (ABC–CLG) that drives business performance – it changed me and made me a better CHRO.

- Learning from very talented people who care about you – people that aren't just in it for the money.

- Being pushed out of my comfort zone – I became a better business person.

- Increasing my credibility with the CEO – the consultant added the balance.
- Developing long-term personal relations – these people were great people to engage with.

"Competitive data is available – we don't live in a vacuum
– Hackett, Saratoga, etc. are great sources."

John Lynch, SVP, Corporate Human Resources, General Electric

CHAPTER 130: MY FAVOURITE HR BOOKS

"Most business & HR books are boring – like getting my teeth pulled. However, books from Bill Conaty and Dave Ulrich are the best."

John Lynch, SVP, Corporate Human Resources, General Electric

The following is a list of key business books that influenced my thinking as a CHRO. I hope they bring great value to your own business career.

Good to Great, by Jim Collins (Harper Business, 2001)

This book investigates 28 companies that have made the jump from good to great, and discusses the determining factors for greatness in the long-term. A mediocre company can indeed rise to a superior status. The focus is on management styles and strategies, comparing the successful companies to ones that have failed.

Who Moved My Cheese? by Spencer Johnson (Putnam Adult, 1998)

Change tends to make people nervous and fearful, but there is an effective way to deal with it by preparing oneself for what is to come. This book tries to remove the anxiety and show our positive attitude is most important when trying to ensure success in the future.

Unlock Behavior, Unleash Profits, **by Leslie Wilk Braksick (McGraw-Hill, 1999)**

This book outlines four "behaviour facts" necessary for the success of every leader, and consequently organization. Leadership by management is a difficult behaviour to learn but is the primary driver for success. It affects everyone's behaviour within the organization, has an economic and moral impact and brings out the best in everyone if practiced properly. Nothing will change until the behaviours of leaders change.

Winning, **by Jack Welch (Harper Business, 2005).**

After 40 successful years at General Electric, Jack Welch became known for his management style. This book offers guidance and advice through Welch's anecdotes on work, and life in general, for people who are passionate about success and want to learn from the best. It looks at the inner workings of GE, competition and strategies to deal with such, and finding the balance in your career and personal life.

Talent Masters, **by Bill Conaty and Ram Charan (Crown Publishing Group, 2010)**

Combining Bill Conaty's 40-year career at General Electric with Ram Charan's global experience of advising top companies brings a book filled with insight on the importance of extracting human talent within the organization to advance one's business to the next level.

A Leader's Legacy, **by James Kouzes and Barry Posner (Jossey-Bass, 2006)**

In this book, Kouzes and Posner discuss leadership and legacy through four categories: Significance, Relationships, Aspirations, and Courage. Through a series of essays, the authors try to answer important questions every leader must ask in order to leave a strong legacy.

Execution, **by Larry Bossidy and Ram Charan (Crown Publishing Group, 2002)**

This book shows the importance of execution in order to achieve the results you want as dictated by the authors who have extensive experience and knowledge within the business world. This is done through the 3 core processes of every organization: operations, strategy, and people.

War for Talent by **Ed Michaels, Helen Handfield-Jones and Beth Axelrod (Harvard Business Review, 2001)**

This book is written by McKinsey & Company consultants who exposed the war for leadership talent in 1997 as an important indicator of good organizational perform- ance and one that will persist for at least the next 20 years. This means attracting, molding, and retaining talented managers and recognizing the importance of human capital. Surveys were done at over 120 companies with 13,000 executives in order to be able to offer advice on how to build a stronger talent pool.

The New Rational Manager, **by Charles Kepner and Benjamin Tregoe (Princeton Research Press, 1997)**

This is an updated book from the 1960's in which Kepner and Tregoe developed logical and simple step-by-step methods in a flowchart manner to help managers find the problem within their company, analyze it and ultimately solve and make a decision on the matter.

Forced Ranking, **by Dick Grote (Harvard Business Press, 2005).**

In this hands-on book, Grote, a performance management expert, argues that with the proper understanding and use of forced ranking, it offers a great tool to evaluate performance success, future leaders, and growing talent.

New books to consider

The Power of Why, **by Amanda Lang (Harper Collins Canada, 2012)**

Lang shows the importance of being curious and asking questions in order to positively affect our work and personal lives. Through interesting studies, she offers practical advice on how to trigger your inner curiosity, improve relation- ships and advance your life.

Stepping Up: How Taking Responsibility Changes Everything, **by John Izzo (Berrett-Koehler, 2011)**

In this book, Izzo re-tells inspiring stories urging people to see themselves as the drivers of happiness in one's life. We must be in charge of change in our own lives in order to bring positivity, power, and less stress. He discusses seven principles that bring this change.

Chief HR Officer: Defining the New Role of Human Resource Leaders, **by Patrick Wright, John Boudreau, David Pace, Libby Sartain, Paul McKinnon, and Richard Antoine (Jossey-Bass, 2011)**

This book discusses the role of the CHRO in today's world. It is therefore an excellent resource for both aspiring and current CHROs by providing guidance from leaders in this industry by discussing skill-sets, management, ethics, leadership, and talent.

The Behavior Breakthrough: Leading Your Organization to a New Competitive Advantage, **by Steve Jacobs, et al. (Greenleaf Book Group, 2013)**

Steve Jacobs and his co-authors introduce the neglected game-changer in the world of business: Behavioral Leadership®, which focuses on crafting these desirable shifts in everyday habits, behaviours, and routines. The premise is based on Applied Behavioural Science, a discipline that has been researched and taught in major universities for decades.

HR from the Outside In: Six Competencies for the Future of Human Resources, **by Dave Ulrich, Jon Younger, Wayne Brockbank and Mike Ulrich (McGraw-Hill, 2012)**

Can HR deliver value to "the business"? Yes, it can and must. And that's just what this book from Dave Ulrich and his co-authors is about. Following on the heels of *The Why of Work and HR Transformation*, it's filled with tips for guiding and empowering HR professionals – and entire departments – so that HR might bring benefits of a different kind to everyone at your organization.

Culture Connection, **by Marty Parker (McGraw-Hill, 2012)**

This book is filled with advice from top business leaders. These leaders know what they are talking about: each represents an organization that has been a previous winner of "Canada's 10 Most Admired Corporate Cultures" and whose performance has outperformed their peers. Culture isn't just connected to performance; it drives performance. Today's top companies invest in their corporate cultures.

"The HRC Chair and CHRO are great sounding boards for each other on effectiveness, particularly on how they or their positions are being received/interpreted by various constituents."

James Olson, Board Director

CHAPTER 131: LES' TOP 10 HR MODELS

> "As a CHRO, you need to provide insight, be practical,
> deliver, make a difference, create value and document it."
>
> Peter Goerke, Group Human Resources Director, Prudential PLC

I have used the following HR models in companies I have worked in and with companies who have engaged me as an HR consultant. They include models from various experts in the field, and I have also included several of my own.

(1)   Q4 Leadership /DCOM – Continuous Learning Group

Q4 Leadership[SM] is a model that depicts differences in leaders and how they are getting the right results in the right way, by using positive consequences and by creating high levels of commitment, fostering an environment of Discretionary Performance[SM], high performance, dedicated employees, self-maintaining systems (employees still on task even when the boss isn't looking), and record-breaking results. It includes the Q4 Leadership[SM] Assessment (© CLG), used to determine how leaders rate in getting the right results in the right way.

DCOM® is an acronym for the four cornerstones of high-performing, flexible organizations (Direction, Competence, Opportunity, Motivation). These corner-stones provide the basis for a flexible and adaptive organization capable of high, steady rates of organizational performance. The DCOM® cornerstones are the foundation for long-term, leveraged organizational performance and are the deter-mining factors in high-performing companies.

(2)   ABC Model – Continuous Learning Group

ABC Analysis is an objective method for analyzing behaviour (B) by examining what precedes it – antecedents (A) – and what follows it – consequences (C). The method is used for two main reasons: (1) to understand why or why not certain behaviours occur, and (2) to identify strategies for encouraging desired behaviours and discouraging undesired behaviours. Conducting an ABC Analysis is important because it points to behaviours that are likely to be reinforcing or punishing – for example, to performers when a new product or process is deployed. Implemen-tations can be designed to increase reinforcement or decrease punishment so that successful deployment is more likely.

Note: ABC Analysis is not service marked and the model is common in Applied Behavioural Science. Over the last 20 years, CLG has advanced large scale applications of the model in leading companies around the world.

(3)   Pay for Performance Model – unknown author

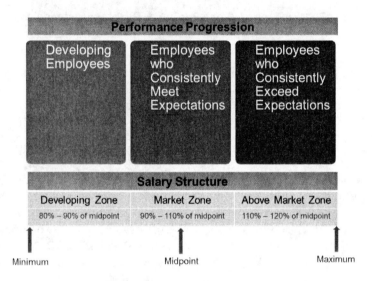

"Pay for Performance" links an employee's level of performance, or contribution to the organization, to the appropriate level of pay. The objective is to manage compensation costs effectively, avoiding over- or under-payment, and appropriately rewarding higher performing employees. The model shown illustrates a pay for performance model for base pay.

External market benchmarking and internal salary structures create the frame of reference. In creating the frame of reference, the organization will decide if the "market zone" is targeted to the 50th percentile of the external market or some other point, dependent on the organization's talent and business strategy. Then the organization will make pay decisions based on this framework.

The majority of the employees in an organization have the skills and experience to perform a given job and consistently meet the expectations of performance for that job. These employees should be paid the market rate for that job. This is fair reward for the contribution made by these employees, and is a good use of company funds. Pay may be below or above the midpoint of this "market zone" depending on performance relative to peers, and considering the employee's potential to move to a more senior job.

Those employees who consistently out-perform their peers and exceed the performance expectations for that job over a period of years, should be paid above the market rate. And employees who are newly-promoted into a level or are still developing their skills and experience should be paid below the market rate.

Using a pay for performance framework like this allows the organization to be fact-based and smart about how it spends its compensation dollars. If a fully-competent employee who consistently meets expectations, or an employee who consistently exceeds expectations, is paid below market, the organization is setting itself up for dissatisfaction and turnover. On the other hand, if an employee who consistently meets expectations is paid above market, the employee is being overpaid for the contribution made, and the organization has less money available to allocate to the higher performing employees.

(4)   Hunter Harrison's Five Guiding Principles

- Principle 1: Service – doing what you say you'll do.
- Principle 2: Cost control – continuously fine-tuning processes.
- Principle 3: Asset Utilization – sweat the assets.
- Principle 4: Safety – 100% compliance.
- Principle 5: People – nurture & develop.

(5)   Organizational Design Principles – Les Dakens

Key elements to review

1. Link to business strategy – does the current organizational structure enable the function to support the company's strategic goals? Why does this function exist – their purpose?

2. Amount of leadership – determine the number of managers relative to total number of employees – average number of employees supervised.

3. Span of control – determine how many employees report into each manager. A good benchmark is 6-10 professionals and 20-30 unskilled employees.

4. Layers of management – determine how many layers from the President to the lowest level job in the function. More than 5 levels is excessive.

5. Value added test – if you owned the business, would you have this function in your company (purpose and value added review)? Or, if a strategic buyer bought this company, would they continue with this function/organizational structure.

Benefits for a lean organization

1. Faster decision making.
2. Reduce bureaucracy.
3. SG&A savings.
4. Develop people faster.
5. Empower employees.
6. Greater line of sight.
7. Eliminate mud in the middle.

(6)   Kepner Tregoe's Problem Solving and Decision-making – SAPADAPPA

Organizations face significant demands to develop leaders at all levels who can effectively resolve issues. KT Problem Solving & Decision-making equips the leaders of tomorrow with the necessary Clear Thinking Skills that become the foundation of effective leadership and issue-resolution management. The common language and process are essential for effective, efficient collaboration across teams, functions and geographies.

The workshop teaches KT clear thinking processes which provide individuals with the capacity to "cut through the clutter" of business complexity, act decisively, and address the most complex challenges confronting your organization.

(7)   Executive Leadership Coaching – Les Dakens

Key Focus Areas:

1. Strategy and Vision – do you know where you want to go and how to get there?
2. People – do you have the right people to help you?
3. Structure – are you organized properly to achieve your strategy?
4. Processes – do you have the right processes to deliver the work?
5. Systems – do you have the proper information to make decisions?
6. Rewards – does your incentive plan reward the right performance?
7. Team – does the team function well as a group?
8. Leadership behaviours – do you know how to influence the right behaviours (ABC)?

"You are being watched by every person who comes into contact with you – inspire them to follow you."

(8)   SARAH – unknown author

This simple acronym has helped leaders deal with emotional reactions to change.

S – Shock at the news

A – Anger that it is happening

R – Rejection of the news

A – Acceptance of the reality

H – Help is accepted

(9)   Org Builder – Boston Consulting Group

OrgBuilder is a systematic and data-driven capability that supports organization change. It leverages battle-tested methodologies to deliver measurable results down to every last position and person. OrgBuilder can help to quickly visualize an organization's people data, as well as estimate opportunity size through an Efficiency and Effectiveness Diagnostic.

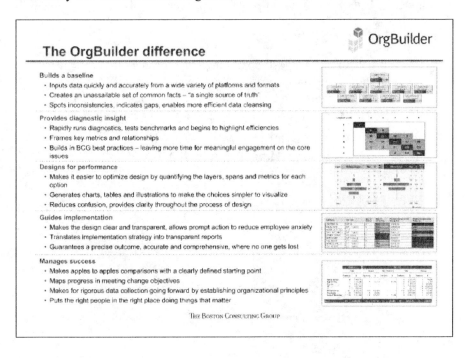

(10) What You Are Is Where You Were When! – Morris Massey

Morris Massey is back with his newest program, What You Are Is Where You Were When... AGAIN!

For over 30 years, Morris Massey addressed the issues of values, diversity, generational conflicts, and gender in his best-selling videos. With a classic combination of humour, and no-nonsense directness, Morris has helped all of us all develop tools for working together. In particular, Morris has presented a framework for understanding all these differences in his original program What You Are Is Where You Were When.

Now, Morris Massey has updated this ground-breaking program with What You Are Is Where You Were When... AGAIN!

What You Are Is Where You Were When... AGAIN! presents a framework for understanding and working with all different types of people. Morris takes on assumptions about race, religion, age, and gender, and will help you develop strategies to deal with your homegrown prejudices and acceptance of others.

As Morris says in the program, "There's a reason we have two ears…but only one mouth. If you want to know what people want…what people need–ASK them!"

"Elevate HR to a position of power and primacy in the
organization, and make sure HR people have the special qualities
to help managers build leaders and careers. In fact, the best
HR types are pastors and parents in the same package."

J. Welch and S. Welch, *Winning*
(New York: Harper Business, 2005), p. 98

CHAPTER 132: THE CHRO OF THE FUTURE – BOLD PREDICTIONS FOR 2040

> "The role continues to evolve; it is different today than it was ten years ago and different from what it will be ten years from now. Industries will die, be born, and transform. The competitive dynamics within industries will change. Technology will drive new products, processes, and ways of doing business. Competitors will emerge from around the globe. With each of these developments will come new expectations and demands from the CHRO role. However, what will not change will be the needs to know the business, know how to lead, know people, and know yourself. Those will form the constellation from which CHROs can navigate the landscape."
>
> P. Wright, J. Boudreau, D. Pace, E. Sartain, P. McKinnon, and R. Antoine, *The Chief HR Officer: Defining the New Role of HR Leaders* (San Francisco: Wiley, John & Sons Inc., 2011), p. 302

> "Prediction is very difficult ... especially if it is about the future."
>
> Nils Bohr, Physicist

> "I have seen the future and it is very much like the present, only longer."
>
> Kehlog Albran, *The Profit*

> "I never think of the future, it comes soon enough."
>
> Albert Einstein

> "The future isn't what it used to be."
>
> Anonymous

If you're reading this it means you've stayed with me for 38 years' worth of stories and a few hundred pages of excellent Carswell typography – which means you're now ready to hear about the future!

This is, of course, the part of the book where I'm supposed to commend you for reading this far, bid you farewell and, applying all my knowledge, experience, expertise and foresight, crack open the door to the coming decades and give you a glimpse into the future of the CHRO.

This is much easier said than done, but fortunately I've had excellent inspiration throughout my career, and today is no different as we gaze into the crystal ball. My thanks to Dave Ulrich and Bill Conaty for their superb insights.

Here's what I think our future will hold for the CHRO role:

1. The people hired as the CHRO will be better educated than in the past – a Master's level degree will be a requirement.

2. The skills needed to influence the CEO, C-suite and Board will reach a level equal to a world-class "peace negotiator."

3. The CHRO will become the "hot asset" in the job marketplace, similar to the IT surge leading up to the Y2K event.

4. The expectations regarding workforce planning should mirror precise military planning in the execution.

5. Combining the CHRO role with the Chief Legal Officer or the Chief Information Officer will remain tempting for many companies – much to their peril.

6. The CHRO should design their team structure to resemble an internal consulting service and outsource the rest of the HR function.

7. Executive compensation practices & expertise will be commoditized and be decided by Boards.

8. Succession planning and talent development will be the number one priority for all managers due to the renewed talent war.

9. Hire to retire costs will be on the fingertips of every CHRO.

10. Manager and employee self-service capability will be a constant "unsatisfied" thorn in the side of the CHRO.

11. The CHRO role will become the "must have experience" for many COO and CEO succession plans.

12. All government relations activities will become part of the CHRO accountability due to their unique skills.

13. The CHRO should be the "master executive coach" for all C-suite players.

14. CHRO's will be expected to take on a Board Director role in another company for developmental purposes.

15. Financial metrics will be equally weighted with qualitative evaluations for people related activities.

There you have it – 15 predictions about where the CHRO role is headed. If you like, you can make a photocopy of this page and keep track over the years and see how many I get right; and drop me a line sometime in the future to let me know what you think.

I also think that in the next 25 years or so we will see some dramatic changes in the employment landscape, particularly in the area of employee-employer relationships.

So here then are my 10 predictions for the year 2040, about how vital employment relationships will change and how the HR function will change as it adapts to a new reality – especially with respect to talent issues.

1. Fixed-term employment contracts for all salaried employees. Knowledge workers will want specified individual terms and conditions for their pre-determined employment relationship. Unions will be replaced by talent agents who negotiate the employment contracts .The HR department will be talent buyers.

2. Salaried employees will work from their home offices. They will attend in-person meetings as the rare exception. The HR group will have a coaching relationship with each employee to ensure connectivity to the organization.

3. Employees will buy their health and medical programs from external marketplace vendors. The healthcare system (medical staff and hospitals) will be nationalized. The HR function will not be involved in the procurement of these services.

4. Employees and employers will be mandated to contribute into a national pension plan run by a consortium of large banks. There will not be any employer-sponsored pension plans.

5. Training and development programs will see increased use of Information Communication Technologies and advanced forms of virtual learning will

become the norm in all areas of corporate activity including technical and vocational. The gaming world and education will converge to create a new interactive form of virtual learning.

6. Multi-level organizational structures will be replaced by flat-line docking. Employees will receive their work instructions from computer systems that are pre-coded for each position. The HR group will monitor roles to ensure the programming is up-to-date. This will entail the complete gutting of the middle-management level.

7. All employees will be share owners or formal stakeholders in their organizations (for profit and non-profit institutions). They will vote on the company's strategic plan and other critical priorities such as executive compensation. The HR function will be the Ombudsman for employee complaints to the Board of Directors.

8. The C-suite executive team will be reduced in size due to multi-functional consolidation. The CEO will have four key players on their team: The talent buyer executive, the financial capital executive, the customer selling executive, and the product-making executive. All other functions will be outsourced.

9. Robotics will replace the majority of unskilled and semi-skilled jobs in the service and manufacturing industries.

10. Human beings will live and work much longer. People will work to 90 years old and retirement will extend to 120 years. Medical care and new science will continue to prolong human life.

Predicting the future of the HR world is fraught with risk, but if I was to trust anyone's predictions it would be Dave Ulrich. Find more of Dave's insights in Appendix 14.

"Be naive and optimistic. A key component to stepping up
is believing you have the ability to make a difference."

J. Izzo, *Stepping Up: Why Taking Responsibility Changes Everything*
(San Francisco: Berrett-Koehler Publishers, Inc., 2012), p. 156

Alzheimer's Disease – Losing Your Legacy of Life

As you may know, my mother died of Alzheimer's disease. So many families in North America have been affected the same way and, as our society ages, the prognosis does not look good – more and more people will die of this withering disease every year.

No one – regardless of race, gender, financial ability or any other factor other than age – is immune from the possibility of getting Alzheimer's. Too many people from all walks of life have been struck down, with more to come, and as a society we will lose so much, in addition to the needless suffering of loved ones.

I have a family history of Alzheimer's as does my wife, Marijane, and it is frankly my own fear that this disease will rob Marijane and I of the opportunity to enjoy a long life together.

Accordingly, I am active in supporting a number of different organizations all dedicated to erasing the threat of Alzheimer's from our society – including the donation of all proceeds from the sale of this book. It is our hope that the medical community, supported by government and private funding, will find a cure soon.

Thank you for your purchase of this book. I hope you enjoyed it. In any event, please know that you have made a valuable contribution towards a very good cause.

Les Dakens

Appendices

APPENDIX 1: LEADERSHIP LESSONS FROM THE 'GREAT ONE'

By Shannon Klie,
Canadian HR Reporter
(Toronto: Thomson Reuters)
October 19, 2009

'Passing the puck' increases engagement and performance

In 13 seasons with the National Hockey League, Eric Lindros, whose career was plagued with injuries, amassed 865 points, of which 57 per cent were assists. His favourite position on the ice was in front of the opposing team's net so he could have the best chance at scoring a goal. He never won a Stanley Cup championship.

In contrast, during 20 seasons with the NHL, Wayne Gretzky amassed 2,857 points, of which 69 per cent were assists. His favourite position on the ice was behind the opposing team's net so he could get the puck to the player in the best position to score. He won four Stanley Cup championships and was inducted into the Hockey Hall of Fame in 1999.

Lindros and Gretzky are perfect examples of two different leadership styles, according to Les Dakens, former senior vice-president of HR at CN Rail and a principal with Pineridge Consulting in Toronto. Lindros exemplifies a leadership style that gets results but doesn't engage the team, so it's not good in the long term, said Dakens at a Strategic Capability Network event in Toronto last month. On the other hand, Gretzky exemplifies a leadership style that gets results by helping others score.

Dakens used this analogy to help get line managers at CN Rail on board with a cultural shift in 2001. While the company had dramatically improved since privatization in 1995, the new CEO felt there was still room for improvement and that would come from shifting from a "kick-butt-and-take names" leadership style to a more collaborative and engaging one, said Dakens.

But it was hard to get managers and supervisors to change a leadership style that had made the company so successful, he said. CN had to let go of one high-profile leader who wouldn't change his ways — which showed all employees senior management was serious — and the company also gave leaders who adopted the new engaging leadership style more recognition and greater opportunities for advancement.

"The message to supervisors was, 'You better start using your employees because you can only get so far on your own,'" he said. "If we can get people engaged, they'll contribute more, there will be better discretionary performance and that's going to take our game to the next level."

In the end, the shift paid off. In 1995, CN Rail had an operating ratio (an industry standard measurement where a lower score is more desirable) of 89 compared to an industry average of 80. In 2001, after six years of a leadership strategy that included reducing headcount by 10,000 employees, cutting expenses and "kicking butt," the ratio dropped to 72, said Dakens.

After shifting to the engaging leadership culture, the ratio dropped even further to 62 in 2007 and the value of CN stock doubled from 2001.

"Regardless of what you're trying to do with your culture, if it's not going to generate better performance, you've got a tough sell," he said.

Part of the new leadership style was learning how to manage employee behaviours that contributed to success. Before the shift, supervisors expended about 80 per cent of their efforts on the antecedents of behaviour — such as telling employees to perform a certain way.

But it's the consequences of behaviour — feedback such as thanking an employee for doing a particular task or recognizing his effort — that have the greatest impact on the likelihood of a behaviour being successful and repeated.

To focus more on consequences, CN introduced a performance appraisal process where employees would be ranked at one of three levels: entry level, skilled or outstanding railroader. After the scorecard was introduced, employees emailed Dakens to tell him that during their career with the company — some as many as 30 years — they had never had a supervisor tell them they had done a good job before.

"You can treat everyone the same and get mediocrity or you can treat everyone differently and let the stars come out," said Dakens.

Moving to a more engaging leadership style doesn't mean managers let poor performance slide, he said. An engaging leader will still confront an employee but instead of using commands and fear of termination to get her to change, the engaging leader will work with the employee to figure out why the performance is substandard.

"It's not scorched earth," he said. And, once the performance improves, instead of ignoring the employee, the engaging leader will recognize that contribution, said Dakens.

Organizations are fond of proclaiming, "People are our most important asset," but very rarely behave as if this is the case, said Robert Potvin, founder of executive coaching firm CDC Coaching, who worked with Dakens at CN during the cultural shift.

This is because boards often see and promote leaders who are good at managing "up" — managing their boss — and these people often aren't good at managing their subordinates, said Potvin at the same SCNetwork event.

"They tend to get stuff done by pushing and by intimidating," he said. These leaders are bright but lacking in emotional intelligence — the ability to understand and manage their own emotions and those of the people around them, he said.

A better way to lead people is to figure out what motivates them to do the job and never assume it's the same for every employee, said Potvin.

Coaching can help leaders develop emotional intelligence and better engage employees for better performance, he said. But the leaders have to have organizational support, be motivated to change and already be competent in the technical aspects of the job.

A coach asks people the right questions so they come to their own conclusions, he said. It's about helping leaders understand organizational rules, seeing themselves as others see them and better understanding the people around them and what motivates them. "You have to understand what people really need," said Potvin. "Changing your mindset about where the other person is coming from is pretty important."

APPENDIX 2:   TAKE YOUR SEAT AT THE TABLE

By James Grossett, CHRO, Agrium

An expression I have heard multiple times throughout my career is "HR deserves a seat at the table." Every time I hear it I cringe, because no one has to give you anything. It's like saying "HR deserves to be respected." Of course HR does, but the only way HR will be respected is if they earn it. And, as I've always said, "Respect is earned in the trenches every single day."

I have headed up HR for five different companies. The common theme with every company I joined was that I replaced someone who was retiring, and the company was looking for a "turnaround" within HR and each one wanted HR to be a driving force for change. So, four times I've walked into a new company where the HR team didn't have a "seat at the table." Nor did anyone hand it to me on my first day on the job. It had to be earned, not just by me, but by the entire HR team.

How to Take Your "Seat at the Table"

First, it starts inside. You can't expect others to believe in you unless you first believe in yourself. I've seen many smart and talented HR professionals who, quite frankly, don't believe in themselves. Part of believing in yourself starts with "standing up for what you believe in." My HR teammates at Agrium have heard me say many times, "If you can't stand up for what you believe in, then you basically don't believe in anything."

Earning a seat at the table will not happen immediately. At Agrium, it took about a year for the cultural shift to start taking hold, and it simply got stronger with each passing year. Without a doubt, HR "taking its seat at the table" was a critical element to this turnaround.

Tone at the Top

It all starts with the tone at the top and cascades down to the entire HR team. As a team, you're only as strong as your weakest link. That philosophy applies to every single person in HR, whether it's a team of 10 or 100 people. On my third day at Agrium I met with the entire Corporate HR team, from my direct reports through to the administrative assistants. I did it to introduce myself and let people know who I was and how I liked to operate. I basically said that there were three things I needed to figure out:

1. What works and what doesn't work in HR at Agrium?

2. Mapping out a new game plan going forward for the next 3 years.

3. Who is going to be on the bus to help us drive that new game plan?

First 90 days

In the first 90 days I focused on two things. First, I got to know each member of the HR team so I could assess who had the right skill sets that we needed going forward. Second, I went across the organization and travelled to as many sites as I could and I asked one basic question of the top 100 leaders in the Company: "What works in HR and what doesn't work?" The key theme coming out of these one-on-one meetings was quite simple: "HR doesn't deliver on its commitments." With this response, it was easy to figure out why HR didn't have a seat at the table.

Getting the HR Team Aligned

In my fourth month, I arranged for a 3-day HR off-site at a dude ranch up in the Rocky Mountains. All the key HR leaders located in our Calgary Corporate office were present, as well as the top 30 HR people from three different business units. The objective was to map out a 3-year HR Strategy. I facilitated the session, with everyone still getting to know me and to understand my style. They had heard me talk about HR needing to drive change in the organization and stand up for what we believed in, but most of them weren't exactly sure how to do it. The session also gave me a chance to understand their individual goals better, which would help to create alignment within the team.

By the final day of our off-site, we had developed a straw man of our 3-year strategy, which we presented to our CEO in the afternoon. We wrapped it up by heading outside and I asked everyone to form a circle. I stood in the middle, with a blanket on the ground. I told everyone how proud I was of what they had accomplished over the 3 days and our game plan for the future. I then pointed to the highest mountain peak in the distance. I told everyone that we were about to start a journey up to the top of that mountain. There would be many challenges along the way, but once and for all HR needed to be known across Agrium for "delivering on its commitments".

With that statement, I removed the blanket and revealed a large rubber mallet and an 18-inch railroad spike. I held the spike as each of them took a swing at driving it into the ground to symbolize that HR was going to "put a stake in the ground" in front of our CEO and commit to delivery of its commitments. I took the last, final swing, and then, with the help of our CEO, handed out plaques to each person. On the plaque was a 6-inch railroad spike and above it the words, "Deliver on Your Commitments".

We needed to earn our seat at the table. I believed we could do it; I just needed to convince everyone else in HR that we could do it and get them to really believe we could do it. The 3 days of mapping our 3 year HR Strategy engaged people's minds, but the last exercise of hammering the railroad spike into the ground did something that was even more important. It was the first step towards starting to engage people's hearts. As a CHRO, you have to engage people's minds and their hearts. Only by engaging both, do you actually begin to tap into a person's full potential.

Gaining Respect with Senior Leadership

I noticed very early in my tenure that the executive team would tell HR what to do and had very little respect for the function. I was going to have to earn that respect. Over the next year, my words and actions, and ultimately also those of my HR team, led to HR "earning its seat at the table." There would be many challenging moments along the way, but in the end our accomplishment was fairly simple: we earned the seat at the table by providing tangible value and HR solutions to the business.

A few weeks after our offsite session, I reviewed the 3-year HR Strategy with the senior leadership team at our monthly meeting. They were all very positive and supportive. With this promising endorsement, I decided to make a bold move. I closed by saying, "I'm a firm believer in putting a stake in the ground, and then delivering on my commitments. So I commit to all of you right now that in 3 years Agrium will be one of the Top 100 Employers in Canada." I paused to let that sink in and then I said, "Right now we're about as far away from achieving it as you can get. If in 3 years we even come close, you ought to hold a parade for everyone in HR because they will have a come a long way. But if we don't, you should fire me because as far as I'm concerned, that's why I was hired."

Why did I make such bold statements? This executive team had not respected HR or its people in the past, and the only way I was ever going to shift how the entire organization thought of HR was to start with this executive team.

The 3-year HR Strategy became a formal document, but at the beginning it was a Gantt chart that laid out 27 initiatives that HR was going to accomplish on a quarterly basis over the next 3 years. We had a plan, and we had made promises, but now we needed to deliver on our commitments without any exceptions. To mark the beginning of the first quarter of the plan, I told my peers at our monthly meeting what HR was going to do in the next 3 months. At the end of that quarter, I told them what HR had accomplished, which matched the plan exactly. For the next two quarters, I repeated the same routine: reporting what HR promised and what it delivered. At the end of the fourth quarter, as I stood up to share what HR had done to meet its commitments, one of my peers said, "Sit down, we know HR did everything it said it would do." At that moment, I knew HR had credibility and was now known for delivering on its commitments. Or to put it another way, HR had earned its seat at the table.

Standing Up for Your Beliefs

I have learned in my career that to be successful you have to look for opportunities to make an impact. One of these opportunities occurred a few months into my new role. Aware that the annual salary adjustment process was about to take place, I asked to see the data on performance and salary adjustments from the previous year. On the 10-point performance rating scale, 90% of the workforce was rated between 6.5 and 7.0. Salary adjustments ranged from 2.5% to 3.5%. Meaning, the lowest performers received 2.5% and the highest performers received 3.5%.

The leaders had essentially rated everyone to the mean and as a result, the concept of "pay for performance" was non-existent. Soon after seeing this data, I met with the CEO, COO and CFO. I wanted to discuss the upcoming salary adjustment process and to suggest a new idea. I told them that 90% of the company the previous year had been rated between 6.5 and 7.0 and that the salary increases ranged from 2.5% to 3.0%. I explained to them that "it is absolutely impossible that nearly our entire workforce is performing at the exact same level…it's not the real world." I then recommended that the company implement "forced ranking." I told them it was the only way I knew of that would allow us to begin to shift the culture of the company, and that although it would create tremendous angst across the organization, it was necessary. To my surprise, there was no resistance to my suggestion and the three leaders assured me of their full support.

It was my belief that forced ranking was the right thing to do. I pulled my compensation people and HR business partners together and outlined the plan to them. I emphasized that I knew this was the right decision and that I needed their support and commitment. I warned them that upon the distribution of my note across the organization there would be a strong reaction from company leaders. I added that I needed them to be strong and to stand their ground by supporting this course of action.

Within days of the note being sent out, there was the predicted reaction. The VP of Manufacturing for our dozen wholesale plant sites located across North America called to tell me how upset all of his plant managers were with the idea of implementing forced ranking. I arranged for a conference call with these plant managers, and included four senior HR people. They were reluctant, sensing a confrontation, but I needed to make a point and assured them that I would do all the talking. In the Calgary meeting room with me were the VP, Manufacturing and four HR people. On the phone, there were 12 angry plant managers. As soon as the conference call commenced, three plant managers, one at a time, told me how stupid forced ranking was and said it didn't apply to them because "all of their people were great performers." After the third plant manager spoke, I said "I'm going to assume that the rest of you feel exactly as the three people who just spoke." After a prolonged silence, I said, "I will take that silence as a yes."

I proceeded to stand up for what I believed in, saying, "I understand and hear your concerns. Yet, there is not a doubt in my mind that this is the right thing to do. This meeting ends in 53 minutes. So we can spend the next 53 minutes debating, or we can spend it talking about how we are going to constructively make this happen." There was silence for around 20 seconds and then one of the plant managers said "Help us understand how we implement this."

At the end of the meeting, one of the HR people said, "In the past, HR would have let them do what they wanted." My reply was "Well, I believe in this and I need each of you to believe in it as well." I would like to think that I was showing them how to stand up for what you believe in and earn people's respect. I know that those four HR people shared that story with others. It was another step towards earning the organization's respect and a seat for HR at the table. Did that conference call earn the respect of those plant managers? Perhaps not right away, but it did get them thinking and it was the first step in earning their respect.

Over the next two years, each of the plant managers approached me, saying, in essence, "I'm sorry, I owe you an apology, implementing forced ranking was one of the best things we could do." Forced ranking made the plant managers differentiate on performance. The result was the classic bell curve, with the top 10% identified as "Top Performers" and rewarded accordingly. The bottom 10% were also identified, and for the first time, action was taken with low performers. A culture that rewarded mediocrity was being replaced with a culture that rewarded high performance. We were developing a true "pay and reward for performance" culture. The plant managers could see the positive impact it was having on their operations. HR now had their respect, and had a seat at the table in view.

Only as Good as the People You are Surrounded By

In my career I've been blessed to work with many talented and bright HR people. For HR to be successful, some "game changers" are needed. These are people who serve as examples of how to stand out by delivering on commitments. The first two people I hired at Agrium: Stella Cosby and Leslie Sarauer, were game changers. Stella was hired as head of Organization Development and Leslie as head of Total Rewards. Agrium would not have earned its seat at the table and gained the success it has without these two individuals

Where Are We Now?

Before I close this chapter I should answer the question of whether Agrium became one of the Top 100 Employers within 3 years. The answer is affirmative. I occasionally turn to look out my office window at the highest mountain peak, which symbolized the journey of our HR team., On the opposite side of my office I see a wall covered with pictures of Agrium receiving awards for being among Canada's Top 100 Employers, Canada's 10 Most Admired Corporate Cultures, and for being one of Canada's Best Diversity Employers. There remains a space on the wall, a place for one more award's picture, which will be hung up shortly. Agrium was recently named one of the Top 50 Global Employers of Choice and Integrity by Cambridge University. This achievement didn't happen by accident. To receive such an award a company must have the right organizational culture, senior leadership of and, of course, HR leadership.

Agrium has come a long way over the past 10 years. The company's increasing success has been the result of an organization-wide effort. However, the HR team has been key to this success. We too stood up for our beliefs and earned the organization's respect. I am very proud of the entire team.

APPENDIX 3:   WORKING WITH HUMAN NATURE TO CHANGE CN

By Les Dakens
Canadian HR Reporter
(Toronto: Thomson Reuters)
September 21, 2009

Railway giant focuses on new tools, behaviours to boost engagement

Change has many enemies. Prime among them is success, especially when paired with complacency. Why change, the standard thinking goes, when you're successful? The problem is success is often fleeting and tied to context. When that context shifts, continued success requires continued change.

In 2001, when I joined CN as senior vice-president of HR, the company was a considerable success story. Lean and profitable, it had the best operating ratio in the industry at 72, compared with the industry average of 80, and the lower the better. Competitors copied its moves and savvy investors snapped up the stock.

On the face of it, there was little reason to undergo much further change. There had been plenty of dramatic change since CN's initial public offering (IPO) in 1995. Up until that point, the company had been a government agency, which lost a dismal amount of money. After the IPO, under the leadership of CEO Paul Tellier, the mandate had to change. The goal became simple, clear and urgent: Build value.

This new focus included aggressive attempts to capture a bigger market share. To attract and keep customers, operations had to become more efficient and stream-lined. Managers had to actively manage the business while the workforce was shrunk by one-third. The company shed assets that were not part of the core mission of the new CN. Acquisitions and mergers broadened the reach of the railroad.

After all that change and turmoil, it was a new world for CN — it had gone from worst in the industry to the best. It was not, however, a time for CN to rest on its laurels. The executive leadership was determined success was not going to get in the way of progress.

CN ignored complacency and committed to continued improvement. It was not a small commitment — it meant a search for new tools to make that change and a focus on different leadership behaviours. The goal was to achieve a profitable enterprise by building a culture that fully engaged every employee and encouraged them to give their best.

Opportunity beckons

What kept fuelling change at CN was a sentiment among senior leadership there were still opportunities for the company – for new markets, more efficiencies and better service levels in operations. Deeper value could be reached through a mix of tactical and strategic moves. The drive for achievement remained strong.

There were still pockets in the organization that worked much the way things had been done when CN was a government agency. Management had a long-standing behaviour of putting a higher premium on keeping the peace than enforcing the rules. Management had abdicated its authority for so many years that employees had developed feelings of entitlement. Resistance to change was deeply rooted.

The drive for achievement among the leadership team made a real difference for CN. To capitalize on opportunities to improve the business, the nature of the company's leadership had to change, too. The leadership weren't just going to be the sponsors of change – they were going to be part of it. Leaders had to see themselves differently, think in new ways and take the risk of acting in a radically changed way. It was a challenge the team was ready to accept.

For whom the bell tolls

Another enemy of change is short-term thinking. Customers, suppliers and technology change constantly, competitors re-imagine themselves and markets shift. Social, economic and political trends take off in new directions.

Fortunately, in a company where most of the energy is expended on daily operations – the goal of a railroad, after all, is to keep the trains running – CN had some long-term thinkers in the executive ranks and on the board. They could see changes that were coming at the company. Just as important, they understood change would take time.

For instance, there was a strong possibility in 2001 that changing demographics were going to be a nightmare for CN. With fewer people in the generations behind the baby boomers, a shortage of employees at all levels was predicted.

This meant leadership turnover, heightening the need for succession planning, which hadn't received much attention during the upheaval of privatization. Another issue was how to replace skilled workers in the unionized ranks. Training at this level, when it had occurred, had been sporadic at best.

We couldn't run a company without skilled, knowledgeable workers at all levels. Nor could CN advance without people who would be job-ready when promoted. On-the-job learning is an expensive option and there were going to be thousands of replacements across management and unionized employee ranks.

The law of unintended consequences

The previous change at CN during privatization had produced some very good outcomes. The company led the industry in every major metric, shed legacy assets no longer needed and leaders were more focused on the business. But the changes also created some less desirable outcomes. The time had come to deal with them.

An employee survey done shortly before I arrived revealed much of the unionized workforce had low levels of job satisfaction. Rather than being engaged actively in the company's success, employees felt they were sitting on the sidelines.

To have a committed, engaged workforce, management was going to have to change. There were very few managers who thought coaching and shaping the behaviour of employees were parts of their job. They had some vague idea HR could do coaching while management's job was to get people jumping to their orders and bringing in results.

Under the circumstances, it was hardly surprising relations with the unions were strained. A lack of trust was the outcome of all the rapid change in the previous years. Productivity gains would prove elusive if the relationships were not repaired. The company has 12 unions and more than 100 collective agreements. Managing the union portfolio at CN is complicated but it would be a necessary ingredient in achieving change to keep the company at the top of its industry.

Culture change

In taking a close look at what needed to be done, it was obvious just tackling issues on a piecemeal basis was not the best method. The past showed as one issue was fixed, another would pop up – which would create an endless to-do list. At that point, we didn't need a list, we needed a plan.

The start was making sure everyone understood the vision for the company. When Hunter Harrison succeeded Paul Tellier as CEO in January 2003, he introduced five guiding principles. His message was simple and direct: Focus on service, cost control, asset utilization, safety and people. CN would not only continue to outpace other railroads, it would lap the competition. The guiding principles gave all employees a shared focus, a way to think and talk about the business, and a common reference point in making decisions. Tremendous effort went into communicating the principles, all the way down to the front-line.

With the goal of changing the culture to one of a committed, engaged workforce, it was necessary to identify the right issues to tackle. Any change initiatives had to have a business case, but would also have to contribute to broad organizational culture change. Only by changing the culture was CN going to achieve the greater success desired.

We needed the right tools to make change happen, faster and better. We found those tools in applied behavioural science – the science of why people do what they do and how to motivate them to higher levels of sustained performance through proper reinforcement. The idea could not have been simpler: To make change, work with human nature, not against it.

On a practical basis, we had to apply the right mechanics of change. We needed managers and employees who would serve as sponsors for change. The reasons for change had to be articulated clearly and strike a compelling chord with people. Having a way to measure outcomes from change was critical, as was communicating the results. If people were going to change, they had to see there was a tangible payoff for their efforts.

We also had to understand the journey was not going to be easy. People were comfortable with what they knew. Getting them to listen to change messages at odds with that comfort level would be difficult. Fear, apathy, indolence and political self-interest, as well as other enemies of change, were all going to be in play.

Nor was culture change going to happen quickly. In a company as big as CN, it would be a mammoth undertaking. While we needed quick hits to sustain the drive along the way, it was going to take years to ensure a new way of doing things was embedded in the culture. And, while corporate would seed the beginning of the change initiative, the divisions were going to have to pay for most of it. For them to open their wallets, they had to see results. What we did had to work, or change efforts would die quickly.

APPENDIX 4:   PLAYING HARDBALL WITH TOMATOES – THE ARTICLE

By Sue Craig
Financial Post Magazine
November 1994

Heinz workers in Leamington, Ontario, didn't need a mediator, "they needed God." Instead they got Les Dakens, negotiator extraordinaire.

Leamington, Ontario is the home of Canada's largest tomato processing plant. Since 1910, workers at H.J. Heinz have earned good wages ($17 an hour at last notice) happily churning out a wide variety of ketchups and other food products for a Canadian market safely protected by high tariffs. Heinz and Leamington grew up together. Living there was like having a rich uncle named Henry Heinz; chances are he could always find you a job, and you always had time for him. The town's recreation complex is named after Frank T. Sherk the company's first Canadian president. A giant tomato-shaped tourist sits in the middle of town and every year thousands of people turn out to the annual tomato festival. "If it wasn't for Heinz, Leamington as we know it wouldn't be here," said Jim Ross, a former Heinz employee and Leamington's mayor.

Les Dakens is the H.J. Heinz Co.'s first North American vice-president of human resources. The no-nonsense manager, who has closed several plants and laid off hundreds of people in his 12 years in the food-processing industry, was hired by the world-famous maker of ketchup just a few years after Brian Mulroney ushered in the Canada-U.S. free trade pact.

Everyone in Leamington knew what Les Dakens was hired to do. With falling tariffs, the Pittsburgh-based food processor realized it needed to rationalize its North American operation. The cost of doing business in Canada, says Jim Krushelniski, the company's North American vice-president of operations, was simply becoming too high. Dakens was ordered to negotiate with the 800 members of United Food and Commercial Workers 459, carve $3.8 million out of the collective agreement, or close the plant.

Employment levels at the Leamington facility, which once employed one in every 10 people in town, have dropped from 1,400 people in 1988 to around 800 today. And the consensus around the Heinz head office is that if somebody other than Dakens had gone into Leamington to streamline the operation, the town might have changed from a single-industry community to a zero-industry one.

He kept the plant alive, he saved the company money and, most significantly, he created a template for Canadian management in a global economy. It wasn't only Dakens' deft negotiating skills that came into play; it was his whole North American approach to business.

"Free trade created a number of jobs like mine," explains Dakens in an interview from his modest office at Heinz world headquarters in Pittsburgh, where he spends about three quarters of this time. "It forced companies to begin looking at North America as one market place."

The president and CEO of H. J. Heinz Canada is John Crawshaw. He says Dakens – a square-jawed, steel-eyed executive who eerily resembles Toronto Maple Leafs Coach Pat Burns – represents the way of the future for corporate Canada. "The '90s demand a different type of manager," says Crawshaw. "In the '70s and '80s it was the tried-and-true methods of management that preserved the status quo. Now we need people like Les who have a vision to change and are able to communicate what they want." And Crawshaw as well as Dakens' former boss from Cadbury Beverages Inc. Doug Tough – Dakens left Cadbury for Heinz in 1990 – agree that one of Dakens' greatest strengths is his ability to work within the North American marketplace. "He has a very good broad perspective of the issues that affect business on a North American level," said Tough, whose company was one of the first to transform itself into a North American operation after the passage of free trade.

Les Dakens' sensibility and strengths personify the Canadian economy. He is a cross-border commuter whose wife works in Toronto as a consultant. He spends most of his time in the States but has a cottage north of Toronto. His knowledge of one-industry towns is informed by the fact that he was raised in the uranium mining town of Elliot Lake, Ontario. Further, and typical of his roots, he spent Saturday mornings playing hockey and dreaming about playing in the big leagues.

The only problem was, he was trapped in a five-foot-seven-inch frame. Those who know Dakens say despite giving up on his dream of being in the NHL, he still has much in common with many of hockey's shortest superstars. "It is a mistake to presume size precludes competence, and those who underestimate Les will find out the hard way they have made a mistake," says Tough.

Being a little guy on the team meant Dakens matured into a feisty competitor; a fighter, even. It came in handy when he got to Leamington.

Dakens hadn't negotiated a labor contract in years. But his reputation preceded him. People worried when he showed up to bargain. "It was sort of like when the L.A. Kings brought in Gretzky," said Bryan Neath, the Ontario assistant to the Canadian director of the United Food and Commercial Workers (UFCW). "Everyone had a good idea they were after something."

Heinz president Crawshaw began the bloodshed in January when he announced to the workforce he needed to cut $10 million from the Leamington operation. Around $2 million would be saved through equipment upgrading. The process to cut the rest would be a little more painful. The company began by laying off 200 people, the first sign of the difficult contract negotiations to come.

Provincial mediator Bob Pryor, who worked with the two sides for almost two months, was skeptical he would ever emerge with anything even remotely resembling a deal. "I remember the first time I met with them," says Pryor. "I had never seen anything like it. They all had $3.8 million tattooed on their foreheads. I realized right away they didn't need me, they needed God." One of the union's negotiators once laughed that the hotel he stayed at during the talks didn't even provide bibles for bedside reading. What did follow was a carefully planned company strategy that captured national headlines and put the fear of God into the people of Leamington who could see their future slipping away, like ketchup from a bottle.

This left the $3.8 million that Dakens had to find in the collective agreement. In early March the company stepped up the pressure on the workers with Crawshaw announcing there would not be a 1994 tomato season if a contract wasn't reached by March 31. This move threatened the livelihood of almost 70 area farmers and their families who grew 200,000 tonnes of tomatoes worth around $20 million for Heinz.

"Heinz is our major source of income," says farmer Bill Wiper, who has grown tomatoes for Heinz for three decades. Despite the threat, the UFCW's Neath, who became the union's chief negotiator, remained steadfast in his position that he was negotiating for the members, not the farmers.

But by effectively negotiating in the media, Dakens had succeeded in starting a tidal wave of public pressure against the workers who battled for months over the decision to accept concessions or lose their jobs.

It worked, but not quite well enough. The negotiating committee recommended acceptance, concessions and all. But the numbers held tight.

After rejecting a second company offer in mid-April, which Heinz billed as its final, the company's gun-to-the-head negotiating tactics went into high gear. Dakens again made front-page headlines in the local papers when he fired off 450 layoff notices to workers, some of whom had worked at the plant for more than 20 years. "Maybe people thought we were bluffing," Dakens said. "I guess I should have told them at the outset that I'm not a good poker player."

The same week the layoff notices went out, Heinz flew most of its management to Pittsburgh to begin the process of moving Leamington's production lines to the United States. They left behind a plant full of workers wondering what to do next. Eventually the members blinked, with workers asking for Dakens to return to the table.

Paul Gardner, the ministry of labor director of mediation, was called in to help with the talks. "I don't do this often," he remarked at the time, noting the last strike he helped settle was at Ontario Hydro. Despite the pressure, Dakens still refused to budge from his demand for $3.8 million. In the end, the members voted to accept a concessionary package that included wage roll-backs of 50 cents an hour. In return, Heinz agreed to pay stiff financial penalties should they leave Leamington during the life of the four-year contract.

"It would have been easy to close the plant in a lot of ways," says Dakens. "But I think at the end of the day the union and Heinz can be proud that we as Canadians saved Canadian jobs."

In the future, Dakens' biggest fight will no doubt be meeting the ongoing challenges of free trade. "In the past the only time you would see an aggressive Canadian was on a hockey rink when they had to keep their elbows up to compete in the corners," says Dakens. "Americans are aggressive in many more walks of life. And with free trade, Canadian businesses will have to become more aggressive or they won't survive."

And when Dakens left Leamington he left behind a plant full of employees much more aware of their own mortality. It's no secret on the line that in four years when the workers' collective agreement expires, the tariff that once protected the goods they make will be completely gone. And it's no secret that if the plant can't compete with its American counterparts, Dakens will be back. "If you can't remain competitive, you don't survive," he says.

On the other hand, the workers are playing a game they seem destined to win. For example, for the first time in the plant's history Leamington exported ketchup to the United States. Leamington was also picked to produce the recently launched USA Toddler baby-food line, a product sold solely in the U.S. And the town just agreed to give Heinz a $150,000-tax break. It's the sort of signal, says Mayor Ross, that should tell Heinz that everyone wants them to stay in town.

APPENDIX 5: NOTES FROM CLAUDE MONGEAU

Conversations

> "The single biggest problem in communication
> is the illusion that it has taken place."
>
> George Bernard Shaw

Dear fellow railroaders,

If the quote above sounds familiar to you, it is because I referred to it in a Note earlier this year, when I announced the Survey on Employee Communications, which was completed in May. Thanks to the thousands of you who participated and I'll be writing to you about the survey results a little later in the summer.

But this Note isn't about that kind of large scale communications; magazines, web sites, e-mails, smart phones and so on. Today I want to talk to you about, well…., talking…. and listening. … about the everyday conversations that we usually don't have time for every day.

At CN, we're very action-oriented, with a lot of take-charge people who like to get things done. That's a good thing, but we also need to make sure we take the opportunity to speak with the people who report to us, and to our supervisors, our colleagues, our suppliers and our customers, as often as we should. These are the conversations that are crucial to our goal of achieving the next level of Operational and Service Excellence. Keeping each other informed about what's going on, setting clear objectives and providing feedback should be second nature, but we know that's not always the case.

Sometimes we address the issue by instilling a process to promote conversations. For example, a new initiative to encourage conversations is designed to help us inform customers about service exceptions. It's a program called iAdvise that our COO Keith Creel summarized in a recent note to all employees. This will help us provide information to customers when we're not going to be able to deliver traffic as expected. Our customers have identified this as a sticking point, and it's going to become an important component of our First-Mile, Last-Mile focus.

July 6, 2012

As well, it's mid-year EPS (Employee Performance Scorecard) review time for many of us, as we are expected to complete our one-on-one assessment meetings with our supervisors by the end of July. These are conversations about tracking our personal objectives which are set at the beginning of the year and ensuring real progress is made on development activities. We also have an annual EPS process for those of us who are unionized which focuses on performance and recognition. This provides an opportunity to connect with supervisors in the spirit of dialogue and coaching that needs to be ongoing throughout the year. While EPS is a formal process, it shouldn't be a formality. It should never be about going through the motions so we can check something off the to-do list. These conversations should be meaningful and I count on everyone involved to make them truly impactful.

Communicating as an investment

We are pretty proud about how we think outside the box at CN when it comes to running our railroad and the service we can offer customers. It's not a bad idea to think outside the box about our individual careers as well, and to take ourselves outside of our comfort zones. I do that regularly with my own direct reports on the Leadership Team. It's of great benefit that they will also challenge me in our conversations and sometimes take me out of my comfort zone as well.

You should talk to your supervisor about your aspirations and see what steps you can take to work towards your goals. If you don't take the time to speak about what you want to achieve, and how you think you can get there, you might be doing yourself a real disservice.

They say that talk is cheap. That's only true if you don't back it up with some action. If we genuinely communicate more often, and engage each other more by talking, listening and acting on our conversations, they can become an investment of time that pays off for us as individuals and for CN as an industry leading company.

Claude Mongeau
President and CEO

Face to face

Dear fellow railroaders,

Last week I was in Illinois on the Joliet Subdivision, where I spent some time with one of our Engineering mega-gangs as they performed their important work on our tracks. This crew of about 40 are in the midst of surfacing and replacing some 70,000 ties on 35 miles of double track. I was pleased to see the fantastic teamwork displayed by this group, which was comprised of employees from the EJ&E, IC, GTW, CCP and WC. In addition to the veterans from these organizations, there were also newly hired railroaders who had recently signed up with CN.

This team from a diversity of backgrounds is pulling together to maintain a safe operation on our network. Of very special note, the team has also gone two years injury-free, which is a hallmark of great railroading. As I was chatting with the folks there, it occurred to me I really should tell you all how much I enjoy meeting our CN teammates whenever and wherever I can.

In the year and half since becoming CEO, whether it's been at the Transcona shops in Winnipeg, meeting new hires at our intermodal yard in Toronto or at CN Family Day at Taschereau Yard in Montreal, I always receive a warm welcome from you. These are not situations where anyone is giving me status reports on projects, or productivity studies, or anything "official." I just like taking the opportunity to introduce myself, shake hands and casually talk about our company, our industry and whatever is on your minds. It's wonderful to see how engaged our people are, how proud they are when we talk about their roles at CN, and how seriously everyone takes their responsibilities.

September 15, 2011

It's encouraging to see the enthusiasm from the many young people we've hired recently, but I also see tremendous passion from our folks who have been part of our railroad for decades, and that combination is a major reason why we're the top railroading team in the business.

I have spent most of my professional career in offices, but two years ago I did seize the opportunity to travel throughout CN's network for a few months when I was "Chief Railroader in Training," just prior to taking on my duties as president. It was great to have that hands-on experience learning how to change out brakes, check air pressure hoses, line a switch, and many other railroading skills. Eventually, I completed my training to become a qualified conductor. The best part of that time was being able to meet with so many of you in person. You can really learn a lot about railroading by meeting face to face and engaging with experienced railroaders in the field.

Nowadays, my schedule makes it challenging to be able to visit with as many of you as I would like, and I aim to meet with more of you whenever I can. But even if I don't have the chance to drop in on your work location in the immediate future and speak with you directly, I still want to tell you how proud I am to be part of this tremendous CN team, and what a first class job you do to help keep CN the industry leader.

Claude Mongeau
President and CEO

APPENDIX 6:   HUNTER CAMP – A TRUE STORY

Postcard from Hunter Camp

Hunter Harrison preaches his "how we do what we do & why" gospel to CN's next-generation leaders

By Pat Foran,
Editor *Progressive Railroading*
March 2007

It'll take time for Canadian National Co. to inculcate 20,000-plus employees with the principles of "precision railroading," a concept President and Chief Executive Officer E. Hunter Harrison has championed since the late 1980s. It helps to have believers out there, walking the talk, and CN does. But Harrison would like to have more.

One way is for Harrison to reach more of them himself. Enter "Hunter Camps," two-and-a-half-day sessions at which the process-oriented Harrison imparts his "how we do what we do & why" message to 20 employees who've been identified as leadership candidates.

"It's not unlike a preacher. Every Sunday morning, they try to convert people," says Harrison, who's been at CN for eight years and in the rail industry for 40. "What we're going through is a culture change. These camps are a way for us to get to the masses quicker."

Helping Harrison preach the precision gospel is CN Senior Vice-President-People Les Dakens, who details the ways CN aims to effect cultural change through the ABC (Antecedent-Behavior-Consequence) model of managing performance. "Many of us went to Boy Scout camp and learned about rules, and a little about life," says Dakens. "Campers also would rally around the flag, which is kind of what we're doing here."

CN began conducting the camps in 2003 so that Harrison could connect with up-and-comers in CN's operating department. Now, the goal is to "Hunterize," as Dakens puts it, 2,000 of the railway's 3,500 non-union employees by 2008's end.

"People are really responding to the message," Dakens says. "You'll see people from IT and finance get a better understanding of the railroad, and the operating folks get a better appreciation of what they are doing to support the railroad. It's helping everybody connect the dots."

I had the privilege of witnessing Harrison and Dakens try to reach 22 more CNers during a camp held Dec. 4-5, 2006, at The Breakers Hotel & Resort in West Palm Beach, Fla.

Why they're here

The campers seem to be in pretty good spirits as they trickle in for the first session. Participants include trainmasters, superintendents, payroll managers, legal counselors and labor relations execs from across the CN system. Seven have been with CN for more than two decades; three, fewer than four years. One's been with the railroad only six months.

"We'll spend a lot of time speaking about behavior and how all of us as leaders have to influence behavior," Dakens tells the campers as they settle into their seats. "It's also a great opportunity to network."

And to engage in dialogue with the CEO. "The more questions you ask, the better he is," Dakens says.

Not that it takes much for Harrison to lock in. He's a very visual orator; Harrison's hard-scrabble vocabulary is a tonal match for his homespun storytelling. Sometimes, he'll relate anecdotes as if he were conducting a self-Q&A, posing a question and answering it in rapid-fire fashion. Other times, he'll shift gears in mid-thought, challenging campers to keep up.

"I'm impatient," Harrison acknowledges. "I'm also demanding. But I'm asking people to stretch."

By doing so, he's stretching, too. "Instead of solving problems himself, he's teaching others to do it," Dakens says. "That's partly what Hunter Camp is all about."

As attendees soon learned, Hunter Camp is also all about Mr. Harrison cutting to the chase. After succinctly summing up the North American rail realm since the Staggers Act and CN's post-privatization successes, Harrison asked campers to keep four words in mind:

- Leadership. "We looked in the mirror back in '98-'99 and said, 'We have some weaknesses in this area,'" Harrison says. "Why? We haven't taken the time to train. Why is that a problem? Because there's so much change going on."

- Change. "In rapidly changing times, experience can be your worst enemy," he says, paraphrasing oil magnate J. Paul Getty. "Reflect on that for a moment."

- Why. "It's the most powerful three-letter word in the world," Harrison says. "Just tell people why we do what we do. If you will take time to explain to people why we have to change, people learn to accept the change better."

- Mud (as in misinformation, miscommunication or anything that muddles the message). "Mud consumes organizations, folks," he says. "I'm trying to run around it because some of you leaders are builders of mud pies – 'I know what they said, but here's what really matters.' That's something we've got to change."

Harrison brandishes these five words frequently during the next two days. "Stay with me on this," he says.

Just as they have with the precision railroading concept that Harrison championed during his late 1980s-to-late-1990s reign at the Illinois Central Corp. and honed for the past eight years at CN.

Precise & principled

Precision railroading is all about providing good service – or doing what you say you're going to do – at an acceptable cost, Harrison says. It's about developing dock-to-dock trip plans for individual shipments rather than scheduling terminal-to-terminal transit times for trains. Meet your schedules, and you'll reduce terminal time and improve asset utilization.

"We've done great, but we're in eighth grade with the scheduled railroad," Harrison says. "We're not close to a PhD. But there's power here."

Particularly if they stick to CN's five guiding principles: service, cost control, asset utilization, safety and people.

"Every process change is not a miracle," he says, citing example after example of CNers working through the "mud" and shoring up previously poor-performing yards and terminals. "We're all better than we give ourselves credit for, or we hold too much in reserve."

Witness CN's massive MacMillan Yard. "In 1998, it was probably the worst operating yard I've ever seen," Harrison says. "Today, it's the best."

Implementing remote-control technology made a difference, but changing the Toronto yard's "early quits" culture did wonders. Dwell time has been nearly halved since the late 1990s.

"Now, the place is world class," says Harrison. "But why didn't anyone stand up and say this was wrong? How did that evolve?"

He's getting into it now, he's zeroing in: "See how things happen? See how things work, how cultures can become in-bred? Guess what it does? You compromise service, you compromise safety."

One mind-set change Harrison believes CNers clearly have embraced is the need to get better at asset utilization. "We reduced the (locomotive) fleet by 30 percent, from 1,900 to 1,300, by simply changing switches," he says. "We worked with locomotives, rail cars – a lot of things. We started to gain momentum. And guess what? The operating ratio came way down."

But there's still room for improvement

"Remember, it's not just about moving cars and trains – it's about doing the right thing," Harrison says. "Every time you misbehave and make the wrong decision, there's a price to pay."

Nowhere is that more apparent than on the safety front. A culture that historically permitted the breaking of rules continues to frustrate Harrison.

"I am a stickler for the rules – I don't want people to interpret what we're saying," he says. "When I got to CN, I said 'zero tolerance' and people said, 'What?' That kind of culture is hard to change. Sometimes what it takes is to shake people into doing the right thing."

By "shake," Harrison means a "significant emotional event" (SEE), citing a term he picked up from behavioral consultant Morris Massey, whose video on that very subject campers will view at the end of Day One. SEEs run the gamut – from workplace injuries (or worse) and disciplinary action on the job, to myriad personal crises at home.

Cultivating change

Unfortunately, railroading has more than its share of tragic SEEs, says Harrison, recalling a four-year-old deadly collision between two CN locomotives that could've been prevented.

"Again, it's just so hard to change culture," he says. "I don't want to have to change it one funeral at a time."

But that's often the way cultures do change, he concedes. Nevertheless, CN must try harder to embrace and effect change.

"This is about people, folks," he says.

He sheds his sport coat as he comes out from behind a makeshift lectern and sits on a table. He's a little closer to the campers.

"People," he says, letting the word linger. "They're assets, not liabilities."

And CN leaders and leaders-in-training must think and act accordingly.

"Here's why: If you think they are liabilities, you will contract out everything," Harrison says curtly, as if he were gearing up for a combative conversation. "We're a railroad; we insource."

He isn't finished.

"We don't just say these things in this room – we act like we talk in this room," he says, borderline angrily. "Last week, we talked about how much contract work we've been doing. Well, we're not going to contract track work out. I believe in keeping a stable workforce. So I said, 'No more contracting.' People abuse it, they're going to lose it."

Bottom line: CN must continue to recruit the right people, clearly define their roles, nurture them, reward them and, ultimately, figure out how to retain them. If people understand what's expected of them, have the tools they need to do their job and are rewarded when they do it, CN leaders will be able to say that they're actually exercising leadership.

"If you take 'people' and the other four pillars, season them heartily with integrity and passion – and passion, in my view, is just caring – and you know what we're about," Harrison says. "If you can unleash the power of people, it's amazing what can be done."

On that note, the campers break for lunch.

The afternoon session is a little less intense, as Harrison spends less time talking theory and more on practical problem-solving approaches.

"How you make the transition from this environment, where it's easy to talk about, to the real world – that's the real challenge," he says. "Some of you are thinking, 'I can't do this by myself.' You're right. That's why we need champions to stand up."

Conflicts & questions

To identify them, campers must know their direct reports better, he says. They'll also need to be more proactive on the problem-solving front.

To that end, campers were asked to come to the session ready to share a challenge they're facing, with Harrison offering potential solutions and thought processes a precision railroader would use to "do the right thing," as he puts it.

A camper says he's having trouble supervising people he "hired out with" in the 1950s. "They're basically looking to retire, criticizing management, and so on," he says. Harrison's response: You can't win over everybody. "Be upfront, be fair and ask them to produce," he says.

And if that doesn't work, the supervisor might need to create an SEE.

"One way to deal with cancer is you cut it out before it spreads," Harrison says. "The tragic thing is, we created that employee. If for 30 years this has been allowed to go on, and somebody comes in and suddenly says 'change,' it's not going to be easy. But good leaders make the tough calls."

Other campers offer up challenges – from issues surrounding the implementation of an onboard locomotive recording system ("A bad thing in this world is too much supervision, but the worst thing in the world is a weak supervisor.") to questions about how to appropriately accommodate a disabled worker. ("I don't believe in light duty, and I don't believe in modified duty ... but if our policy is too restrictive or doesn't fit, call me.")

The afternoon session ends with campers viewing the aforementioned Massey "SEE" video.

Have Harrison's words resonated with campers today? Have they bared their professional souls enough to Harrison's liking? Are they buying in?

He'll let them know soon enough.

Campers begin Day Two by watching another Massey video, "What You Are is Where You Were When." The overriding theme: Ignore people's values at your own risk.

"When we ignore them, we can seriously screw up," Massey says in the video. "What people think is right, wrong, normal – you name it and you're correct. The truth is, it's OK to be different."

After the tape ends, Harrison offers up what he terms a "reality check" based on his observations the day before.

"How many of you felt a little uncomfortable because it was difficult, because it didn't fit your hymnal?" he asks. "I could see it. A lot of you were formed with different values, different type cultures. And that's one of the things we're trying to gauge."

He pauses ... then says loudly: "If you don't think I didn't see mud in this room, you're wrong. A few of you – I'd say four of you – are still saying, 'B.S. – I'm not buying it.' Look, you're going to make yourself difficult doing that. Decide to buy in or not, but don't turn your back on the cultural differences. You have to be aware of them."

It's just one of the things campers will have to be aware of if they have any thought of becoming a "true, good leader," Harrison says as he offers a few tips:

- Be a good follower. That means taking direction and recognizing that rail-roading is a team effort, he says.

- Know your role – or "understand where you fit in the pyramid," as he puts it. "You can't individually go off and do your own thing."

- Communicate the game plan – or the "Why?" – effectively.

- Instill confidence. "If they don't have confidence in you, they'll waver," he says.

- Inspire people. "It's one way to get people to stretch. We're all better than we think we are."

Would-be leaders also need to manage and reward performance, as well as apply consequences, which Dakens will delve into later.

"A lot of people have a hard time telling people they're not doing their job," Harrison says. "But, again, the real great leaders make the tough calls."

It's lunch time, and campers originally were going to spend the afternoon golfing, fishing or otherwise recreating. But it's a windy, rainy day in West Palm Beach, so they elect to finish the session this afternoon. And they'll do so without Harrison, who's preached enough for one camp.

"These sessions are always learning sessions for me – I hope they are for you," he tells the campers. "We've got a long way to go ... but you're part of the best-operating railway in the world right now. We've been doing things that are unimaginable – especially with the operating ratio, which isn't the be-all, end-all. But it indicates we're doing things right."

That shareholders are happy – and customers are getting happier – is another indication, Harrison adds.

"All I ask you to do is keep getting better – execute on a day-in, day-out basis," he says. "Do what we say we'll do, and we'll all continue to have success."

Getting 'Hunterized'

After Dakens discusses the ABC performance model, the CN leadership model and organizational development continuum, he thanks the campers for being active participants, each of whom receives a bronze-coloured "Hunter Camp" pin. He also tells them what to expect when they get back home.

"Somebody will say, 'Oh, you went to a Hunter Camp. Isn't that cute? You're going to get Hunterized,'" Dakens says. "Is there a little bit of brainwashing at Hunter Camp? You bet. The point here is for the message to sink in."

Campers also will be grilled about getting to go to West Palm Beach. Don't sweat it, Dakens tells them. You deserve it.

"We're at the top and we want to stay there," he says, reiterating Guiding Principle #5 ("CN is powered by passionate people."). "That's what this thing is all about."

APPENDIX 7:   BOARD DIRECTOR INTERVIEWS
– BIOGRAPHIES

Top HRC Profile

Name: **Jim Olson**
Position: **Board Director**

Biography:

Mr. Olson has 35 years of experience in the food and beverage industry, including 17 years in senior executive roles for major global food and beverage manufacturers. He is the retired Senior Vice-President, Operations of PepsiCo International, a global food and beverage manufacturer. From 2002 to 2006, he held this position for PepsiCo's Europe, Middle East and Africa division and was responsible for all manufacturing, distribution, purchasing and engineering. From 1999 to 2002, he served as Vice-President, Operations of Ernest & Julio Gallo Winery, one of the largest global wine production companies, where he was responsible for all vineyards, procurement, production, bottling and distribution operations. Additionally, from 1990 to 1999, Mr. Olson served as Vice-President of Operations for Frito-Lay Canada, Walkers Snack Foods Limited (Frito-Lay International, UK division) and Frito-Lay Latin America.

Mr. Olson is currently a director of Maple Leaf Foods where he is also Chair of the Human Resource and Compensation Committee and a member of the Audit Committee. He is also a former Director of Winn-Dixie Stores , Snack Food Ventures Europe (a PepsiCo/General Mills joint venture in Western Europe), and the European Snacks Association.

Top HRC Profile

Name: **Dr. Chris Bart**
Position: **Principal and Lead Professor**
Company: **The Directors College at McMaster University**

Biography:

Dr. Chris Bart is the Founding Partner and Co-Chair of The Schreiber Bart Group and the world's leading expert on mission and vision statement effectiveness. He is also the Founder, Principal and Lead Professor of The Directors College at McMaster University, Canada's first university accredited corporate Director Certification program.

Dr. Bart authored the Canadian business best seller (2012), *A Tale of Two Employees and the Person Who Wanted to Lead Them* as well as the widely acclaimed publication *20 Essential Questions Corporate Directors Should Ask About Strategy (2013)*. He also has two new books scheduled for release this fall: *Achieving the Execution Edge: 20 Essential Questions Corporate Directors Need to Get Answered About Strategy Execution (with Elliot S. Schreiber)* and *The Mission Driven Hospital*.

Through his pioneering research and teachings, Dr. Bart has become highly sought after by organizations seeking to develop vision and mission statements that get results. His practical approach for bringing mission statements to life has inspired business leaders and audiences around the world.

As a Professor of Strategic Market Leadership (Strategy and Governance) at McMaster University's DeGroote School of Business, Dr. Bart has published over 160 articles, cases and reviews. He currently serves as Associate Editor of the *International Journal of Business Governance & Ethics*.

Dr. Bart is listed in *Canadian Who's Who*. He is currently a member of the Board of The Schreiber Bart Group as well as Terra Firma Capital Corporation (TII.V) and its Audit Committee. He is a past Director of St. Joseph's Hospital, the Harshman Foundation, the Canadian Foundation for Education and Research on Finance, the United Way, and Eagle Precision Technologies Ltd. (a former TSE listed company) where he chaired its Compensation Committee.

Top HRC Profile

Name: **Purdy Crawford**
Position: **Corporate Director**

Biography:

Purdy Crawford is a Canadian lawyer and businessman.

Purdy Crawford is the "Dean Emeritus of Canada's corporate bar", a native of Five Islands, Nova Scotia, and a graduate of Mount Allison University, Dalhousie Law School and Harvard Law School. He pursued his legal career with Osler, Hoskin & Harcourt LLP, practicing primarily in the corporate/commercial area. He joined Imasco Limited as CEO in 1985, retiring as CEO in 1995, but continuing as non-executive Chairman of Imasco Limited, CT Financial Services Inc. and Canada Trustco Mortgage Company until February 1, 2000.

Crawford sat on the boards of several large Canadian companies. He was Chair of the Pan-Canadian Investors Committee for Third-Party Structured Asset Backed Commercial Paper, is the former Chair of the Five-Year Review Committee, appointed to review securities legislation in Ontario, and is also the former Chair of the Securities Industry Committee on Analyst Standards. In 1996 he became an Officer of the Order of Canada and in July 2007, he was elevated to Companion of the Order of Canada. He was inducted into the Nova Scotia Business Hall of Fame in 1997 and became a Fellow of the Institute of Corporate Directors in 1999. In 2000 he was inducted into the Canadian Business Hall of Fame and named Ivey Business Leader of the Year. In April 2003 he was named one of the five 2002 Public Policy Forum honorees and in October he was named The Conference Board of Canada's 2003 Honorary Associate. In 2007 he received the Yee Hong Golden Achievement Award and was honoured as a Champion of Public Education by The Learning Partnership. He is Chancellor Emeritus of Mount Allison University.

Top HRC Profile

Name: **Gordon Ritchie**
Position: **Board Director**

Biography:

Gordon Ritchie served as a member and then Chair of the HRC at Maple Leaf Foods Inc. In addition to 17 years as a Director of Maple Leaf Foods, Gordon served as a Director of a number of leading Canadian public and Crown companies (Telemedia, Laidlaw Inc., Laurentian Bank of Canada, AIG United Guaranty Canada, Canadair Ltd., De Havilland Aircraft of Canada Limited, Federal Business Development Bank, and Export Development Canada), frequently as Member or Chair of the corporate HRC. Prior to his business career, Gordon was a federal official for 22 years, culminating in service as a Deputy Minister and as Ambassador for trade negotiations responsible for the Canada-US free trade agreement. He is the author of *Wrestling with the Elephant: The Inside Account of the Canada-US Free Trade Negotiations.*

Top HRC Profile

Name: **Edward C. Lumley**
Title: **Vice-Chair**
Company: **BMO Nesbitt Burns**

Biography:

The Honourable Ed Lumley has been Vice-Chairman of BMO Nesbitt Burns since 1991. From 1986 to 1991, he served as Chairman of the Noranda Manufacturing Group of companies.

The previous 10 years were spent in the Parliament of Canada where he served as a Minister of the Crown holding several portfolios including Industry, International

Trade, and Science & Technology. During this period he was also responsible to Parliament for various Crown Corporations, Boards, and Commissions including the Federal Business Development Bank, Export Development Corporation, among others. His colleagues in the all-party Canadian Association of Former Parliamentarians selected Mr. Lumley to be the second recipient of their Lifetime Achievement Award.

Prior to his public service Mr. Lumley was a successful entrepreneur. During his career he has served on the Board of a number of National and International Corporations such as, Air Canada, Bell Canada Enterprises, Canadian National, Dollar Thrifty Automotive Group Canada Inc., Magna International Inc., Chrysler Canada Incorporated, and Mercedes Benz Canada Inc.

Born and raised in Windsor, Mr. Lumley is in his third term as Chancellor of the University of Windsor where he graduated with a Bachelor of Commerce degree in 1961. His unwavering support of the university resulted in the naming of the Ed Lumley Centre for Engineering Innovation, a $112 million plus building that was the largest capital investment in the campus's history.

Ed and his wife Pat have been married for over 50 years. They have 5 children and 13 grandchildren.

Top HRC Profile

Name: **Geoff Beattie**
Position: **Board Director**

Biography:

Mr. Beattie received a law degree from the University of Western Ontario and served as a partner in the Toronto law firm Torys LLP before joining The Woodbridge Company Limited (where he served as President from 1998 through December 2012). The Woodbridge Company Limited is a privately held investment holding company for the Thomson family of Canada and the majority shareholder of Thomson Reuters, where Mr. Beattie served as Deputy Chairman from 2000 through May 2013 and as Director from 1998 through May 2013. He has served as Chairman of Relay Ventures since June 2013. He also serves as a Member of the Board of Directors of Royal Bank of Canada (where he serves as Chairman of the Risk Committee) and Maple Leaf Foods Inc. In addition to his public company Board memberships, Mr. Beattie is a Trustee of the University Health Network in Toronto

Top HRC Profile

Name: **David Emerson**
Position: **Board Director**

Biography:

The Honourable David Emerson is a Director and Chair of several Canadian and global companies, including Maple Leaf Foods Inc., Finning International Inc., New Gold, Stantec Inc., TimberWest Forest Corp., and the Institute for Corporate Directors.

He has served as a Minister in the Government of Canada in the roles of Minister of Foreign Affairs, Minister of International Trade and Minister of Industry. He has also served as President and CEO of Canfor Corporation, President and CEO of the Vancouver Airport Authority and Chairman and CEO of Canadian Western Bank.

Mr. Emerson holds Bachelor's and Master's degrees in Economics from the University of Alberta and a Doctorate in Economics from Queen's University.

Top HRC Profile

Name: **Yvonne Jackson**
Position: **Board Director**

Biography:

In 1970, Yvonne received her B.A. in History from Spelman College. Upon graduating, she joined the management training program with Sears, Roebuck & Co., became a merchant, and was appointed Personnel Manager. In 1979, she became an Executive Recruiter for Avon Products, Inc. From 1980 to 1983, Jackson started as Manager of Employee Relations and Staffing, and then became Director of Headquarter Human Resources. In 1982, she left that role to attend the Harvard Business School in the PMD program where she received a Certificate in Management Development in 1985. She returned to Avon's New York office as the Director of Manufacturing Redeployment where she was responsible for rationalizing the US manufacturing plants. In 1986, she was named Director of Human Resources, International and subsequently named Vice President. She remained in that role for 4 years. In 1989, she became Avon Products Vice-President of Human Resources for the North American division.

Jackson went on to work for Burger King Corporation in 1993, Compaq Computers in 1999, and in 2002 the pharmaceutical company, Pfizer, Inc. as Senior Vice-President of Human Resources and Chief People Officer for those three companies. Some of her key responsibilities as Senior Vice-President were building management tools to strengthen business growth and development, launching communication and retention programs, structuring global human resource strategy and leadership and talent management/advancement programs, and developing human resource training and development programs.

Jackson recently formed her own management and human resources consulting firm, Beecher Jackson Inc. She is the recipient of numerous awards and honours. She currently serves on the Board of Spartan Stores and as Compensation Committee Chair. She also serves as Vice-Chair of the Association of Governing Boards of College and Universities (AGB) and is on the Simmons College Board. She is immediate Past Chair of the Board of Trustees at Spelman College, and serves as a former Board Member for Girls, Inc. and for the Institute for Women's Policy. She also formerly served on the Advisory Council for the accounting firm of PricewaterhouseCoopers and on the Board of Winn-Dixie Stores, Inc., serving as Chair of the Compensation Committee.

Top HRC Profile

Name: **Peter Gleason**
Position: **Managing Director & CFO**
Company: **National Association of Corporate Directors**

Biography:

Peter Gleason is Managing Director and Chief Financial Officer for the National Association of Corporate Directors (NACD), the only national association devoted exclusively to serving the information and educational needs of corporate directors. Mr. Gleason also serves as Treasurer for the NACD Board of Directors and as Chief Operating Officer of NACD's Center for Board Leadership. The Center engages in substantive research projects focused primarily on helping establish and refine leading practices to enhance board performance.

Mr. Gleason is a member of NACD's national faculty and is a frequent presenter on the subjects of corporate governance, executive and director compensation, risk, strategic planning, Board process, and Board evaluation. He has served as the host of NACD BoardVision, has appeared on CNBC's Squawk Box and Power Lunch, Reuters TV, NPR's Marketplace, and is regularly quoted in the national media. He oversees all of NACD's research and publications, and has served as a Commissioner on each Blue Ribbon Commission report issued over the past 12 years, including the most recent releases on The Diverse Board, The Effective Lead Director, Performance Metrics, Audit Committees, and Risk Governance.

Mr. Gleason is a Director of Nura Life Sciences, LLC, a privately-held, development-stage health-care company. He also serves on the International Professional Practices Framework Oversight Council of the Institute of Internal Auditors. Formerly, he served as a Director of The Patriot Fund and was also a member of the Executive Advisory Panel for the Open Compliance and Ethics Group (OCEG).

Before joining NACD, Mr. Gleason was a Management Consultant with both Ernst & Young and Pritchett & Associates. In addition, Mr. Gleason spent 8 years in the Research Department at Institutional Shareholder Services including service as Vice-President and as Director of U.S. Research.

Mr. Gleason is a graduate of Dartmouth College, has an MBA with concentrations in both Finance and Marketing from Virginia Tech, and is an NACD Board Leadership Fellow.

Top HRC profile

Name: **Stan Magidson**
Position: **President and Chief Executive Officer**
Company: **Institute of Corporate Directors (ICD)**

Biography:

Stan Magidson, LL.M., ICD.D

Mr. Magidson is President, Chief Executive Officer and a Director of the Institute of Corporate Directors (ICD).

Prior to joining the ICD in July 2010, he was a partner in the Calgary office of Osler, Hoskin & Harcourt LLP, and head of Osler's business law practice in Western Canada. With over 30 years of legal experience, Mr. Magidson has extensive experience in mergers and acquisitions, corporate governance and corporate finance matters.

In 1999, he was seconded to the Ontario Securities Commission, where he built the team that is primarily responsible for the securities regulation of take-over bids and M&A transactions in Canada. Mr. Magidson has been actively involved in the policy implications of securities regulation, having served as Chair of the Securities Advisory Committee to the Alberta Securities Commission.

Before his appointment to President and CEO, he served on the ICD Board of Directors and was Chair of the ICD Calgary Chapter.

Top HRC Profile

Name: **Sarah Raiss**
Position: **Board Director**

Biography:

Sarah Raiss is currently a Board Director of Canadian Oil Sands, Shopper's Drug Mart Corporation, Commercial Metals Company, Chair of the Alberta Electric System Operator Board and past Director of Business Development Bank of Canada where she was Chair of the Human Resource Committee. She was President of the Calgary Petroleum Club Board of Governors and sits on the National Board of the Institute of Corporate Directors. From 2001 to 2011 she was Executive Vice-President of Corporate Services for TransCanada Corporation and was responsible for human resources, information systems, aviation, building, office services, real estate, organizational excellence, communications, branding, marketing and other administrative functions. Sarah also has experience in the telecommunications industry in engineering, operations, strategy, merger integration, governance, and marketing. She has a BS in Applied Mathematics and an MBA, both from the University of Michigan. She has completed several courses including: Creating Value Through Finance at Wharton School of the University of Pennsylvania, Making Corporate Boards More Effective at Harvard University, and the Institute of Corporate Directors' (ICD) Directors Education Program. She has an ICD.D designation. In 2003, 2004, 2005 and 2006, Ms. Raiss was listed in Canada's Most Powerful Women: Top 100, and in 2007 she was inducted into the Top 100 Hall of Fame.

Top HRC Profile

Name: **Claude Lamoureux**
Position: **Board Director**

Biography:

Mr. Lamoureux was Chief Executive Officer of the Ontario Teachers' Pension Plan Board until his retirement in 2007. He was appointed to the position in 1990, when the Ontario government established the new independent corporation to replace the Ontario Teachers' Superannuation Fund. An actuary by profession, Mr. Lamoureux took on the role with the Ontario Teachers' Pension Plan following a successful career at Metropolitan Life, where he worked in the company's New York and Ottawa offices.

Mr. Lamoureux serves on the Board of Directors of Atrium Innovations Inc., Maple Leaf Foods Inc., Northumbrian Water Group plc., Xstrata plc., the Canadian

Institute for Advanced Research, and the Ontario Securities Commission Investor Education Fund.

Mr. Lamoureux holds a BA from the University of Montreal and a B.Comm. in Actuarial Science from Laval University, as well as honorary doctorates from Glendon College at York University and from HEC Montreal. He is a Fellow of the Canadian Institute of Actuaries, the Society of Actuaries and the Institute of Corporate Directors.

Mr. Lamoureux is an Officer of the Order of Canada.

APPENDIX 8: CEO Interviews – Biographies

CEO Interview

Name: **Hunter Harrison**
Position: **CEO**
Company: **Canadian Pacific**

Biography:

E. Hunter Harrison is the Chief Executive Officer of Canadian Pacific (CP). He joined CP in 2012. Mr. Harrison served as President and Chief Executive Officer at Canadian National (CN) from 2003 to 2009 and as Executive Vice-President and Chief Operating Officer from 1998 to 2002. He served on CN's Board of Directors for 10 years. Mr. Harrison brings valuable railroad knowledge to CP with almost 50 years of experience in the industry.

Prior to joining CN, Mr. Harrison was President and Chief Executive Officer at Illinois Central Corporation (IC) and at Illinois Central Rail Road Company (ICRR) from 1993 to 1998, during which time he was also a Member of the Board. Mr. Harrison held various positions throughout his time at IC and ICRR, including Vice-President, Chief Operating Officer and Senior Vice-President of Operations. His railroad career began in 1963 when he joined the Frisco (St. Louis-San Francisco) Railroad as a carman-oiler in Memphis while still attending school.

In1989, Mr. Harrison served as Burlington Northern Railroad's Vice-President of Transportation and Vice-President of Service Design. He has served as a Director on several railway companies and industry associations, including The Belt Railway of Chicago, Wabash National Corporation, The American Association of Railroads, Terminal Railway, TTX Company, CN, IC, and ICRR. He has received numerous accolades, including being selected North America's Railroader of the Year by *RailwayAge Magazine* in 2002 and CEO of the Year by *The Globe and Mail Report on Business* Magazine in 2007.

CEO Interview

Name: **Joseph Jimenez**
Position: **President & CEO**
Company: **Novartis**

Biography:

Joseph Jimenez has been Chief Executive Officer (CEO) of Novartis Pharmaceuticals Canada Inc. since 2010. Mr. Jimenez is responsible for leading the company's diversified healthcare portfolio of leading businesses in innovative pharmaceuticals, eye care, generics, vaccines and diagnostics, and OTC and animal health.

Mr. Jimenez joined Novartis in April 2007, in the position of Division Head, Consumer Health.. In this role he led the transformation of the pharmaceutical portfolio to balance mass market and specialty products, and significantly increased the percentage of sales from newly launched products. He also worked to realign the division's commercial approach to focus on the individual needs of customers, and incorporated more technological tools to better connect with patients and customers.

Before joining Novartis, Jimenez served as President and CEO of North American business for the H.J. Heinz Company, and as President and CEO of Heinz in Europe from 2002 to 2006. He was a non-executive Director of AstraZeneca plc, United Kingdom, from 2002 to 2007. He was also an Adviser for the private equity organization Blackstone Group L.P. in the United States.

Mr. Jimenez is a member of the Board of Directors of Colgate-Palmolive Co., New York. He graduated in 1982 with a Bachelor's degree from Stanford University and in 1984 with a Masters of Business Administration from the University of California, Berkeley.

CEO Interview

Name: **Mike Wilson**
Position: **President and CEO**
Company: **Agrium**

Biography:

Mike joined Agrium in 2000 and became President and CEO 3 years later. Under his leadership Agrium has grown significantly, increasing its size and profile in world markets. Mike gathered experience as an executive leader in the chemical industry, working both across Canada and internationally. Prior to joining Agrium, he was the President of Methanex Corporation.

CEO Interview

Name:	**Michael McCain**
Position:	**CEO**
Company:	**Maple Leaf Foods**

Biography:

Michael McCain is President and Chief Executive Officer of Maple Leaf Foods Inc. Mr. McCain joined Maple Leaf Foods as President and Chief Operating Officer in April 1995 and was appointed President and Chief Executive Officer in January 1999.

Prior to joining Maple Leaf Foods, Mr. McCain spent 16 years with McCain Foods Limited in Canada and the United States and was, at the time of leaving in March 1995, President and Chief Executive Officer of McCain Foods USA Inc. He began his career with McCain Foods after graduating from university, and held progressive positions in sales, sales management, marketing management and information systems management. In 1986, he assumed the role of President of McCain Citrus Inc., and was appointed President and Chief Executive Officer of McCain Foods USA Inc. in 1990.

Mr. McCain is a Director of Maple Leaf Foods Inc., McCain Capital Inc. and Chairman of Canada Bread Company, Limited. He is a member of the Board of the Royal Bank of Canada, the American Meat Institute, the Richard Ivey School of Business Advisory Board, the Centre for Addiction and Mental Health Foundation (CAMH), MaRS Discovery District, and the Canadian Council of Chief Executives. Mr. McCain is also co-chairing the current CAMH Capital Campaign. He is a past member of the Board of Trustees of The Hospital for Sick Children and a past Director of the American Frozen Food Institute and Bombardier Inc.

Born in Florenceville, New Brunswick, Michael McCain was educated at Mount Allison University and received a Bachelor's Degree (Honours) in Business Administration from the University of Western Ontario. He has five children and is a resident of Toronto, Ontario.

CEO Interview

Name: **Claude Mongeau**
Position: **President and CEO**
Company: **CN**

Biography:

Claude Mongeau became President and Chief Executive Officer of CN on January 1, 2010.

He joined CN in May 1994 and has held the positions of Vice-President, Strategic and Financial Planning, and Assistant Vice-President, Corporate Development. He was appointed Executive Vice-President and Chief Financial Officer in October 2000.

Prior to joining CN, Mr. Mongeau was a partner with Secor Group, a Montreal-based management consulting firm providing strategic advice to large Canadian corporations such as Bombardier and Bell Canada. He also worked in the business development unit of Imasco Inc., a diversified holding company with subsidiaries operating in the manufacturing, retail, and financial services sectors. His career started in Europe with Bain & Company, a leading American consulting firm.

In 1997, Claude Mongeau was named one of Canada's top 40 executives under 40 years of age by the *Financial Post Magazine*. In 2005, he was selected Canada's CFO of the Year by an independent committee of prominent Canadian business leaders. He is a Board Director at SNC-Lavalin Inc.

APPENDIX 9:   CHRO INTERVIEWS – BIOGRAPHIES

Top CHRO Profile

Name: **Bill Conaty**
Position: **Former Senior Vice-President, HR**
Company: **General Electric**

Biography:

Long recognized as a world leader in his field, Bill retired in 2007 as Senior Vice-President for Human Resources at General Electric, a company consistently ranked as without peer in developing world-class leaders. The management development and training programs that Conaty engineered provided GE with one of the world's most talent-rich management benches. Conaty has served as chairman of the National Academy of Human Resources and was named as a Distinguished Fellow, the organization's highest honour. He currently serves as a personal advisor to CEOs of companies around the world, including Procter & Gamble, Boeing, Dell Inc., Goodyear, LG Electronics (Korea), and UniCredit (Italy). He is a frequent business speaker and is an Advisory Partner at Clayton, Dubilier & Rice. He is co-author of the bestseller *The Talent Masters: Why Smart Leaders Put People Before Numbers*.

Top CHRO Profile

Name: **Peter Goerke**
Position: **Group Human Resources Director**
Company: **Prudential plc**

Biography:

Peter joined Prudential plc in March 2011 as Group HR Director. He is a Member of the Group Executive Committee and a Director of Prudential Services Limited. In addition, he has Group-wide responsibility for Corporate Property and is Chair of the Group Head Office Management Committee.

Peter was born in 1962 and graduated from the University of St. Gallen, Switzerland with a Master of Arts and Master of Business Administration. In 2002, he took an Advanced Management Program at the University of Pennsylvania, USA.

In 1989, Peter joined Abegglen Management Partners, Switzerland, where he became partner. He moved to McKinsey & Company as a Senior Engagement Manager in 1997, and worked in Switzerland and in the USA. In 2000, he joined Egon Zehnder International Inc. in Switzerland, and progressed to Global Head of Insurance Practice.

In 2005, Peter was appointed Group Head of HR of Zurich Financial Services AG. He was a member of their Group Management Board from 2005 – 2011.

Peter was also a Board Director for Zurich Assurance Limited, UK, and a member of the Supervisory Boards for Zurich Alternative Asset Management, USA, and Zurich Vorsorgeeinrichtung, Switzerland.

He is married with one daughter.

Top CHRO Profile

Name:	**John F. Lynch**
Position:	**SVP, Corporate HR**
Company:	**General Electric**

Biography:

John F. Lynch is Senior Vice-President of Corporate Human Resources at General Electric, and is based in Fairfield, Connecticut.

A native of Edinburgh, Scotland, Mr. Lynch worked in a number of management roles in human resources for one of the UK's major finance houses for 18 years. In 1991, he joined the UK Auto Finance business of GE Capital, and in 1994 he was promoted to HR Leader for GE Capital Retail Finance, Europe. The following year he moved to Stamford, Connecticut, to take on the role of Senior HR Leader for GE Capital Global Consumer Finance, now GE Money.

In 2001, Mr. Lynch was elected a GE Company Officer, becoming Vice-President, Human Resources for GE Medical Systems in Milwaukee, Wisconsin (now GE Healthcare). Following the Amersham acquisition in April 2004, John led human resources at the new global headquarters for GE Healthcare in London.

In 2007, Mr. Lynch was appointed Senior Vice-President of Corporate Human Resources, reporting directly to the GE Chairman and CEO Jeff Immelt. In this role he has overall HR responsibility for GE's 320,000 employees worldwide.

Mr. Lynch studied at Blairs College, Aberdeen, and St Andrews College in Scotland. He has three children.

Top CHRO Profile

Name:	**Ferio Pugliese**
Position:	**Executive Vice-President and President of WestJet's regional airline, WestJet Encore**
Company:	**WestJet**

Biography:

Ferio Pugliese became Executive Vice-President and President of WestJet's regional airline, WestJet Encore, in November 2012. He joined WestJet in 2007. Serving in his previous role as WestJet's Executive Vice-President, People, Culture and Inflight Services, Ferio was responsible for overseeing all aspects of WestJet's People (human resources, corporate real-estate and inflight services) department. He and his team were also instrumental in defining and executing people plans that supported WestJet's culture and strategic direction.

Ferio is proud that WestJet was included in Canada's 10 Most Admired Corporate Cultures Hall of Fame, that the company was recognized as one of Canada's Most Admired Corporate Cultures for four consecutive years (2005 to 2009), and was also selected one of Canada's best employers by Hewitt Associates in 2009.

A certified Human Resources Professional (CHRP), Ferio holds a Master of Arts degree in Adult Education from Central Michigan University, a Bachelor of Arts (Honours) in Social Science, and a Bachelor of Commerce (Honours) from the University of Windsor. He is a member of the Conference Board of Canada's Human Resources Executive Council and has worked in various senior leadership roles. Prior to joining WestJet his previous roles included Vice-President, Human Resources at Catalyst Paper Corporation in Vancouver, Director of Human Resources Development at Windsor Casino Ltd., and Director of Human Resources Development at Casino Rama, Carnival Resorts and Casinos.

Top CHRO Profile

Name:	**Katy Barclay**
Position:	**SVP, Human Resources**
Company:	**The Kroger Company**

Biography:

Katy Barclay is Senior Vice-President of Human Resources for The Kroger Co., where she leads all aspects of Human Resources, including leadership development, talent management, succession planning, associate engagement, and total reward programs for Kroger's 343,000 associates.

Kroger, the nation's largest traditional grocery retailer, operates 3,700 supermarkets, convenience and jewellery stores under two dozen names across the country. With more than $96.8 billion in annual sales, Kroger is ranked number 23 on the Fortune 500 list.

Katy has over 30 years of experience in the Human Resources field. Prior to joining Kroger, she was the VP of Global Human Resources for General Motors Corp. During her time with GM, she led the automaker's global Human Resources organization with a strong focus on building the company's strategic HR capability worldwide, redesigning domestic health care and pension programs, organizational restructuring in mature markets, and building a strong footprint in emerging and growth markets.

Katy served in leadership roles for both of her alma maters. She served as President of Michigan State University's Eli Broad College of Business and as Member of the MIT Sloan Fellows Alumni Board. She was a Board Member for the Hispanic Scholarship Fund and the Henry Ford Health Care System, and currently serves on the Board of Directors for the Cincinnati Symphony Orchestra.

Katy was installed in the National Academy of Human Resources 2000 Class of Fellows and currently serves as Chair of the Board for the Academy. She is a three-time recipient of Automotive News's 100 Leading Women and has been named to *Human Resource Executive* magazine's HR Honour Roll. In 2013, Katy was the recipient of The YWCA's Career Woman of Achievement Award.

Katy has two grown sons. She earned a Bachelor's degree in Business from Michigan State University and a Master's degree in Business Administration from the Massachusetts Institute of Technology's Sloan Fellows Program.

Top CHRO Profile

Name: **Dave Ulrich**
Position: **Professor, Ross School of Business**
Company: **University of Michigan**

Biography:

Dave Ulrich is a Professor at the Ross School of Business, University of Michigan, and a partner at the RBL Group a consulting firm focused on helping organizations and leaders deliver value. He studies how organizations build capabilities of leadership, speed, learning, accountability, and talent through leveraging human resources. He has helped generate award winning data bases that assess alignment between strategies, organization capabilities, HR practices, HR competencies, and customer and investor results.

He has published over 200 articles and book chapters and over 25 books. He edited *Human Resource Management* from 1990 to 1999, served on the Editorial Boards of four journals, on the Board of Directors for Herman Miller, and on the Board of Trustees at Southern Virginia University, and is a Fellow in the National Academy of Human Resources.

APPENDIX 10:   CASE STUDIES FOR HRC TRAINING SESSION

Case Study # 1 - Managing Relationships

This Canadian company is a favourite of the stock market, and has operations in Canada and the U.S. The current CEO has been in the role for 3 years and has grown the company. The Board Chair, appointed 15 years ago, has revamped the membership of the Board. The HRC Chair is a very well respected Canadian Director and has been on the Board for 10 years. The CHRO was hired 4 years ago by the previous CEO and HRC Chair.

Behind the public facade of the company, there is considerable conflict within the Board and between certain Board Members and management. None of the conflict is open warfare, but it does create a good deal of tension, which can make it difficult to handle issues. Specifically, there is an uneasy relationship between the Board Chair and the CEO. The Chair wants to control the CEO, who is a bit of a maverick, and does not value any input from most of the Board Members. There are times when he does not bother to attend committee meetings, which really annoys the Board Chair. The Board Chair does not get along with the HRC Chair who has a great deal of influence with most Board Members and has a great relationship with the CEO.

Recently, the Board Chair approached the Corporate Secretary and asked him to arrange to have two requests handled by the CHRO. The first request was to provide a special pension enhancement for his executive assistant in the event she does not find another position when he retires in 2 years. The second request was to have the company provide healthcare coverage for him and his family when they travel to the U.S. This coverage is provided to senior management, who have business reasons to be on both sides of the border, but the Chair only visits the U.S. to stay at his vacation home. The Corporate Secretary has passed on the Chair's requests to the CHRO.

The CHRO has reviewed the requests and believes they are not reasonable and, more importantly, granting them will set a precedent. As the CHRO has pushed back against several other requests from the Board Chair in the past, which has made for an uneasy relationship between them, he has contacted the HRC Chair and the CEO and sought their advice. Both have indicated they support his conclusion.

The CHRO has to decide the best way to approach the Board Chair.

If you were the CHRO, what would you do?

1. Contact the Board Chair directly.

2. Ask the HRC Chair to handle the contact with the Board Chair.

3. Ask the CEO to handle the situation with the Board Chair.

4. Bring in the CEO, HRC Chair to the meeting with the Board Chair.

5. Some other approach?

2011 Les Dakens

Case Study # 2 - CEO Succession Planning

This terrific success story Canadian company has been led by a very dynamic CEO for 8 years. He is nearing 65 and most people expect him to retire in the next 12 months or so. Through the formal succession process, two internal candidates have been identified and development plans have been in place for the last 2 years. The Board and the HRC committee have confidence that the right individuals have been identified.

Each Board Member has spent time with the two individuals during the last 2 years. There is full Board consensus on these individuals. In fact, the majority of the Board has a strong preference for one of these individuals who is currently in the CFO role. This person has done a stellar job in acquiring successful acquisitions which have been accretive from day one. The downside is that the CFO does not have any operating experience and has not run a business unit. He is regarded as a high flight risk if he does not get the CEO role within the next year. The second candidate, the head of Sales and Marketing, is a veteran within the industry. He is 10 years older than the CFO but is willing to commit to at least 5-7 years as CEO if he is selected.

The Board Chair and the HRC Chair had to work together to push the incumbent CEO into identifying and providing development plans for these two individuals. From the start of the process, the CEO has been pushing a third candidate, a personal protégé of his, as his replacement. Although very talented, and regarded as having high potential in the future, the Board feels this individual is not ready to become the CEO but could be promoted to the COO role with the new CEO.

Yesterday, the CEO has informed the Board Chair that he would like to extend his contract by two more years. The CEO feels the market will respond very positively to this extension and it will give him more time to develop his successors, including the third candidate. It is true that the stock market is very nervous about a change in leadership at this time. The Board Chair has called a meeting with the HRC Chair and the CHRO to discuss how they should respond to the CEO's request.

If you were on the HRC, what advice would you give to the HRC Chair and the CHRO on how to tackle this situation?

2011 Les Dakens

Case Study # 3 - Executive Compensation

This large Canadian company has had a spotty track record for the last 5 years. Their new products have been hampered by cost overruns, development delays and significant competitor activities. The company is run by the founding CEO and his total compensation has grown to above the P75 level versus his peers in the industry.

The board has recently been criticized by shareholders and Bay Street analysts for the sagging share price and the high CEO compensation. Several of the Board Members on the HRC have quietly suggested to the HRC Chair and the CHRO that the compensation issue needs to be dealt with at the annual HRC CEO Compensation review meeting to be held next month. Specifically, these Board Directors have been recommending privately that a salary freeze and a reduction in the annual LTIP award is needed to remedy this situation.

The Board's Executive Compensation Advisor has been a staunch supporter of the CEO's pay package design and is not willing to challenge the status quo. A new Board Member on the HRC has proposed replacing this consultant. The long tenured Board Chairman is a close friend of the CEO. He feels the shareholders' and analysts' concerns will die down once the company shows some good news next quarter, and that "the turnaround is underway." In addition, he believes any change in the pay package would be a big de-motivator to the CEO.

The CEO has indicated to the HRC chair and the CHRO that he is actually expecting some recognition in his pay for his leadership during these difficult times. Anything less would be a "slap in the face."

The Board is under considerable pressure to take some action on the shareholder complaints about executive compensation. If you were on the HRC, what would you recommend to the HRC Chair and the CHRO?

2011 Les Dakens

APPENDIX 11: PEOPLE STRATEGY

In order to describe how to develop a People Strategy for your business, I would like to share with you a business article that was written about the People Strategy process at Maple Leaf Foods. The article appeared in the *HR Professional* in 2012.

Maple Leaf Foods: Building a People Strategy to Align with Business Needs

By Jennifer Campbell

The headlines in late October: "Maple Leaf Foods closes plants, cuts 1,550 jobs," the *Toronto Star* wrote. "460 jobs to be cut at Moncton Maple Leaf Foods," CBC. ca announced. The *Globe and Mail* summed it up this way: "Maple Leaf to cut jobs, close plants in sweeping overhaul."

It's an announcement no company likes to make. Yet, sometimes corporate repositioning and the accompanying job losses such as those announced by Maple Leaf Foods (MLF) herald plans to move the organization into a more secure and competitive future.

This was the future President and CEO Michael McCain envisioned when he said at the time of the announcement that the company was creating "a highly efficient, world-class, production and distribution network that will markedly increase our competitiveness and close the cost gap with our U.S. peers."

However, these distribution network changes represent just one element of what Maple Leaf Foods (MLF) calls its "comprehensive value-creation business strategy." The other elements of the strategy focus on driving market share through strong brands and innovation. As a marketing organization that manufactures its own products, Maple Leaf is setting a path to excel on both sides of the equation.

Aligning People Strategy with Business Strategy

Clearly, one of the keys to ensuring the success of MLF's business strategy will be how the company uses and develops one of its critical assets: its people.

In January 2011, the company coaxed one of Canada's top HR professionals out of retirement to take on the task of aligning the restructuring plan with a people plan. Les Dakens, who was previously senior vice-president in charge of "people" at CN Rail, and before that worked with companies such as Cadbury Beverages, H.J. Heinz and Nortel, became MLF's senior vice-president and chief human resources officer. Right out of the gate, he identified the need to design and implement a new people strategy and began working with Cheryl Fullerton, the company's director of HR transformation, to tackle the project.

Fullerton and Dakens began the project some 11 years after the company's previous people strategy came into force. That plan had created an enduring foundation –the Maple Leaf Leadership Edge defined a strong, values-based culture with some industry leading practices, such as their performance assessment and development process.

"It was a well thought-through strategy and one that was well executed," Fullerton says. "But it had been a long time since it was launched and we were ready for a re-focusing. With this new business strategy, it was time to refresh it."

The project began in earnest. A team scoped it out in February and hit the ground running in March. Between March and June, they did an enormous amount of research, Fullerton said, to figure out the areas on which to focus and how to answer the following questions.

"What people strategies will have the biggest impact in driving business success? What initiatives are we going to implement in order to drive that strategy?" Fullerton explains. "How do we sequence that over the next couple of years? What resources will it take, what will it cost the organization? That's when we had to really drill down deep."

Implementation Process

The team undertaking the revamp included members of the HR Council, which is made up of HR leaders from the half-dozen business units, along with the corporate HR leaders. Fullerton, as the lead, identified a small working group to provide counsel and decisions on key elements. To be inclusive, the full HR Council was regularly updated on progress, and involved in providing input on behalf of their business units all along the way.

In other words, HR has a seat on many of the company's key groups. For instance, Fullerton is a member of the MLF Marketing Council, providing input on the people resources needed to implement the marketing plans. Or, taking away from the meetings what HR needs to do to help marketing fulfill its mandate.

Direction and coaching was provided throughout the project from the company's corporate strategy group, which is made up of a small, talented set of visionaries who are responsible for developing the company's business strategy as a whole.

"They're the internal consulting group for strategic projects," Fullerton says. "They have great strategic-thinking capabilities that they bring to any area of the business going through a strategy planning exercise."

The deep-drilling Fullerton mentions above took place when her team started consulting staff about what they wanted from the new strategy. Dakens met with a full three-quarters of the senior leaders, while Fullerton had one-on-one conversations with all executives. She also surveyed and got feedback from the entire HR team. They also incorporated information from employee engagement surveys from the salaried group and those paid by the hour.

"We have a standing process to collect feedback through engagement surveys," Fullerton notes. "(From those), we got a lot of information about the drivers of engagement and strong messages about how important alignment to the overall business is to them – and how important leadership is."

External research was also conducted, including in-depth interviews with a number of other organizations to gain perspective on their integration of people and business strategy, and their best-practices.

Getting alignment between the overall business strategy, the HR strategy and the various business unit and functional strategies was the biggest challenge in the project, Fullerton says. "It is a complex situation, and involved a lot of conversations with a lot of people," she notes.

"Think of six or seven different businesses and trying to get them all aligned," Dakens adds. "That requires some finesse. What was most valuable there was spending time answering questions and talking about what we were trying to accomplish and what impact it would have on the organization."

Final approval on the strategy came in September, though Dakens notes that they could have completed it a month earlier but were delayed somewhat over the summer months due to vacation.

Getting buy-in from the C-suite leaders wasn't a problem, Fullerton says, because the nature of the Maple Leaf Foods approval process meant that group was involved, or at least informed, every step of the way. When it comes to employee buy-in to the new people strategy, it's hard to assess but, Fullerton feels they would approve. Dakens agrees.

"We know what they're looking for and I think over time, they'll say that things have changed, have gotten better," Dakens says. "That's the mark."

Engaging Plant Employees

In the past, Maple Leaf's HR efforts have placed a heavy emphasis on developing leadership in the company, Fullerton says, but not necessarily touching the people in the plants. The new people strategy has a strong emphasis on increasing engagement for this group of employees. The distribution network changes driven by the business strategy highlighted this need.

"We have good leaders in our plants, and we will be helping them get even better by improving their ability to communicate with and motivate employees on the plant floor." Dakens says "A big part of the strategy is engaging the 75 per cent of employees who work in our plants."

The people strategy includes training on behaviour-based leadership with ongoing coaching on this learning for managers in the plants. This is more than a training program, since the managers will immediately apply the concepts to business improvement projects. Success of the learning will be measured directly by success of the improvement projects.

Fullerton says the new plan also has a much greater emphasis on communication with the plant employees–communication about the business, how it operates and how they fit into it. This communication effort is targeted to secure alignment with the organization as a whole, and to strengthen the leadership of those who are managing plant workers on a daily basis. In short, the people-management strategy has to drive the growth outlined in the business strategy. "It's the leadership style that's going to drive us to that commercial success" Fullerton says.

Dakens referred to the project as that of a $5-billion company that's ratcheting itself up on both the commercial and manufacturing side, over three to four years. "So that's a lot of change," he says.

Implementation and Monitoring

Implementation of the strategy will be phased in over three years. There are 25 key initiatives to implement, with another 15 or so sub-initiatives. The team has defined individuals within HR and among executives outside HR to co-champion the initiatives, along with dedicated project leaders who will be accountable for implementing change.

When it comes to evaluating the plan's success, they will track progress for each initiative with performance metrics directly tied to the strategy. One example is to measure the "management internal fill rate." Today, one in every two management position openings is filled from outside the organization. In the future, they want to fill these positions internally 70 per cent of the time.

"If you do a good job of developing your talent, it's a deeper supply talent stream you have to play with. But if you don't, you're always going to be (limited) in people's ability and flexibility to move to new positions in the company," says Fullerton. Similarly, retention rates for high-performing employees will be tracked and the goal is a 95 per cent retention rate with the brightest.

After all that work, Fullerton and her colleagues are keen to get started. "The HR team is extremely energized by having a plan and having a vision," she says. "For anybody, it's very engaging to understand how you fit into the organization and how you can have the biggest impact."

APPENDIX 12: MICHAEL MCCAIN'S WEEKLY MESSAGE TO EMPLOYEES

What's Happening at Maple Leaf

From: McCain, Michael H
Sent: 5/18/2012 12:59 PM

> "The more you praise and celebrate your life,
> the more there is in life to celebrate."

> –Oprah Winfrey

Celebrating our successes was a key takeaway for me from our annual Food Fight offsite, which was held this week. I use a portion of my weekly note every week to celebrate our commercial wins, but I know that there are many achievements across the company. We have momentum over three years, and while there are inevitable ups and downs, wins and losses along the way, we are winning and making exceptional progress on our journey. Our leadership team committed to do a better job of celebrating this, and the little victories along the way. I hope you do also!!

Here are some achievements to celebrate this week…

Prime Portions an Award Finalist!

Great news! Maple Leaf Prime Naturally Portions has been selected as a finalist by the Retail Council of Canada for a Canadian Grand Prix New Product Award. For those of you who haven't yet tried them, they are delicious and offer fantastic convenience. Prime Portions are four individually-sealed boneless, skinless chicken breasts which make them easy to store and freezer ready. This is an example of awesome innovation!

As a result of this recognition, Prime Portions will be showcased in the upcoming spring issues of some of the industry's top trade magazines: *Canadian Retailer*, *Canadian Grocer*, *Western Grocer* and *L'alimentation*. Terrific work Prime team!

Wild about Country Natural Sausages!

Schneiders Country Naturals added more power to its all-star roster with the launch of Fresh Sausages on April 30th with three flavours: Mild Tuscan, Hot Sicilian and Honey Garlic. Our customers are absolutely wild about this product. We shipped HUGE volume to Wal-Mart, Sobeys and Atlantic Co-op last week and expect that this will continue to grow as other customers are getting on board.

Fresh Sausage is a strategic launch for Maple Leaf. Within the total meat category, fresh sausage is one of the largest segments, so it's extremely important that we have a strong branded presence with Schneiders Country Naturals.

I have a load of these stocked up for my long weekend in Georgian Bay!

Special thanks go to Marija Usjak (Associate Product Developer), Harry Cumming (Sr. Product Developer), Christine MacLean (Sourcing Manager, Co-Manufac-turing), Gertrude Semerjian (Manager, Optimization Planning), Mike Sanderson (Sr. Director, Marketing – Innovation), Claire McRonald (Sr. Marketing Manager) and the entire Sales team.

California Goldminer coming to traditional Canadian retailers

Debuting this month, Sobeys Ontario will be the first traditional Canadian retailer to distribute the California Goldminer branded sourdough products in its stores. The California Goldminer Sourdough brand is a Maple Leaf owned brand that has heritage dating back to the 1900s and is one of the few ISB (In Store Bakery) brands made from a real "mother dough" starter. The brand is very popular in the U.S and we anticipate seeing the same consumer excitement in Canada!

This branded launch will bring three new SKU's (Original Square, Cracked Wheat Square and Original Mini Boule) to all Sobeys Ontario stores with planned mar-keting and merchandising support in the form of branded displays in the ISB, flyer ads and demos.

Thanks to all at Maple Leaf Frozen Bakery that made it possible!

Manufacturing Update with Ken Campbell

I had another Manufacturing update meeting with Ken Campbell (SVP Manufacturing) this week covering two main topics. The first was the investment we're making in our shop floor technology called Manufacturing Execution System or MES. There are so many interdependencies with other systems (such as SAP) and other functions (such as Food Safety and Quality) that the team has brought together all the critical stakeholders to hammer out the details of the design and implementation. There is a lot of training required to get supervisors up to speed on this new technology, but Ken assures me that it is manageable and not significantly greater than the training that we would typically see at a new start-up plant.

We also chatted about a new and innovative way to approach energy opportunities best described as "outsourced utilities" deals. These types of deals appear to have tremendous economic advantages, but as with any deal, the devil is in the details. He's working with Rocco Cappucitti (SVP, Transactions, Admin & Corp Secretary) to ensure that if we proceed, that we structure the deal to our advantage.

Thanks, Ken, for the great update!

Food Fight

The theme of this year's Food Fight, our annual strategy conference for senior leaders, was "a breath of fresh air"… and that's exactly what our participants got. In the middle of intense "implementation" day-to-day, we wanted this to be time for the executive team to gather, reflect on the big picture of how far we have come, and what we have left to accomplish, build "broad perspective" and network with colleagues for ideas and support in finishing what we set out to do!

We also selected three significant topics to debate vigorously as a senior executive team, and debate we did!!

One special surprise was that our debates were moderated by Amanda Lang, CBC's Senior Business Correspondent and anchor of the daily show "The Lang & O'Leary Exchange." She did a wonderful job pulling people into the debate and bringing alternate perspectives to the table. In every case, we had people present the case "for and against" and then the audience participated assertively on both sides!

The debates covered three very important and highly emotional topics:

1. Maple Leaf should make innovation THE cornerstone of its culture. Innovation is clearly a critical part of our company and essential to growth. That is not in question. What is in question is should this be THE cornerstone? Does it have to

be to be innovative? What are the consequences of that? What things should be weighed against this? These are enormous and important questions to explore.

2. Maple Leaf Foods' financial targets should be adjusted at the half way point. The clear takeaway from this debate was that our senior management team is confident that we will achieve the 2015 financial targets that we have broadly communicated. But, target setting has many consequential impacts and we explored all of them! We have a track record of success and have materially changed the trajectory of our earnings over the last four years. For this we should be incredibly proud and have great confidence that we will achieve our goals for 2015. I certainly do. We will undoubtedly encounter challenges along the way, but I (along with the senior team) trust that we will get there by 2015.

3. Maple Leaf should commit itself to producing zero waste as an organization. Every participant at Food Fight and likely every employee at Maple Leaf believes that we should do our part to drive the environmental sustainability agenda forward. And in fact, we already are. But, we have been tactical in our approach, we have not yet had a well-defined strategy or explicit goals and plans. Should we right now? Can we do it? Can we now? Is this a "cost" or a "benefit"? Again, enormous questions, and I was blown away at the quality and emotion that went into this debate…very powerful, AND inspiring! Now, speaking of celebrating the wins we do have, here are some environmental ones:

- Maple Leaf has invested over $85 million in environmental control systems and $10 million annually to manage our environmental programs.

- In 2011, we reduced energy intensity by 0.48% compared to the prior year. We also reduced our absolute greenhouse gas generation by 1.2%

- The majority of our raw materials and ingredients come from Canadian sources

- On average, over 90% of our manufacturing waste is diverted from landfills and beneficially reused or recycled

- Our new bakery in Hamilton, Ontario was constructed to Leadership in Energy and Environmental Design (LEED®) Silver standards and is currently in the verification stage prior to certification

- Our newest office in Mississauga, Ontario, which houses our ThinkFOOD! product innovation centre, was built to LEED® Gold standards for the building core and shell

- We sold over 45 million litres of bio-diesel fuel, produced from waste fats and recycled grease and cooking oils

The debates elicited some spirited and very open dialogue. There are clearly many takeaways which require some thought, consideration and counsel from topic experts in the organization. So I have I committed to listening carefully, considering all of the dialogue and using that to shape our forward direction on these topics.

For each debate, two of our Food Fight participants bravely volunteered to lay out the opening arguments on each side before opening the floor to the entire group. A special thanks to Stephen Graham (Chief Marketing Officer), Maryanne Chantler (SVP, Six Sigma), Anne Tennier (VP Environmental Affairs), Kevin Golding (President, Agri-Farms & Rothsay), Debbie Simpson (SVP, Finance) and Barry McLean (President, Fresh Bakery) for stepping up to the plate for this one!

We also had a couple of "team building" events which appeared to be quite popular, as is always the case in our strategy offsite, Food Fight.

It was an absolutely outstanding event, which could never have been possible without the tremendous work from Sean Drygas (Director, Strategy) and Sue Perkins (Executive Assistant, Office of the CEO). Thank you both for your hard work in creating a truly wonderful experience for the team. It was top notch!

Capital Council

On Thursday, I met with the Capital Council to get a view of our capital spending for the remainder of the year. 2012 marks a milestone year in our transformational effort and we have budgeted a dramatic increase in capital spending. This increase is in our "strategic capital" rather than in our base capital where our plant and operators are holding the capital spending at the minimum level required just to maintain the business.

We promised our stakeholders that we would fund our capital needs through a "pay as you go plan" and we are accountable to maintain a specific ratio of earnings for the debt, so we are keeping a critical eye on our spending habits and altering our spending to meet these needs where necessary.

A special thanks to Joyce Chan (Manager, Financial Analysis) and Sid Hathiramani (Senior Financial Analyst) who pulled the analysis together a week ahead of schedule. Terrific work!

Olivieri

I ended a very busy week by attending the Olivieri e-meeting. They have some exciting new innovations in the pipeline, which include extensions in manicotti, cannelloni and their cooking sauces line-up. This is great news, because the business has been volume challenged this year, and these initiatives will form part of a clear and simplified plan to get our volumes and market shares back on track.

There have been some changes in plant management at Olivieri, and I'm pleased to hear that everyone is rolling up their sleeves and pitching in to ensure that our plants are running smoothly. Thanks for your hard work and commitment to make this happen!

Ayr Closure

It is with a heavy heart that we close the Ayr facility this week. We have faced many difficult decisions, but decisions that affect people's livelihoods are particularly difficult and we don't make them lightly. We are proactively trying to find roles for our people at our other plants, and those we cannot place elsewhere in our organization will be treated fairly and with respect, consistent with our values.

I want to extend my sincere thanks to each and every one of our Ayr employees. They did an absolutely outstanding job in supporting the orderly wind up of our operations. I am sure the last several months since we announced the closure in February have not been easy, but despite the hard reality of the decision, they continued to focus on the task at hand and do what it takes to get the job done. Through it all, they continued to ensure the plant operated safely and efficiently to meet our customer requirements.

Thank you for all dedication and hard work you have provided to this plant and to Maple Leaf over the years!

This & That

I had a couple of external commitments this week, but other than that was consumed by Food Fight which is always so intense that it is exhausting by the end, and this year was no exception. It's off to Georgian Bay for the first weekend of the summer season and I am peeing myself I am so excited. I've got my kids with me and a gaggle of their friends so it's me and 10-12 twenty somethings for the weekend. Think that will be fun? Hang on…

Weather looks like a spectacular few days which is also great for business!!

Enjoy…

Leadership Edge
Michael

From: McCain, Michael H
Sent: Sunday, May 22, 2011 8:58 AM
Subject: Wallace McCain; The Legacy & Looking Forward
Attachments: A Perfect Love distribution.doc

"He didn't tell me how to live; he lived, and let me watch him do it."

Clarence Kelland

This will surely be one of the most difficult weeks of my lifetime. It has been often said that there is no more challenging a time to a man, than the passing of his father. Scott & I devoted the largest share of our week to celebrating his life and this week, that is all I will write about.

In our tribute ad, the Maple Leaf family honored our Chairman, Wallace McCain, as businessman, community leader and philanthropist. He was each of these and they are described in great detail in a tribute website www.wallacemccaintribute.ca.

As a businessman, his life mostly began in the world of the New Brunswick Irving family. He and his brother shared a passion for entrepreneurship; they started a frozen food company. The success of that business has been legendary, but, Wallace McCain was different. Following the adversity of a family dispute (which was much more than a dispute about succession), he left McCain Foods and we began our journey here at Maple Leaf Foods. Few people in life have one successful business career. Rare is it that at 65, a person starts fresh again in a new business. Wallace McCain did just that. He was an iconic Canadian businessman.

As a community leader, our father was always on the forefront of "giving back" to his community. He was an avid participant in the political process. He managed campaigns, and he raised a great deal of money for them. In fact, he took pride in telling people he "voted many ways" in his lifetime. Wallace McCain was also active in stewardship of many other community responsibilities including education, health care and the arts. He was a giant of a community leader.

And, particularly in the last five years, Wallace McCain blossomed in what we describe as his third career – a philanthropist. He supported a wide range of important causes, and mostly engaged this third career collaboratively with his life partner of 56 years…his wife Margaret. Generosity was deeply rooted in this man.

Businessman, community leader, philanthropist. These are the Wallace McCain the world came to love dearly. And, he led them all with passion, energy, skill and his characteristic humility.

But, this is not the Wallace McCain I and my family remembered this week. We celebrated the life of a husband, a father, a father-in-law, a grandfather and a stalwart friend. In each of these roles, Wallace McCain nurtured intimate relationships with many hundreds of people. My family found joy and peace hearing the outpouring of affection for this man which came through in the greetings of the thousands of people he touched. They reached out to us over the course of the last few days and it was more comfort than one could ever have imagined.

Finally, I can only say that my relationship with my father was unique and a life blessing. The best way for me to describe this is in the text of my remarks at his funeral, which I am happy to share with you.

I know there are many faiths represented in the Maple Leaf world. I respect that. Mine happens to believe that Wallace McCain, my father, is in a better place now, I will see him again and he is still with me spiritually. That gives me and my family great comfort. I will miss him profoundly. The world will miss him profoundly. But, we are all better off for his existence. He had impact; he made a difference.

His legacy above all else, is laying a foundation for us now to look forward, continue on the journey he began. We are all well equipped for this journey from the gifts he left us – gifts of character; gifts of knowledge; gifts of will; gifts of a wonderful foundation. We will do him proud by carrying that torch forward and continuing to build on the enormous legacy he began.

Looking forward!

That is what Wallace McCain would now want us to do…and it is a wonderful view!

Thank you all for your support. The love and affection has been palpable throughout a very difficult time, and I cannot tell you how much I appreciate it. You all mean the world to me.

Leadership Edge
Michael

APPENDIX 13: LES ON LINE (FIRST AND LAST LOLS)

First LOL

Les on Line #1 – Week of January 24 to 30, 2011

INTRODUCTION

Welcome to the first edition of LOL! This new Les on Line weekly e-mail message has been designed to inform, educate and recognize the HR staff at MLF. In addition, I am sending the LOL to all of the VPs at MLF to provide them with a weekly progress report on HR activities and initiatives.

My first week has been a busy and fun one! Michael was one of the first people I met on Monday and he made sure I felt welcomed. One of my first priorities on day one was to speak to most of you on the Monday morning conference call. I subsequently met many of the Toronto based HR staff in several BU meetings throughout the week. Here were the highlights of my message in all of the HR meetings:

1. Rationale for joining MLF: many of you wanted to know why I came out of semi-retirement to take on the CHRO role. There were three key reasons; A) work with Michael McCain – I like his values and respect him as a business leader; B) MLF is a great Canadian icon and I want to help it remain Canadian; and C) the new Strategic Plan requires a strong HR effort and I want to lead that effort. I felt I could contribute to MLF and have some fun.

2. One Company-One HR function Vision: our customers expect to see the same processes and programs (i.e. compensation, succession planning, talent development, PADS, etc.) regardless of which business unit they work in. We must act as one HR function with best practices throughout the company. This needs to be the rallying cry for the HR team. We have a strong bench of very talented HR professionals who want to do the right things.

3. My Guiding Principles for the HR Function: I use five principles in leading a successful HR team. They include:

    1) We are business people first: we must know what business we are in before we can offer practical solutions. This includes HR staff at home office and in the business units.

    2) We are the people experts: we know how to assess talent and coach managers on managing people effectively. Our business is people.

    3) We are an integrated team: we need to have great hand-offs between the home office and business units. Our customers expect us to operate together (home office & BU HR teams) to solve their business issues.

4) We are both a strategic & tactical partner: our customers want both short term needs met along with tackling more strategic people issues. Our solutions have to be pragmatic and consistent across the company.

5) We are focused on adding value every day: There are many daily opportunities to add value to the business. Ask yourself every day "Did I put the puck in the net today." You will be proud and have fun doing it.

4. Questions to all HR Staff: I asked each of the HR staff at MLF to respond directly to me on two questions: 1) How would our customers rate the HR function at MLF and what is our greatest strength; and 2) If you were the new CHRO, what would be your top three priorities? So far I have received well over 100 responses to-date and they have been terrific. I plan to ask each VP in the company these same two questions.

SALES COUNCIL TRAINING

Richard Lan invited me to be a participant in the first sales leadership training course. All of the sales VPs attended so it was a great opportunity to meet them. Richard's vision is to grow the revenue line by enhancing the selling system we use at MLF. All of the business units are aligned to this common approach. It is another example of the One Company-One Sales function theme. I committed HR's support to this important initiative. The HR staff that work with the sales functions throughout the company need to be very engaged in this roll-out. The future of our company's top line growth is predicated on the success of this new selling system.

TOWN HALL MEETING

I was asked to MC this meeting with home office staff. It was a great chance to meet everyone and give out some great service and values awards. MLF does it better than most companies.

MEETING EXECUTIVES AT MLF

I had the opportunity to meet with ten executives in one-on-one meetings during the week. We had a chance to get to know each other and discuss their answers to my two key questions (mentioned earlier). In particular, I enjoyed my meetings with Barry and Gary, the two largest business unit presidents. It was very clear to me these guys are very talented and passionate. We are in good hands under their leadership. I plan to be their internal "coach" for strategic HR and leadership matters.

INDUSTRIAL RELATIONS

One of the key strengths in the HR group is our collective agreement negotiations expertise. It is very clear to me that Ian Henry and the IR Directors are very talented and results focused. As an example, the recent tentative agreement in Saskatoon was a tremendous success for both the union and company. Congratulations to Ken and Ian. I look forward to engaging with the team.

CHERYL FULLERTON'S NEW ROLE

I asked each of the BU HR leaders to recommend a person to work with me to develop a new People Strategy for MLF. Every person selected Cheryl for this assignment. It would appear our HR Talent Tracker process is working very well. I plan to partner with Cheryl in working with the HR council to develop this People Strategy by the end of June. Jared will provide a person from his Strategic Development group to help facilitate the process.

HRC MEETING OF THE BOARD

Michael, Wayne, Sylvie and I participated in the meeting. We were well prepared for the discussion. It was a wonderful chance for me to meet them and re-connect with Purdy Crawford who was the chair of the HRC at CN (my former company). We have our marching orders from the meeting and Sylvie is leading the charge on several fronts.

CONCLUSION

I want to end this LOL by thanking a number of people. They include the two Tinas and Gemma for their help with my on-board orientation. Thanks to Ian and Bob for inviting me to their national HR conference calls. To Sylvie for her great work on the HRC meeting…to the HR council for providing information prior to my first day…to the many executives who welcomed me to the company especially Mike, Richard and Scott…to all of the HR staff for your warm welcome and wonderfully inspired responses to my two questions…to Wayne for his tremendous efforts to educate me before my arrival…to my wife Marijane for her encouragement to take this role and our little puppy Cassie for adjusting to "Dad" being away.

Finally, I'd like to make a special thank you to Michael for having the belief in me to hire me as his CHRO. On a humourous note, I was asked by one of the HR staff members (who will remain nameless for now) how I would compare my return to the corporate life to Brett Favre's return to the NFL from retirement. As a die-hard Steeler fan, I answered Brett was past his prime and should not have come out of retirement. I need to make sure the same thing is not said about me!! Thanks, have a great week and looking forward to meeting more of you in person this week.

Les

Final LOL

Sent: Wednesday, July 31, 2013 8:16 AM
Subject: Final Les on Line – July 31, 2013

Well, my last LOL to you is enclosed. First, let me congratulate Ian on his appointment as the new CHRO effective tomorrow – he is a very talented guy and I wish him well. Second, my sincere thanks to Cheryl and Leanne for making all 132 LOLs happen in the last 2.5 years – we did not miss a single week.

When I arrived in January 2011, I was very impressed with the MLF Leadership Values, Labor Relations expertise, PAD/DAP focus and the HR Talent.

In the last two and half years, the HR Team has really made a difference. Here are our major achievements:

1. Creating Opportunities to Grow the HR Team – Through the first ever HR Conference, Coaching Sessions with Les, CHRO Awards, HR Manager Case Studies, Functional Talent Reviews, introduction of HR Leadership Track hires and individually meeting every HR Manager & Director. I was very proud to see each member of the team stretch themselves.

2. Creating a One HR Team Culture – We developed our vision, actively moved HR talent across the company, used the Les on Line as a communication vehicle, encouraged standardization in HR processes and most importantly, we "covered each other's backs." This is a much more unified HR Team.

3. Going Toe-to-Toe with the CEO – Michael is such a strong advocate for leadership development; he is like a second CHRO. This situation created great collaboration between us and a few skirmishes. However, I always knew Michael wanted to do the right thing from a people perspective.

4. Coaching Very Talented Managers and Executives – This is our sweet-spot! We enjoy working with people who want to improve themselves and are open to developmental suggestions. In addition, we added more assessment and tools to help managers, including the use of external coaches and peer mentoring. There is no better feeling than to help someone become a better leader and human being.

5. Adding Value to the Business – Developing a People Strategy to support the MLF Value Creation Strategy and introducing performance tools to our leaders, through the Q4 and ABC models, will make us a better performing company. These People Strategy initiatives are taking hold in various Business Units. In addition, the MLF People Strategy was featured in magazine

articles and some of the HR VPs have spoken at various conferences on this topic. This publicity helped to raise our profile, which is always good for business, and reinforces MLF as an employer of choice.

6. Influencing Organizational Design – Tackling the HR function's structure – we reduced the number of VPs and Directors by 50%. In addition, we worked to influence the use of spans and layers across MLF. This was not a popular subject for many but ultimately the company will be better streamlined and more efficient.

7. The CEO Workout Sessions were Transformational – Michael created an extraordinary experience for the 144 participants. Each participant raved about the development they gained as well as the bragging rights to say they spent two days with the CEO. This best practice event, which was supported by the HR group, was a truly rewarding gift to these high potential employees.

8. Supporting the Network Transformation Strategy – The HR team was very active in managing all aspects of the people component. Closing facilities is not easy but the team provided great support to the affected employees. They role modeled the "human" aspect of our jobs.

9. New Areas of Human Resources Support – The creation of the commercial HR group put more emphasis on helping our Sales and Marketing teams with their people issues. Also, the Supervisory Foundations Program has become a terrific forum for developing our most important frontline leaders. These new services will have a lasting impact on MLF.

10. Focus on our Hourly Employees – These hard working people can bring more value to the company with some more TLC. We are optimistic our new hourly training and engagement strategy will enrich their work satisfaction which will add more profit to the bottom line.

On a personal basis:

*   Spending time with the Business Unit Leadership Teams–I personally met all of the Presidents and VPs in my first year. This allowed me to better understand their needs as well as participate in Business Unit e-meetings. I felt very welcomed by the Leadership Teams.

*   Working with Cheryl and Leanne every Sunday to produce the LOL was a great bonding experience. I really appreciate the extra commitment from them. Thank you to Tina Shimbos for owning the distribution list and sending the LOL out on my behalf every Monday.

- Coaching very talented Business Unit executives was a great thrill for me. You can make a difference with peoples' lives.

- Meeting each HR Manager and Director to get to know them better was a wonderful journey – their passion and devotion was contagious.

- Engaging with the Senior Leadership Team (Michael, Scott, Mike & Richard) was a real treat for me. There is no question about their love of the business.

- Developing the People Strategy with Cheryl and the rest of the HR Council was a truly energizing experience – everyone was engaged and believed in what we were doing to support the business.

- Seeing HR members become certified ABC instructors was a great in-house solution for MLF.

- Working with the two HRC Chairs was fun because they were very engaging.

- Watching more executives become shareholders was gratifying – we became a better executive team.

- Coaching Stephanie and watching her grow was a true highlight for me at MLF – she is our future.

- I very much appreciated the administrative support by Tina Shimbos, Tina Di Matteo and Debbie Donaldson. They kept me organized and focused.

- Introducing my wife Marijane and dog Cassie through the LOL allowed me to share my personal life with you – thank you for your kind feedback.

Finally, the HR team is a very gifted group of people and it has been a true honour to have led this team – you are only as strong as your team and I felt like Superman. All the best and I look forward to seeing all of you who are coming to the conference in September.

Les

APPENDIX 14: ADDITIONAL INSIGHTS FROM DAVE ULRICH

I asked Dave Ulrich for his thoughts on the future.

Q: What are the skills and knowledge critical to being a future CHRO and what should be their key performance metrics?

A: We have studied HR competencies for 25 years. Based on that work in 2012, we identified six competencies for effective HR professionals:

Strategic Positioner. High performing HR professionals understand the global business context including social, political, economic, environmental, technological and demographic trends and translate these trends into business implications. They understand the structure and logic of their respective industries and the underlying competitive dynamics of the markets that they serve including customer, competitor and supplier trends. They then apply this knowledge in developing a personal vision for the future of the company. They participate in developing customer focused business strategies and in translating the business strategy into annual business plans and goals.

Credible Activist. HR professionals in high performing firms function as Credible Activists. They do what they say will do. Such results-based integrity serves as the foundation of personal trust that, in turn, translates into professional credibility. They have effective interpersonal skills. They are flexible in developing "positive chemistry" with key stakeholders. They translate this positive chemistry into influence that contributes to business results. A major way through which such influence is established is through consistent, clear and insightful verbal and non-verbal communications. They also have confidence in their opinions about the business. They take strong positions about business issues that are grounded in sound data and thoughtful opinions. They are not only activists for the business; they are also advocates for the importance of HR in driving business results.

Capability Builder. An effective HR professional creates, audits and orchestrates an effective and strong organization by helping to define and build its organization capabilities. Capability represents what the organization is good at and known for. These capabilities outlast the behaviour or performance of any individual manager or system. Capabilities have frequently been referred to as a company's culture. Such capabilities might include innovation, speed, customer focus, efficiency and the creation of meaning and purpose at work. HR professionals can help line managers create meaning so that the capability of the organization reflects the deeper values of the employees.

Change Champion. Effective HR professionals develop their organizations' capacity for change and then translate that capacity into effective change processes and structures. They ensure that the capacity for change on the inside is equal to or greater than the rate of change on the outside. They ensure a seamless integration of change processes at the institutional, initiative and individual levels. They build the case for change based on market and business reality; they overcome resistance to change by engaging key stakeholders in making key decisions and building their commitment to full implementation. They sustain change by ensuring the availability of necessary resources including time, people, capital and information and by capturing the lessons of success and learning from failure.

Human Resource Innovator and Integrator. A major competency of effective HR professionals is their ability to integrate HR practices around a few but critical business issues. The challenge is to make the HR whole more effective than the sum of the HR parts. Occasionally sub-processes within HR departments fail to be unified with different HR processes going different directions. The result is conceptual and process inconsistency. Mixed messages are sent and performance is sub-optimized. On the other hand, high performing HR professionals ensure that desired business results are clearly and precisely prioritized, that the necessary organization capabilities are powerfully conceptualized and operationalized, and that the appropriate HR practices, processes, structures and procedures are jointly aligned to create and sustain the identified organizational capabilities. As they do so with discipline and consistency, they help the collective HR practices to reach the "tipping point" of impact on business results.

Technology Proponent. Technology and information is changing dramatically. For many years, HR professionals have applied technology to the basic HR work. HR information systems have been applied to enhance the efficiency of HR processes including benefits, payroll processing, healthcare costs, record keeping and other administrative services. In this round of the competency survey, we see a dramatic change in the implications of technology for HR professionals. High performing HR professionals are now involved in two additional categories of technological applications. First, HR professionals are applying social networking technology to help people stay connected with each other. They help guide the connectedness of people within the firm and the connectedness between people outside firms (especially customers) with employees inside the firm. Second, in the high performing firms, HR professionals are increasing their role in the management of information. This includes identifying the information that should receive focus, bundling that information into useable knowledge, leveraging that knowledge into key decisions, and then ensuring that these decisions are clearly communicated and acted upon. This is an emerging strategic competency through which HR will add substantive value to their organizations.

INDEX

W

Numerical references